WOMEN ARTISTS & DESIGNERS

AT THE NATIONAL TRUST

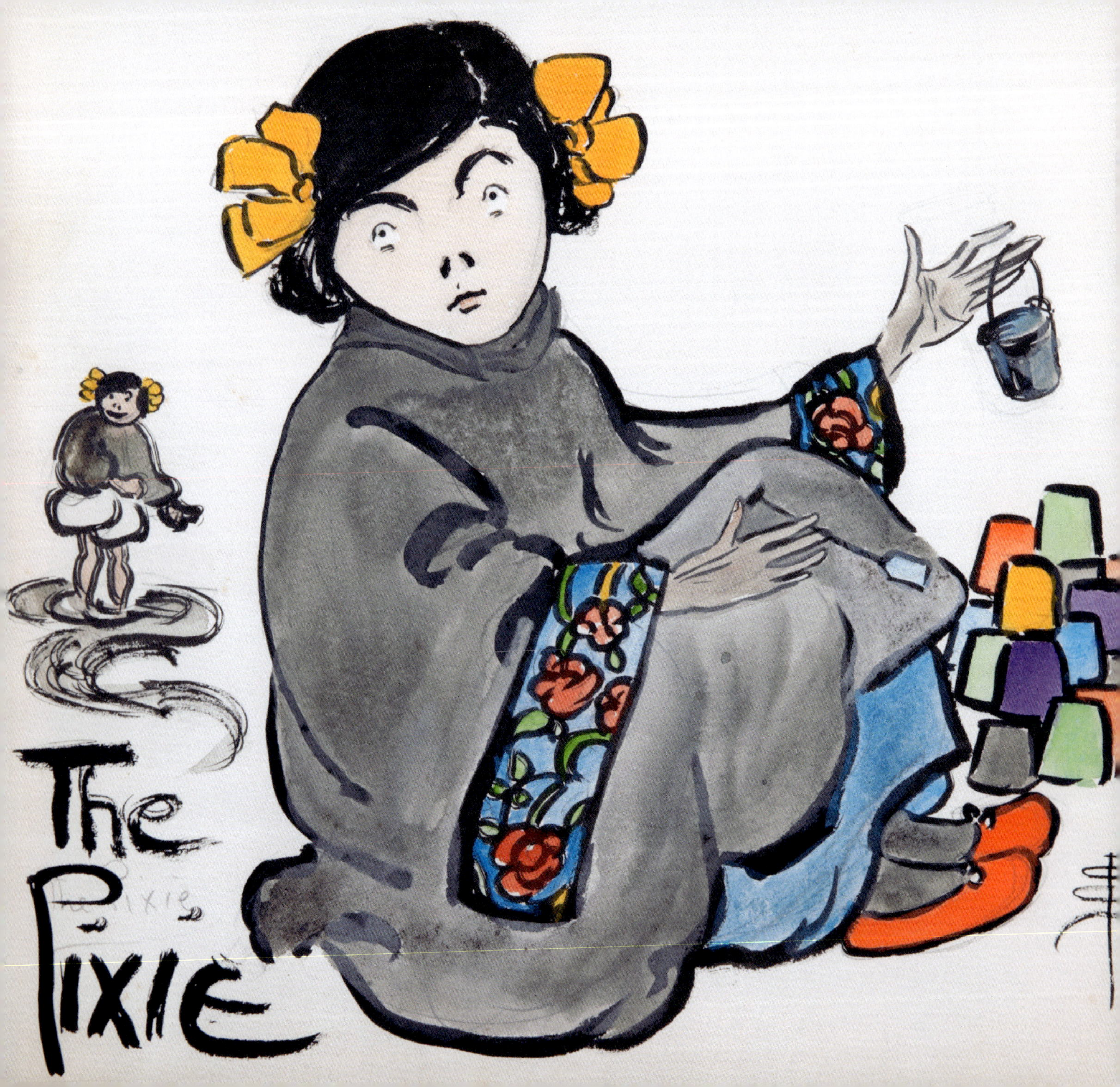
The Pixie

WOMEN ARTISTS & DESIGNERS

AT THE NATIONAL TRUST

Rachel Conroy

Introduction by Sandi Toksvig

With entries by Benjamin Alsop, John Chu, Matthew Constantine, Jane Eade, Miranda Garrett, Mia Jackson, Rachel Jacobs, Joanne Moody, Alice Rylance-Watson, Anna Sparham, Alice M. Strickland and Jonathan Wallis

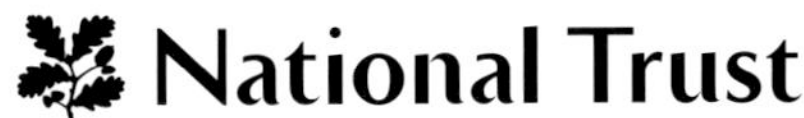

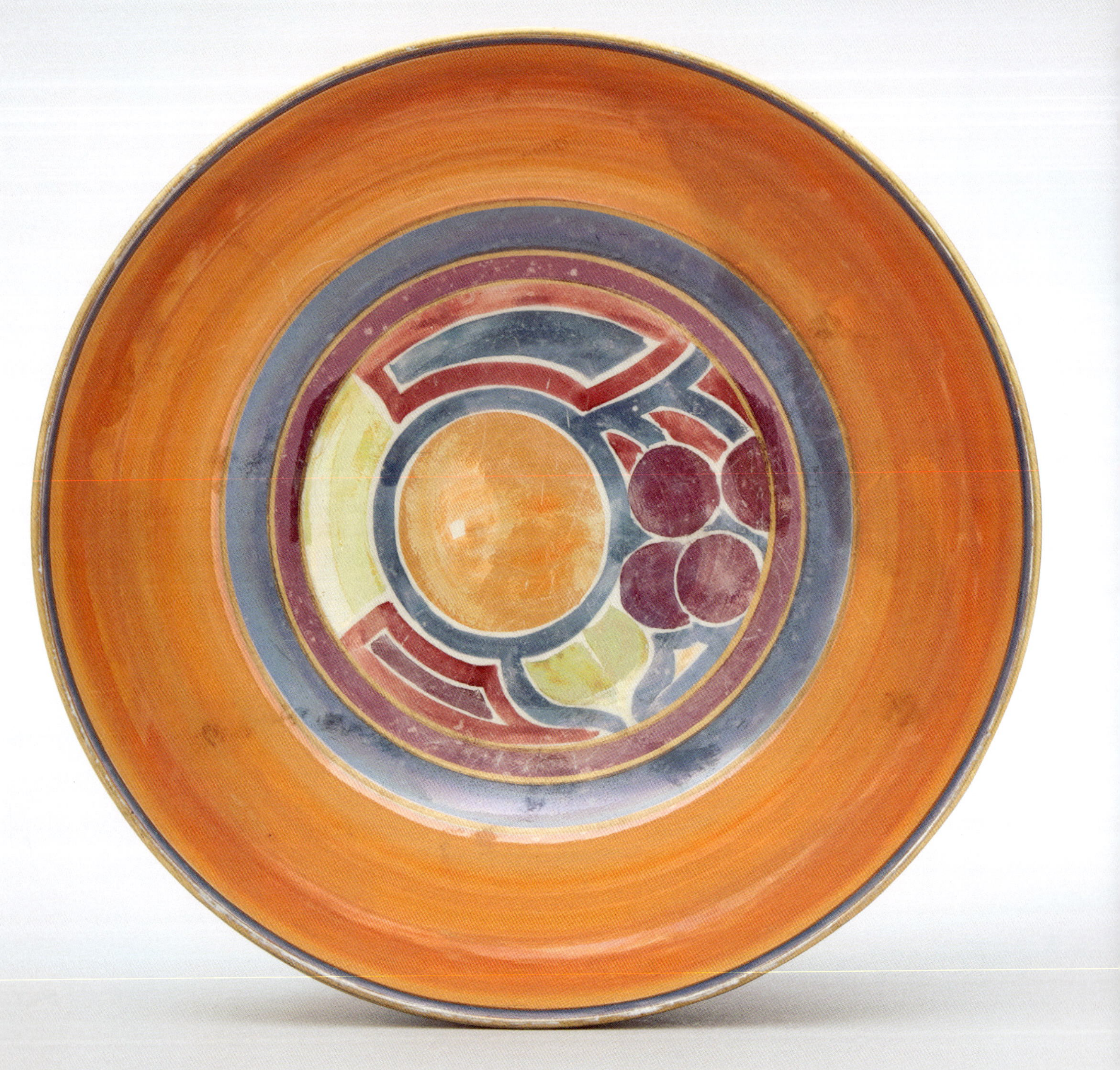

CONTENTS

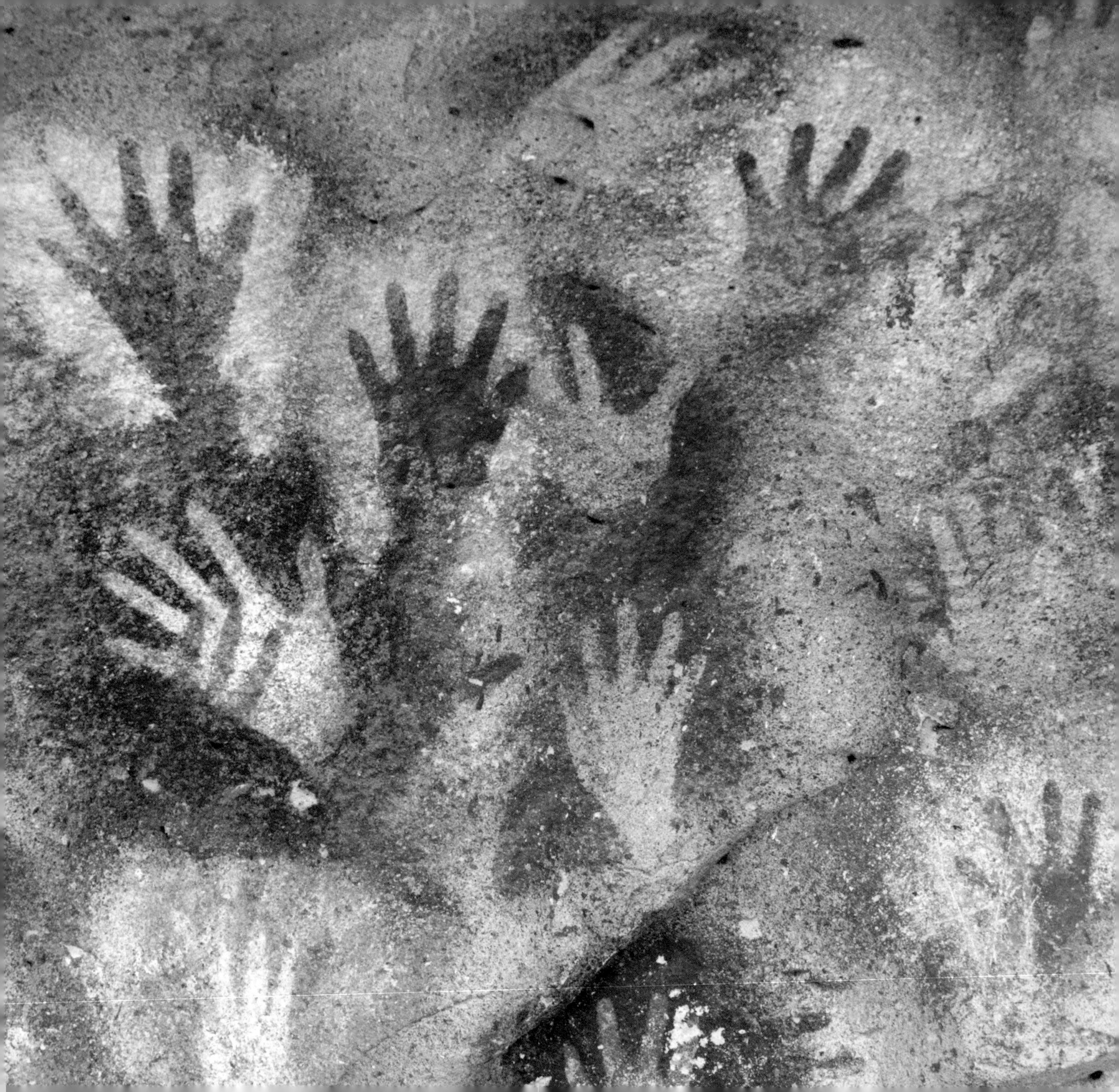

Introduction by Sandi Toksvig

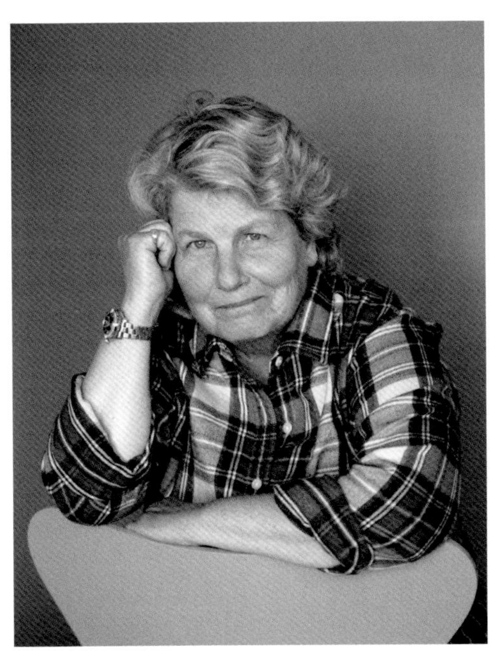

← Between 13,000 and 9,500 years ago, the Cueva de Las Manos (Cave of Hands) in Río Pinturas, Santa Cruz Province, Argentina, was decorated with cave art – including the handprints of women.
↑ Sandi Toksvig in a photograph by Debbie Toksvig

I was once staying at the home of a very wealthy person with an incredible art collection. He went on and on about his many paintings without once noticing that everything he focused on was by a man. On the way to the loo I found a self-portrait by the Italian Renaissance painter Sofonisba Anguissola (*c.*1532–1625) hanging outside the door. This was a woman of such talent that it was recognised by none other than Michelangelo. Now she stood guard over the Ladies. It made me want to weep.

Today, however, I am singing. I am full-throated with joy at introducing this book. When you begin to absorb the fabulous range of work ahead of you in this publication then I expect you will find it impossible to believe that art by women has for generations been overlooked, ignored or belittled.

Back in 1989 I had a poster on my wall created by the Guerrilla Girls, an anonymous artist activist group from New York. It asked the question 'Do women have to be naked to get into the Met. Museum?' And explained that 'Less that 5% of the artists in the Modern Art sections are women but 85% of the nudes are female.' Have things changed? In 2017 the National Gallery published a book for children called *Picture This!* aimed at introducing art to kids. It had 96 paintings in it, of which two were by women.

How is this possible? Art by women is not a new thing. Indeed it may be the oldest thing. All over the world there are prehistoric cave paintings, with some in Argentina, France and Spain dating back approximately 30,000 years. These often consist of handprints and are usually referred to as 'work by cavemen'. We are led to believe that these were passing cavemen on hunting expeditions who did a bit of art on the side. In fact, recent research shows that the majority of these handprints are female, which means that not only were women, presumably, on the same hunting trips, lugging along the kids and a pot big enough for a bison, but they were also creating art – and not just handprints. Huge cave paintings assumed to have been painted by men have now been attributed to women.

The fact is, from the dawn of time women have always been creative to express how they feel, to make their mark on history, or just to let us know they were there. The variety of work produced is magnificent – everything from oil paintings to needlework. Needlework? Is that art? Of course it is, but too often these glories made by women's hands have been denigrated as 'craft'. We all need to look again at something like the Bayeux Tapestry. First of all, not a tapestry but an embroidery – made

↓ *Do women have to be naked to get into the Met. Museum?* Billboard commissioned in 1989 by the Public Art Fund in New York from the Guerrilla Girls, a collective of feminist artists who wore gorilla masks in public to maintain their anonymity. The design incorporates a female nude figure from Jean Auguste Dominique Ingres's painting *Grande Odalisque* (1814, Musée du Louvre, Paris) with added gorilla mask.

→ A scene from the Bayeux Tapestry, which was embroidered by women and tells the story of the Norman Conquest of England in 1066.

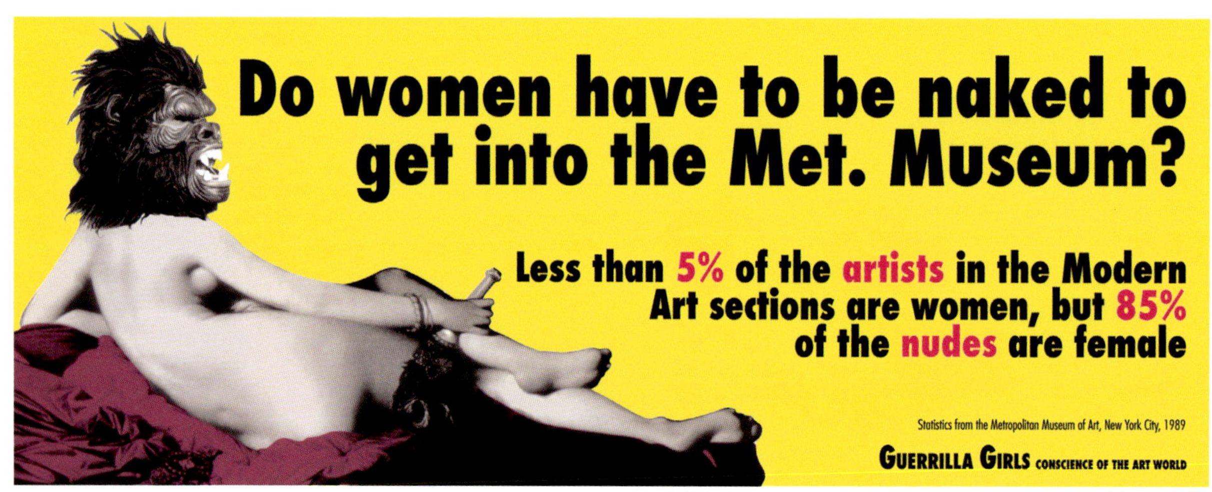

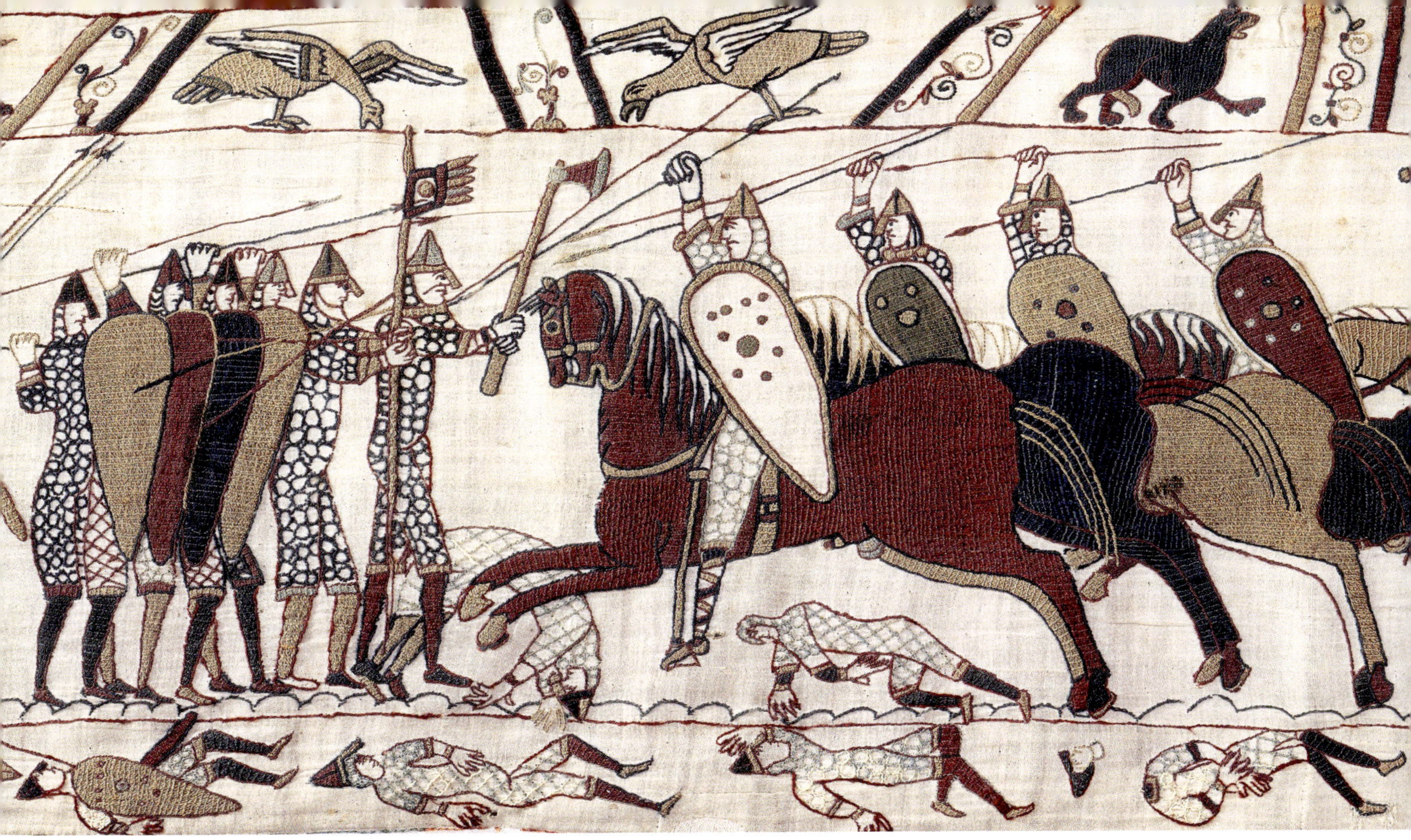

by women but named by men. It is one of the most famous examples of craft that has endured the test of time. A lot of textiles have been lost to history as they are by nature biodegradable, so how unbelievable to be able to see the embroideries at Hardwick Hall in Derbyshire (pages 28–9), which Bess of Hardwick (1527–1608) worked on with Mary, Queen of Scots while the latter was in the custody of the Earl of Shrewsbury. Here is art, but here too is a deeply personal story of two women spending time together. Take a moment to admire the needlework of Lady Marian Alford (1817–88) (pages 124, 125) at Belton House, Lincolnshire, and you will know this is technically intricate and beautiful work. Nevertheless, it was often dismissed as a lesser form of art because it lacks an association with intellect and institutions, an association that has been an endless historical challenge for women.

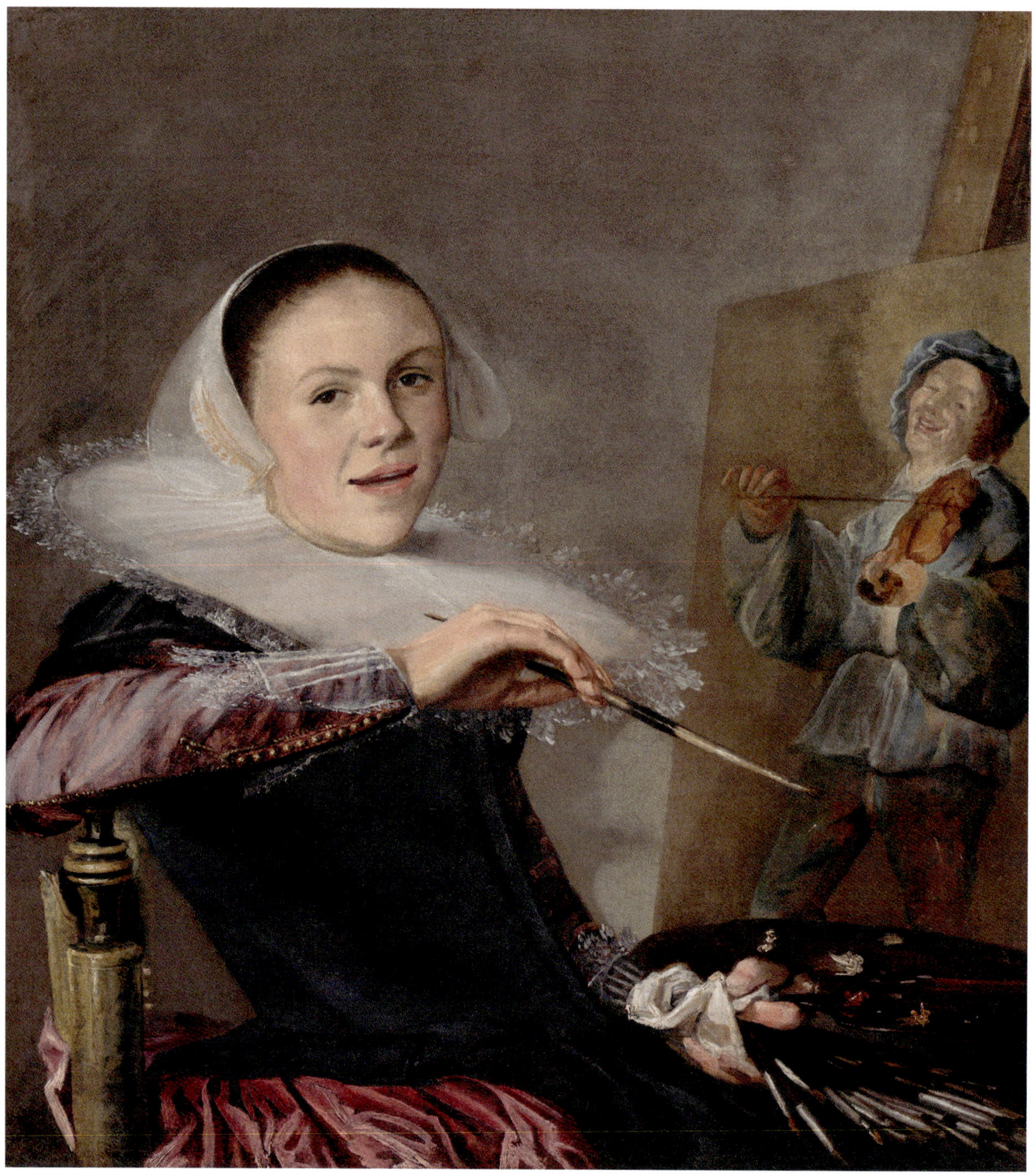

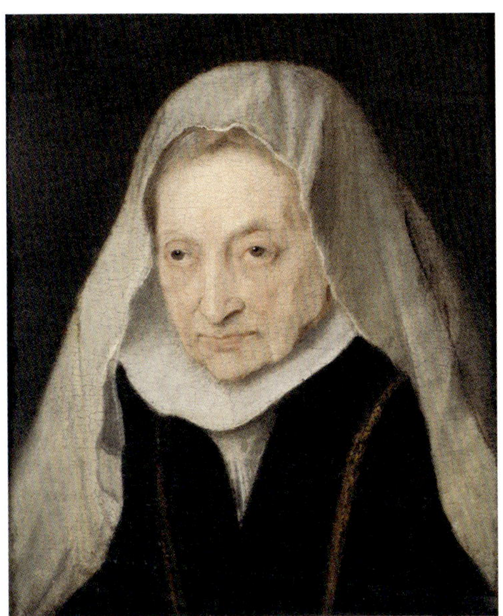

← Self-portrait by the Dutch artist Judith Leyster (1609–60), *c.*1630, oil on canvas, 74.6 x 65.1cm (National Gallery of Art, Washington DC)
↑ *Sofonisba Anguissola*, Anthony van Dyck (1599–1641), 1624, oil on canvas, 41.6 x 33.7cm, Knole, Kent, ‡ 2012 (NT 129883)

Female artists have battled for recognition for centuries. Those whose work was recognised were sometimes then belittled by having their work attributed to someone else. It was too good to have been done by a woman. The Dutch Golden Age painter Judith Leyster was so admired that after her death and for hundreds of years all her work was attributed to either a contemporary male painter called Frans Hals, or to her husband. It wasn't until 1893 that she was rediscovered. The clue, when anyone bothered to look, was the initials JL in the corner of the paintings. Marvel at the work of her contemporary Rachel Ruysch (1664–1750) (page 14) at Dudmaston in Shropshire. Check out the stunning engravings by Marie-Louise-Adélaïde Boizot (1744–1800) (page 78) at Waddesdon Manor, Buckinghamshire, and know that she was much praised but also had her work mistakenly attributed to her brother.

How I should have loved to walk through the National Trust's collection with the art critic John Ruskin (1819–1900), who once declared that there '[had] never been ... a lady who could paint'. We would stand before the work of Winifred Hope Thomson (1864–1944) (page 156) in Dorneywood, Buckinghamshire, and ask him to think again.

The depth and breadth of the Trust's collection is inspiring. There is everything from paintings and sculpture to pottery, photography, illustration and more. There are names you will recognise and those with whom you will be making a first acquaintance. How exciting! How thrilling to feast your eyes and soul on this smorgasbord of delight.

The portrait of Sofonisba Anguissola by Anthony van Dyck (left), which hangs at Knole in Kent, makes me feel as though she is looking at me. That she demands I keep singing from the rooftops that women artists matter. That the work in this book matters. For centuries it's been hard to be a woman and make art, and even harder to be recognised for it. We need to rethink how we collect and curate material about women in all walks of life, including art, so that we don't lose the past and we can inspire the future. Well done to the Trust – now go and have the best time!

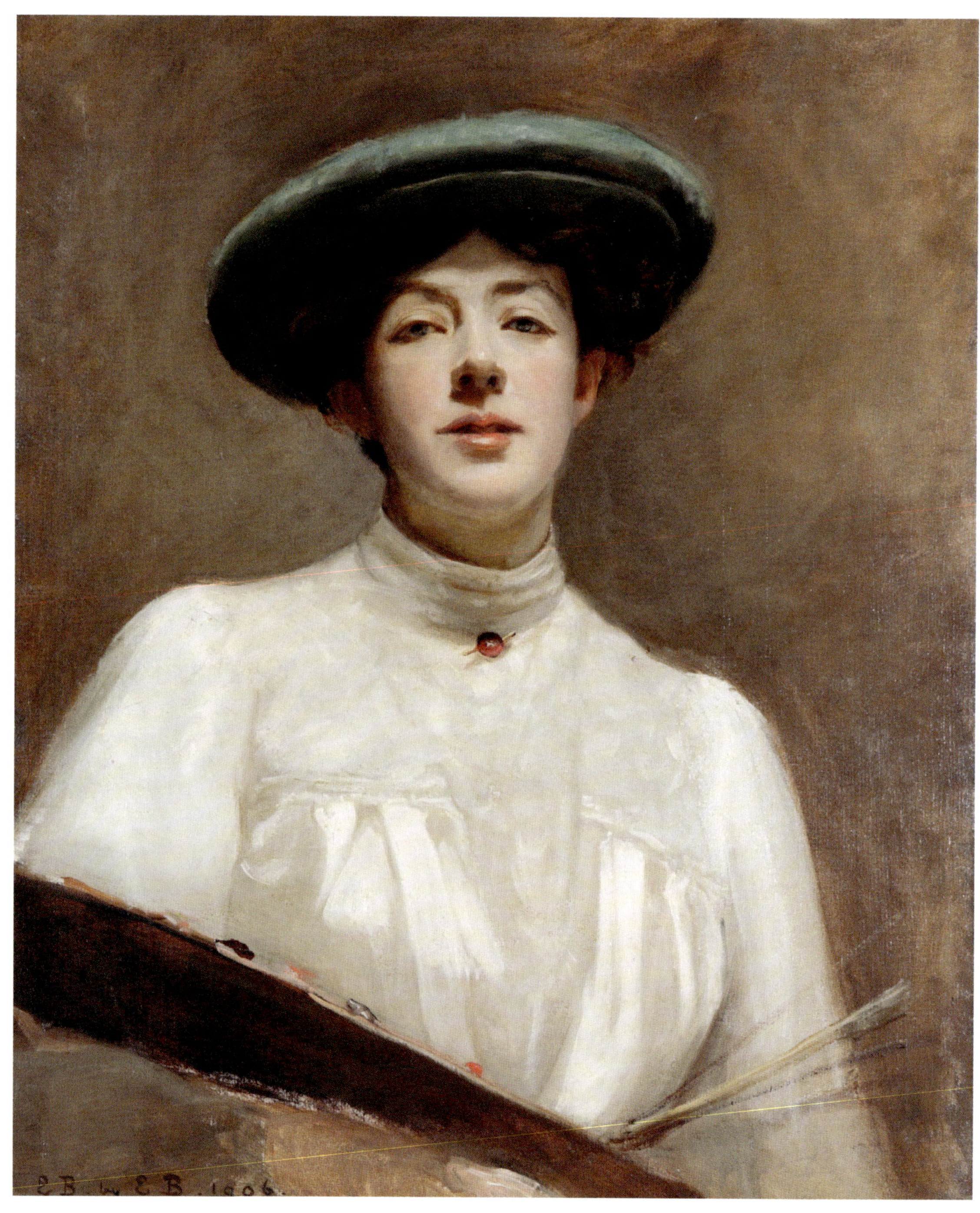
E.B. by E.B. 1906.

By brush, scissors and spade

This is the first major publication from the National Trust to focus on the women artists and designers represented in its collections. It is exciting – and timely – to share a selection of them in these pages.

From the outset, I wanted this book to span a period of history that reflects the immense chronological scope of the National Trust's collections and places. It is arranged broadly in chronological order, taking into consideration the period at which the women were most active. It needed to include the work of fine and applied artists – pots and paintings – and to touch upon other aspects of design, such as gardens, interiors and fashion. By the very nature of their intrinsic connection to people and place, the National Trust's collections probably include more work by amateur artists and makers than most major public collections. It was therefore essential that this book embraced both professional and amateur practice (and all that sits between) so that it reflects the special character of many of our places as material repositories of the creative women who have lived or worked in them. For this reason especially, it is a book that could only have been written using the collections of the National Trust.

This book could have been written many times over and it goes without saying that the selection is, inevitably, a subjective one. Some of the objects you will see in these pages sit completely at home in the

← *Self-portrait*, Evelyn Blacklock (1872–1948), 1906, oil on canvas, 74 x 61.3cm, Dudmaston, Shropshire (NT 814180)

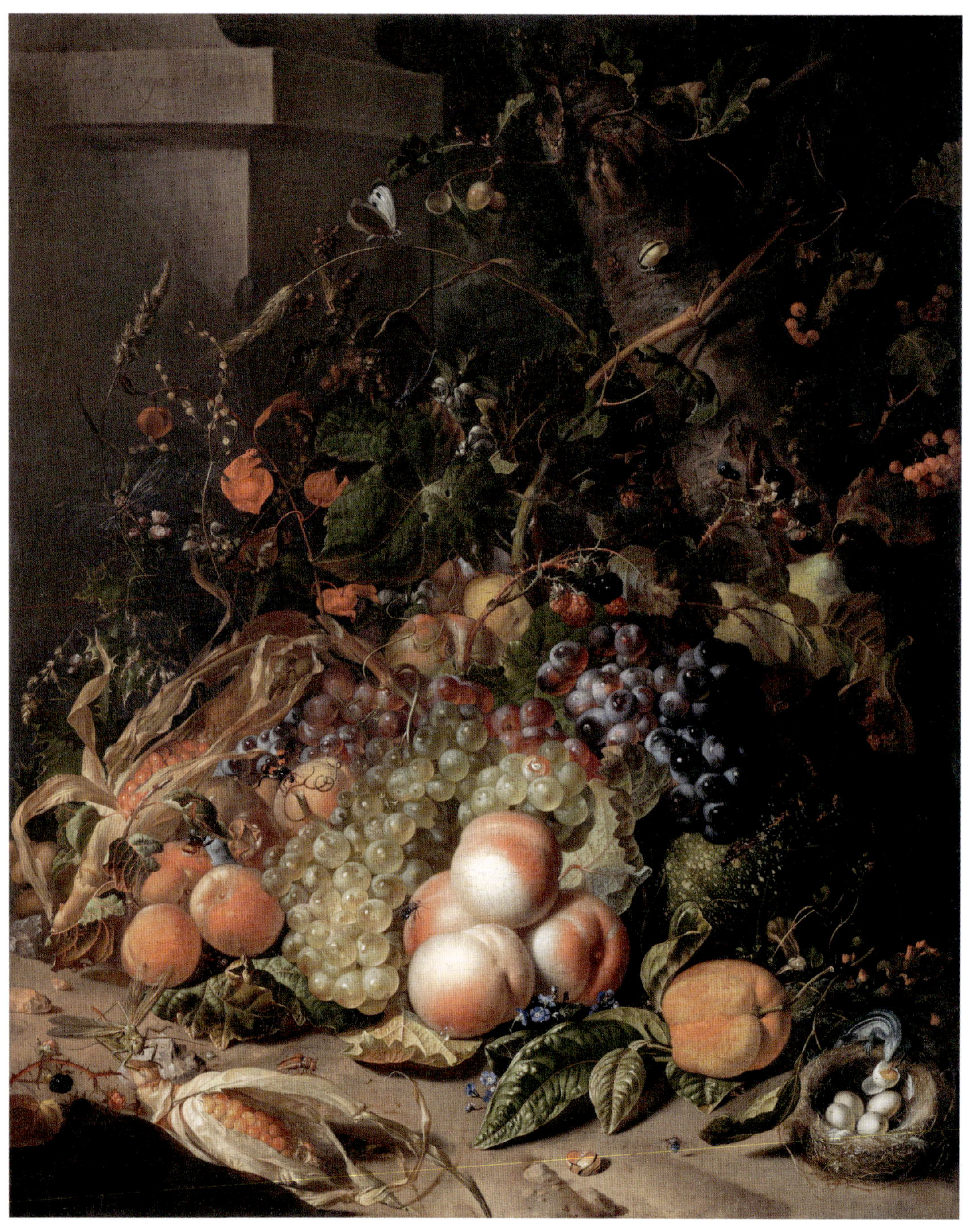

places intrinsically associated with their makers – perhaps even in the very rooms in which they were brought into existence. Others would slot seamlessly into the collection of a major museum or art gallery. Some objects are of considerable historic or cultural significance, while others could be regarded as of minor importance (at least when considered in isolation). Some bear little or no relationship with the place at which they now reside, but are such striking examples of the work of a particular woman that I could not resist including them. Whatever the context, they all have compelling and important stories to tell.

It is fair to say that any collection is in a constant cycle of growth and stasis when it comes to the body of knowledge that sits around it. Part of the wonderful challenge of developing the content for this book was to add the names of many women back into our records – to rearticulate the relationship between the thing and the hand that made it. This was not always an easy task and, in some ways, the selection reflects the bias of my own interests as a specialist in applied art – the three-dimensional stuff – with perhaps even more of an interest in the everyday than the extraordinary (the National Trust is incredibly fortunate to have an abundance of both). So alongside works by Barbara Hepworth (page 233) and Lavinia Fontana (page 30) are others that might also be found in your own home or your neighbour's, such as the mass-produced ceramics designed by industry pioneers Susie Cooper (page 214) and Susan Williams-Ellis (page 239), or a Peter Rabbit board game, brought to life by Beatrix Potter's enduring illustrations (page 184).

The entries in this book attempt to find a comfortable balance between the personal and creative biographies of the chosen makers and I hope they offer enough both to satisfy curiosity and encourage the reader to follow up their own threads of interest, and to form connections across different entries. The women and works occupying these pages are drawn from across the many places that are in the care of the National Trust. They span six centuries – from Bess of Hardwick's needlework, wrought stitch by stitch, by window- and candle-light in the 1570s (pages 28–9), to Tabitha Jussa's contemporary photographic portraits (page 248), inspired by the history of the women working at the Hardmans' studio in Liverpool. I'm conscious that gaps become particularly apparent during the last few decades and there are also more fundamental issues around representation within the collection, particularly in relation to

← *Still Life with Fruit, Bird's Nest and Insects*, Rachel Ruysch (1664–1750), 1716, oil on canvas, 76.2 x 57.1cm, Dudmaston, Shropshire (NT 814164)

women of colour, cultural diversity and class. The voids, I hope, will narrow as the National Trust's portfolio of properties – and perhaps its collecting practices – develop in the future.

The National Trust's collections include stellar works by professional artists who are an integral and recognised part of the canon of art history, such as Rachel Ruysch (1664–1750), whose paintings of glorious groups of flowers (page 14) led to international (and financial) recognition in her lifetime. Although, unfortunately, the Trust's collections do not include her work, a portrait of Italian Renaissance painter Sofonisba Anguissola (*c.*1532–1625) by Sir Anthony van Dyck (page 11) presents a noble vision of this remarkable and celebrated artist, then in her nineties and almost without sight. Evelyn Blacklock's confident self-portrait, palette in hand (page 12), is a wonderful example of the type of amateur artistic practice our collections so richly and uniquely represent. The collection at Dudmaston also includes her portraits of family members (including Bo the Pekinese dog), horse paintings and watercolours, offering a depth of insight into her influence and interests. Sarah Lethieullier, Lady Fetherstonhaugh (1722–88), probably made her fabulous images at Uppark, West Sussex, but they combine highly detailed images of birds, animals, fruit and flora from around the world in an almost collage-like effect (opposite).

Placing artist and artwork within their social and historical contexts has been enriching and fascinating in equal measure. While many lived lives of privilege and relative ease, others flourished in the face of every kind of adversity, from entrenched prejudices to the effects of war and personal tragedy. The painter Mary Beale (page 36) had to leave London for a time to escape the terrifying ravages of the bubonic plague, Elisabeth Vigée Le Brun (page 84) fled France during the Revolution and spent the rest of her life in exile from the home she loved, and the family of goldsmith Louisa Courtauld (page 70) – persecuted for their Huguenot faith – came to England as refugees. Many of the women explored here were involved in the fight for female suffrage, including interior decorators Rhoda and Agnes Garrett (page 130), actress Edith Craig (page 173) and ceramicist Mary Seton Watts (page 142).

The dressmaker, artist and gallerist Amy Kotzé (page 179) is a woman I have thoroughly enjoyed getting to know through her work and life story. A skilfully decorated dish at Nuffield Place in Oxfordshire, perhaps

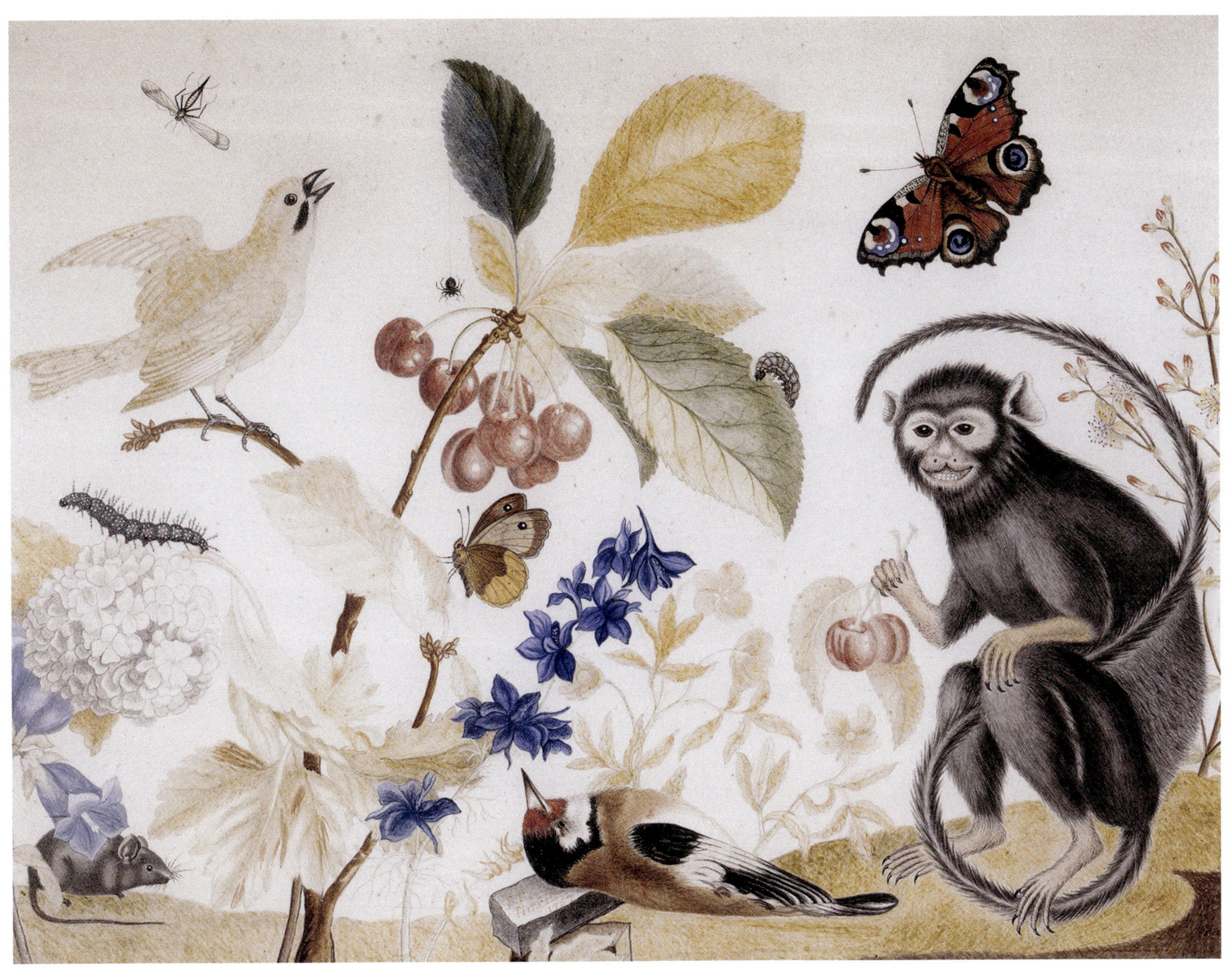

↑ *West Indian Little Black Monkey with Birds, Butterflies and Flowers*, Sarah Lethieullier, Lady Fetherstonhaugh (1722–88), 1757, watercolour on parchment, 42 x 51cm, Uppark, West Sussex (NT 138308.1)

unique in a public collection, was a key that unlocked her life and restored her to her rightful place alongside her better-known contemporaries. Needlework samplers – long an essential part of skills education for girls – are present in huge number across our collections and are often relatively anonymous, but the example by teenage Agnes Grange (page 110), a tenant at East Riddlesden Hall in West Yorkshire, is potent because it is linked to both place and life experience. It was created during a period of bereavement, and it is tempting to imagine the meditative comfort that the hundreds of tiny stitches might have provided her.

Some of the women in this book, such as Ruysch and Blacklock, picked up a brush, others deftly wielded their scissors, sank their fingers into wet clay, picked up a spade, or threaded a needle with silk. Some drew upon the worlds and people they knew most intimately, while others expanded their (and our) collective horizons, in some cases literally venturing into 'new' worlds, or developing innovative modes of creative expression. I have particularly enjoyed looking at the extraordinary work of Maria Sibylla Merian, whose amazing books, sitting in the libraries at Hardwick Hall in Derbyshire and Blickling Hall, Norfolk, meld artistic expression with scientific rigour (page 39). Her work on metamorphosis helped to disprove the theory that insects spontaneously emerged from mud or decaying organic matter. Susanna Drury's meticulous views of the Giant's Causeway in County Antrim (pages 50–3) were the 18th-century equivalent of 'viral' images – reproduced, circulated, discussed and admired far and wide. Their impact, however, went beyond sensation – they helped to advance the science of geology.

The 17th-century artist Joan Carlile (page 35) supported her family through her practice, while others, including Rebecca Orpen (page 137) and Rhoda Delaval (page 60), expressed and articulated family connections through theirs. Orpen's self-portrait includes a miniature version of her sketch of her second husband, Edward Dering; a second, on her easel, portrays the home they shared. Still others, such as the painter Mary Ellen Best (page 107), her potential limited by societal expectations, stopped working after starting families of their own. Elizabeth Ratcliffe's astonishing mother-of-pearl models were made during her time as a servant at Erddig, where she was afforded the luxury of time to work on her creations (page 74), although an underlying question remains – who benefited most from her talent?

→ *Annie Theodosia Wilson, Mrs Charles Francis Benthall*, Ethel Walker (1861–1951), c.1940, oil on canvas, 60 x 50cm, Benthall Hall, Shropshire (NT 509821)

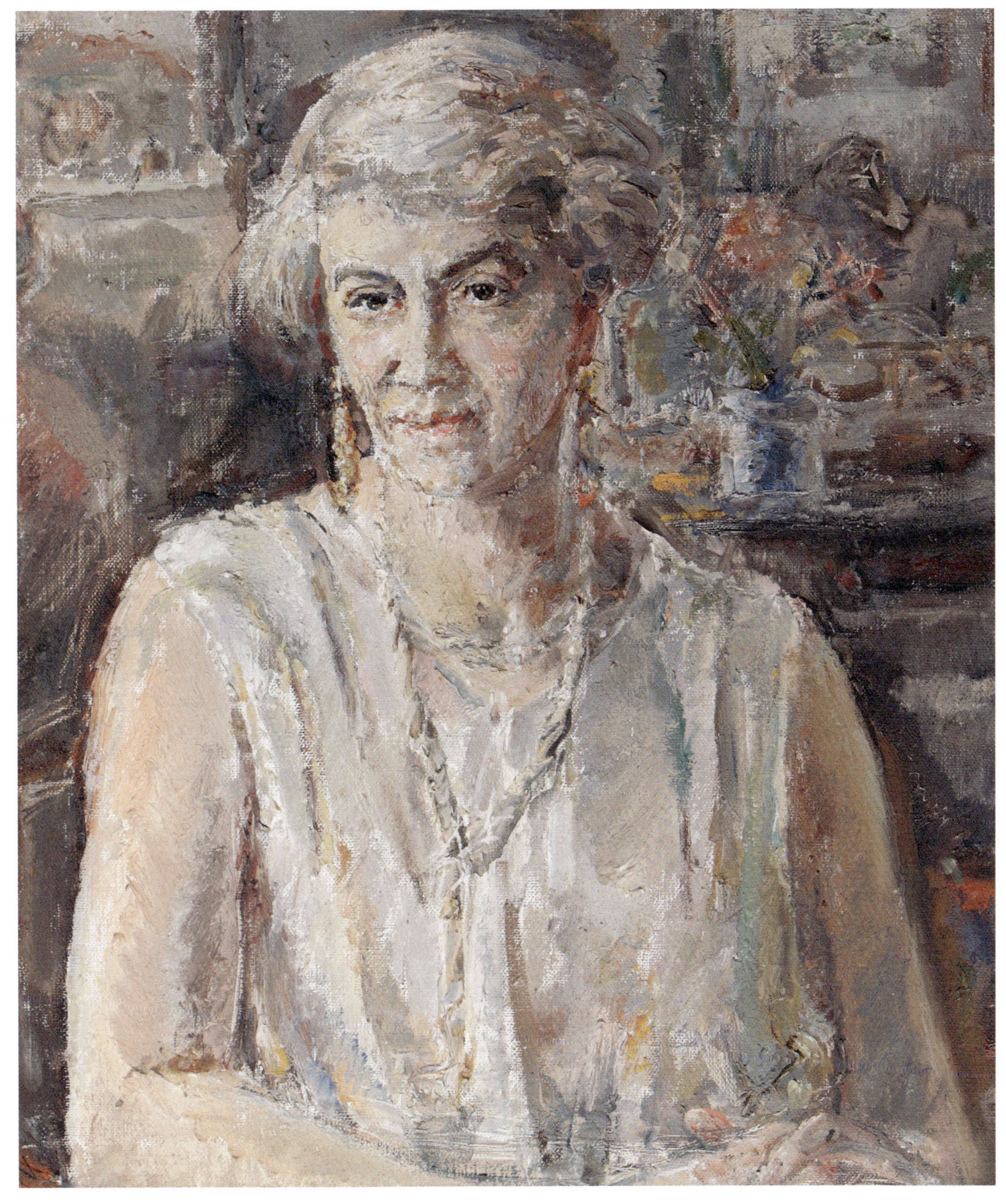

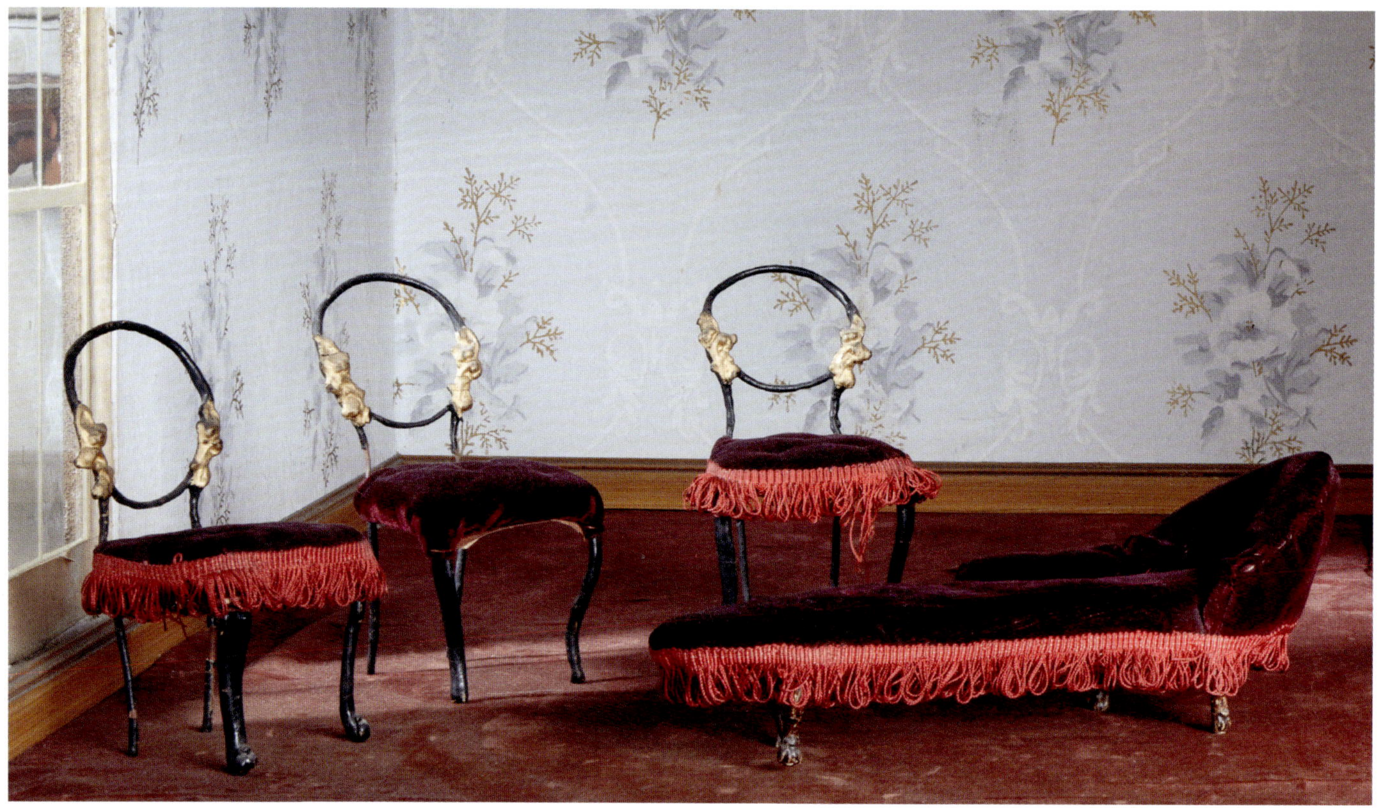

↑ Set of doll's house furniture made by The Ladies' Guild, 1852–8, wire with velvet upholstery, 11 x 6.5cm (chairs), Calke Abbey, Derbyshire, ‡ 1985 (NT 288980)

Some of the women in this book have had their contributions under-acknowledged or overlooked in their time or beyond it, particularly if their work was produced with male partners or associates. Until relatively recently, the creative genius of May Morris (page 153) was overshadowed by that of her father, William Morris, whose legacy she worked so hard to ensure. The pivotal role of Ray Eames (page 236) in the designs created in partnership with her husband, Charles Eames, was also frequently underplayed. Barbara Hepworth (page 233), Harriet Hosmer (page 128) and Pamela Colman Smith (page 170) each actively experienced and reacted to forms of prejudice directed at their gender or sexuality (or both). Ethel Walker (1861–1951) has been described as one of the first lesbian artists to openly explore her sexuality through her paintings, which were predominantly of women (page 19). Although she had a remarkably successful and celebrated career she is not widely known today. It has been interesting to observe that some of the women – including Walker – discovered (or perhaps were only free to pursue) their creative talents later in life. Elizabeth Creed (page 46), the creator of remarkable *trompe l'œil* wall paintings and lyrical epitaphs, seemingly did not set out with her brush and ladder until widowhood, in her sixties. Constance Spry (page 221), at one time the most fashionable floral artist in the country, found her niche as a second career, having first worked in education and social reform.

Education is a thread that connects many of the women in this book – whether through a lack of access to the same training as their male counterparts, or through their roles as teachers. Marian Alford (page 125) was one of the founders of the School of Art Needlework (later the Royal School of Needlework), which, over 150 years later, still provides specialist training for the next generation of embroiderers. At Calke Abbey a group of tiny pieces of doll's furniture, crafted in the 1850s from bonnet wire with plush velvet upholstery (opposite), was created by girls aged 8–17 years old, who were members of The Ladies' Guild. The guild was established to help women and girls who were experiencing poverty by providing them with skills and employment. Caroline Southwood Hill managed the programme, and her teenage daughter Octavia (1838–1912), one of the founders of the National Trust, came to manage the girls in the toy-making workroom – an experience that had a profound effect upon her.

While I feel I am only scratching the surface of what the National Trust's collection can offer for our understanding, appreciation and enjoyment of the work of women artists and designers, it is a privilege to be able to do it. I hope it might inspire you to learn more about someone you discover in these pages, to get to know a new type of creative practice or method of making, or to see a property that is familiar to you through a different lens. Perhaps you might pick up a camera, needle, pencil or shell and create a masterpiece of your own.

Rachel Conroy
Senior National Curator,
National Trust

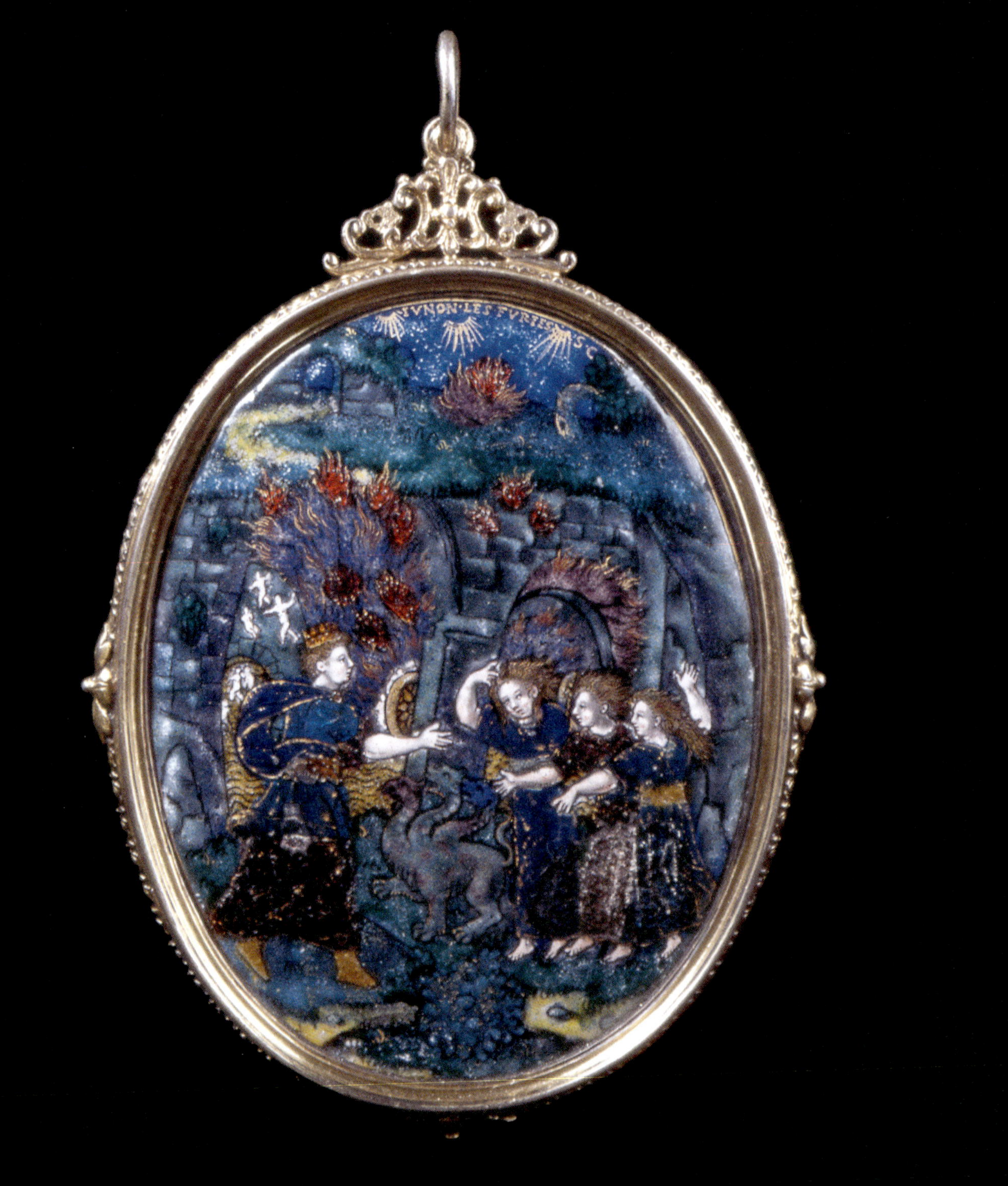
IVNON·LES FVRIES
S C

'FAINTLY IMPRESSED FOOTPRINTS'

Writing in 1876, Ellen Clayton noted in her biographical history of women artists in Britain that they had 'left but faintly impressed footprints on the sands of time. They do not glitter in the splendour of renown, like their sisters of the pen …'

The few professional women painters working in Britain during the 16th century were mostly from continental Europe, where some women enjoyed greater freedoms and could make their living as artists. Levina Teerlinc (*c.*1510–76), for example, was a highly paid Flemish miniature painter at the Tudor court, who had been trained by her father. Sofonisba Anguissola (page 11) defied social convention further, as she was able to access a formal art education in Italy, where her father arranged for her to undertake an apprenticeship with a painter. Other major figures of the period include Rachel Ruysch (page 14), Judith Leyster (1609–60; page 10) and Artemesia Gentileschi (1593–*c.*1653). Women such as Maria Sibylla Merian (page 39) and, before her, the Flemish artist Clara Peeters (*c.*1587–after 1636) worked at the intersection of art and science – both shared and advanced knowledge of flora and fauna through their work. In France, Suzanne de Court (page 33) produced enamel works of exceptional quality, and her distinctive figurative style is instantly recognisable. Unusually, she also often signed her work – the only woman enameller to do so.

← *Juno and the Furies*, mirror back, Suzanne de Court (active 1575–1625), *c.*1600, copper, enamel, gold, velvet and wood, 17 x 11.5 x 1.4cm, Waddesdon Manor, Buckinghamshire, ‡ 1990 (Waddesdon 4131)

The 17th century saw the first British women to practise as professional artists, although it was still unusual for them to run their own studios – Joan Carlile (page 35) and Mary Beale (page 36) are rare exceptions. A larger circle of women worked in related trades but are harder to trace. Over 120 are listed as members of the Painter-Stainers' Company, representing a network of women in London working or involved in related trades between 1660 and 1740, probably undertaking a wide range of painting and decorative work, many training their own apprentices. Mary Ashfield (active *c.*1670–80) was one of several women frame-makers working at this time. She supplied fashionable carved and gilded frames to artists including her husband, Edmond Ashfield (Chirk Castle, Wrexham). She also supplied frames for portraits of the 'Fire Judges', who adjudicated on legal disputes following the Great Fire in 1666, commissioned by the Court Aldermen of the City of London.

Needlework formed an important part of the education of girls from wealthy families, affording them a practical and creative skill. Embroidery was often taught from mother to daughter, but there were also academies offering more formal training. A beautiful casket decorated with raised embroidery was created in 1671 by Hannah Trapham to safeguard her most treasured personal items (opposite). Creating the panels for this box showcased her meticulous skills in using silk to sew and sculpt her tiny figures in brightly coloured, fashionable outfits. 'Japanning' was another popular craft. It was used for updating all manner of household objects – furniture, frames or tea-caddies – in imitation of highly desirable Japanese and Chinese lacquer (an early form of upcycling). A japanned table and candlestands at Lyme, Cheshire, might have been decorated by Elizabeth Legh (1643–1728), whose sister sent her a small quantity of varnish for a 'Tryall' in 1681. The colour, now green, was originally a vibrant blue; a 1688 recipe for 'Blew-Japan' varnish suggested a heady mixture of smalt (ground glass tinted with cobalt), fish glue and white lead to create the effect.

The remarkable buildings created by Bess of Hardwick are rightly celebrated, but other women made significant contributions to the field of architecture. A notable example is Lady Anne Clifford (1590–1676, right), who spent much of her life fighting to regain her family estates, which had been left to her uncle by her father in 1605. A historic entail meant that they should have passed to her as the eldest surviving child,

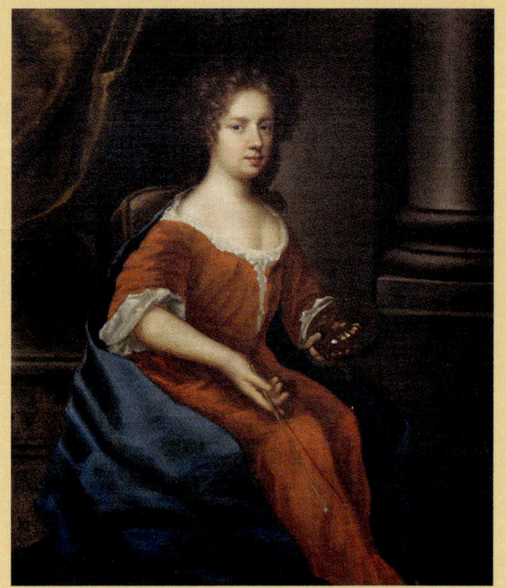

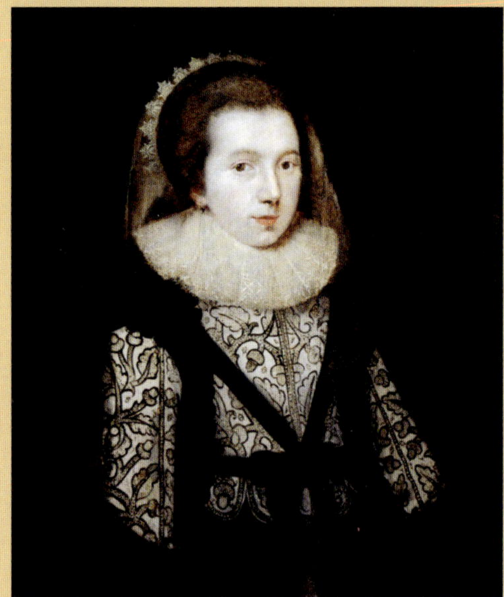

↑↑ Self-portrait by Mary Beale (1633–99), *c.*1675, oil on canvas, 45.7 x 38.1cm (West Suffolk Heritage Service)
↑ Portrait of Lady Anne Clifford, British School, *c.*1620, oil on panel, 75 x 62cm, Nostell, West Yorkshire, purchased by private treaty, 2010 (NT 959447)

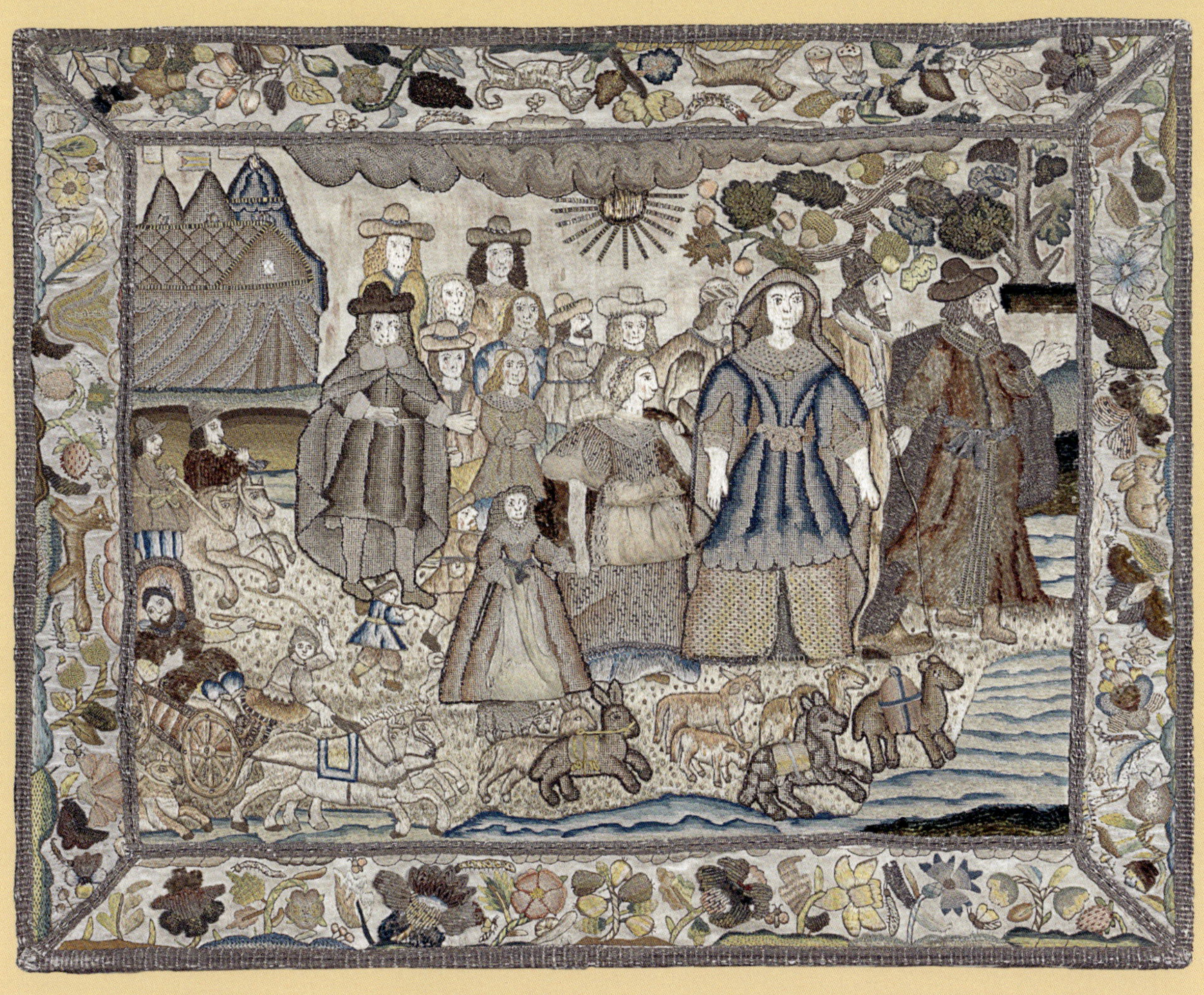

↑ Box lid with raised embroidery, Hannah Trapham (active *c.*1671), 1671, wood, silver, silks, chenille, metallic thread, silver-gilt braids, lace, mica and pearls, 18.5 x 41.4 x 33.5cm, Sudbury Hall, Derbyshire, ⁑ 1967 (NT 653275)

regardless of gender (less than a third of eligible women received their rightful inheritance at this time). Four decades later Clifford finally took possession of her estates. She led the design and delivery of an impressive programme of architectural projects, including the sympathetic repair and restoration (rather than updating) of five family castles in Yorkshire and Cumbria damaged during the Civil War. Each is emblazoned with an inscription of her titles, her claim to the land on which it stood and her role in its restoration – an inescapable statement of her reclaiming of her birthright.

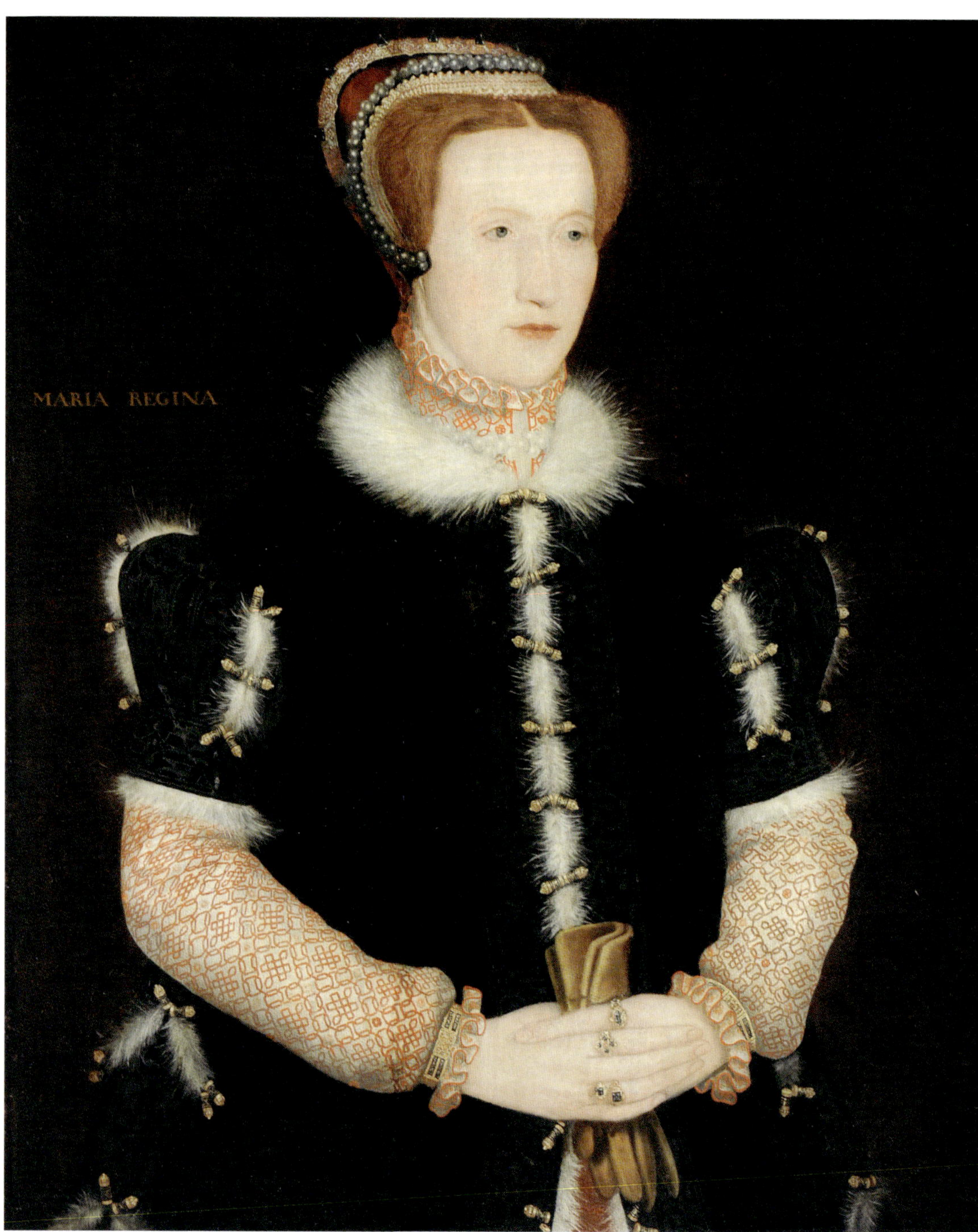
MARIA REGINA

An embroidered encyclopedia

BESS OF HARDWICK (1527–1608)

← Elizabeth Hardwick, later Talbot ('Bess of Hardwick'), Countess of Shrewsbury, by a follower of Hans Eworth (*c.*1525–after 1578), *c.*1560–69, oil on panel, 115 x 100cm, Hardwick Hall, Derbyshire, ‡ 1958 (NT 1129165)

The interiors and collections at Hardwick include examples of some of the most fascinating and rare textiles to survive from the late 16th century. Elizabeth (Bess) Talbot, Countess of Shrewsbury, gave over entire rooms at Hardwick to create space for her professional embroiderers, but she was also a skilled maker herself and some of the most characterful pieces are the product of her own needle.

Textiles held a particular place in elite households during this period. The extraordinary cost of the materials – silks, gold threads, continental velvets – and the skilled labour needed to produce them meant they were the epitome of luxury. They were also a source of warmth, a marker of taste, a prompt for conversation and an outlet for creativity. Bess took an active interest in the design, development and production of the tapestries and embroidered textiles that adorned the beds, walls and furniture in her homes at Hardwick and elsewhere.

Embroidery featuring flower or plant stems (called 'plant slips', as 'slipping' was the practice of pulling up single stems with roots to propagate new plants) became increasingly fashionable at this time. The collections at Hardwick include a group of octagonal plant-slip panels (pages 28–9), most bearing the prominent initials of their maker – ES for Elizabeth Shrewsbury. It is possible that they were originally incorporated into five wall hangings of green velvet embellished with cloth of gold and silver described in a 1601 inventory of the property. The embroideries show stylised trees, flowers and plants, from leaf to root, accompanied by an occasional hen, snail or butterfly. Most are copied from illustrations in botanist Pietro Andrea Mattioli's 1558 *Commentary on Dioscorides*. The examples shown here include stinking iris, gourd and laurel. Around the edge of each octagon is a Latin motto, taken from sources including Erasmus's *Adages* (1500).

→ Group of needlework octagons, five with the initials 'ES' for Elizabeth Shrewsbury, *c.*1570, linen canvas worked with silk and wool in cross and tent stitches, 35.5cm (width, each octagon), Hardwick Hall, Derbyshire, ‡ 1984 (NT 1130604)

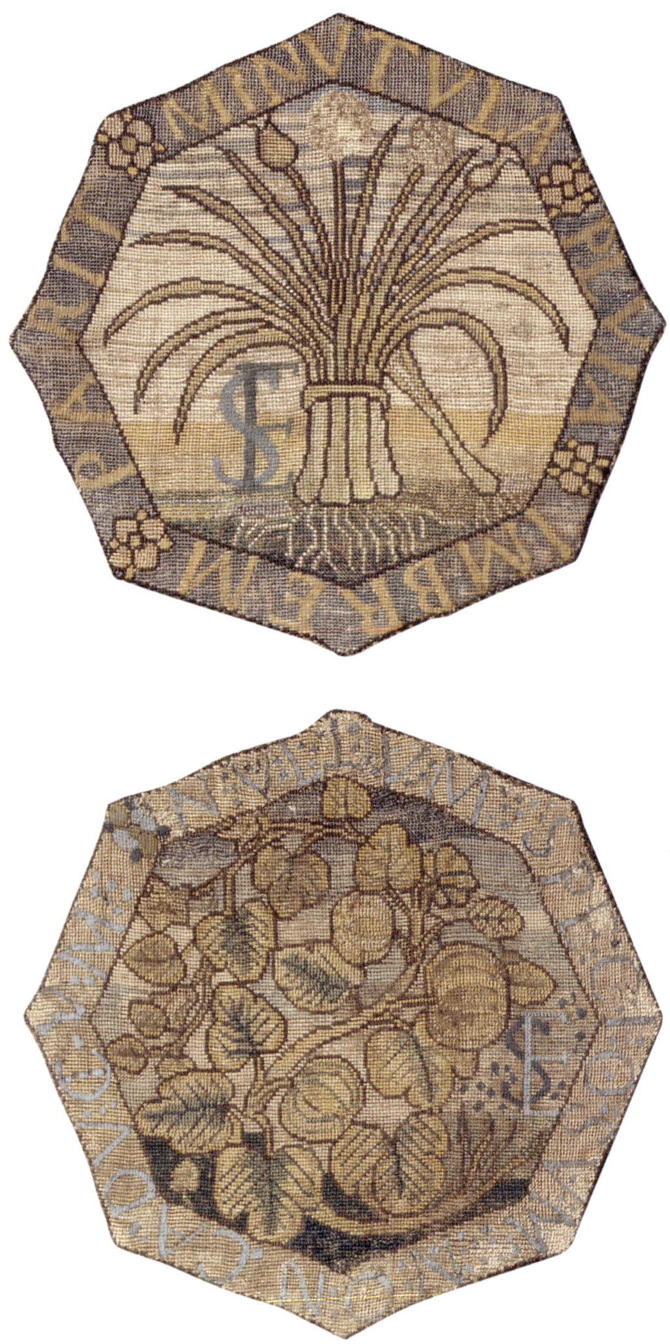

Bess worked on the embroideries with Mary, Queen of Scots (1542–87) while the latter was incarcerated and in the custody of the Earl of Shrewsbury. A recent interpretation of these works argues that they are a form of information management – a means by which Bess could engage in intellectual experiments in a language that, as a woman, society more readily permitted her to use. They form a virtual collection of plant specimens and mottoes published in wool and silk, but also acted as an educational tool for Bess when learning the Latin phrases. A panel with a leek, for example, is circled with the text *Minutula plvia imbrem parit* (little drops make up the shower), using a visual memory prompt as well as a mnemonic pun based on the homophone leek/leak. RC

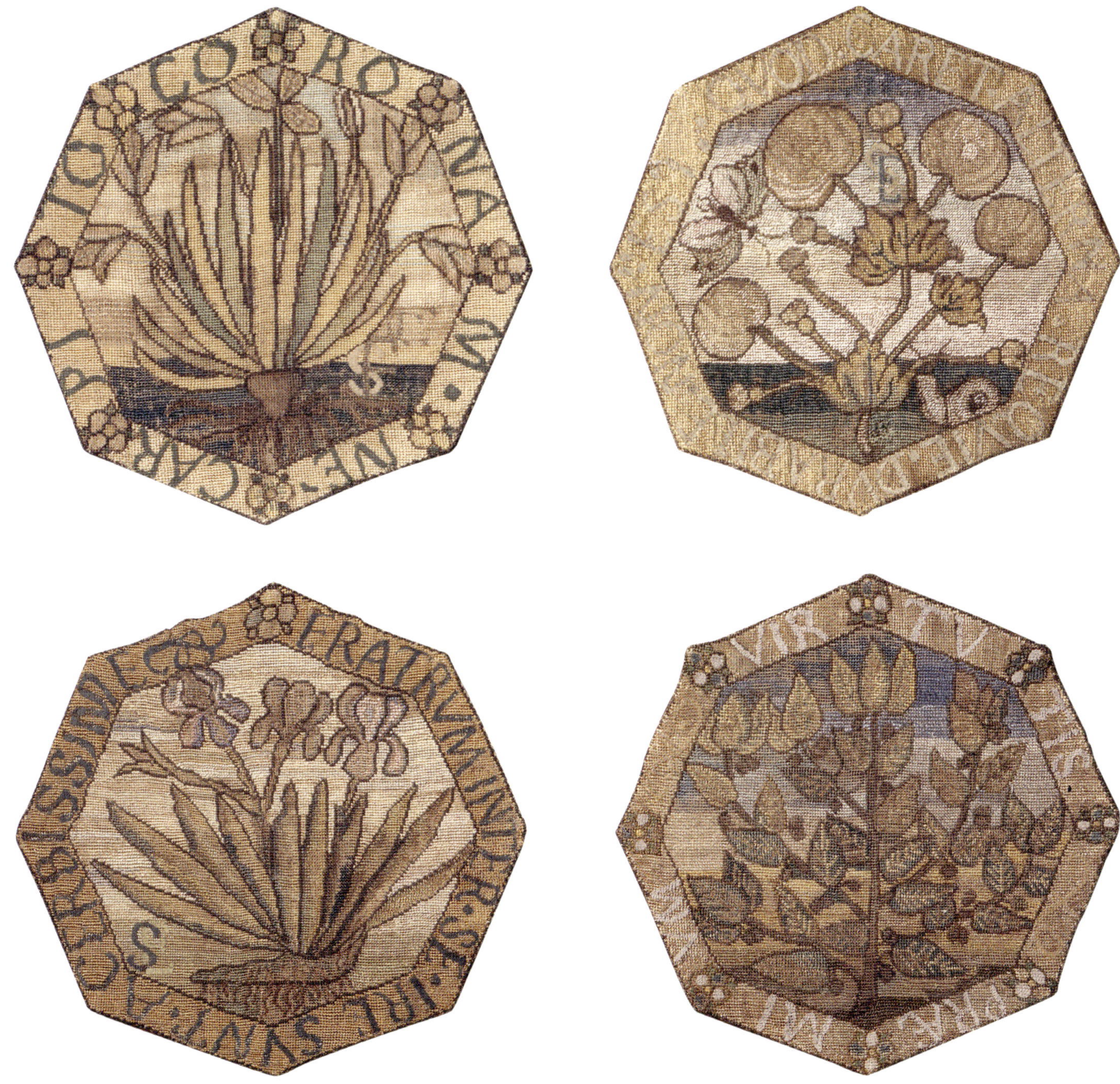

Sumptuous detail

LAVINIA FONTANA (1552–1614)

Lavinia Fontana is thought to be the first Western woman to have had a prosperous career as a traditional painter outside a court or convent. To have attained this distinction during a period of outstanding artistic achievement in Italy makes it all the more remarkable. As well as being the first Italian woman known to have had her own studio, she was also the mother of 11 children, of whom, tragically, only three would survive her. Initially trained by her artist father, Prospero, Lavinia's education included Latin, music and an introduction to humanist scholarship, befitting Bologna's reputation as a centre of female learning.

In this stately portrait (opposite) a gentlewoman of Bologna is sumptuously dressed in a gown of pearly silk embellished with a pattern of gold studs and buttons. Swathed in pearl jewellery, she is seated in a red chair with a narrow silk hanging of green behind, reminiscent of a throne canopy. The colours of white, green and red may be an allusion to the theological virtues of Faith, Hope and Charity. Pigment analysis has revealed that shell gold (paint containing powdered gold) has been used for decorative highlights to the painting, along with silver for the dress. Fontana's remarkably detailed attention to the costume and jewellery of her sitters, particularly the rich fabrics of Bologna's thriving silk industry, must have made her an attractive choice for the city's numerous patrons.

The sitter, although unidentified, may appear in another late work of Fontana's, the ambitious and monumental painting *The Visit of the Queen of Sheba to King Solomon* (1599). Fontana's work appears to have become more experimental following her father's death in 1597 and her years of child-rearing. As with Sheba and Solomon, this portrait shows evidence of changes made by the artist during painting, for example to the back of the chair and the position of the sitter's left hand. JE

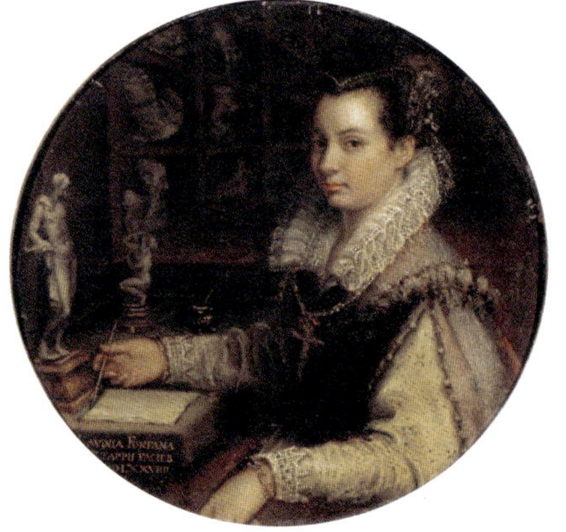

↑ *Self-portrait in a Studio*, Lavinia Fontana, 1579, oil on copper, 15.7cm (diameter) (Uffizi Gallery, Florence)
→ *An Unknown Noblewoman Seated in a Chair*, Lavinia Fontana, c.1599, oil on canvas, 105.5 x 84cm, Petworth, West Sussex, ‡ 1956 (NT 486252)

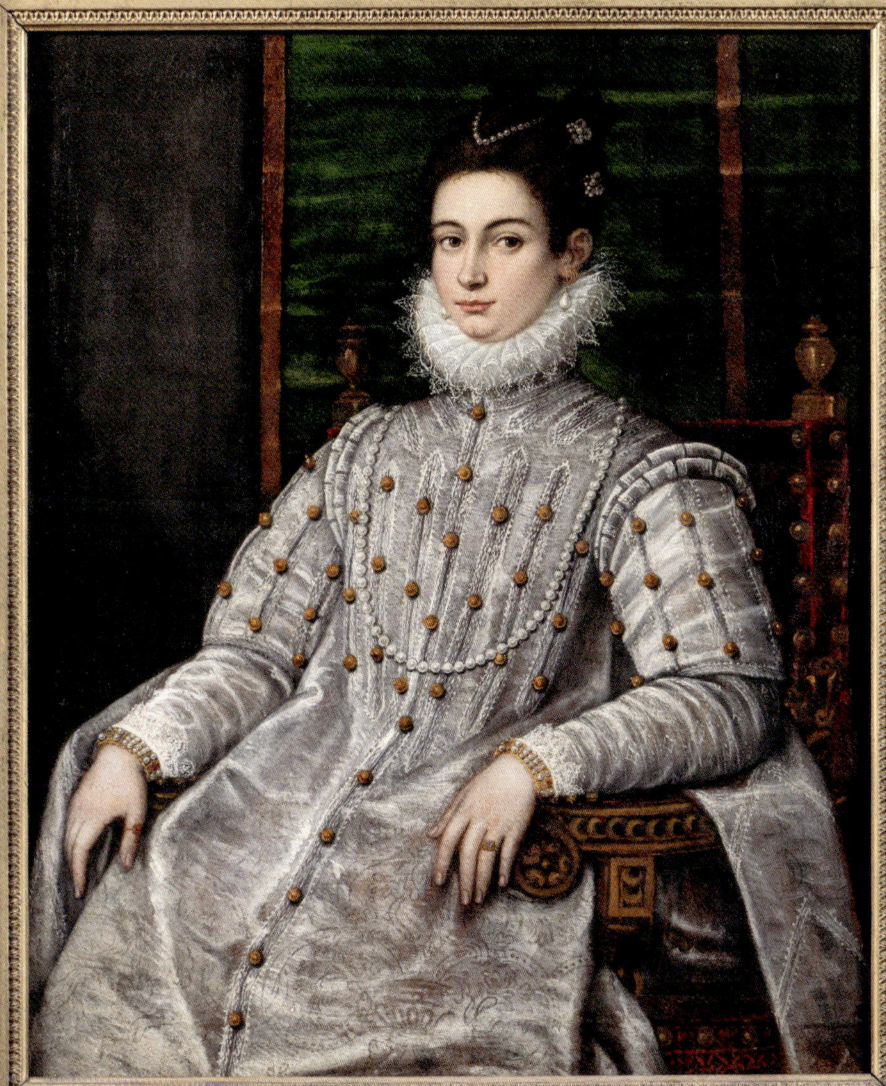
327. Att. to LAVINIA FONTANA

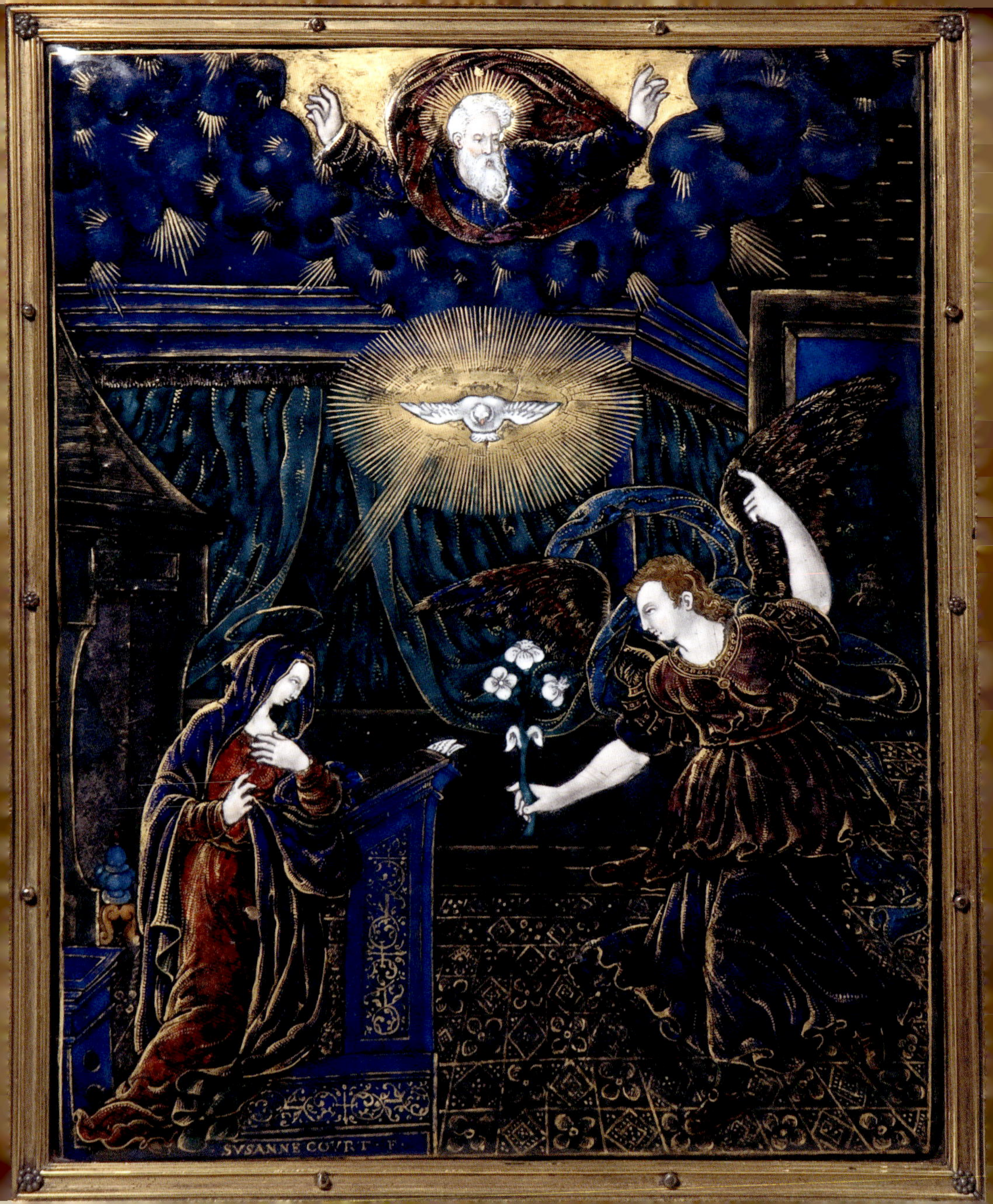
SVSANNE COVRT · F ·

Shining example

SUZANNE DE COURT (active 1575–1625)

← *The Annunciation*, Suzanne de Court, *c.*1600, copper, enamel, gold, velvet and wood, 30 x 24.8cm (with frame), Waddesdon Manor, Buckinghamshire, ⁑ 1990 (Waddesdon 3163.1)

This lustrous enamelled plaque of *The Annunciation* (opposite) was made around 1600 in Limoges in south-west France, a major centre for enamel production from which a number of prestigious makers supplied courtly clients. Unusually, it was made by a woman, Suzanne de Court, one of only two known female enamel painters in Limoges at the time. She often signed her work, as here on the lectern. Although little is known of her life, she came from a dynasty of enamel painters and it is thought that she probably ran the de Court workshop.

The intense, almost shimmering colour is a result of the painted enamel technique, in which ground glass is mixed with metal oxides, laid over copper and silver foils, and fired, creating the luminous effect seen here. The plaque is one of 12 depicting stories from the life of Christ. As was usual for this kind of enamel, the design is based on a contemporary print, in this case by Flemish artist Cornelis Cort (1533–*c.*1578). Plaques such as this were highly regarded by collectors and could be treated like paintings or set into furniture or even the panelling of rooms. De Court's workshop also made more functional objects decorated in enamel, such as mirror backs (page 22) and serving dishes.

The plaque's presence at Waddesdon is thanks to another woman, Alice de Rothschild (1847–1922), who inherited the estate from her brother Ferdinand in 1898 and assembled a collection of Renaissance works of art for the Smoking Room in the Bachelors' Wing. She was a passionate, independently minded and discerning collector, and bought other pieces by Suzanne de Court, as well as inheriting them from Ferdinand. In 1917 this plaque was bought for £2,000 (the equivalent of around £120,000 today) with another from the same set. MJ

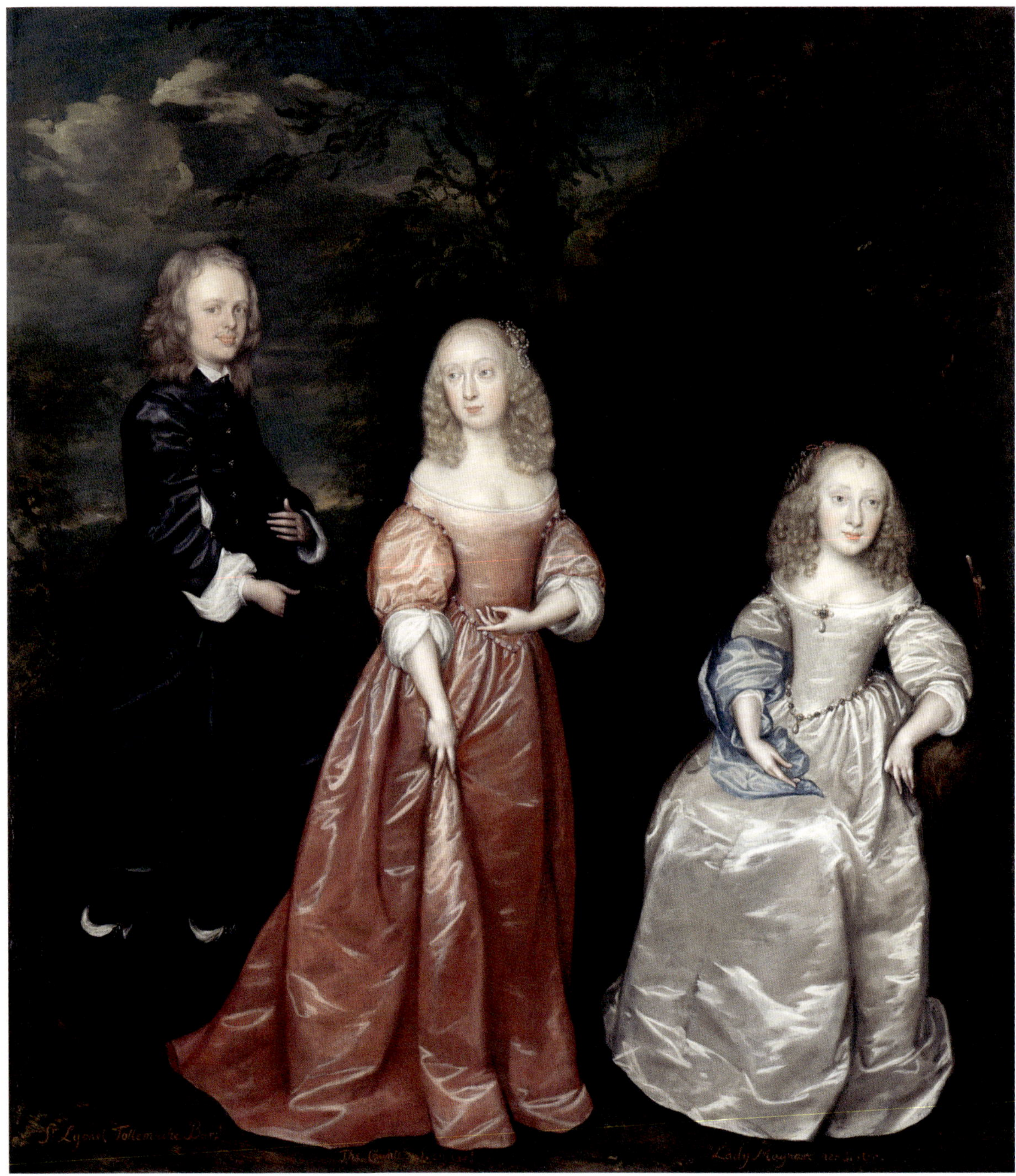
Sr Lyonel Tollemache Bart
Lady Maynard

Friendship

JOAN CARLILE (*c*.1606–79)

← Elizabeth Murray, Countess of Dysart, with her first husband, Sir Lionel Tollemache, and her sister, Margaret Murray, Lady Maynard, in a painting of *c*.1648 by Joan Carlile (Carlell, Carliel), oil on canvas, 109.2 x 92.7cm, Ham House, Surrey, acquired by HM Government, 1948, and transferred to the Victoria and Albert Museum; transferred to the National Trust, 2002 (NT 1139727)

'And in Oyl Colours we have a virtuous example in that worthy Artiste Mrs. Carlile', wrote William Sanderson in *Graphice … or, The most Excellent Art of Painting* (1658).

Joan Carlile, then in her early fifties, was probably self-taught. Greatly influenced by the work of Sir Anthony van Dyck (1599–1641), like her younger contemporary Mary Beale (page 36) she appears initially to have painted for pleasure until the family's financial situation led to her opening a studio in the artist's quarter of Covent Garden in London in 1653.

Occupying the centre of this unusual family portrait (opposite) is Elizabeth Murray, Countess of Dysart, who would later inherit Ham House in Richmond. The Carlile and Murray families were neighbours and the park at Richmond is the likely setting of this painting. The two families were already acquainted through the court as Joan's husband, Lodowick, and Elizabeth's father, William Murray, were Grooms of the Privy Chamber and Bedchamber respectively to Charles I and Queen Henrietta Maria.

Despite the awkward arrangement of the figures, the individual heads are skilfully and delicately rendered, and the lustrous silk fabrics and jewels painted in a rapid, confident manner. The painting has an experimental quality and probably began life as a portrait of the two sisters. Conservation work in 2019 revealed a thinly painted tree trunk in the space between Lionel and Elizabeth, suggesting that the figure of Lionel may have been added as the composition progressed.

Following her death, Carlile was talked of as a noted copyist of Old Masters for the royal court. Her only known works today, however, are portraits, ranging from small oils on panel or copper (including one of Elizabeth's mother, Catherine) to the type of full-length portrait illustrated here. JE

‘Dearest Heart’

MARY BEALE (1633–99)

Mary Beale (née Cradock) was one of 17th-century England’s most commercially successful portraitists. Her reputation aged 25 was such that she was included in a list of notable painters in oil by the historian William Sanderson in 1658, along with her older contemporary Joan Carlile (page 35).

In 1652 she had married Charles Beale (bap.1631–1705), a civil servant and artists’ supplier (or ‘colourman’), and moved to London, attracting a broad clientele of gentry, nobility, clergymen and friends. She developed a lifelong friendship with the painter Sir Peter Lely (1618–80), who commended her work. After a period in Hampshire seeking refuge from the plague, and with her husband’s job uncertain, they set up a studio in Pall Mall with Beale as the main breadwinner and Charles as studio manager to his ‘Dearest Heart’. It is to Charles’s detailed notebooks, just two of which survive, that we owe our knowledge of her sitters and prices, and of the couple’s joint experiments trying different pigments and supports. Her manuscript *Observations* (1663), on the materials and techniques employed ‘in her painting of Apricots’, is the earliest known text of its type by a female artist.

The sitter in this thoughtful portrait (opposite) is unknown. It appears to have begun as a head study, the white chemise and pink silk drapery possibly left unfinished. The sitter bears some resemblance to Moll Trioche, whom Beale painted as a *Penitent Magdalene* in 1671. Or perhaps it is Moll’s sister Kate, who would become Beale’s studio assistant in 1681, when Charles recalls her undertaking a number of paintings for the purpose of ‘study & improvement’.

The picture may be mounted on its original strainer, although the canvas has been lined at an unknown date onto a coarse twill. A drawing after this portrait by one of Mary Beale’s sons, Charles (1660–1714), is in the collection of the British Museum. JE

→ *An Unknown Girl*, Mary Beale, c.1670s, oil on canvas, 63.5 x 53.3cm, Castle Ward, County Down, purchased with a grant from the Ulster Land Fund, 1967 (NT 836226)

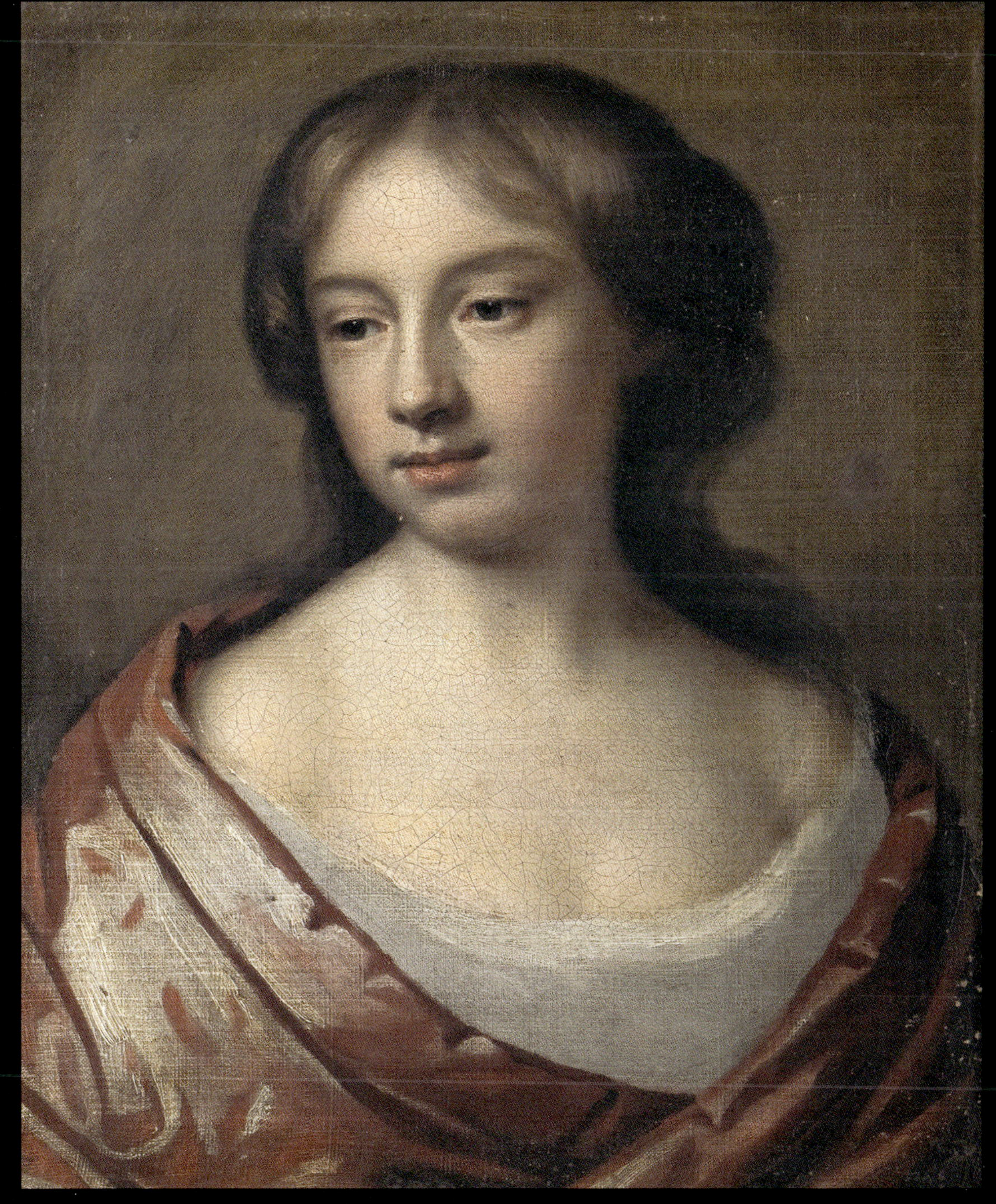

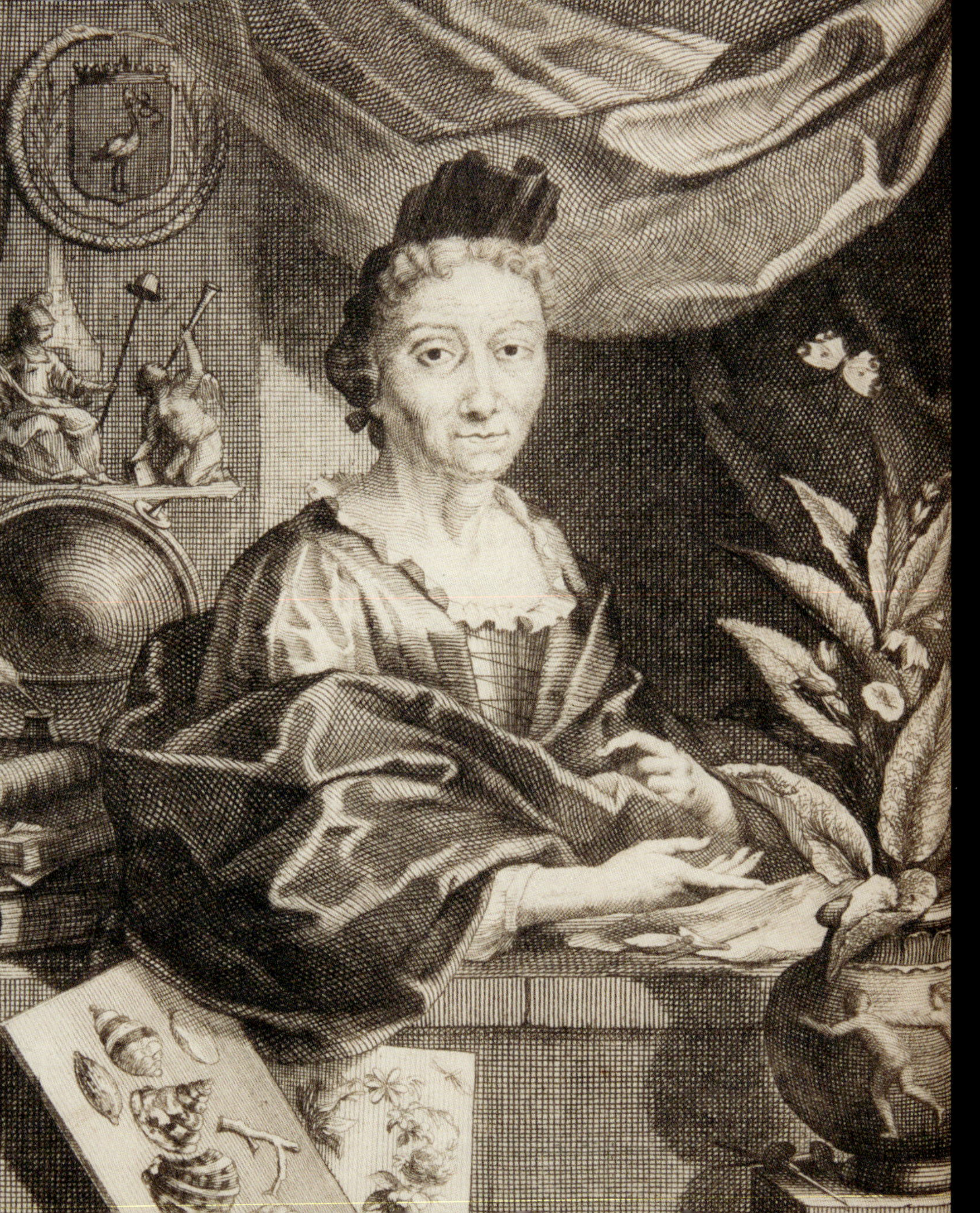

A life scientific

MARIA SIBYLLA MERIAN (1647–1717)

Over 300 years ago Maria Sibylla Merian and her daughter, Dorothea (1678–1743), boarded a ship and began a remarkable adventure together.

Born into an artistic German family, Merian was a pioneering entomologist, botanist and naturalist. She is considered one of the founders of zoology as a modern scientific discipline. Merian worked as an engraver and watercolour painter and published three volumes of botanical engravings between 1675 and 1680.

In 1699 they set sail on a voyage to study the flora and fauna of Suriname that lasted two gruelling months. At the time of their visit, the country was a Dutch colony. Merian observed and recorded the horrific conditions in which enslaved people were living, while also benefiting from their local expertise.

Maria and Dorothea spent two years in Suriname studying and recording plant and animal species at first hand. The resulting publication, *Metamorphosis Insectorum Surinamensium* (1705), contained 60 illustrations and descriptions focusing on insect species at various stages in their life cycle and the plants that sustained them. Admired for its scientific rigour and exceptional artistic expression, many of the book's observations were entirely new to Western science. The edition in the collection at Blickling was published in 1726 and includes 12 additional plates, at least one of them attributed to Merian's eldest daughter, Johanna (1668–1723). Both Johanna and Dorothea were trained by their mother and assisted in the creation of her books.

Merian's compelling images – a perfect marriage of science and art – were re-imagined as source material for the decoration of Chinese and German ceramics. A pair of porcelain plates at Belton (one of which is shown overleaf) are illustrated with insects and flowers from four different plates in Merian's third *Raupenbuch* (caterpillar book), published in 1717. Born over 160 years after Merian, the artist Mary Ellen Best (page 107) is among those who would later make their own copies of Merian's work. RC

← Maria Sibylla Merian in an etching and engraving by Jacobus Houbraken (1698–1780) after Georg Gsell (1673–1740), published as the frontispiece of *Erucarum ortus, alimentum et paradoxa metamorphosis*, 1718, Hardwick Hall, Derbyshire, ‡ 1958 (NT 3131202)

↙ Plate, 1725–40, China, hard-paste porcelain with enamels based on Merian's illustrations, 23cm (diameter), Belton House, Lincolnshire, acquired with the assistance of the National Heritage Memorial Fund, 1984 (NT 433399)

→ *Cassava Root with Garden Tree Boa, Sphinx Moth and Treehopper*, Maria Sibylla Merian, etching and engraving on paper, published in *Dissertation sur la generation et les transformations des insectes de Surinam* (Plate V), 1726, Blickling Hall, Norfolk (NT 3008465)

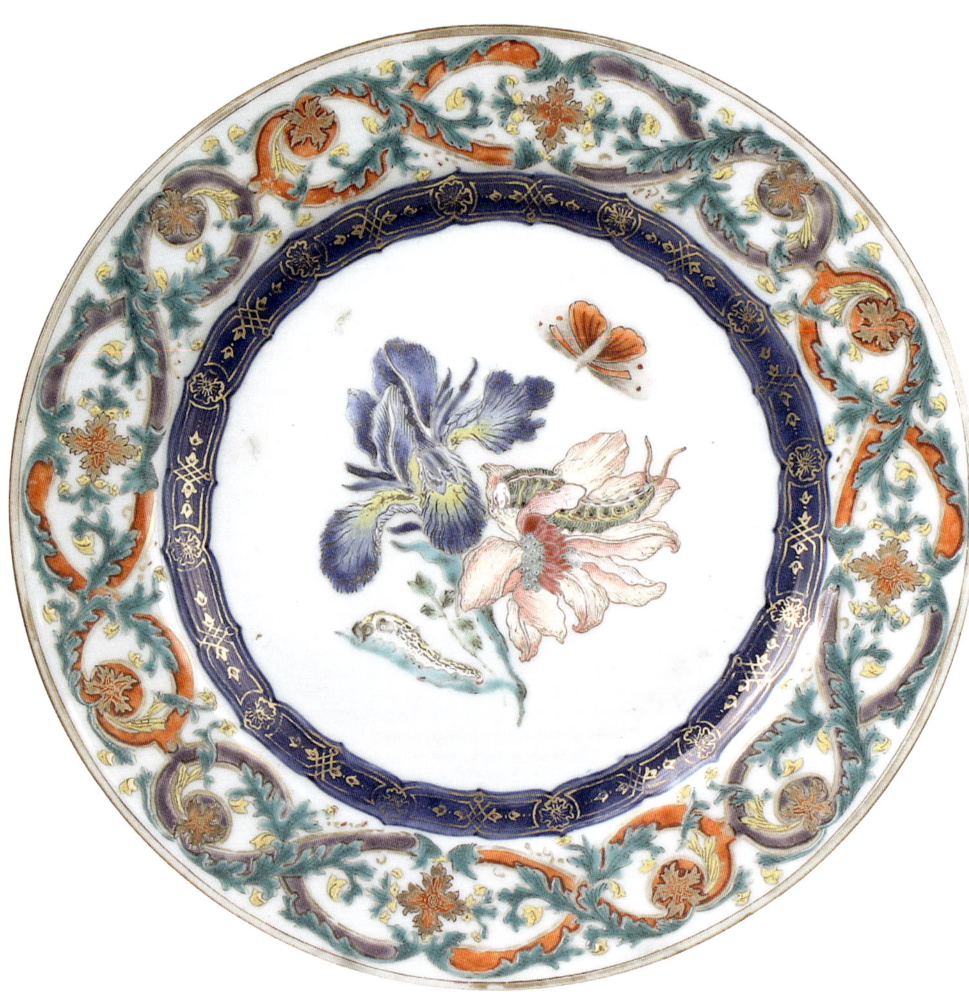

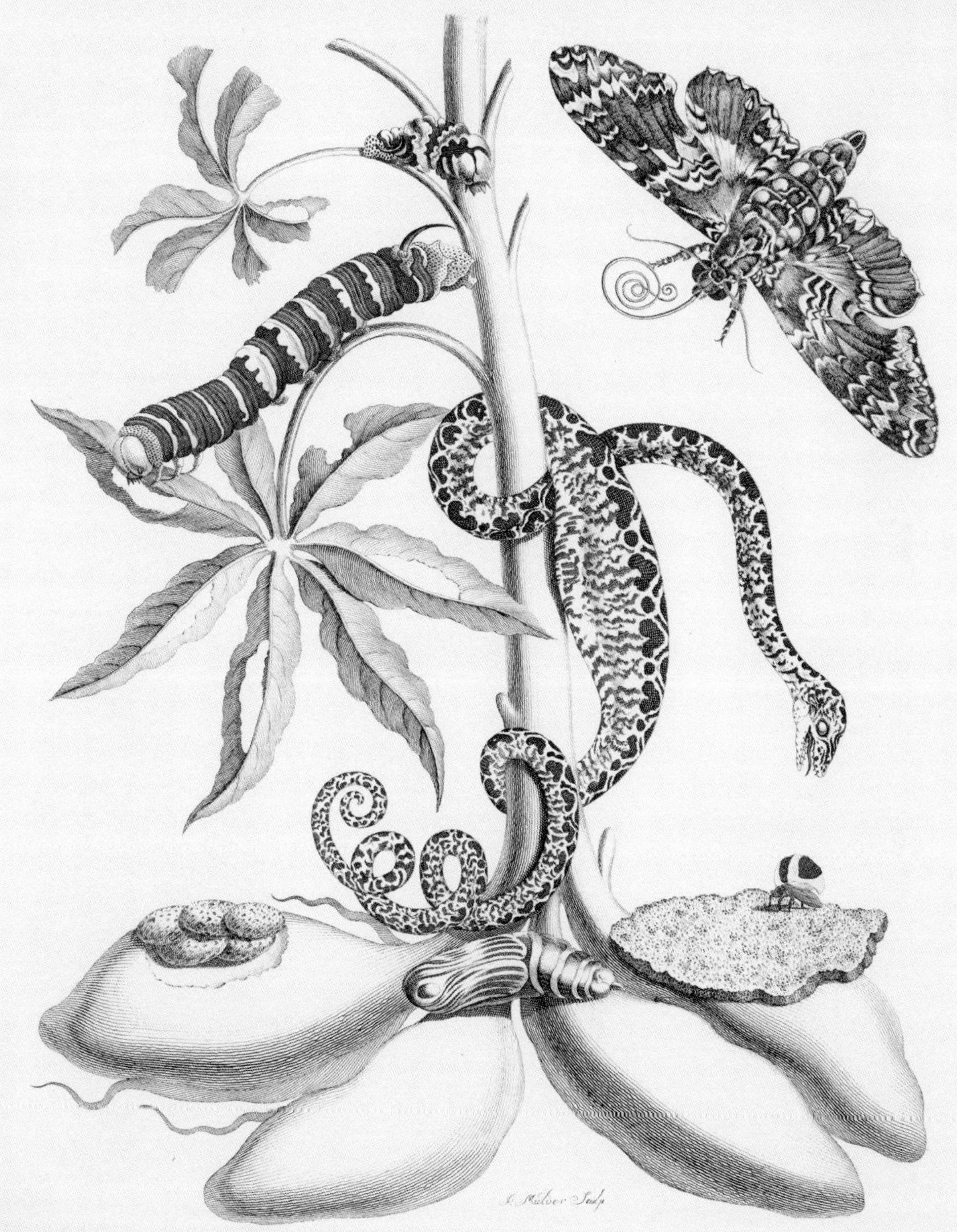
J. Mulder Sculp

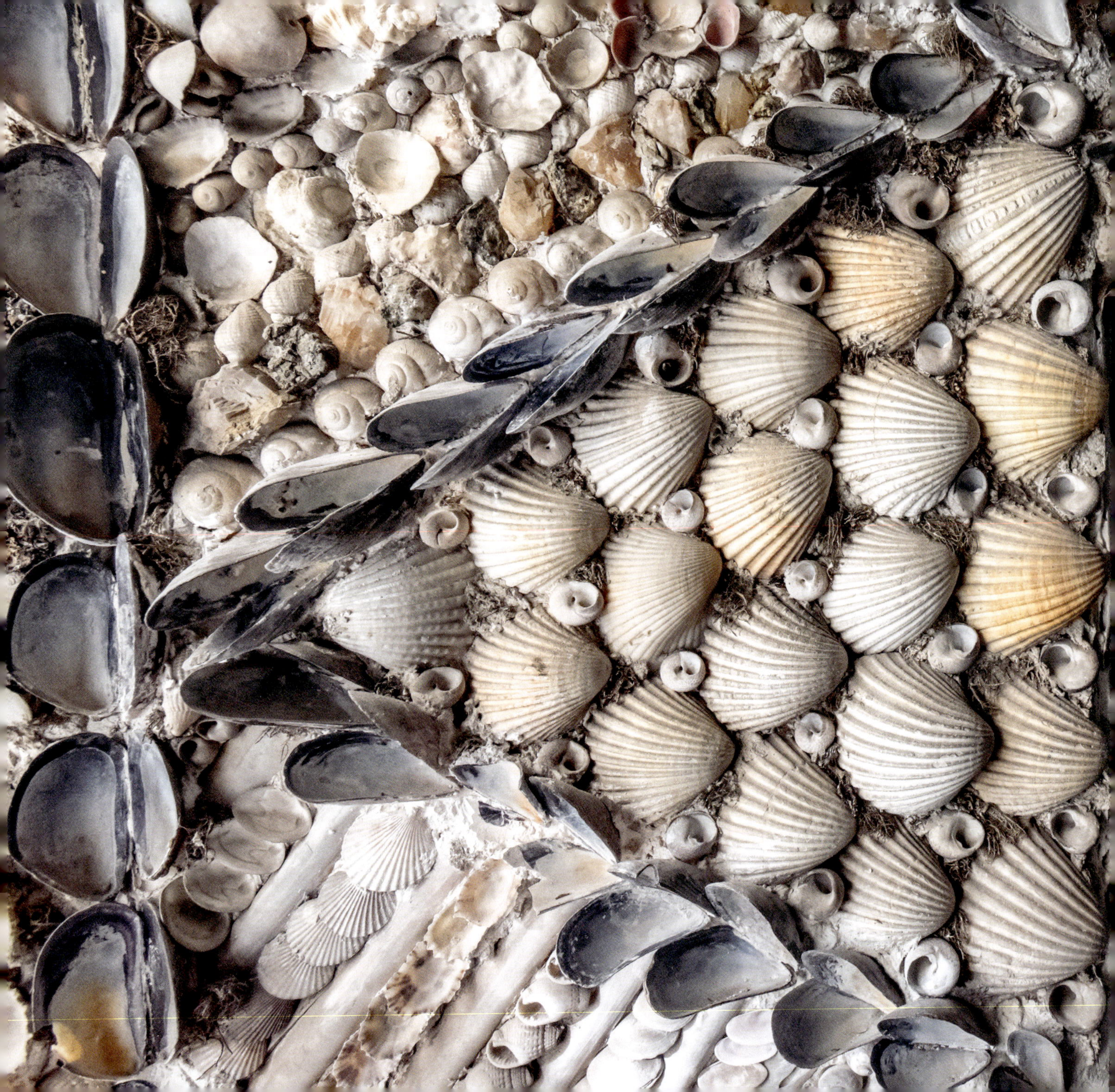

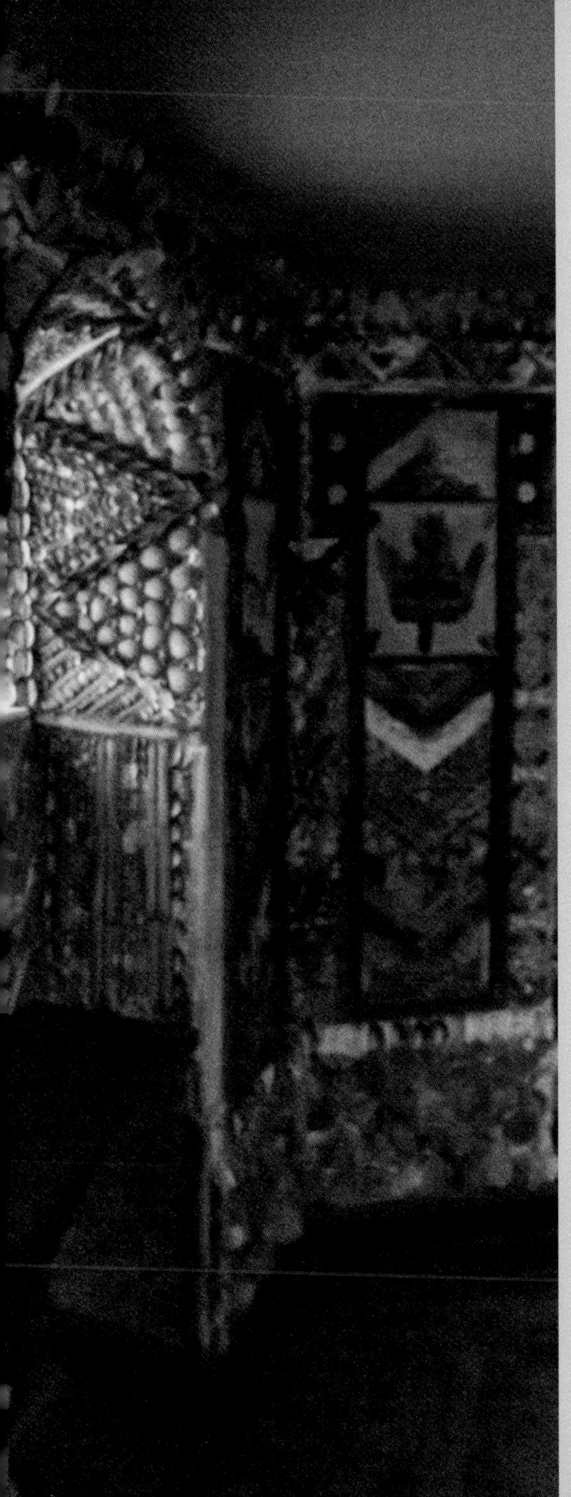

EXPANDING OPPORTUNITIES

During the 18th century, many more women in Britain began practising professionally as artists and sharing their work publicly at exhibitions. Women joined the established academies – painter Angelica Kauffman (page 66) and botanical artist Mary Moser (1744–1819), for example, were founding members of the Royal Academy of Arts.

Although there was a long gap before the next woman was admitted to the Academy, hundreds showed their work at its summer exhibitions, including major figures such as painter Maria Cosway (1760–1838) and sculptor Anne Damer (1748–1828). Unlike men, women art students were not permitted to study from life, but (generally) had to rely upon casts and sculptural forms to develop their practice. By the middle of the century, the number of women in Britain pursuing a formal education in art had grown considerably and a new wave of professional painters, sculptors, engravers and designers emerged. Mary Gartside (c.1755–1819) was an exhibiting artist, flower painter and teacher. In 1805 she published the first of her instruction books for the 'polite art' of watercolour painting – a copy sits in the library at Tatton Park, Cheshire (page 260). The book includes a treatise on colour theory, which is probably the first published by a woman.

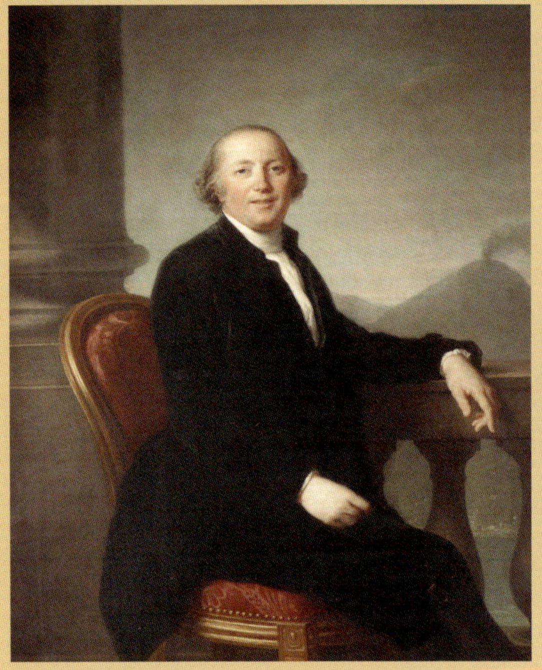

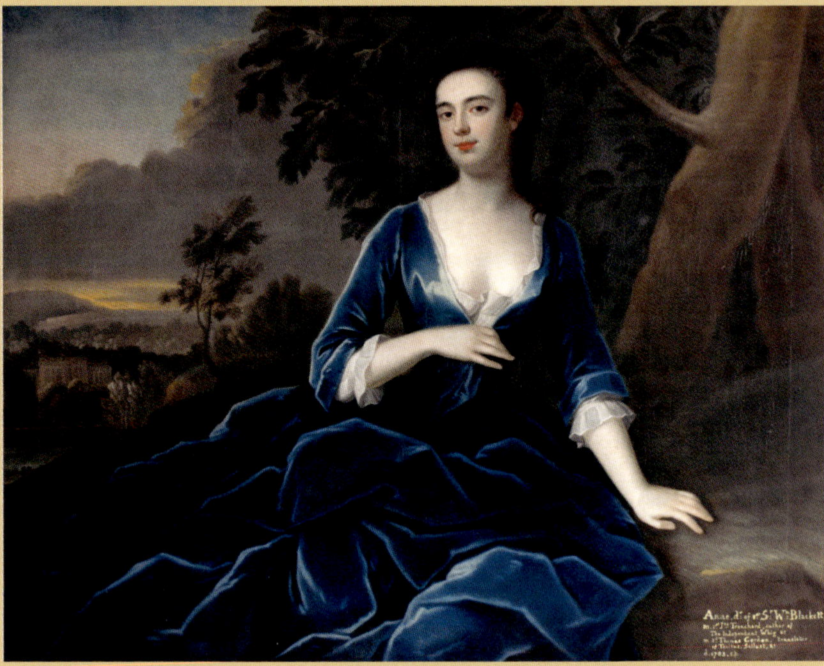

As had often been the case for painters, printmakers and engravers – such as Elisabeth Vigée Le Brun (page 84) and Marie-Louise-Adélaïde Boizot (page 79) – it was still not unusual for skills to be passed on through generations of the same family. This was so for Viennese painter Maria Verelst (1680–1744, example above right), whose family escaped to England when their home city was attacked in 1683. Apprenticeships were not available to many women. Fewer than one per cent of apprentices at the Goldsmiths' Company, which regulated the trade in objects made from precious metals, were women, and most were from the middling or gentry classes. This was typical for many of the different London livery companies – and membership was essential if a woman wanted to work in a skilled occupation. Apprentices had to be at least 14 years old and typically served for seven years with an experienced mistress or master. After their apprenticeship, they could register with the relevant livery company as a 'freewoman', which enabled them to work as independent makers and take on apprentices of their own.

The level of ambition, imagination, creativity and commitment that works by Elizabeth Ratcliffe (page 74) and the Parminter cousins (page 91)

⇇ Detail of decoration in the Shell Gallery at A la Ronde in Devon, a home that was shaped by the highly individual creative vision of cousins Jane Parminter (1750–1811) and Mary Parminter (1767–1849).

↖ *Frederick Augustus Hervey, 4th Earl of Bristol and Bishop of Derry*, Elisabeth Vigée Le Brun (1755–1842), 1790, oil on canvas, 100.3 x 74.9cm, Ickworth, Suffolk (NT 851764)

↑ *Anne Blackett*, Maria Verelst (1680–1744), *c.*1723, oil on canvas, 121 x 156.2cm, Wallington, Northumberland (NT 584413)

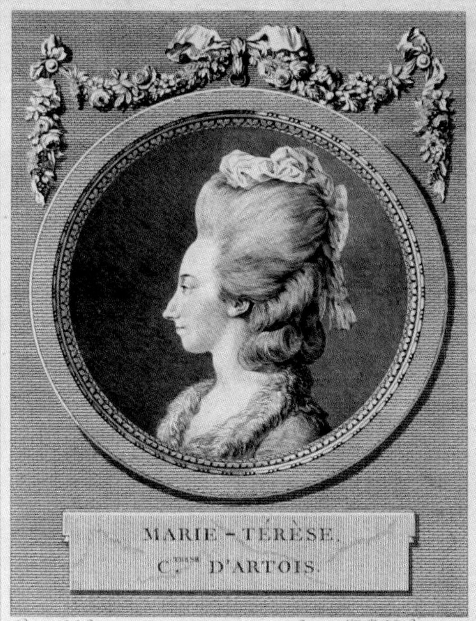

↑ *Marie-Térèse, C.tesse D'Artois* (Countess of Artois), Marie-Louise-Adélaïde Boizot (1744–1800), after Louis-Simon Boizot (1743–1809), 1778, etching and engraving on laid paper, published by Jean Jacques Flipart, 33.3 x 24.7cm (mounted), Waddesdon Manor, Buckinghamshire, Gift of Dorothy de Rothschild, 1971 (Waddesdon 6324)

represent is nothing short of extraordinary. Each took inspiration from places far from their homes in 18th-century North Wales and Devon – whether through the privilege of being able to travel overseas or having access to inspiring source images. Embroidery and other forms of needlework continued to be an important part of the creative lives of women and girls. Other practices, such as cut paperwork, quillwork (paper filigree), shellwork and collage, were incredibly popular polite pastimes. Everything from sand to seaweed, stone to silk was used to make art.

The legal rights of women – including their ability to own property or practise a trade – were still largely tied to their marital status, and widows often had more independence. Anna Maria Garthwaite (1690–1763) and her widowed sister Mary established a remarkably successful business in Spitalfields, London, designing patterns for the most sumptuous silks and brocades. Widows could also become freewomen following the death of their husbands, enabling them to continue in business. This was the case for many women in the goldsmithing trade, such as Louisa Courtauld (page 70). Grace Coxed (active 1700–35) ran a large London furniture business, with multiple workshops and retail spaces based at St Paul's Churchyard. Twice widowed, she went into partnership with her brother-in-law, the cabinetmaker Thomas Woster, at the request of her deceased second husband, who had been in the trade.

Just as women worked in textiles, millinery, book production and other trades, they were also heavily involved in the ceramics industry, although the contribution of most workers is impossible to trace. Following the death of her husband, Mary Chilwell (active 1730–50) operated a pottery in Vauxhall, London, making tin-glazed earthenware. Elizabeth Barston (d.1704) and her daughter Ann ran the Norfolk House Pottery, making similar wares in Lambeth. Although Josiah Wedgwood capitalised on the opportunity to engage aristocratic women in the production of his designs (page 81), the contribution of the many women and girls working in the British ceramics industry during the 18th and early 19th centuries – painting or printing decoration onto pots, modelling porcelain flowers, or preparing clay to be thrown or moulded – was critical, but their labour remains largely unacknowledged.

‘From her industrious and pious hands’

ELIZABETH CREED (1642–1728)

The Painted Parlour at Canons Ashby is designed to trick the eye. The impressive ‘marble’ pilasters that encircle this wood-panelled room are not made from stone but emerged from the brush of Elizabeth Creed (née Pickering).

Creed was a talented mural painter and epitaph writer, beginning to practise both in her sixties, during widowhood. In her 1876 book on women artists, Ellen Clayton described ‘many churches … decorated with altar pieces and various artistic adornments from her industrious and pious hands’. Some of Creed’s best surviving works are in St Mary’s Church at Titchmarsh and Canons Ashby, Northamptonshire.

Creed probably worked at Canons Ashby in 1708–17, when it was being remodelled by her cousin Edward Dryden (d.1717). The work attributed to her at the property is often in a skilled but playful *trompe l’œil* style and on a large scale, using tricks of perspective to suggest things that are not quite what they seem. A life-size ‘dummy board’ gives the impression that a soldier of the Scots Guards is standing by the door in the Great Hall. High up in the church, cupids pull back a sumptuous red curtain by the stained-glass window. The Painted Parlour (pages 48–9) is the most ambitious of Creed’s work at the house. The fluted pilasters with ornate, cut-out capitals, architrave and cornice are all painted to replicate marble. Creed has not only painted beautiful pink marbling in variegated colours, but given the illusion that the pillars and cornice are carved, when they are in fact flat surfaces. Above the door another painting imitates a swagged wooden carving.

Creed’s creative talents also extended to portraiture in pastel and oils, and to teaching drawing and needlework to local women – she is even recorded as providing healthcare to her local community. Following the death of her daughter Jemima (d.1705), Creed established a school and chapel in Ashton, Northamptonshire, providing local children living in poverty with a free education. The charity she established in Jemima’s name continues today. RC

→ Self-portrait attributed to Elizabeth Creed, c.1660–70, pastel on paper, 56.5 x 46cm (frame), on loan to Canons Ashby, Northamptonshire (NT 494880.2)

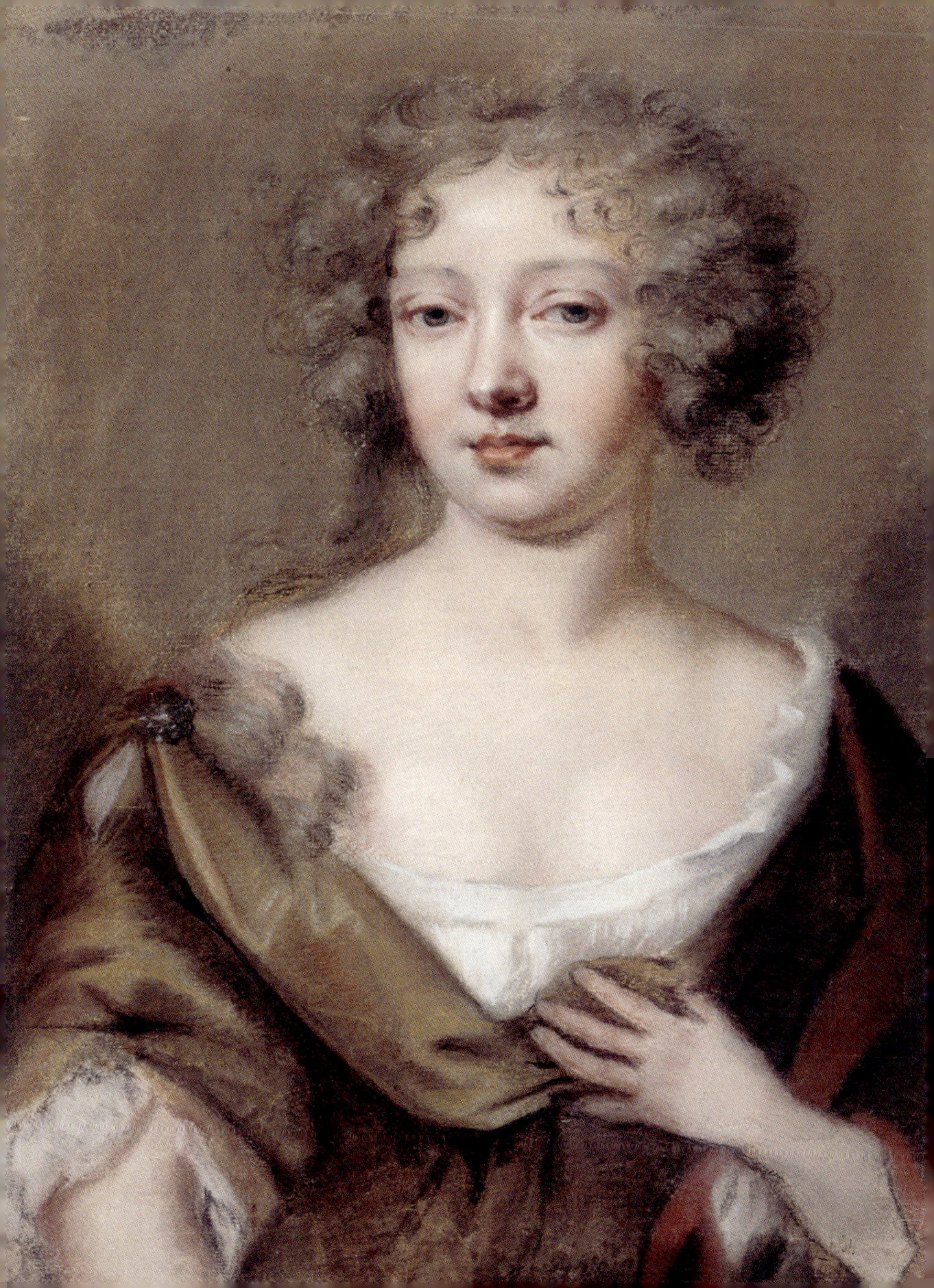

↓→ The Painted Parlour at Canons Ashby, Northamptonshire, acquired with the support of the National Heritage Memorial Fund, 1981

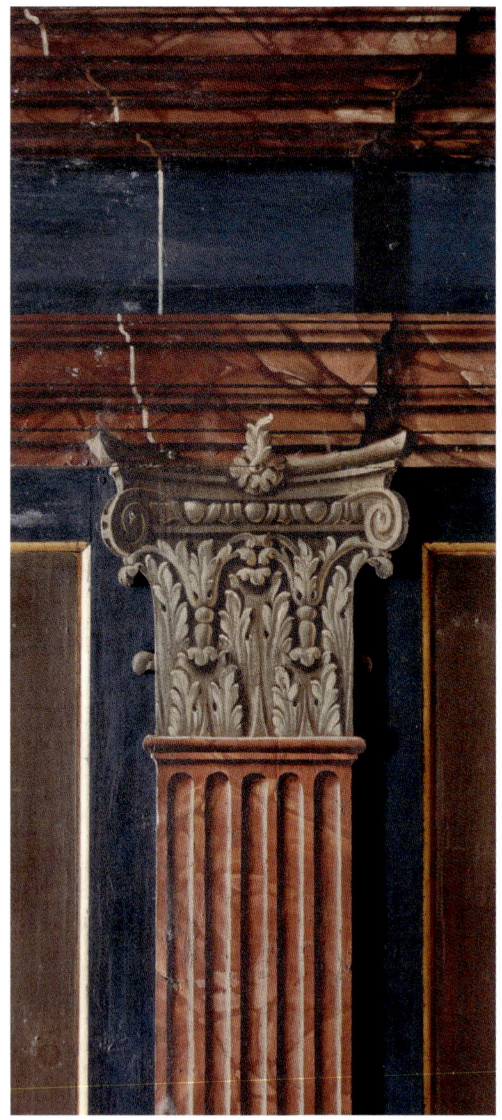

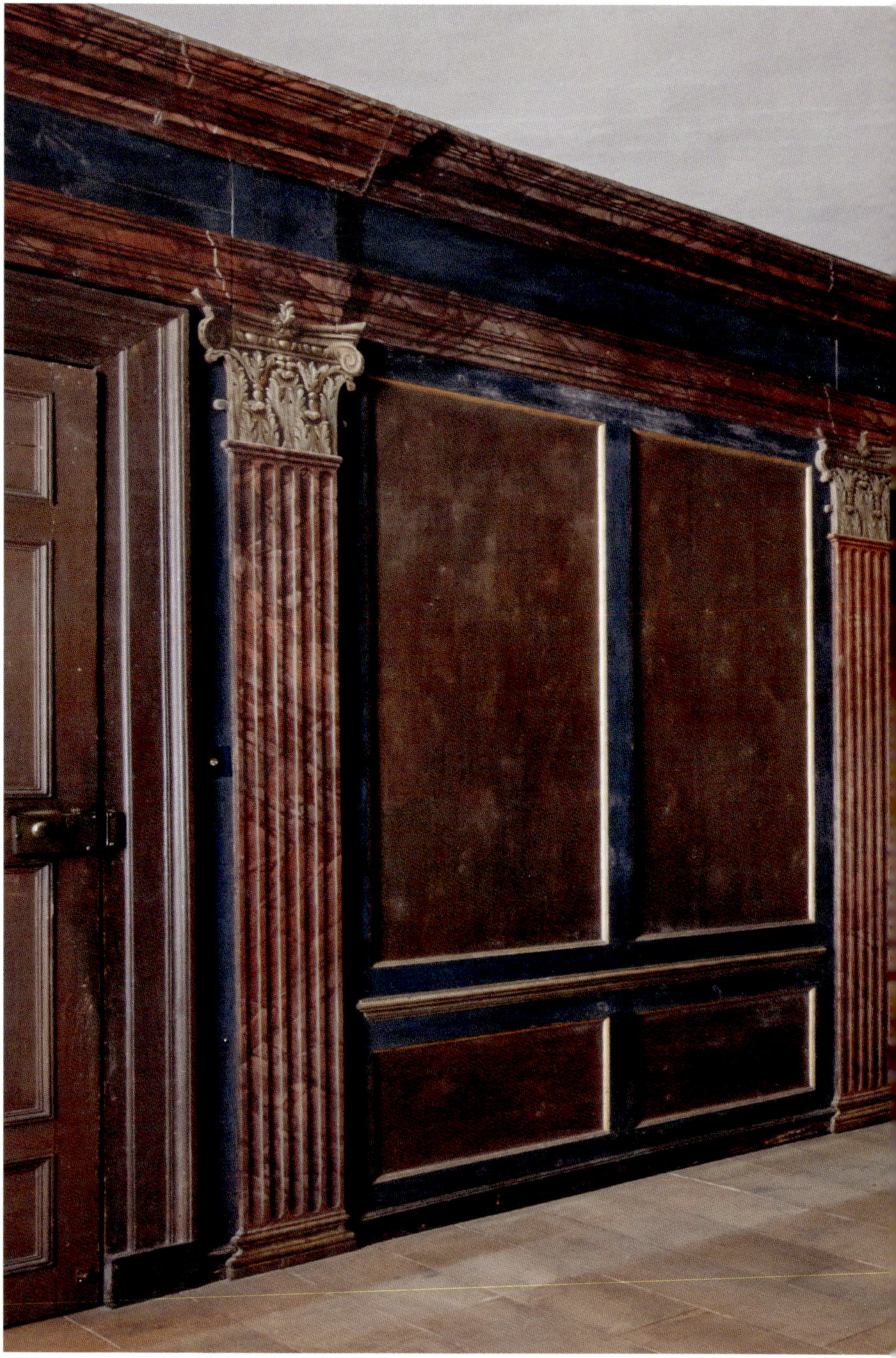

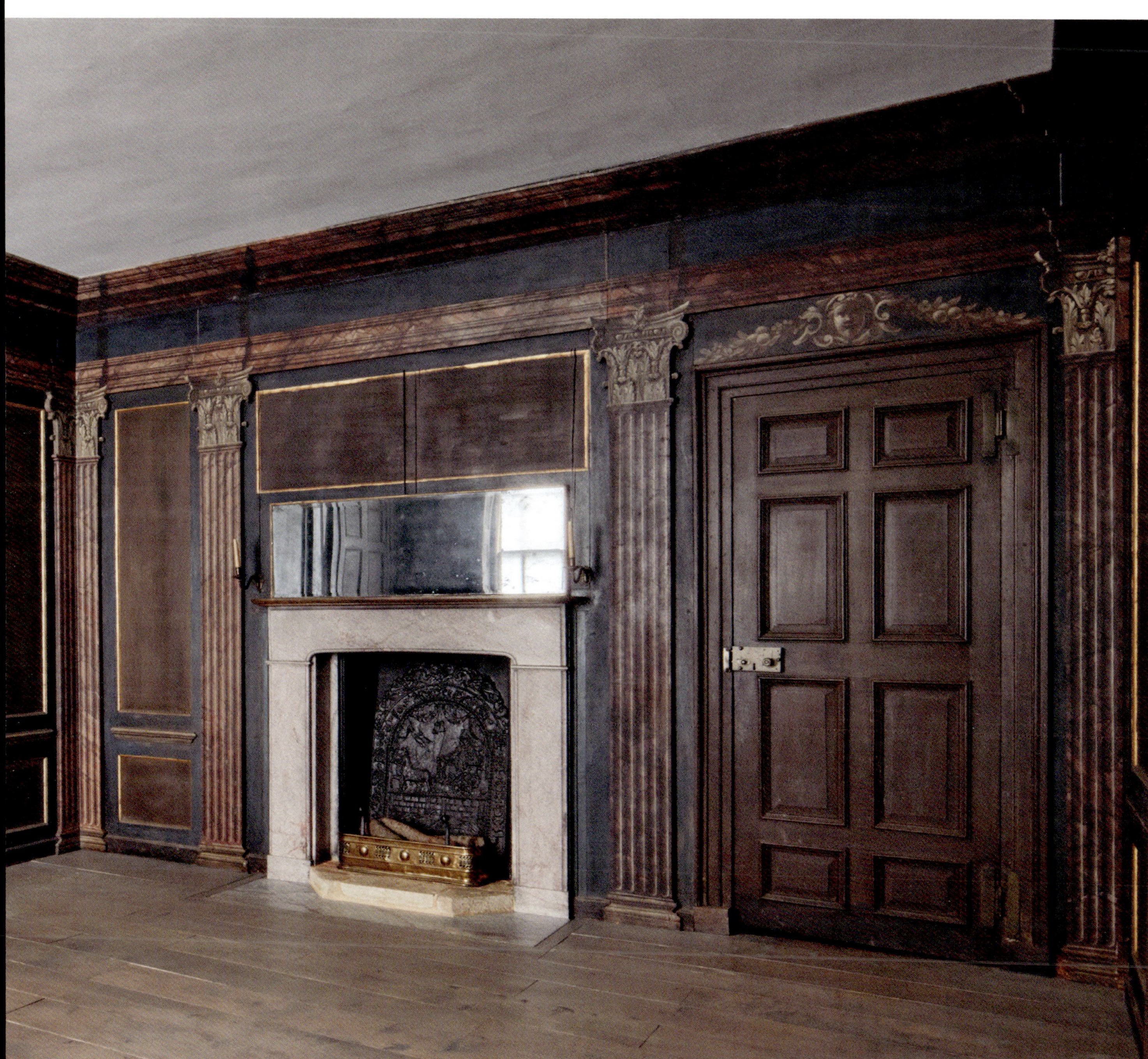

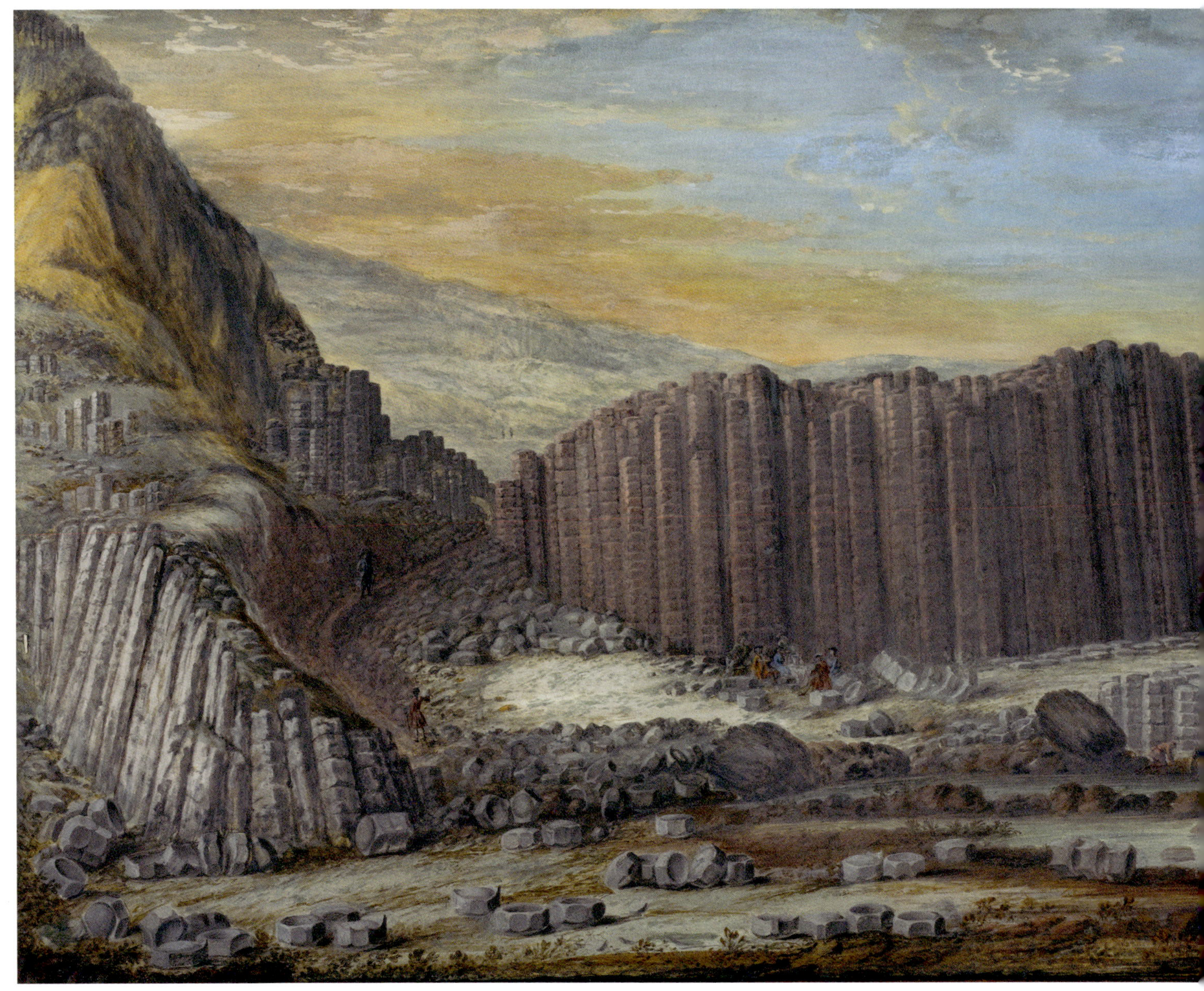

↑ *The East Prospect of the Giant's Causeway*, Susanna Drury, *c.*1739, watercolour on paper stretched over board or canvas, 33.5 x 67.5cm, Springhill, County Londonderry (NT 216679)

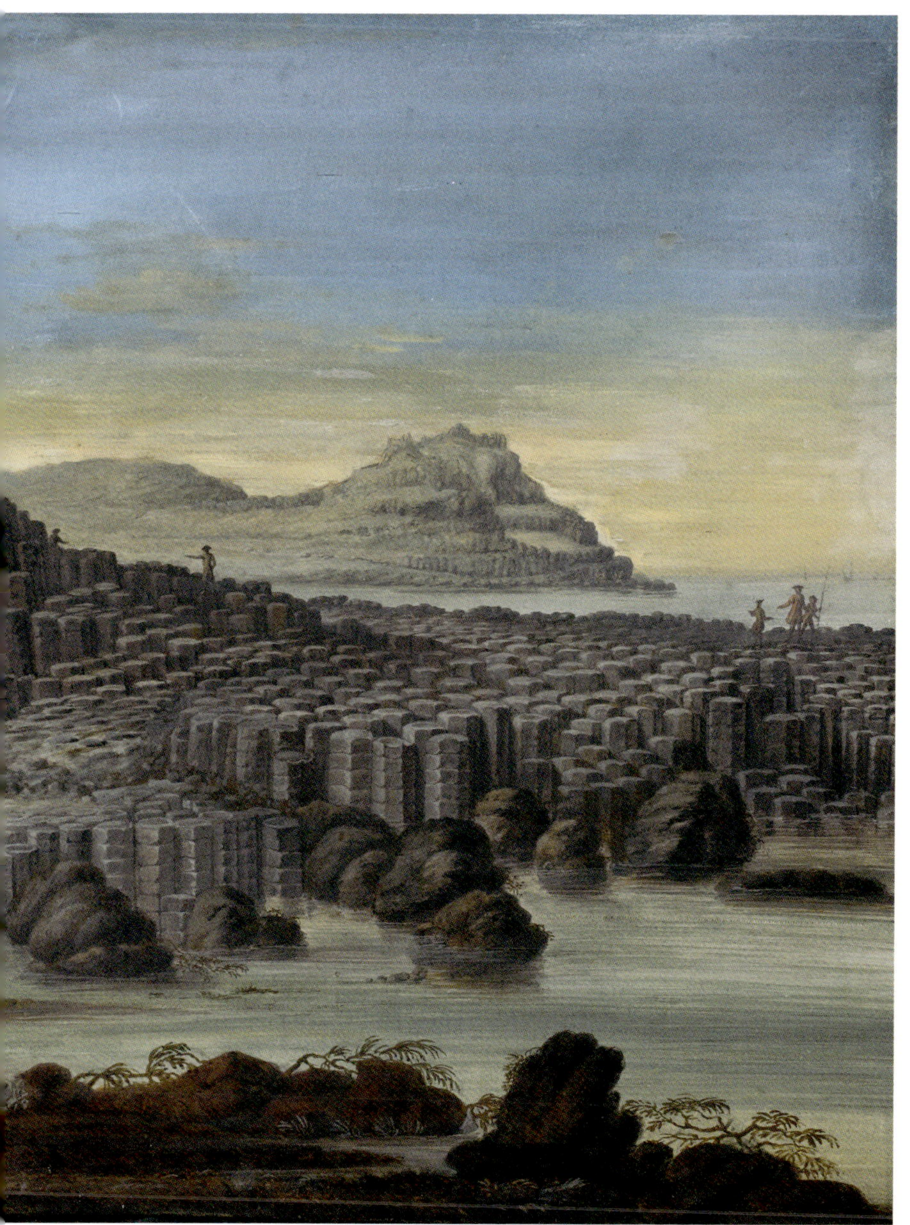

A worthy cause

SUSANNA DRURY (1698–1770)

In the early 1740s, thanks to Susanna Drury, the world came to know the spectacular basalt columns that rise out of the landscape to form the Giant's Causeway in County Antrim. Her intricate, luminous paintings were the first accurate depiction of this remarkable geological feature and caused a sensation when reproduced as prints a few years later.

Drury's pictures were produced at a time of increasing scientific interest in rock formation, and geologists used her depictions to corroborate their theories of the volcanic origins of basalt. Beyond her enduring images, little is known of Drury's life. She probably trained in London and her family eventually came to live in Ireland. She spent three months at the Causeway creating her works, painting outside on the exposed North Atlantic coast. In 1740 Drury won a prize for her Causeway landscapes from the Dublin Society. Two pairs of paintings showing the east and west prospects are known, and are now at Springhill House in County Londonderry and the Ulster Museum in Belfast. By 1744 her views had been engraved and published in London by François Vivares (1709–80) and were beginning to circulate in continental Europe.

Recounting her own trip to the Causeway in October 1758 ('I am still in amazement at the stupendous sight'), the artist Mary Delany (1700–88) compared the natural wonder in front of her with the Drury prints owned by her sister, saying, 'the prints you have represent some part of it very exactly, with the *sort of pillars* and the remarkable stones that compose them of different angles, but there is an infinite variety of rocks and grassy mountain *not at all* described in the prints, nor is it possible for a poet or a painter, with all their art, to do justice to the awful grandeur of the whole scene'. That being said, Delany – whose intricate botanical paper mosaics would later also enrapture those who saw them – said, with much admiration, 'I can do nothing so exact and finished.' RC

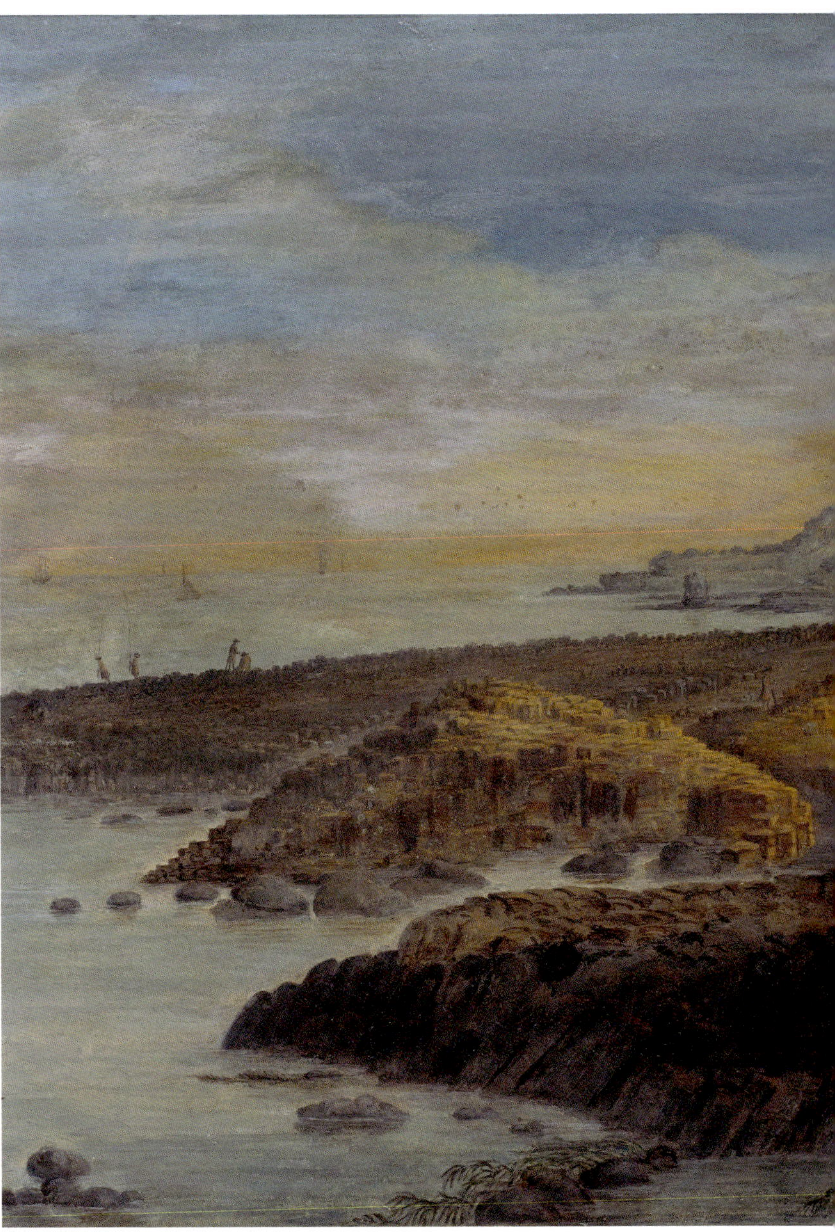

↓ *The West Prospect of the Giant's Causeway*, Susanna Drury, c.1739, gouache on vellum, 34 x 68.5cm, Springhill, County Londonderry (NT 216681)

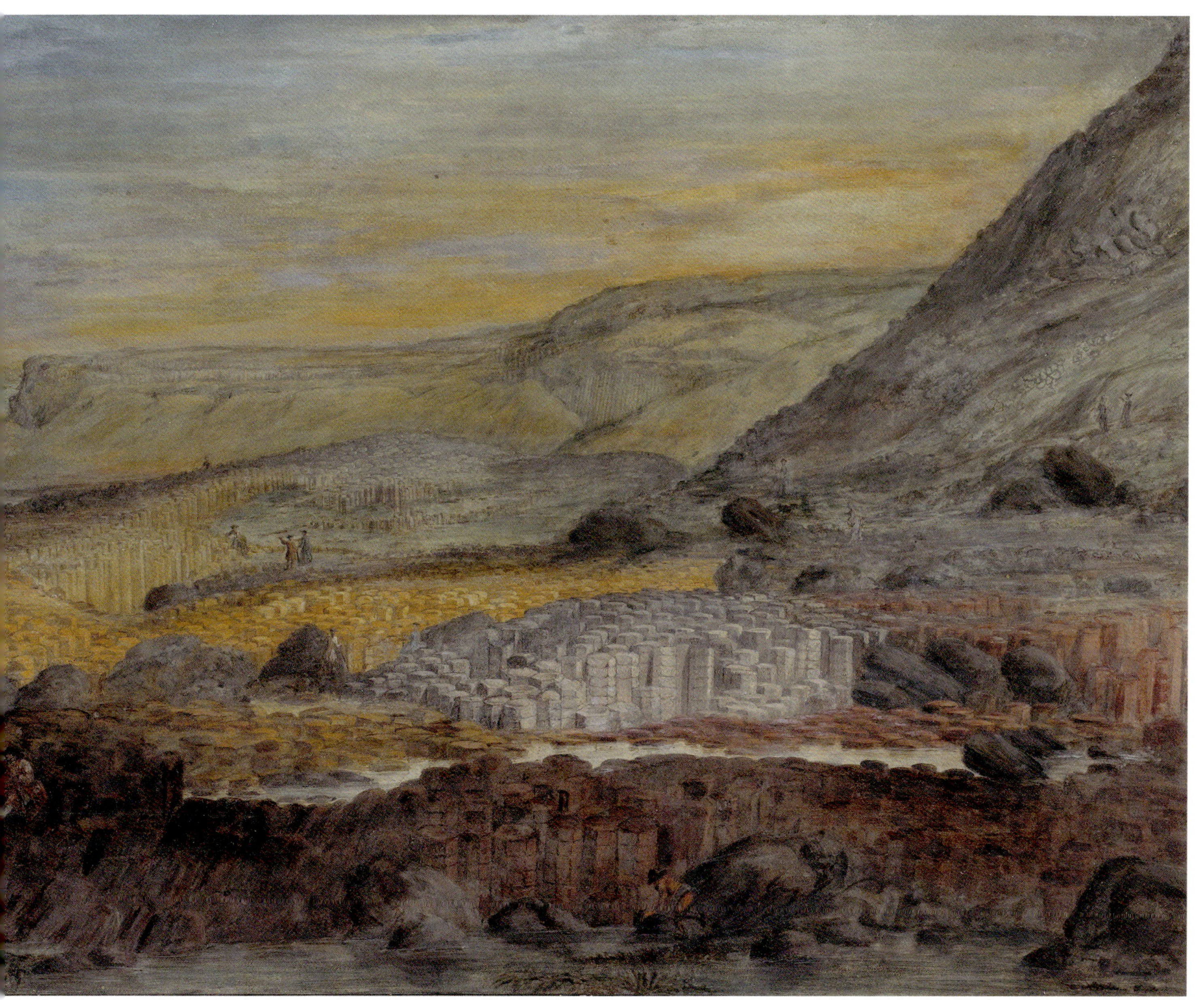

‘The queen of pastel’

ROSALBA CARRIERA (1673–1757)

Rosalba Carriera was at the forefront of pastel’s emergence as a fully developed art form in the early 18th century, ultimately becoming its most famous and commercially successful practitioner. Even 100 years after her death, she was still being hailed as ‘the queen of pastel’. Based in her native Venice, she established an international clientele for her works and was celebrated for her unprecedented virtuosity. Using both wet and dry sticks, she deftly worked their bright pigments with paintbrushes, tiny combs, rolled-up paper and her fingertips. Carriera developed her shimmering effects just as the taste of European elites in the visual arts was turning towards a greater luminosity, intimacy and sensuous lightness of touch. Through considerable business acumen and professional ambition, she not only exploited this new direction in art – now referred to as Rococo – but also played a significant part in shaping it.

In Britain her legacy survives principally in the works brought home by grand tourists – wealthy young men completing their education with an Italian ‘gap year’. The more discerning of these might visit Carriera’s comfortable studio and acquire one of her allegorical or character studies, perhaps depicting a young woman in the typical dress of the Tyrolean Alps – then one of the main routes between Britain and the Italian peninsula. Others might commission a portrait of themselves in extravagant Venetian fashions as a souvenir of their time in a city notorious for its parties and casinos. Her rarer portrait drawings, in simple chalk or ink, reveal the acute character observation that underpins her more flamboyant pastel creations.

Aware of the great distances over which her fragile pastels were transported, Carriera would habitually slip a little print of the three Magi behind their stretchers as a protective talisman. Examples of these have recently been identified or discovered with works at Tatton Park and The Vyne – a testament both to their maker’s professional care and her spiritual life. JC

→ *Francis Whithed*, Rosalba Carriera, 1741, pastel on paper, 57.1 x 50.2cm, The Vyne, Hampshire (NT 718711)

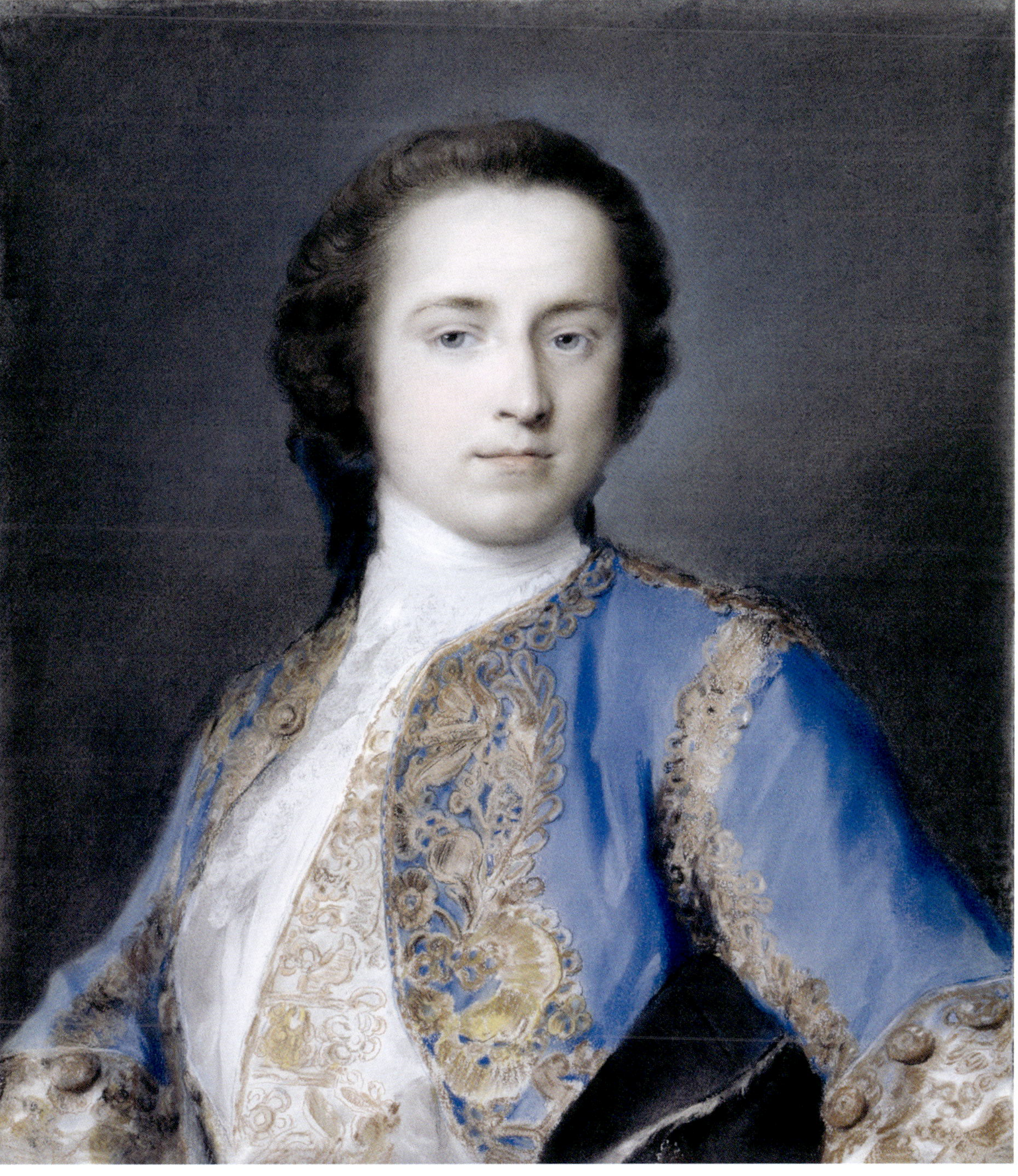

↓ *John Chute*, Rosalba Carriera, 1741, pen and brown ink over traces of pencil on paper, 20.3 x 14cm, The Vyne, Hampshire (NT 718722)
→ *Tyrolese Girl*, Rosalba Carriera, 1729, pastel on paper, 45.7. x 33cm, Tatton Park, Cheshire (NT 1298229)

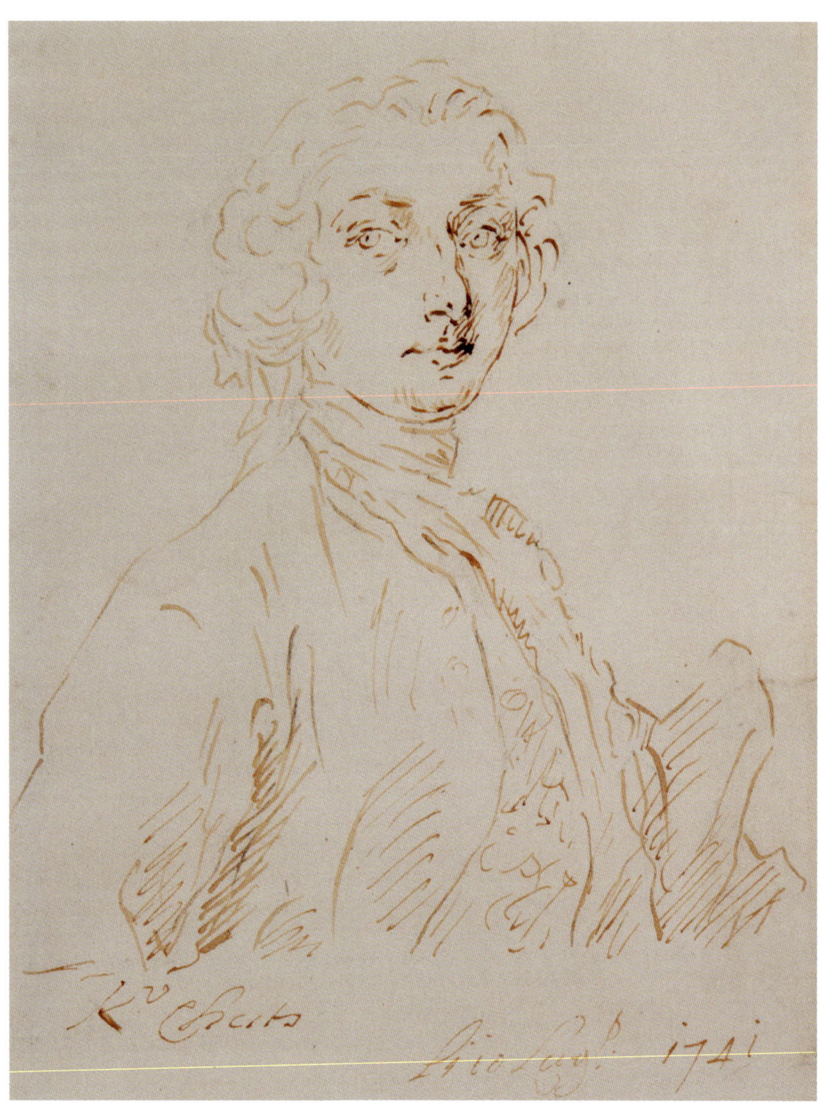

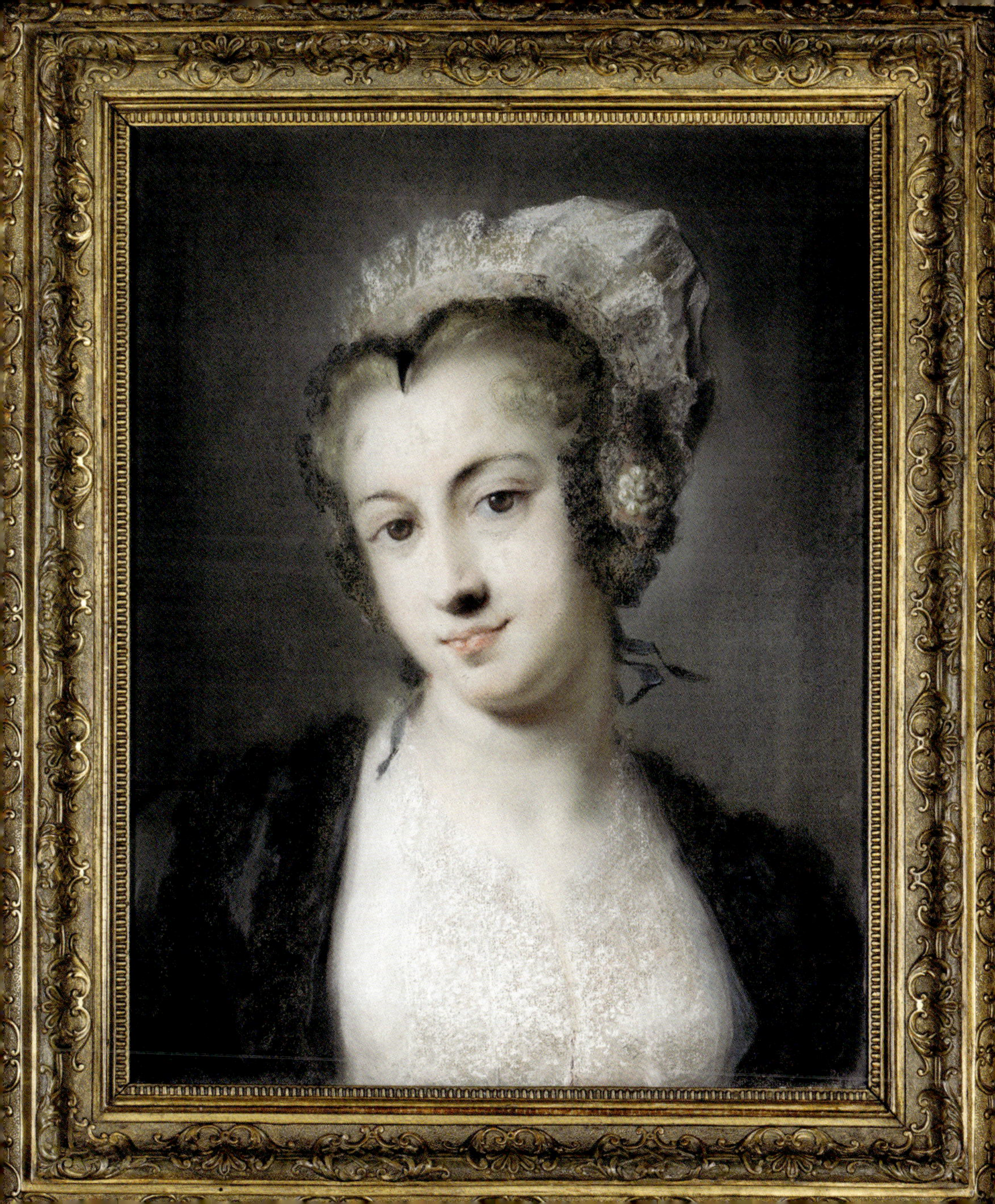

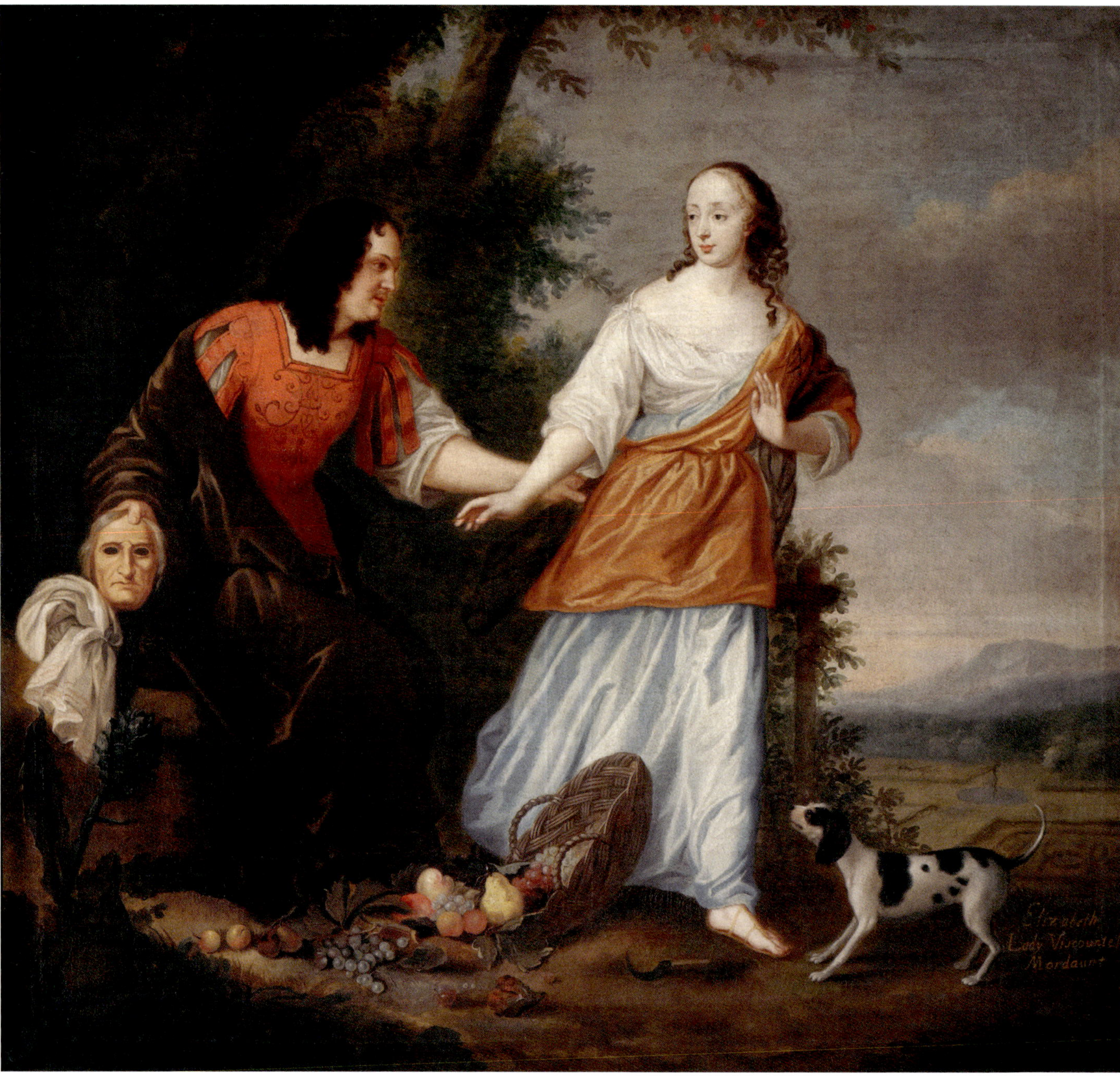
Elizabeth
Lady Viscountess
Mordaunt

The triumph of love

MARY HOTCHKIS (d.*c*.1786)

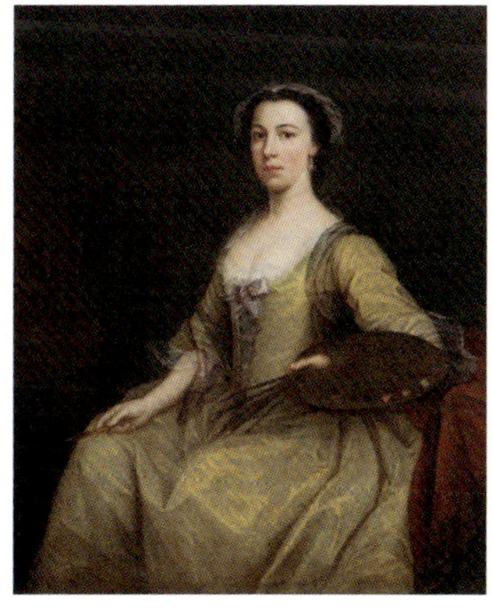

← *John, 1st Viscount Mordaunt and his wife Elizabeth Carey as Vertumnus and Pomona*, Mary Hotchkis, after an original by Princess Louise Hollandine of the Palatinate, before 1744, oil on canvas, 132.1 x 132.1cm, Castle Ward, County Down, purchased with a grant from the Ulster Land Fund, 1967 (NT 836191)

↑ *Mary Grace* (née Hotchkis), self-portrait, *c*.1760s, oil on canvas, 119.4 × 97.2cm (Santa Barbara Museum of Art, Gift of Mrs Lenore Adams)

This dramatic painting (opposite) is a rarity for being one of the few 18th-century copies signed by the artist. That it is by the otherwise little-known painter Mary Hotchkis, and reproducing the work of another woman, makes it all the more remarkable.

Hotchkis appears to have been self-taught, possibly with the help of Stephen Slaughter (1697–1765), an artist and Surveyor of the King's Pictures who painted a descendant of the Mordaunts in 1744. Her copy of *Vertumnus and Pomona* must have been completed before Hotchkis married Thomas Grace in December 1744, as thereafter she exhibited under her married name.

Along with artists such as Maria Cosway (1760–1838), Hotchkis was viewed by contemporaries as an exemplar of female professional independence. In 1762 she exhibited several works with the Incorporated Society of Artists, including what may be the self-portrait illustrated here (above left).

Elizabeth is probably depicted with her soon-to-be husband, John, Viscount Mordaunt. Vertumnus and Pomona were Roman deities of the seasons, trees and fruit of the orchard. According to Ovid, Vertumnus disguised himself as an old woman in order to infiltrate the garden of his beloved Pomona and woo her. The painting is unusual in depicting the moment at which a desperate Vertumnus drops his disguise and reaches for the startled goddess, who has previously rejected his advances. Pomona is shown as if about to flee, her fruit basket dropped in surprise. In Ovid's version, her heart is finally captured by her youthful suitor.

The Mordaunts were staunch Royalists and at the heart of a spy ring known as the Great Trust, Elizabeth passing messages directly between her husband and the future king Charles II (1630–85). Elizabeth probably sat for Princess Louise in The Hague. Both the original painting and Hotchkis's copy descended through the families of Elizabeth Carey's daughters. JE

The painterly Delaval

RHODA DELAVAL (1725–57)

Rhoda Delaval was the oldest of the generation who became infamous as 'The Gay Delavals' of Seaton Delaval Hall, Northumberland. While her younger siblings established reputations for lavish theatrical antics, Rhoda channelled her creative energies into becoming an accomplished artist.

In February 1744 she began lessons with her family's favoured portraitist Arthur Pond, who had his studio in London. Throughout the spring and summer months until 1750, Delaval paid Pond a monthly fee of four guineas (the equivalent of around £750 today) for her instruction, plus occasional extras for materials. It was one of the few ways a woman of Delaval's generation could access professional training.

Delaval found her family to be convenient and interesting models, and a number of the works attributed to her are portraits of siblings. One of the most notable is a self-portrait with her brother Francis. In it she portrays herself as 'Painting' and Francis, the lively theatre-lover two years her junior, is cast in the role of 'Poetry' (page 62). In 1751 Delaval's marriage to Edward Astley gave her access to that family's art collections, enabling her to copy a portrait of their famous ancestor, the Civil War commander Jacob Astley (page 63). While such copying was a way of honing technique, it also took skill to achieve convincingly.

Delaval's undoubted talent, her close association with Pond and the lower status traditionally granted to 'amateur' endeavour have conspired to limit our understanding of her art. At least six substantial paintings are either attributed to Delaval or could be, if subjected to deeper study. Are there more, perhaps overlooked as the work of either her teacher or another professional?

For over a decade Delaval painted intimate glimpses of her family, yet we still understand her best from the chatty, easy-going letters she wrote to her sister-in-law. She died in 1757, at just 32 years old, leaving us a tantalising artistic legacy to explore. JM

→ *Rhoda Delaval, later Lady Astley*, Arthur Pond (1701–58), *c.*1750, oil on canvas, 76 x 64cm, Seaton Delaval Hall, Northumberland, ‡ 2009 (NT 1276704)

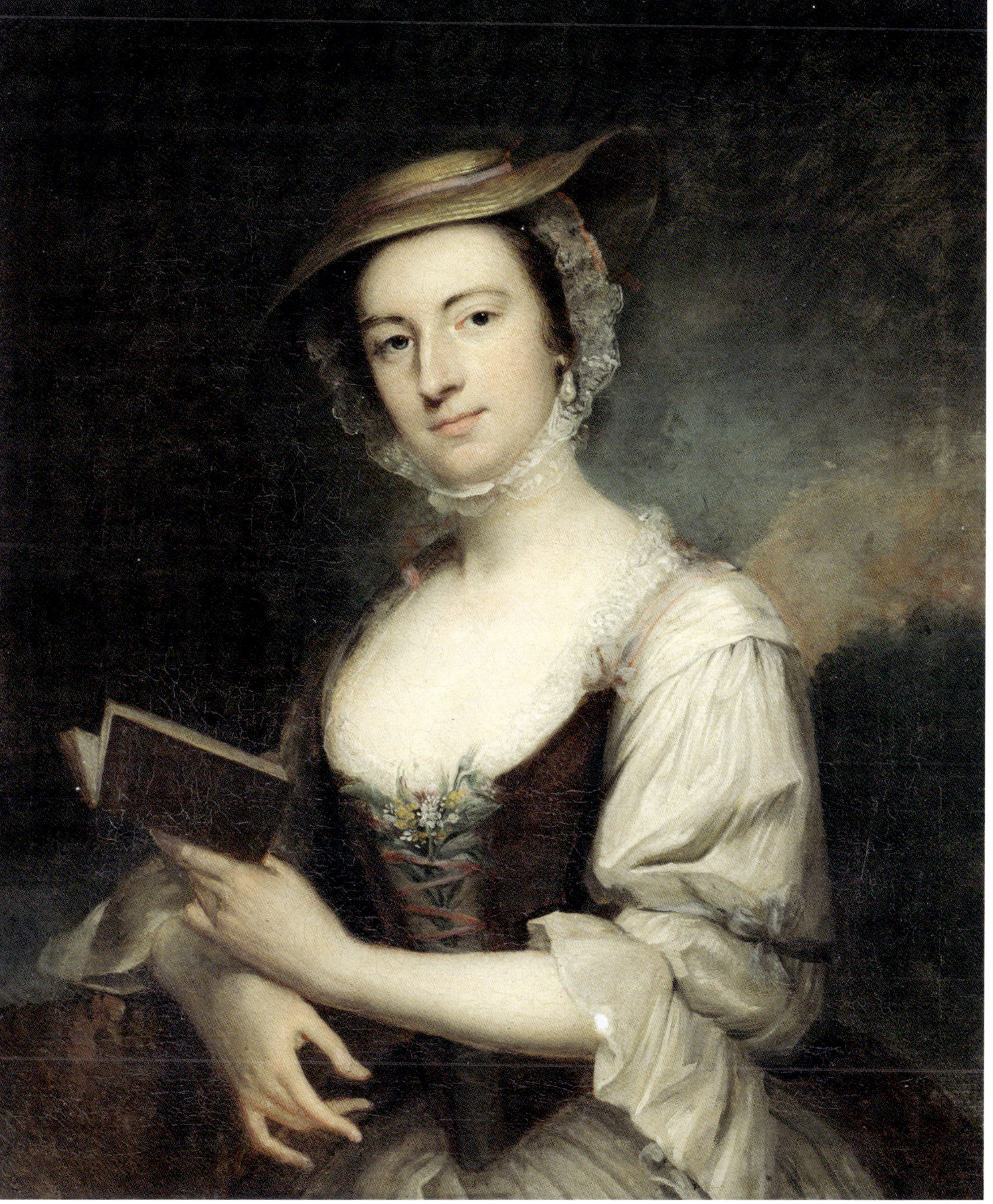

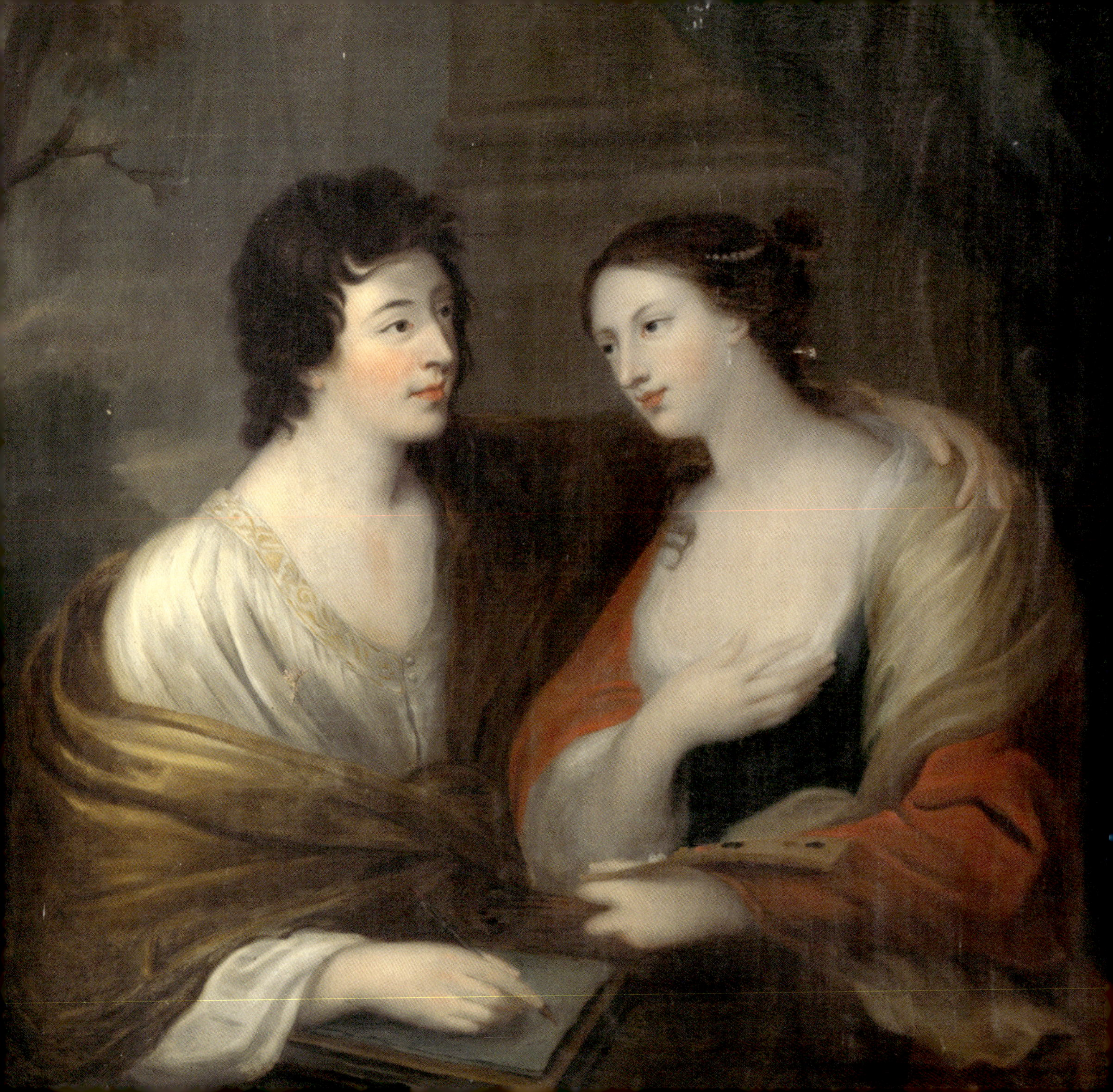

← *Rhoda Delaval, later Lady Astley, and her brother, Sir Francis Blake Delaval (1727–71), as 'Painting and Poetry' (after Luini)* (detail), Rhoda Delaval, Lady Astley, *c.*1745–57, oil on canvas, 114 x 115cm, Seaton Delaval Hall, Northumberland, private treaty sale, 2012 (NT 1276899)

↓ *Sir Jacob Astley, 1st Baron Astley of Reading (1579–1652),* Rhoda Delaval, Lady Astley, *c.*1745–57, oil on canvas, 74 x 61cm, Seaton Delaval Hall, Northumberland, ‡ 2009 (NT 1276692)

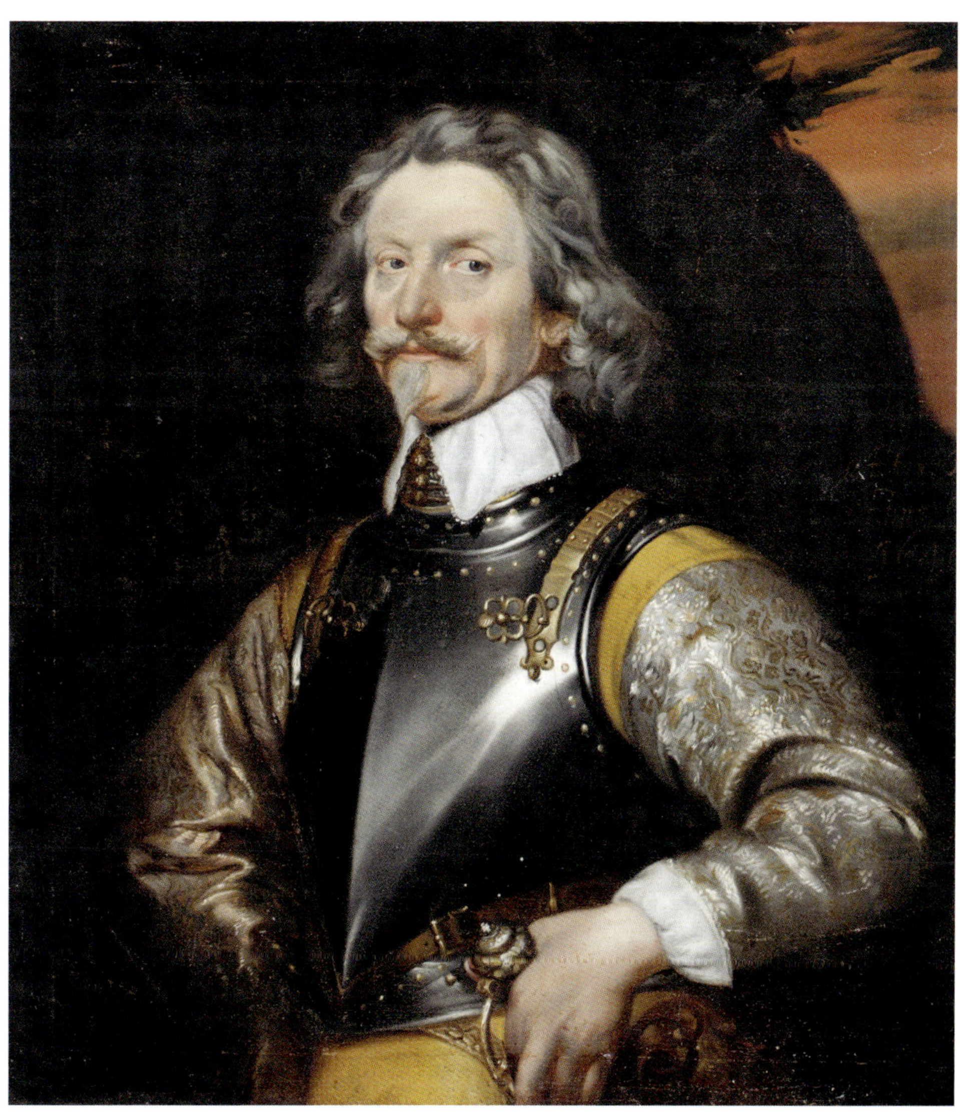

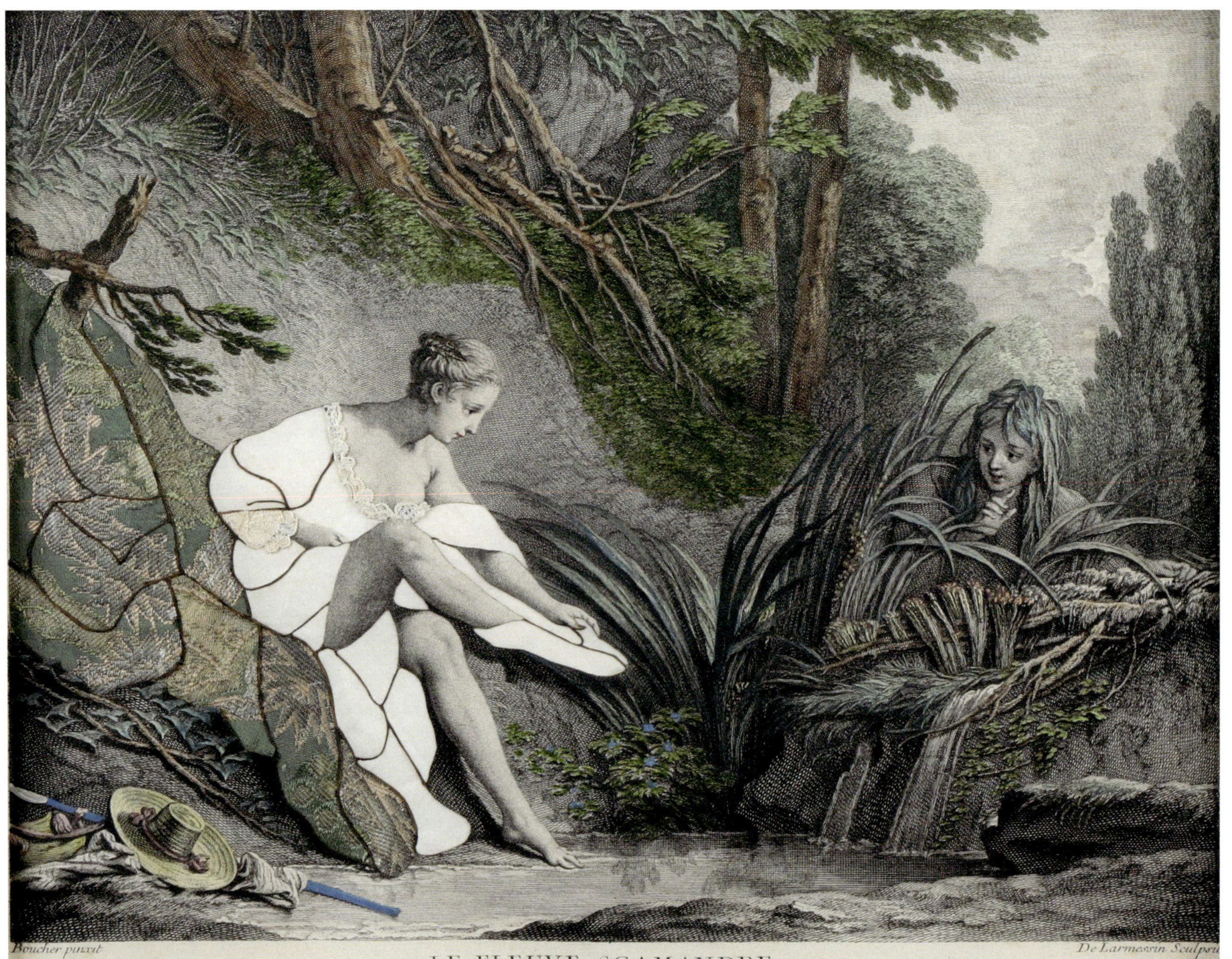

Boucher pinxit — De Larmessin Sculpsit

LE FLEUVE SCAMANDRE

Pour vos Ieunes Apas le Scamandre embrasé
Sort d'entre ses roseaux : Cest un Dieu qui vous aime :
Un Dieu! mais S'il n'estoit qu'un mortel deguisé….
Point dexamen : aidez à vous tromper vous même

M.r Roy.

a Paris chez De Larmessin graveur du Roy rüe des Noyers a la 2.e porte cocher a gauche entrant par la rüe S.t Jacques. A.P.D.R.

Dressed to express

SABINE WINN (1734–98)

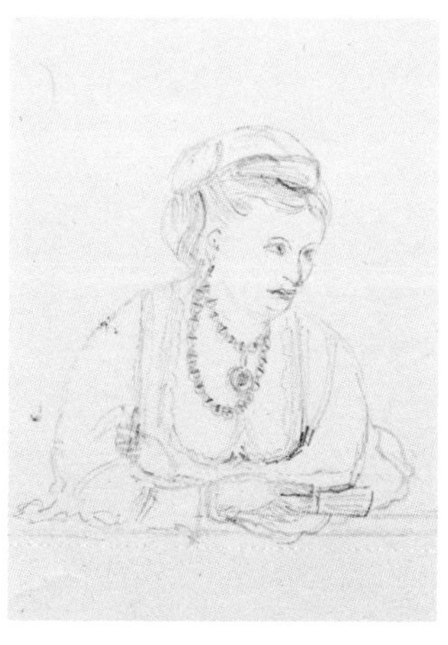

← Detail of print dressed by Sabine Winn, 1761–5, engraving by Nicolas Larmessin IV (1684–1755), *Le Fleuve Scamandre*, 1743, after François Boucher (1703–70), paper, silk, lace, brocade, hand-colouring, 36 x 40cm, Nostell, West Yorkshire, ‡ 1986 (NT 960084.9)

↑ *Sketch of a woman (possibly Sabine Winn)*, Esther Sabine Winn, c.1780, pencil on paper, 11 x 18cm, Nostell, West Yorkshire (NT 3232788)

In the early 1760s Sabine Winn picked up her scissors and began to create a series of works that would become her personal masterpiece. They began as a group of 16 French prints from the risqué *Suite de Larmessin*, given to her by her new husband. Winn's incredible skill, dexterity, vision and patience transformed them into something far more interesting and personal. Her unique creations are 'dressed prints', in which parts of the costume in the image are meticulously cut out and adorned with pieces of textile pasted onto the back, probably taken from her own garments.

Born in Vevey, Switzerland, Winn moved to London and then to Nostell in West Yorkshire in 1765, a few years after her marriage. Because she could not speak English well and her husband was often travelling, she struggled to settle into life in Yorkshire, preferring the company of French-speaking friends in London. The process of creating her pictures might well have been a comforting reminder of home. The technique is one that she had presumably mastered before leaving Switzerland, as it had been fashionable in continental Europe during the late 17th and early 18th centuries.

The prints show Winn's remarkable understanding of fabric. Grains are laid to suggest drapery, and patterns arranged to give a sense of movement. There is extraordinary attention to detail – from the tiny French-knot buttons sewn onto garments, to slivers of original paper left overlaying the fabric to create structure. Minute pieces of lace are used to embellish the neckline and cuffs of a simple white linen dress. Winn has painted areas of colour onto the print to add further realism and interest, adding a lush green to the background foliage and giving the bather, who is removing her stockings, rosy pink lips. The fabric draped over a branch behind her, now faded but preserved on the back, was originally rich shades of green and vibrant coral.

Once her work was complete, each picture was backed with card, framed and a hand-written label affixed, confirming the piece as her own creation. It is rarely possible to attribute dressed prints to an individual, which gives Winn's work particular importance. RC

Making history

ANGELICA KAUFFMAN (1741–1807)

As a popular history painter, Angelica Kauffman succeeded where most artists in 18th-century Britain fell short. History paintings, which drew their subjects from literary, mythological and religious sources, were considered the most prestigious of visual art forms for their intellectual and technical ambition. They also posed a commercial challenge in a contemporary art market geared towards the more domestic genres, especially portraiture. Kauffman's exceptional success in this field earned her a place as one of the first members of the Royal Academy of Arts in London: one of just two women to gain this distinction, and the last for over 150 years.

Swiss-born, Kauffman demonstrated an early talent for music as well as painting, but ultimately chose art as her profession; a crossroads in life she later depicted in this allegorical self-portrait (right). This path led her to Italy where, along with other artists, she looked afresh at the ancient sculpture and classically inspired pictures of the previous century. A new, restrained form of

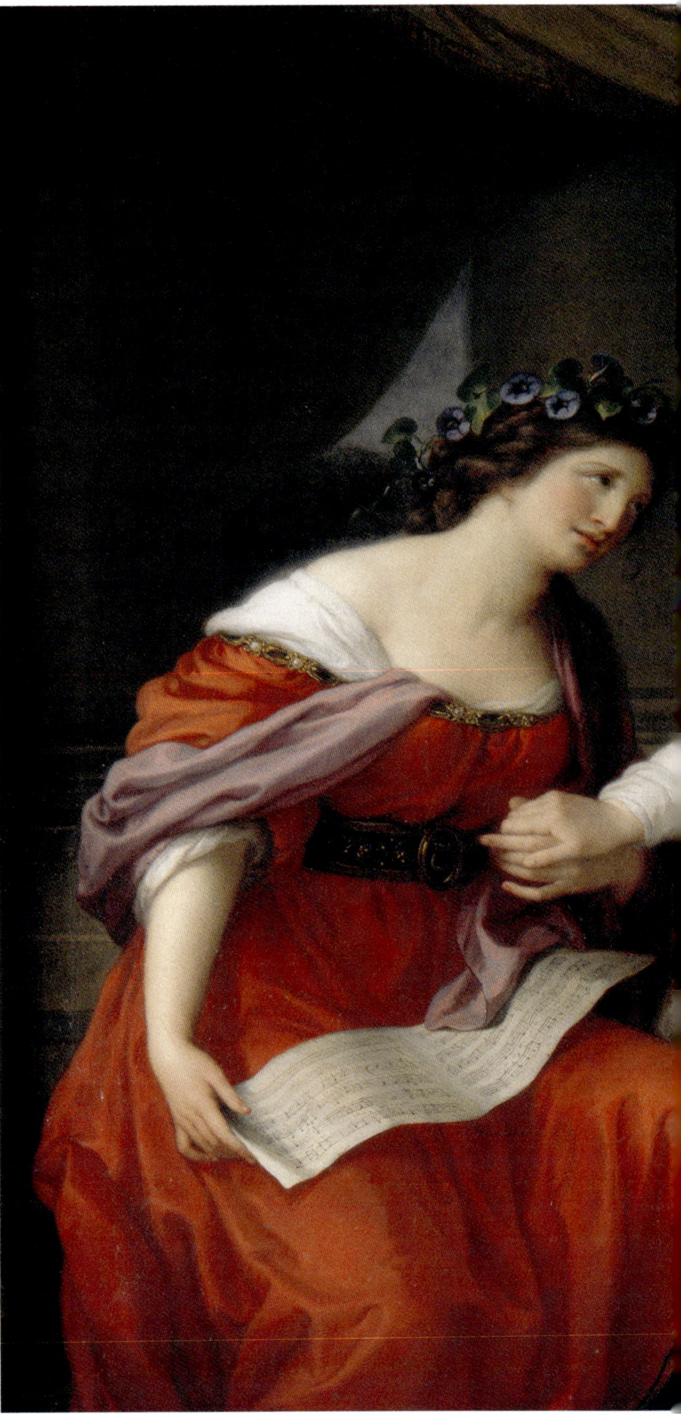

→ *Self-portrait of the Artist Hesitating between the Arts of Music and Painting*, Angelica Kauffman, 1794, oil on canvas, 180 x 249cm, Nostell, West Yorkshire, purchased by the National Trust by private treaty with the aid of a grant from the Heritage Lottery Fund, 2002 (NT 960079)

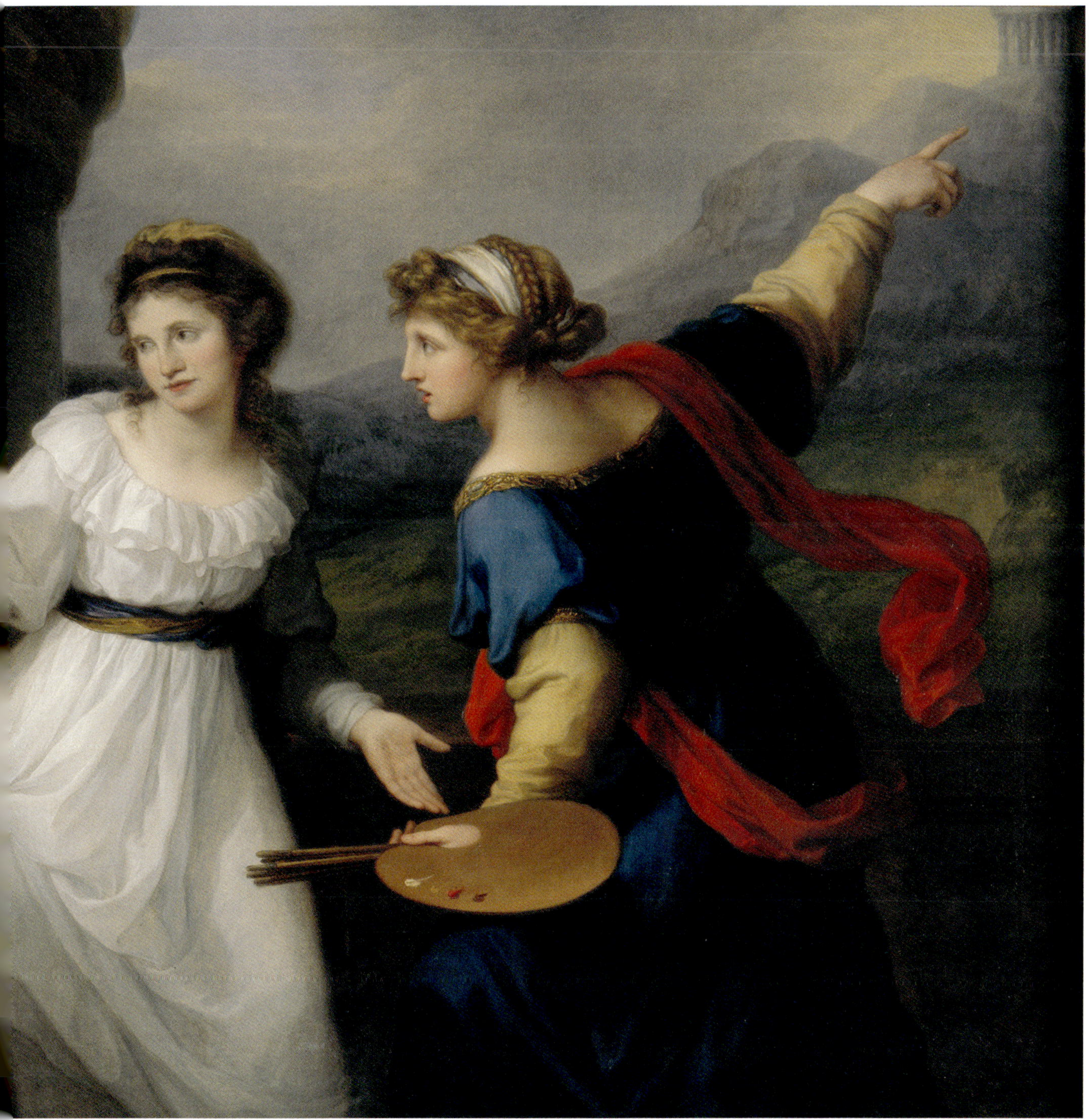

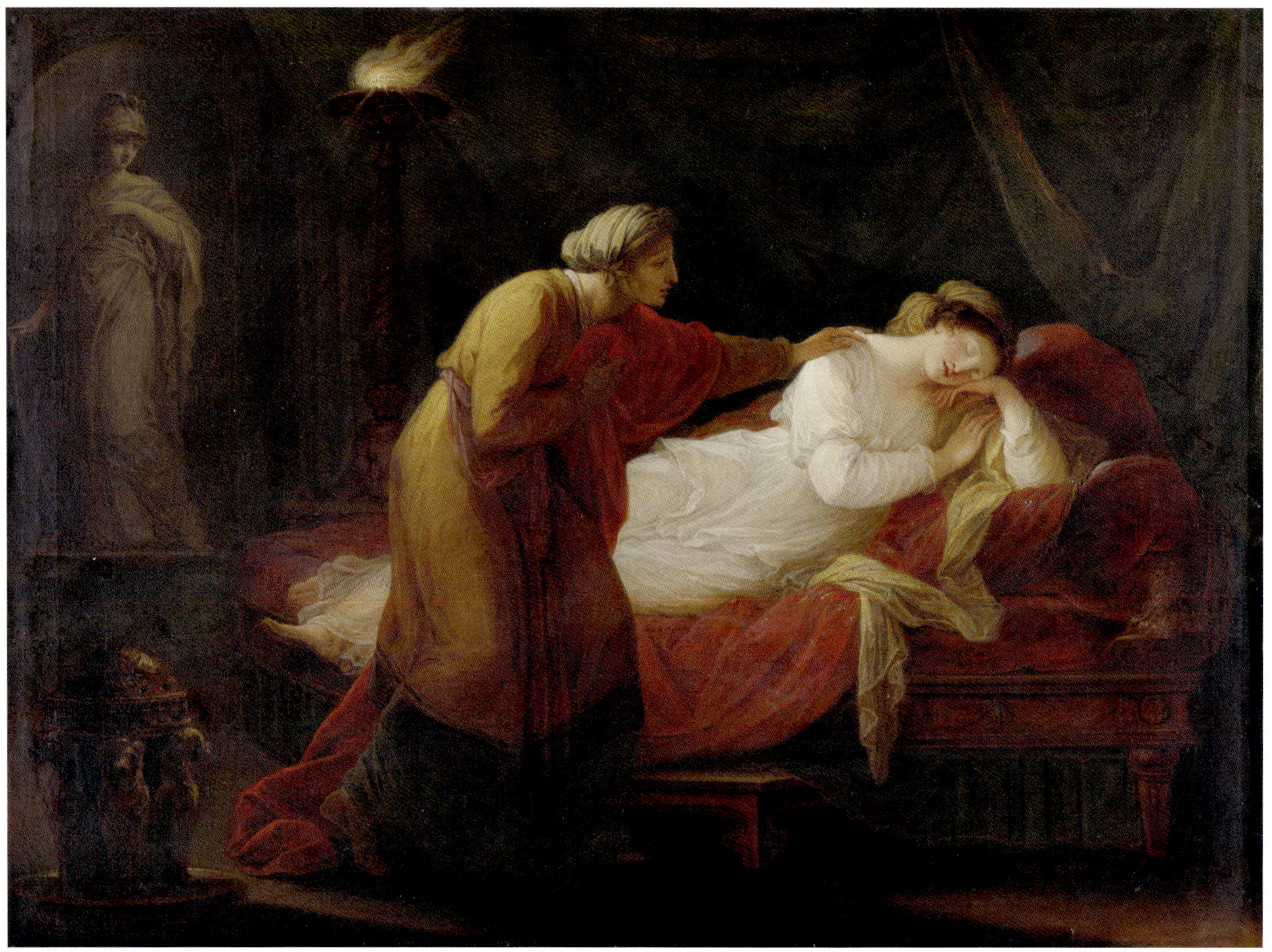

history painting emerged, known as Neo-classicism, to which Kauffman added a distinctive spin – typically foregrounding women characters and often emphasising their fortitude.

High repute in Italy provided inroads to London, where she arrived in 1766. Over the next 15 years Kauffman went from strength to strength, thriving in the country's unique atmosphere of commercial innovation. As well as producing paintings for the nobility, she contributed regularly to the new public exhibitions, branching out

← *Penelope and Euryclea*, Angelica Kauffman and studio, *c.*1773, oil on canvas, 78.7 x 104.5cm, Stourhead, Wiltshire, acquired with funding from the Monument 85 Fund and a private donation, 2023 (NT 732643)
→ *Two Virgins Awakening Cupid*, figure group after Angelica Kauffman, William Duesbury & Co., *c.*1778–90, Derby, biscuit porcelain, 30.5 x 19cm (figure group), Dunham Massey, Cheshire (NT 929315)

into sentimental and modern literary subjects with a view to mass appeal. Capitalising on the ornamental potential of her style, she became the foremost supplier of designs for framed furniture prints, so-called for their primarily decorative function. 'Angelicamania' in turn led to the incorporation of classical compositions inspired by her works into all manner of household goods, from Chippendale commodes to Wedgwood creamers. JC

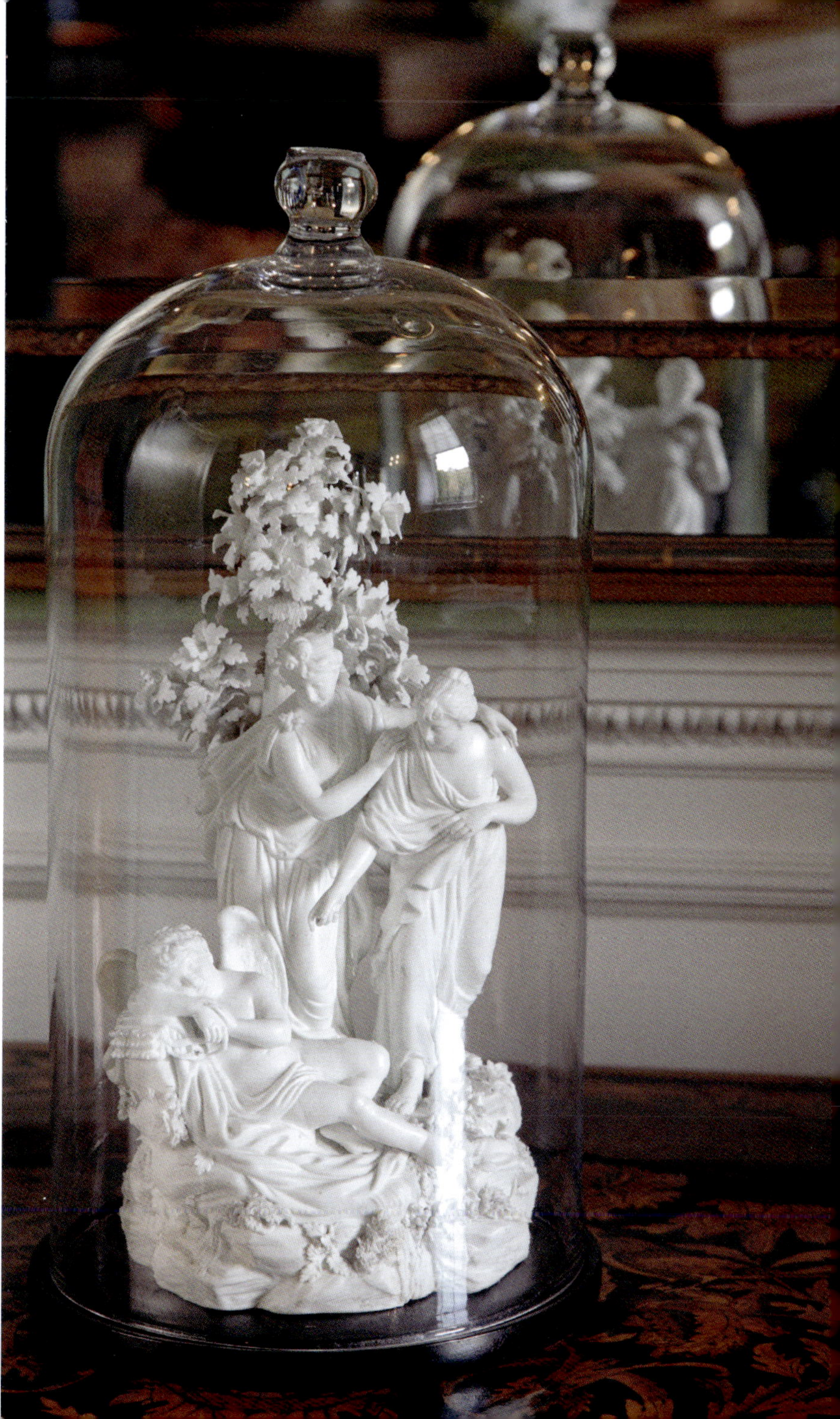

The business of luxury

LOUISA COURTAULD (1729–1807)

By the 18th century London was home to many Huguenot (French Protestant) craftspeople, who had fled to London from France to escape religious persecution. Louisa Perina Ogier came to England as a baby after her father, a silk weaver, moved as a refugee to Spitalfields, the area of London most closely associated with the production of sumptuous silk cloth.

It was her marriage to Samuel Courtauld (1720–65), a second-generation goldsmith from one of the most acclaimed families in the trade, that established Louisa's connection to the business. Courtauld was in her mid-thirties when, following the death of her husband, she took control of the family firm, as many widows then did. Unlike the many anonymous women who were involved in goldsmithing as workers or suppliers, Courtauld's prominent role as a wealthy businesswoman means that her contribution to the trade is more easily recognised today.

A 1768 bill describes Courtauld as a 'jeweller, goldsmith &c.' based at 21 Cornhill, opposite the Royal Exchange. During her early years in business she had pieces marked with her own initials 'LC' in a lozenge-shaped punch, indicating her status as a widow. She later registered a mark with her business partner, George Cowles (d.1811), and another with her son Samuel (1752–1821). This meant that every piece of silver to come out of Courtauld's workshops was stamped with her initials – and she would be held legally accountable for any deficiencies, particularly if the purity of the metal was not up to standard.

Courtauld dealt personally with retailers, as well as with her royal and noble clients. The goods produced in her workshops were of a remarkably high quality and responded to the latest fashions. Her clients included Sir Nathaniel Curzon of Kedleston (1726–1804), who ordered a remarkable set of three condiment vases based on Greek vases published by the antiquarian William Hamilton, a set of tea canisters with a sugar vase, an argyll (gravy warmer) and other pieces in the fashionable Neo-classical style. In 1777 Curzon settled his account with Courtauld, which then amounted to £142 3s 6d (over £12,000 today). RC

→ Set of four candlesticks with the armorial crest of Sir Nathaniel Curzon, Louisa Courtauld and George Cowles, 1771–2, London, sterling silver, 35.5cm (height), Kedleston Hall, Derbyshire (NT 108941)

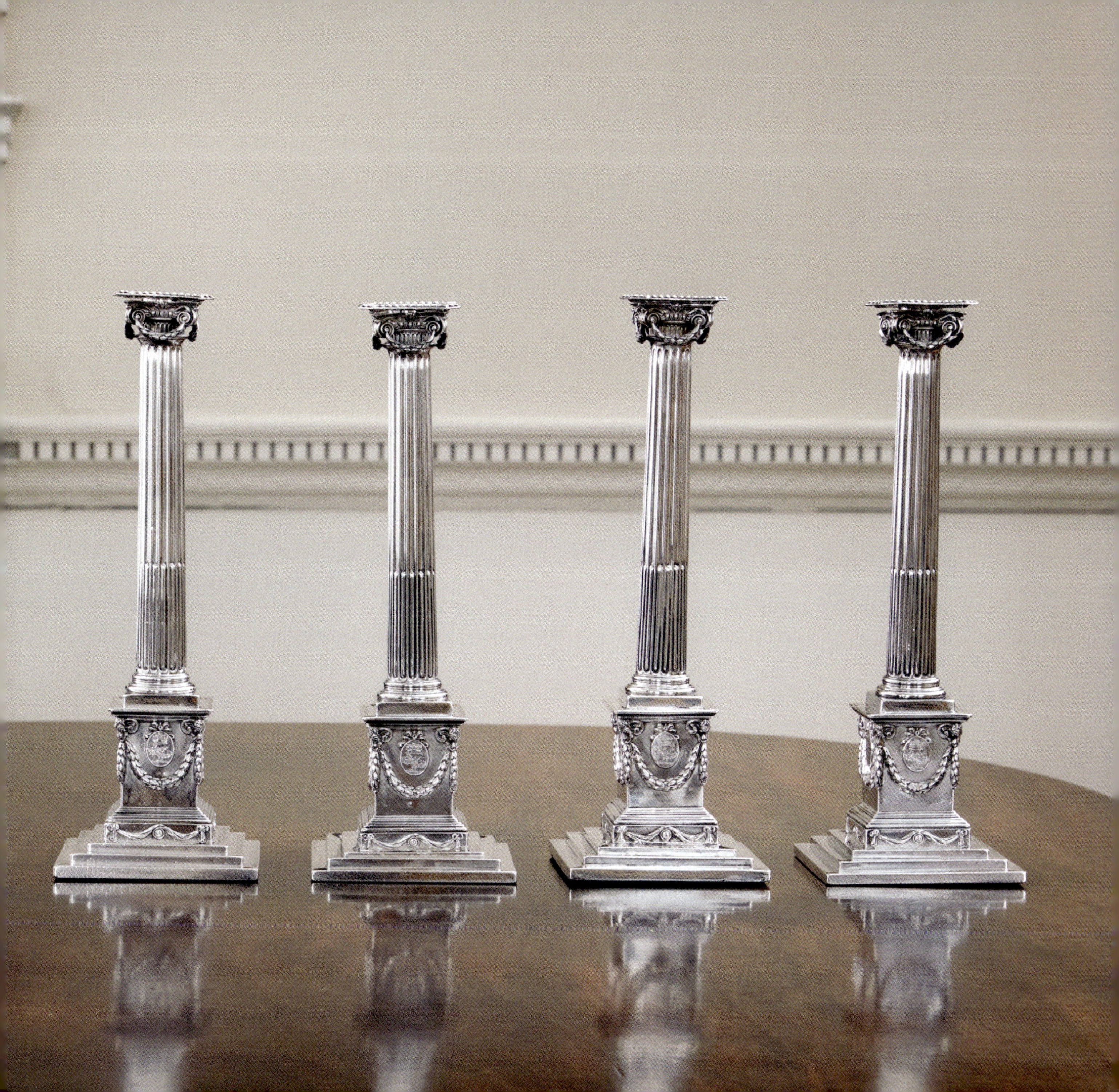

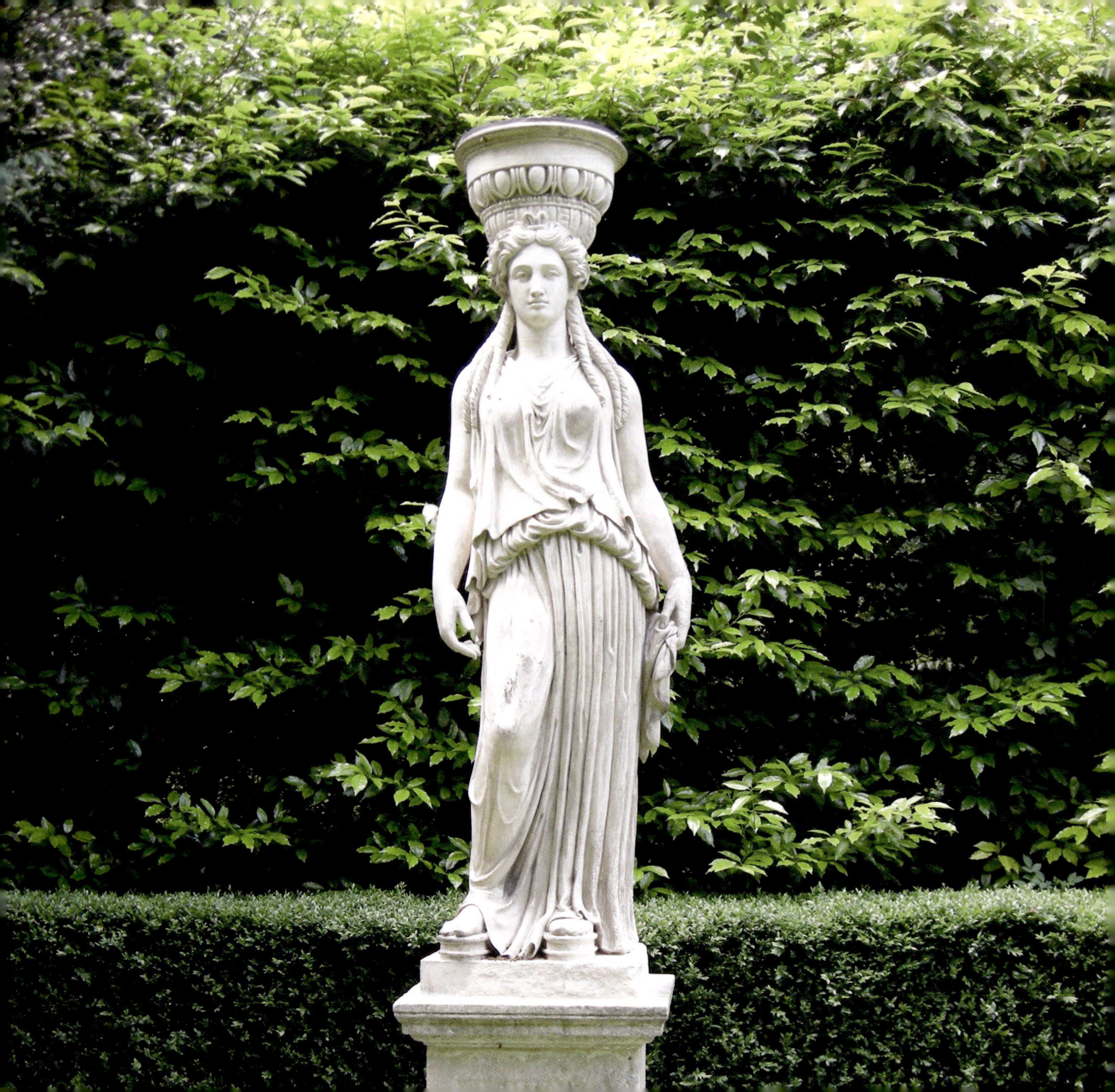

A formula for success

ELEANOR COADE (1733–1821)

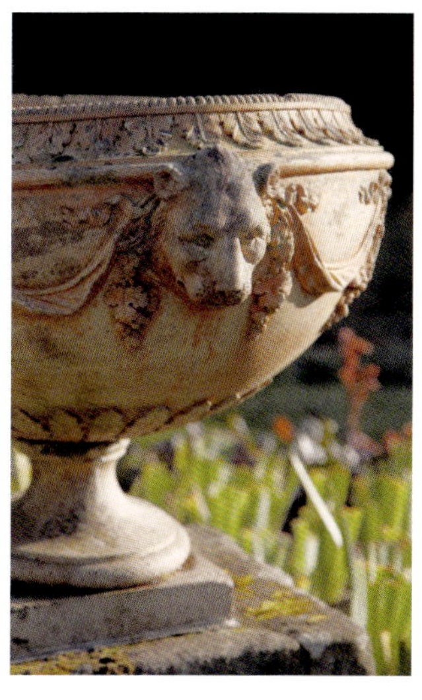

← Caryatid, Coade's Artificial Stone Manufactory Co., Lambeth, 1793, Coade stone, 192 x 60 x 40cm, Anglesey Abbey, Cambridgeshire (NT 516655)

↑ Garden urn, Coade's Artificial Stone Manufactory Co., Lambeth, 1790, Coade stone, 92 x 115 x 76.2cm, Ardress House, County Armagh (NT 247727)

Eleanor Coade developed Coade stone, an innovative artificial stone made from a highly durable type of ceramic that was perfect for outdoor use. Her ornamental sculpture added an enduring beauty to hundreds of gardens and buildings.

Coade established her Lambeth manufactory at a time when British industry was dominated by men. In 1769 she took over the premises of an ailing artificial stone factory run by Daniel Pincot, developing the new, closely guarded formula that would bear her name. Pincot continued in the business but was dismissed by Coade a few years later for falsely presenting himself to clients as its proprietor. She made her position abundantly clear in an advert in *The Daily Advertiser* in September 1771 – 'no Contracts or Agreements, Purchases or Receipts, will be allowed by her, unless signed or assented to by herself' – she was indisputably in control of this business.

Coade brought in sculptor John Bacon (1740–99) as superintendent and he improved the quality of design, working mostly in the fashionable Neo-classical style. She supplied mould-made architectural ornaments, garden sculpture and monuments to the most eminent architects of the day, including Robert Adam, James and Samuel Wyatt, and John Soane. The caryatid shown opposite – one of six in the gardens at Anglesey Abbey, Cambridgeshire – is probably from a group used by Soane in the rebuilding of Buckingham House, London.

The company's 1784 catalogue includes 778 different designs, including one matching an urn (left) now at Ardress House, County Armagh. In 1799 Coade went into partnership with her cousin and the business was renamed Coade & Sealy. A London showroom was opened and the company was granted Royal Appointments by George III and the Prince Regent, who were clients. Coade continued to run her business until her death in 1821, aged 88.

Next time you are wandering through a garden and spot what looks like a carved stone urn or figure, perhaps look again – is it what it seems, or has Mrs Coade's formula tricked you? RC

Model servant

ELIZABETH RATCLIFFE (*c.*1735–*c.*1810)

In the State Bedroom at Erddig a delicate bunch of roses, pinks, carnations and violas (opposite) has drawn admiration for almost 250 years, in spite of the caterpillar crawling up one of the stems. It is just one of many remarkable creations by Elizabeth (Betty) Ratcliffe, lady's maid.

Ratcliffe occupied an unusual and privileged position, as her employers encouraged (and benefited from) her creativity. Her work was cherished and valued by the Yorke family – specially commissioned stands display and protect her wonderful models of a pagoda and the *Ruins of the Temple of the Sun at Palmyra* (pages 76–7). Ratcliffe had access to high-quality materials and, perhaps most importantly, the time granted to her to create work. When requested to draw a copy of a print for the writer and antiquarian Thomas Pennant, she was able to ask Philip Yorke, head of her household, for a necessary 'sheet of the finest grain'd white Vellum'. A letter suggests the commission was negotiated through Yorke's wife, Dorothy, after Pennant had 'beg'd of Mamma' to let Ratcliffe undertake the work.

This blurring of social and hierarchical boundaries was not without tension. In a letter of 1768, the year after Ratcliffe completed her pagoda, Dorothy wrote to Philip, her son, expressing her concern that Ratcliffe 'is at work for you: but pray my dear do not employ her in that way again for one year at least as all her improvements sink in drawing & then I shall have no service from her'.

The model of the temple, glittering with mother-of-pearl, is particularly ambitious. It was inspired by Robert Wood's 1753 publication of engravings of the Roman ruins in Syria, although it is far from a slavish recreation. Ratcliffe has taken key recognisable architectural elements and placed them in a wild, silvery landscape, with vegetation trailing across the doorway and pillars. It is possibly the work Ratcliffe mentions in her 1770 letter to Philip Yorke, 'I yesterday received the honour of your letter and will do the utmost of my power and endeavour to execute, what you are pleas'd to request instead of Comand, as I shall ever think it my Duty, to a Family, I am so particularly oblig'd to.'

Given her imagination and skill, what would Ratcliffe have created had she been able to do so purely on her own terms? RC

→ Flower picture, attributed to Elizabeth Ratcliffe, *c.*1775, straw-work, paper, wire and wool, the gilt wood frame possibly by Thomas Fentham, 66 x 39cm, Erddig, Wrexham (NT 1151845)

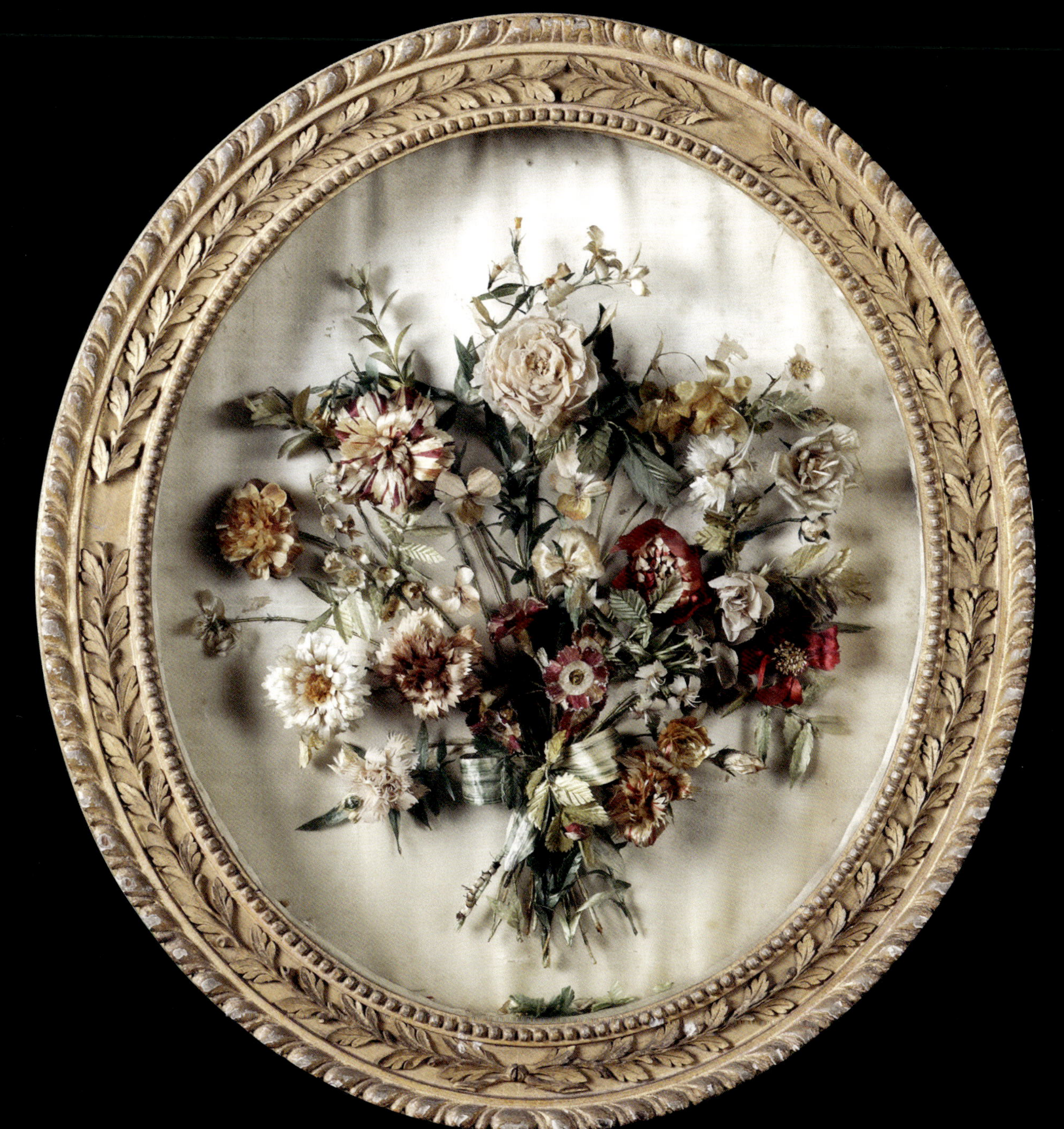

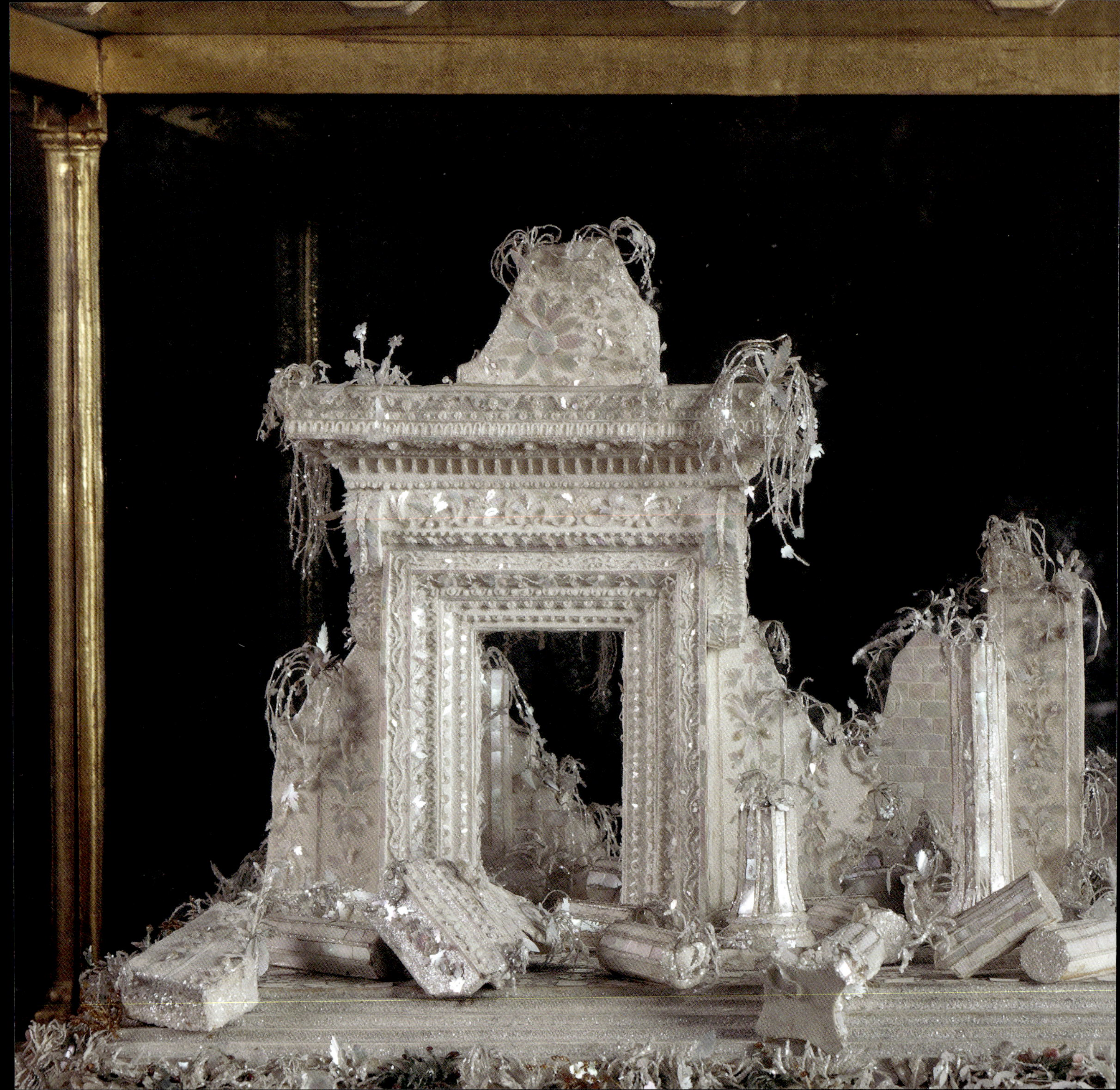

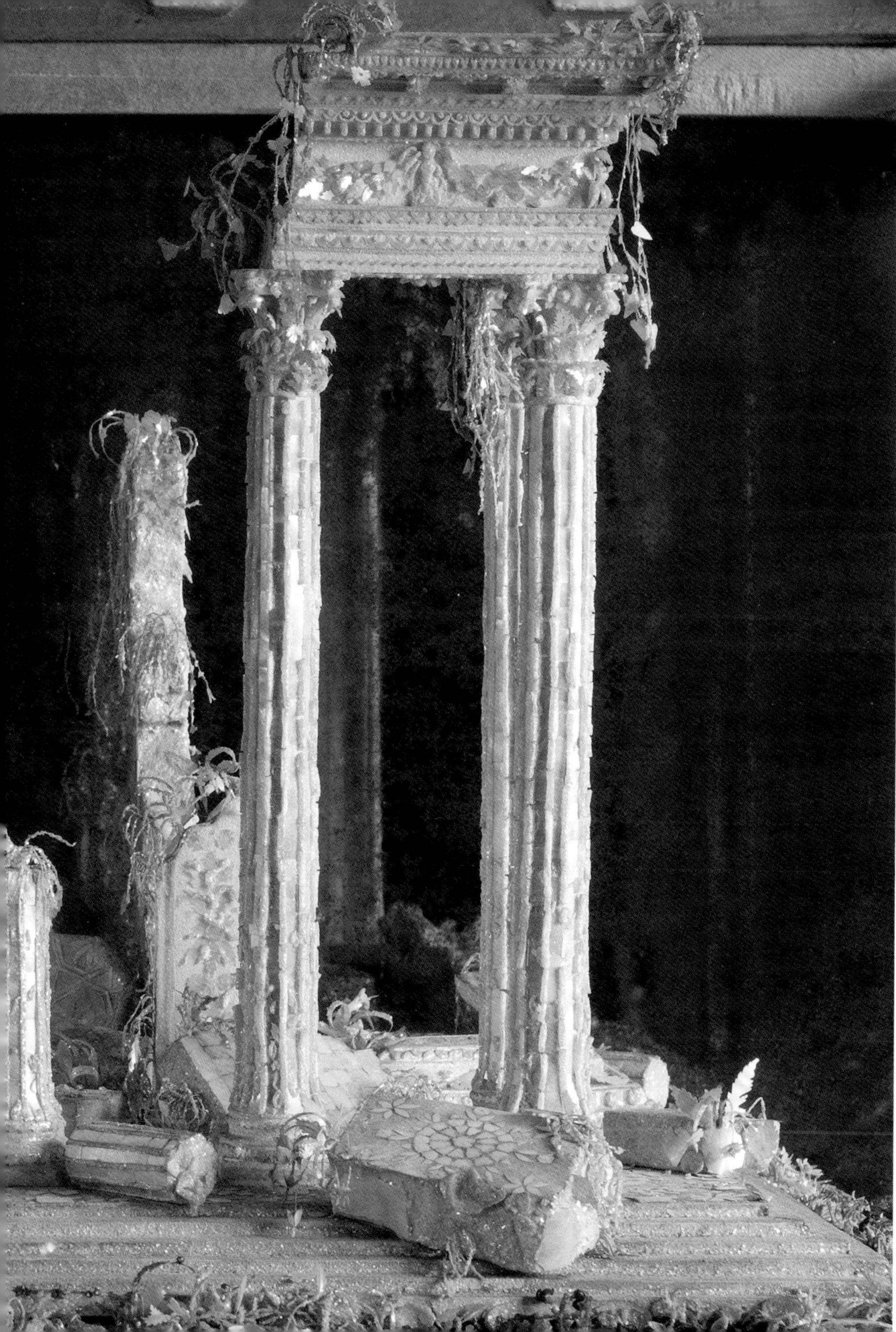

← *Ruins of the Temple of the Sun at Palmyra*, Elizabeth Ratcliffe, 1773, wood, mother-of-pearl, mica and glass, 162 x 89 x 61cm (case), Erddig, Wrexham (NT 1147092.1)

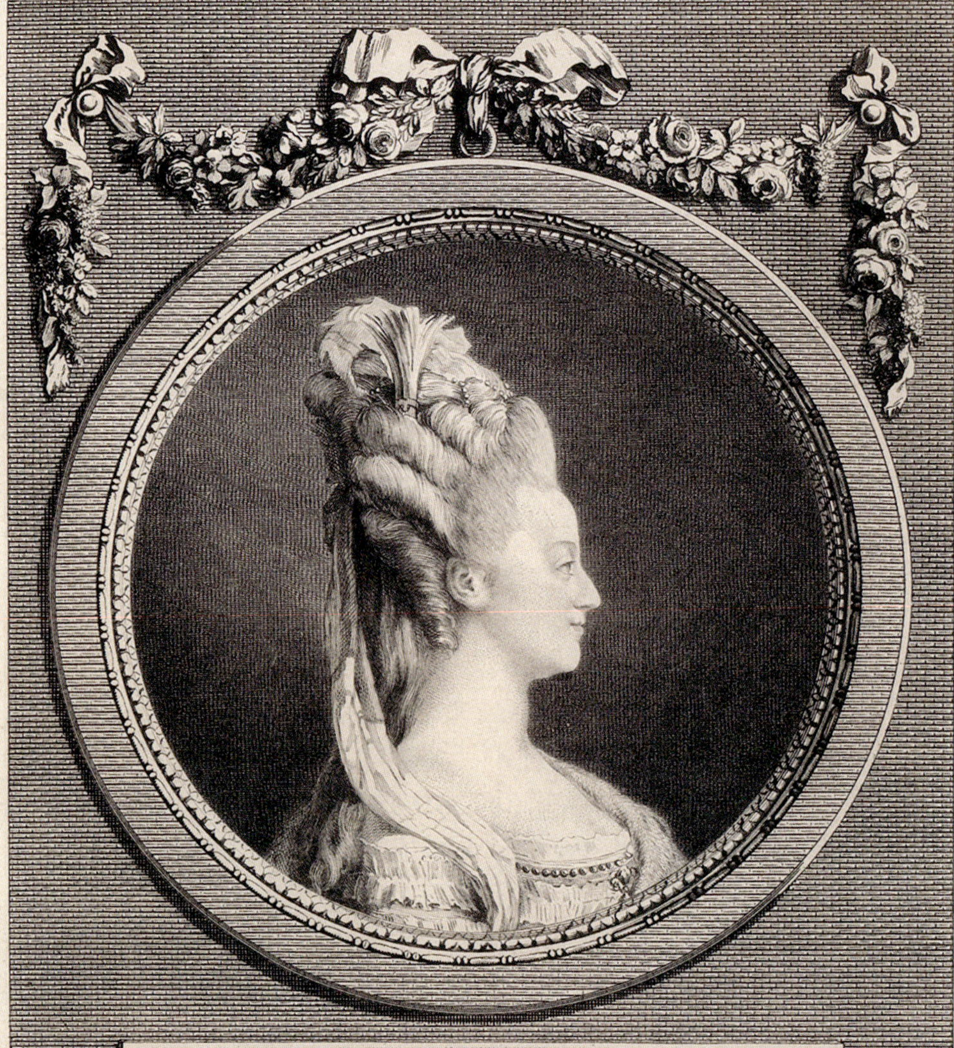

MARIE ANTOINETTE
d'Autriche Reine de France.

Dessiné par L. S. Boizot. *Gravé par Marie L.se A.de Boizot 1775.*

Se vend à Paris, chez J. J. Flipart Graveur du Roy, Rue d'Enfer pres la place S.t Michel chez le Limonadier.

The royal line

MARIE-LOUISE-ADÉLAÏDE BOIZOT (1744–1800)

← *Marie Antoinette d'Autriche Reine de France* (of Austria, Queen of France), Marie-Louise-Adélaïde Boizot, after Louis-Simon Boizot, 1775, etching and engraving on laid paper, published by Jean Jacques Flipart, 31 x 23.7cm, Waddesdon Manor, Buckinghamshire, Bequest of James de Rothschild, 1957 (Waddesdon 4232.3.6.6)

Marie-Louise-Adélaïde Boizot was a highly regarded printmaker known for her faithful portraits of French royals and her reproductions of Dutch 17th-century and contemporary French paintings.

Born into a family of artists, Boizot studied drawing with her father, the painter Antoine Boizot (1702–82), and engraving with Jean Jacques Flipart (1719–82), who also published many of her prints. She often engraved after designs by her brother Louis-Simon Boizot (1743–1809), a sculptor and the artistic director of the sculpture studio at the Sèvres porcelain manufactory.

Boizot's portraits of Queen Marie Antoinette (1755–93) – made the year her husband, Louis XVI, became king, and Marie-Térèse, Countess of Artois (1756–1805; page 45), are two examples from a larger series of portraits after Louis-Simon, whose designs reference the classical tradition of portrait medallions and medals, either produced as cameos, intaglios (engraved gems) or cast in plaster, porcelain or metals. Intaglio printmaking is also a sculptural process. The final printed image is the result of a series of lines and grooves cut into a metal plate, which is then transferred onto paper through the medium of ink. The printmaker's signature during this period was often accompanied by the Latin words *sculpsit* or *sculpebat*, sharing the same root and meaning as the word 'sculptor'.

Boizot's work was praised, and her prints can be found advertised in French periodicals. In 1776 the weekly *L'Avantcoureur* published a rave review of Boizot's *La Liseuse* (The Reader), after a painting by Jean-Baptiste Greuze (1725–1805), but mistakenly attributed the work to her brother. It quickly printed an apology accompanied by a statement insisting that no distinction could be made between men and women in terms of taste and artistic talents. The apology went on to observe that some women, such as 'Mademoiselle Boizot', had even made successful careers as artists. RJ

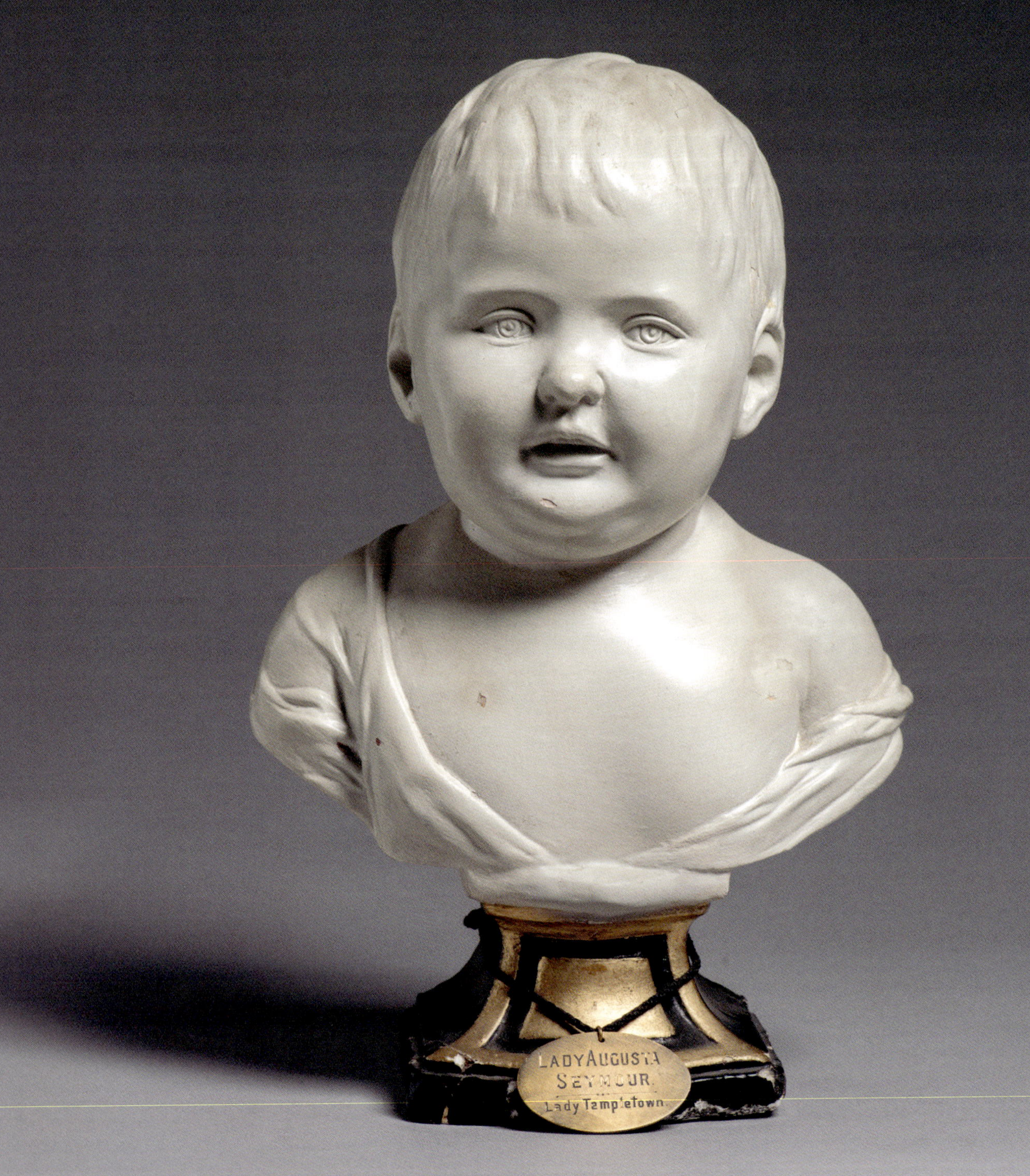
LADY AUGUSTA
SEYMOUR
Lady Templetown

‘A Lady of great Taste’

ELIZABETH BOUGHTON, LADY TEMPLETOWN (1746/7–1823)

← *Bust of Lady Seymour as a Child*, Lady Templetown, *c*.1800, plaster, 37 x 25cm, Ickworth, Suffolk, ‡ 1956 (NT 852216)

Elizabeth Boughton, Lady Templetown, was an artist working across several disciplines, including painting, sculpture, wax modelling and cut-paperwork. The artist John Downman described her as ‘a Lady of great Taste and her Works greatly admired’.

Lady Templetown is best known for the ‘cut Indian paper’ designs she produced for Josiah Wedgwood’s jasperware between 1783 and 1789. She was skilled at making images and silhouettes from cut paper, which was a popular polite creative activity, typically practised by women. Unusually, she was able to develop this into a professional practice.

William Hackwood (*c*.1757–1836) translated Lady Templetown’s work into low reliefs that could be applied to the surface of vessels, plaques and small personal items, such as brooches. She created at least 15 designs for Wedgwood, who – no doubt seeing an opportunity to monopolise on her social cachet – acknowledged her role as designer in his 1787 ornamental-ware catalogue. He wrote that she and Diana Beauclerk (1734–1808), ‘whose exquisite taste is universally acknowledged, have honoured me with the liberty of copying from their designs’.

The example here (overleaf) shows a woman and child reading – it could be the one described in the 1787 catalogue as *Study*. Her designs encompassed fashionable Neo-classicism and ‘romantic’ subject matter. They ranged from scenes illustrating domestic virtues and interpretations of contemporary literature to depictions of goddesses and cherubs. Two series of designs – *Domestic Employment* and *Maternal Affection* – may have been created in collaboration with her relative Emma Crewe (1741–*c*.95), who also supplied imagery for Wedgwood.

Born into an aristocratic family, Lady Templetown was bedchamberwoman to George II’s daughter Amelia. In 1769 she married courtier Clotworthy Upton (1721–85), who owned plantations and enslaved people on Grenada and Dominica. His Grenada estate was left in trust to Elizabeth upon his death. RC

↓ Bowl decorated with figures from Lady Templetown's *Domestic Employment*, *c.*1790–1800, jasperware, Wedgwood, Stoke-on-Trent, 6 (height) x 12.8cm (diameter), Stourhead, Wiltshire (NT 730523)
→ *Elizabeth Boughton, Lady Templetown*, portrait miniature, Anne Mee (*c.*1770–1851), *c.*1795–1800, watercolour on ivory, 7.5 x 5.9cm, Ickworth, Suffolk, ⁑ 1956 (NT 851902)

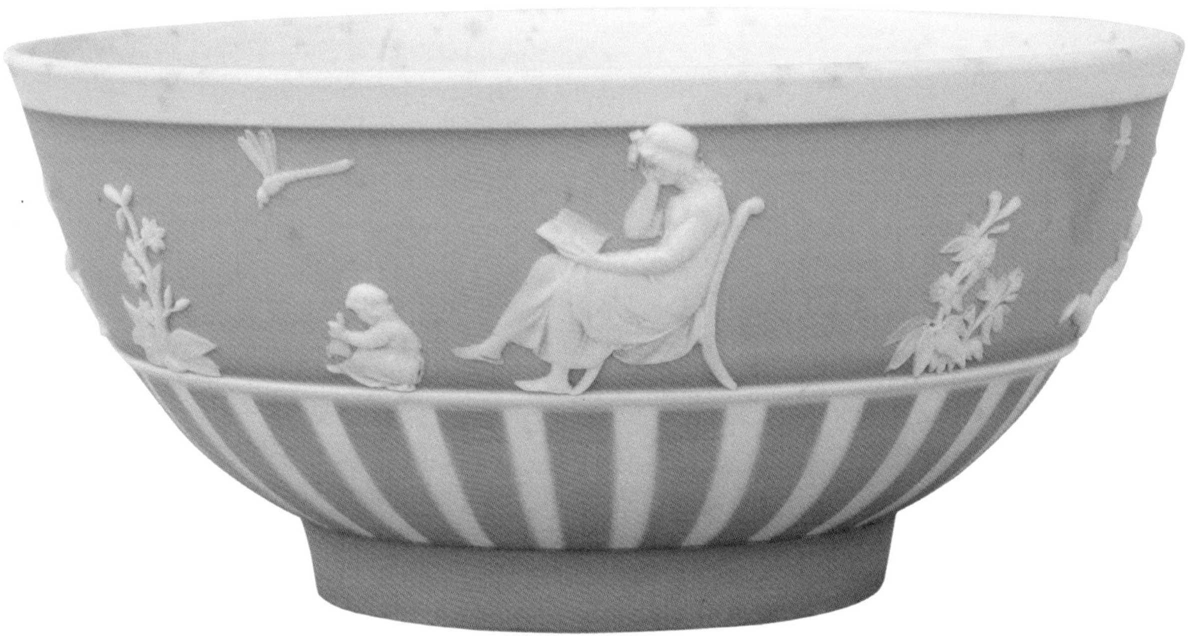

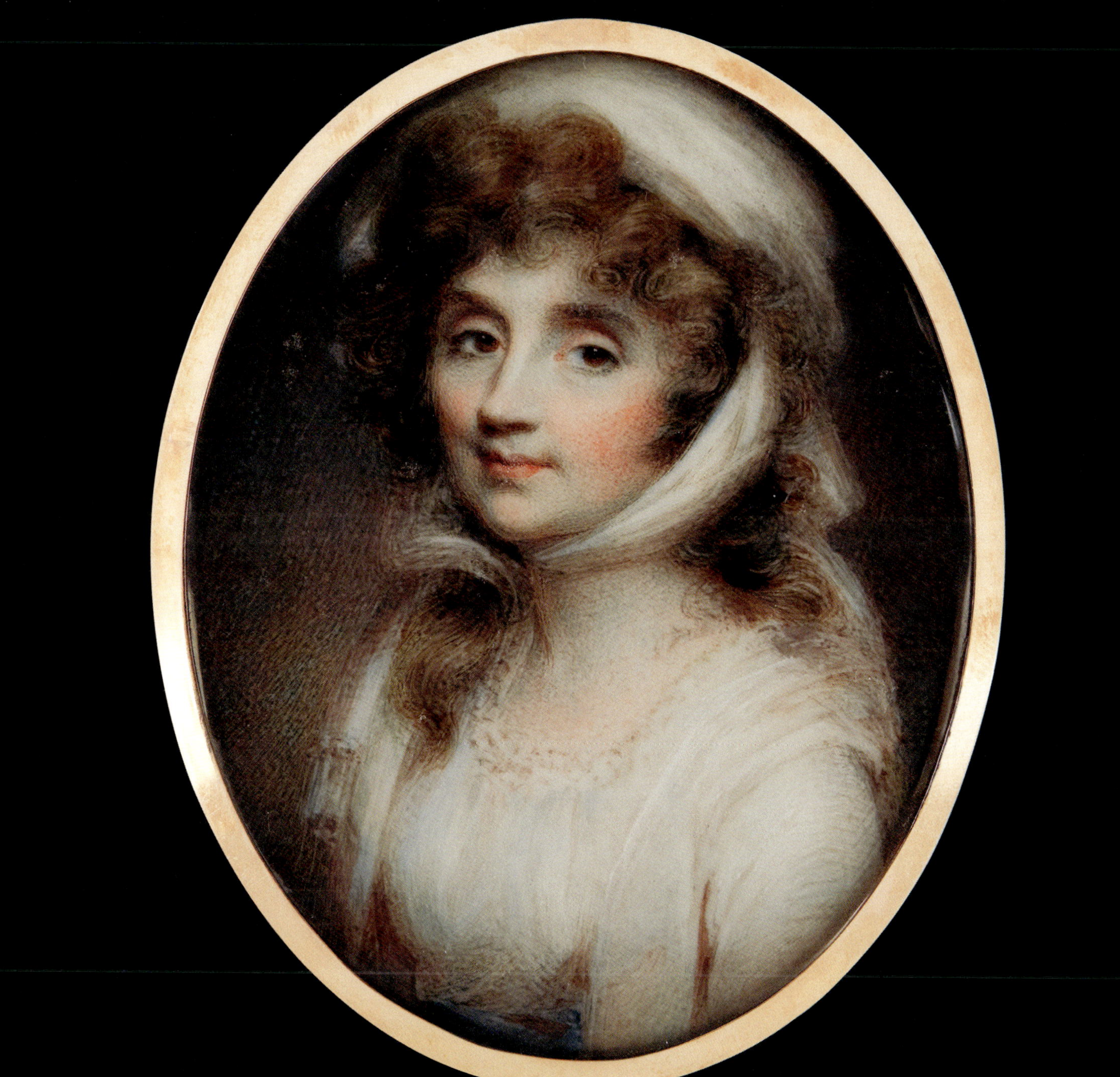

A revolution in portraiture

ELISABETH VIGÉE LE BRUN (1755–1842)

The portraits of Elisabeth Vigée Le Brun embodied the profound cultural and intellectual changes that shook France in the lead-up to the political revolution of 1789. Throwing off aristocratic conventions, she painted her sitters in relaxed poses and unrestrictive clothing. Spontaneous-looking expressions caught fleeting moments of individual sensibility; glistening eyes and open-mouthed smiles, baring straight white teeth, were a startling innovation.

Ironically, she perfected this new approach to portraiture at the epicentre of pre-revolutionary privilege: the court of Queen Marie Antoinette (1755–93). The queen and her intimates embraced these new ideas of 'natural' behaviour – emphasising the authentic flow of feelings of parenthood and friendship – and found in Vigée Le Brun their perfect image-maker.

In her self-portrait in a white turban (opposite), Vigée Le Brun promotes exactly this talent for expressing tender human emotion in paint. Engaging the viewer with a warm smile, she airily sets to work on the likeness of her beloved daughter, Julie.

Unlike many of her royal and noble patrons, Vigée Le Brun escaped the guillotine but fled into exile. Roaming Europe's other centres of artistic patronage in the years that followed, she found a ready market for her likenesses. She painted the Earl of Bristol in Naples (page 44), for example, and in England the Duchess of Dorset, whom she visited at Knole in Kent. But despite these warm welcomes, she never regained the unique sense of freedom and creativity she had known in pre-revolutionary France. For the rest of her long life, she mourned that lost world. JC

→ *Self-portrait*, Elisabeth Vigée Le Brun, 1791, oil on canvas, 99 x 81cm, Ickworth, Suffolk, ‡ 1956, transferred to the National Trust, 1990 (NT 851782)

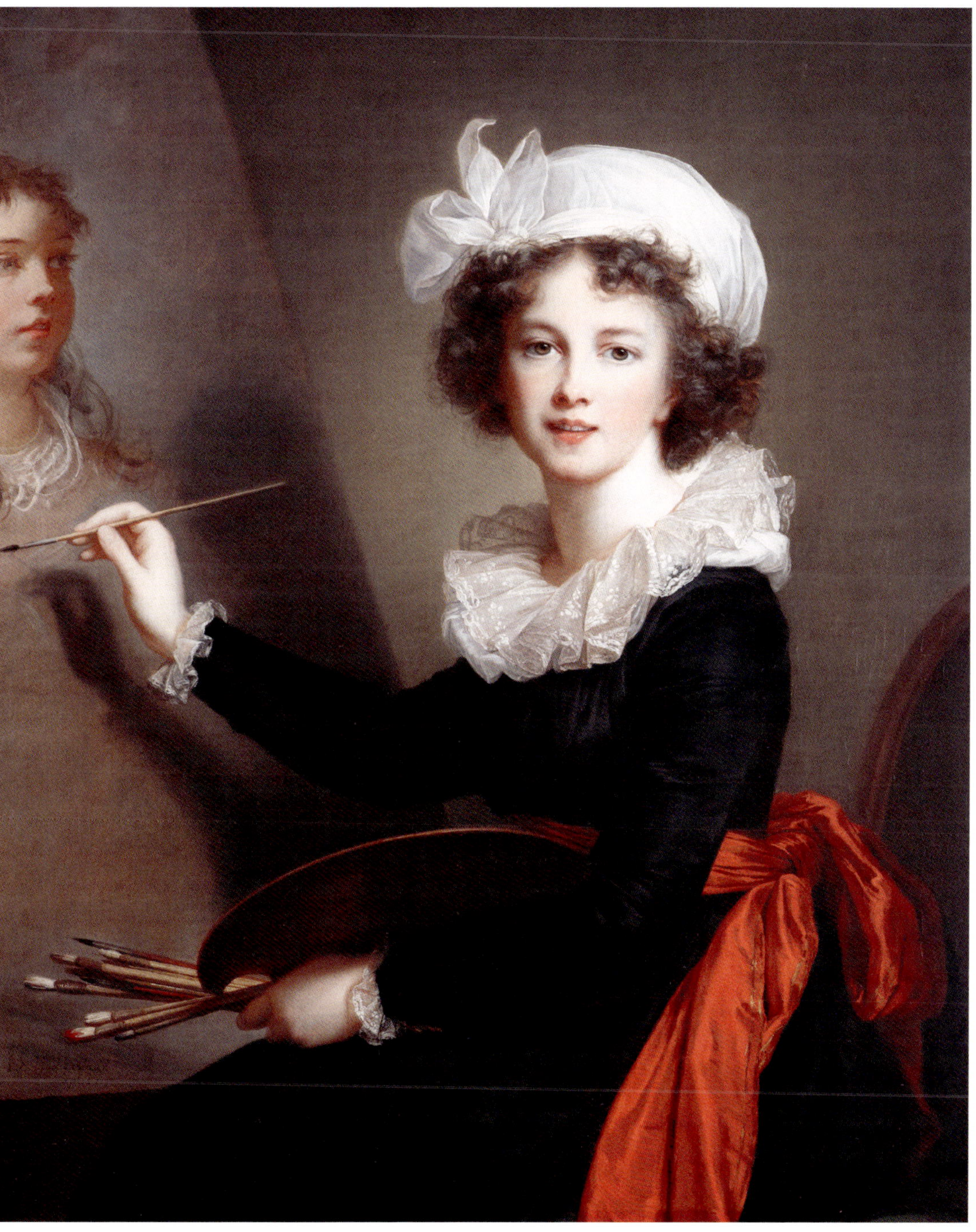

A passage to India

ANNA TONELLI (*c.*1763–1846)

The life and work of Anna Tonelli was profoundly shaped by conflict in Europe and colonial India. A trained portraitist, she built up a clientele in Britain in the 1790s for her intimate pastel likenesses and exhibited at the Royal Academy of Arts. She maintained this professional practice while working as a companion and governess in aristocratic households, including that of the Clives of Powis Castle, Powys. An accomplished singer and harpsichordist, she taught her charges music as well as Italian and drawing.

Born in Florence as Anna Nistri, she married the violinist Luigi Tonelli, with whom she had two children in around 1789–90. The arrival of the French Revolutionary Wars in the Italian peninsula, and the disruptions this caused in the portrait market, probably informed her decision to move to Britain alone. Her letters reveal a tact and warmth of personality that must have been invaluable in the complex negotiation between public artistic practice and private domestic service; Henrietta, Lady Clive, described her as 'a treasure'. However, correspondence also documents the strain of separation from her war-torn country and her own children, whom she supported by her income.

These financial considerations led her to accept an invitation from the Clives to accompany them to India in 1798, where Lord Edward Clive had been appointed Governor of Madras by the East India Company. This three-year stay culminated in a 1,000-mile tour through Tipu Sultan's recently defeated Kingdom of Mysore as part of Lady Clive's entourage. Tonelli's skills were deployed for diplomatic aspects of this journey, which pushed her art in new directions. The intricate detail of her portrait of Maharaja Sarahbhoji of Tanjore (page 89) responds to the type of picture that Indian artists, trained in late-Mughal miniature techniques, had developed to appeal to the taste of European colonists, known as 'Company School' painting. JC

→ *The Hon. Rebecca Clive, Mrs Robinson*, Anna Tonelli, 1797, pastel on paper, 24.5 x 19.7cm, Powis Castle, Powys, ‡ 1963, transferred to the National Trust, 1991 (NT 1180505)

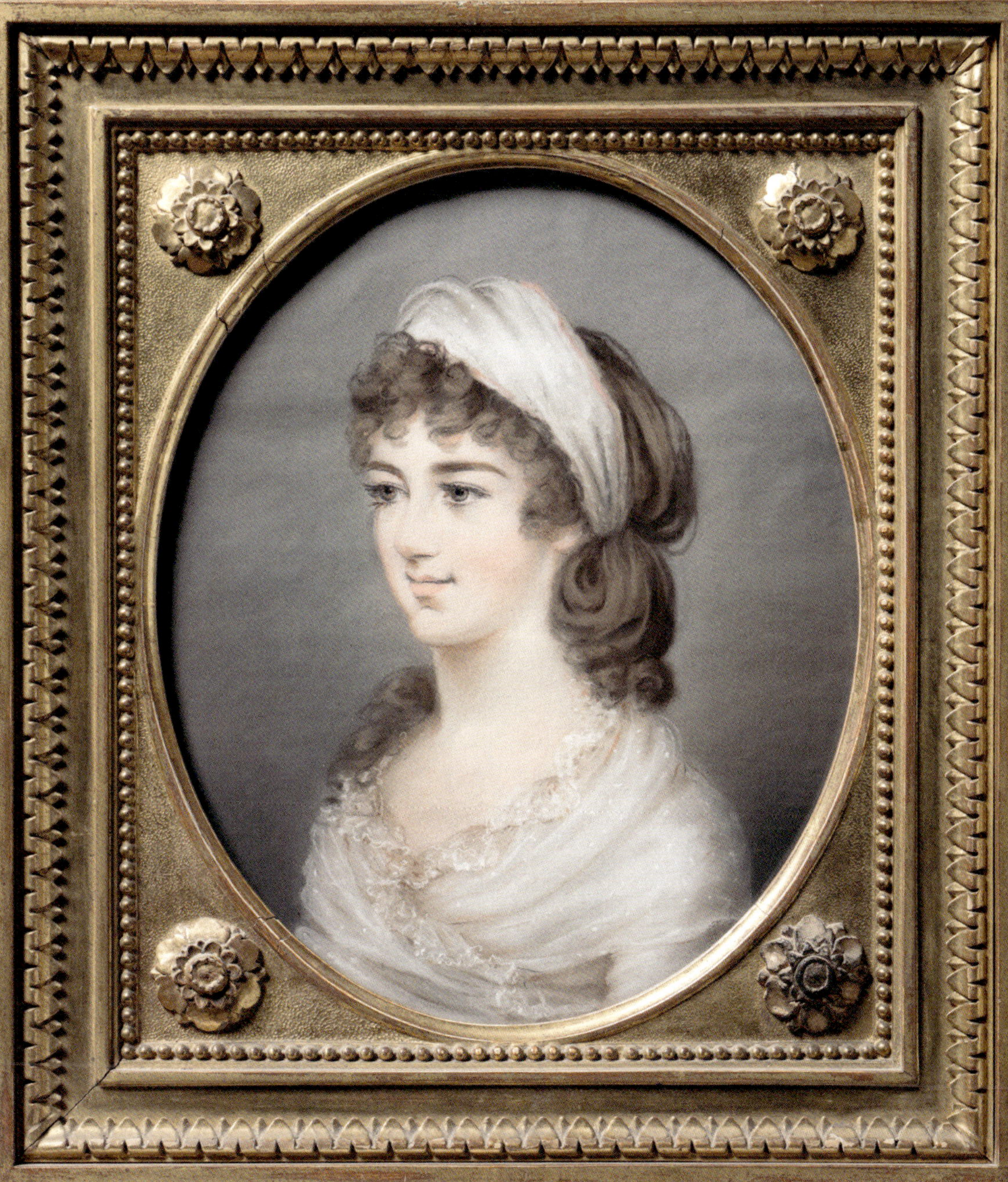

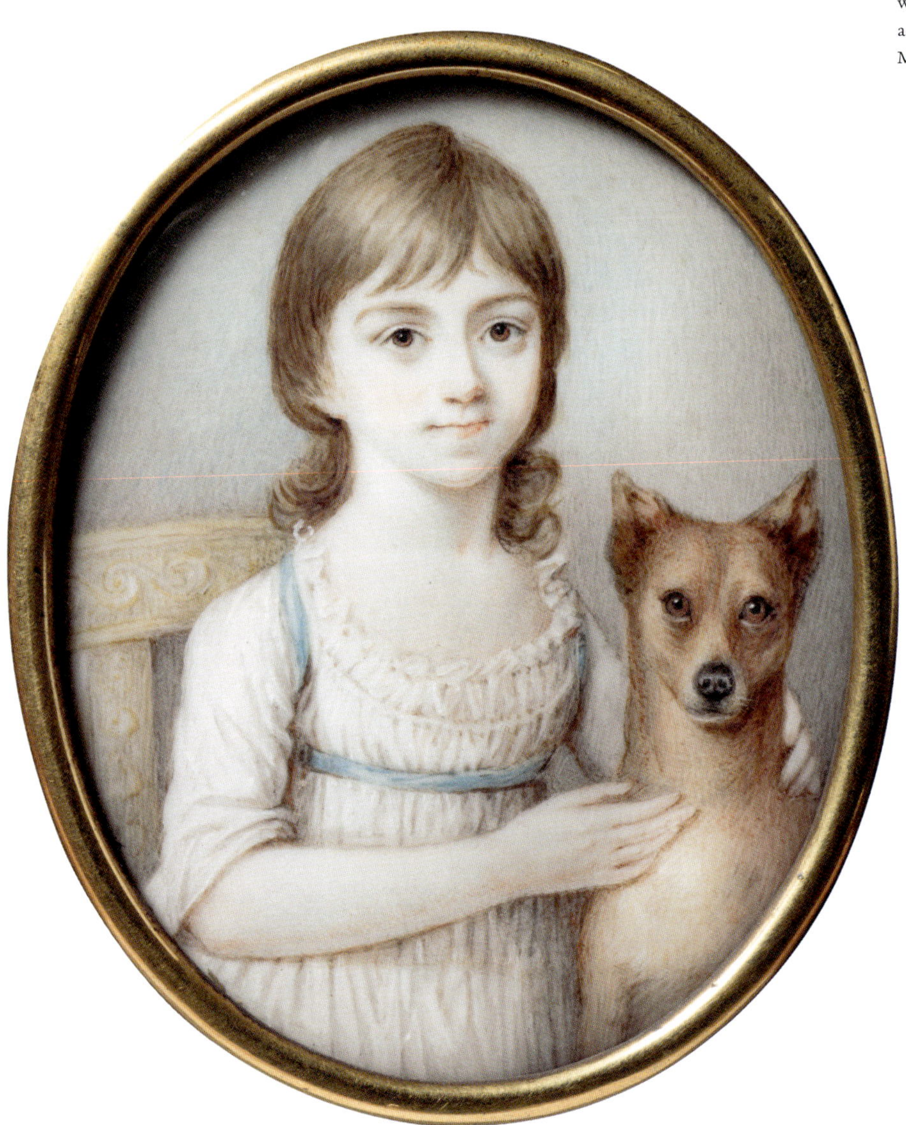

↙ *Lady Henrietta Antonia Clive with a Dog*, Anna Tonelli, c.1799, watercolour on ivory, 8.9 x 7cm, Powis Castle, Powys, ‡ 1963, transferred to the National Trust, 1991 (NT 1181046)

→ *Maharaja Sarahbhoji of Tanjore*, Anna Tonelli, 1800, watercolour on paper, 20 x 21.5cm, Powis Castle, Powys, acquired with funding from The National Heritage Memorial Fund, 1999 (NT 1180777)

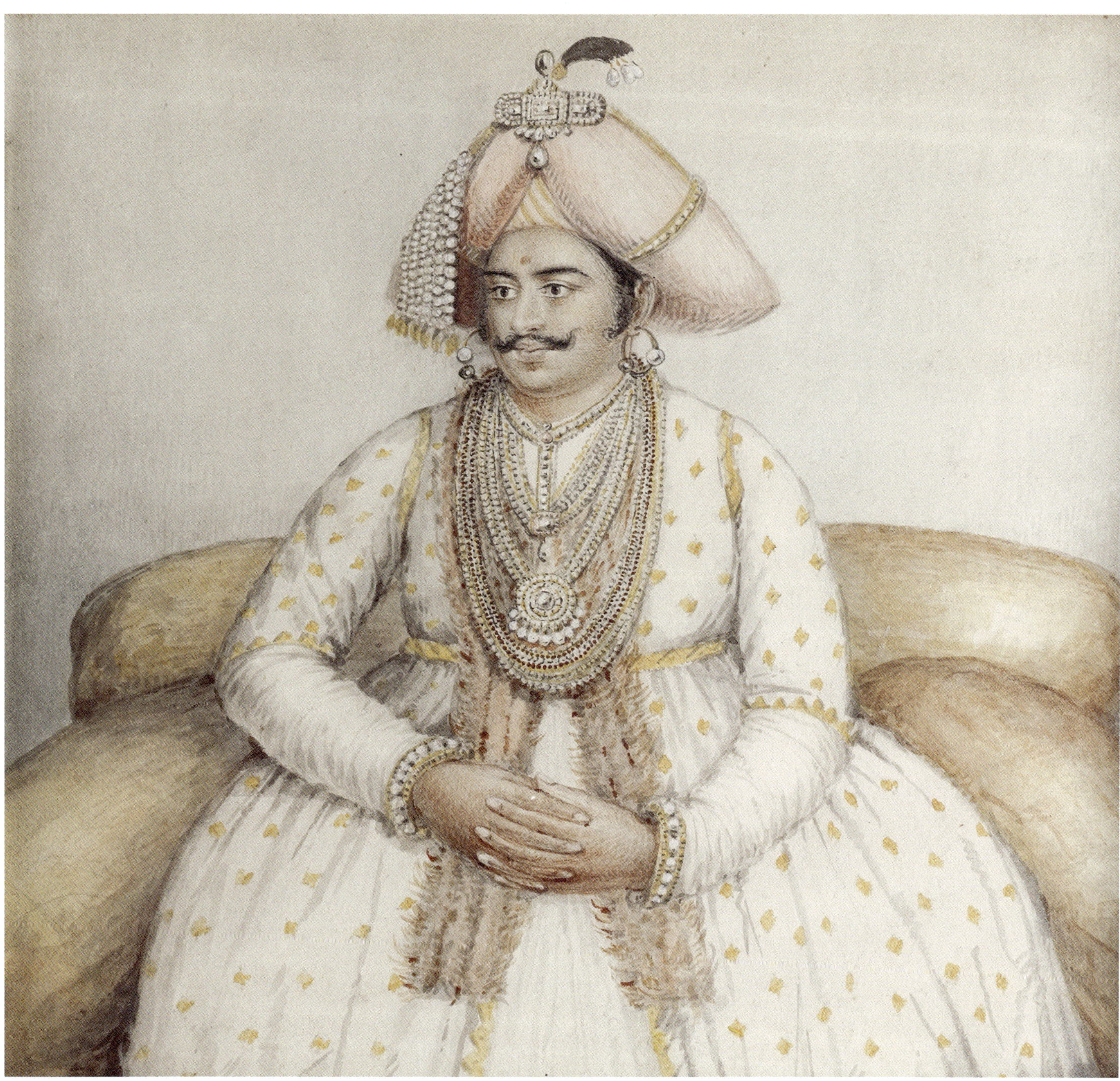

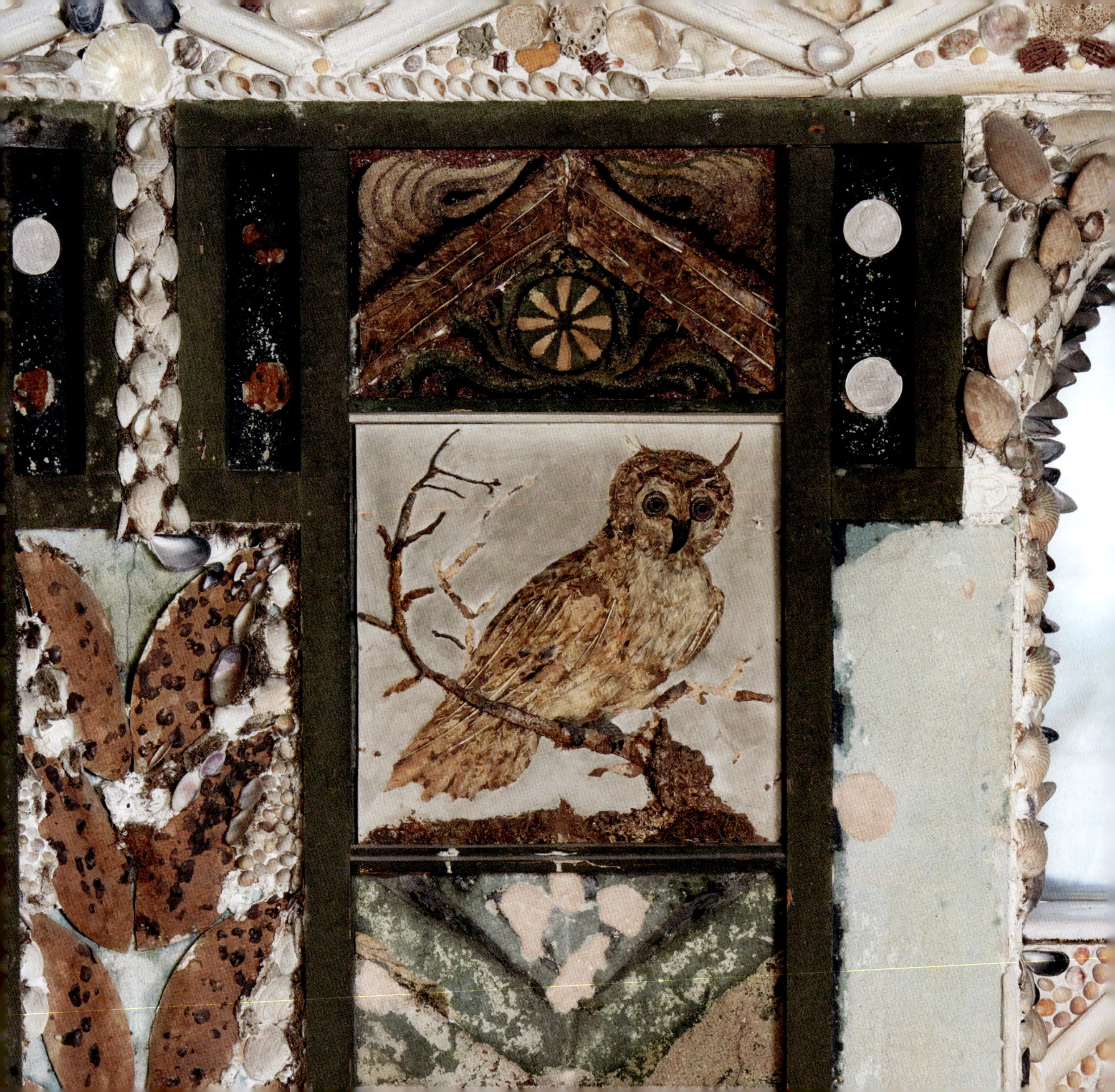

Creative cousins

JANE PARMINTER (1750–1811) AND MARY PARMINTER (1767–1849)

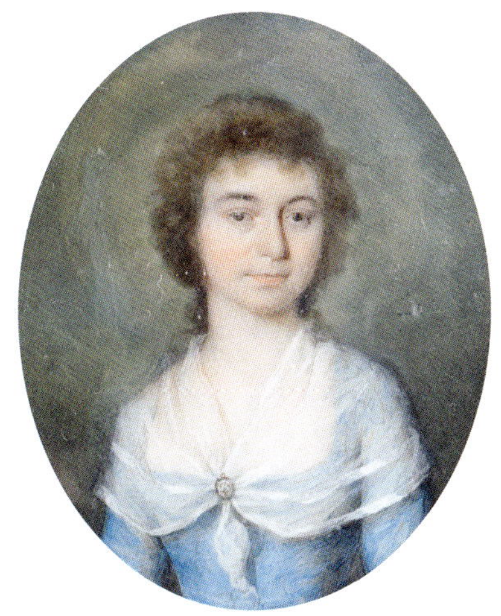

← Detail of decoration in the Shell Gallery at A la Ronde, Devon
↑ Portrait miniature of Mary Parminter, attributed to Ozias Humphry (1742–1810), c.1784, watercolour on ivory, 5.7 x 4.8cm, A la Ronde, Devon (NT 1313488.5)

In around 1799 Jane Parminter and Mary Parminter moved into their new Exmouth home, A la Ronde. This extraordinary 16-sided house was built by the cousins after their European grand tour with Jane's sister Elizabeth (1756–*c.*1790) and another female friend. In between visits to places of cultural interest, in 1786 the intrepid group climbed Mont Buet in the Alps, making them the first women to scale an Alpine summit of over 3,000 metres. A trip to the Basilica of San Vitale in Ravenna, Italy, may have been one of the sources of inspiration for the design of their future home.

A la Ronde contains remarkable friezes and decorative schemes using materials such as feathers, shells, lichen, cut-paperwork and found objects. We do not know whether they were created by the Parminters themselves or commissioned by them and worked by others (perhaps a combination of both), but it is clear that the cousins had a highly individual creative vision for their home. Some objects can be confidently attributed to the two women – including a series of delicate framed collages made using sand and seaweed, and a number of painted and découpaged chairs. A work table decorated by the Parminters with shells, micro-mosaics, intaglio seals, hardstone specimens and other souvenirs collected during their grand tour has recently been interpreted as a memorial to Elizabeth, who died shortly after their return from Europe. Fan-leaves, prints and other objects collected during their travels are also incorporated into the rooms, many of them displayed in their overflowing cabinet of curiosities.

In addition to creative expression, benevolence was central to the Parminters' life. They built a chapel near to A la Ronde, Point In View, that incorporated almshouses for unmarried women and a school for disadvantaged girls. It was a stipulation of Mary's will that their home should pass only to unmarried female relatives. RC

↓ Detail of a silhouette group showing Jane Parminter, Francis Torond (1742–1812), 1783, glass, paint, wood, paper, 52.5 x 91cm, A la Ronde, Devon (NT 1312028.1)

→ Collage made by Jane and Mary Parminter using sand, seaweed, paper and paint, 1780–1810, 35.5 x 46cm, A la Ronde, Devon (NT 1313698.3)

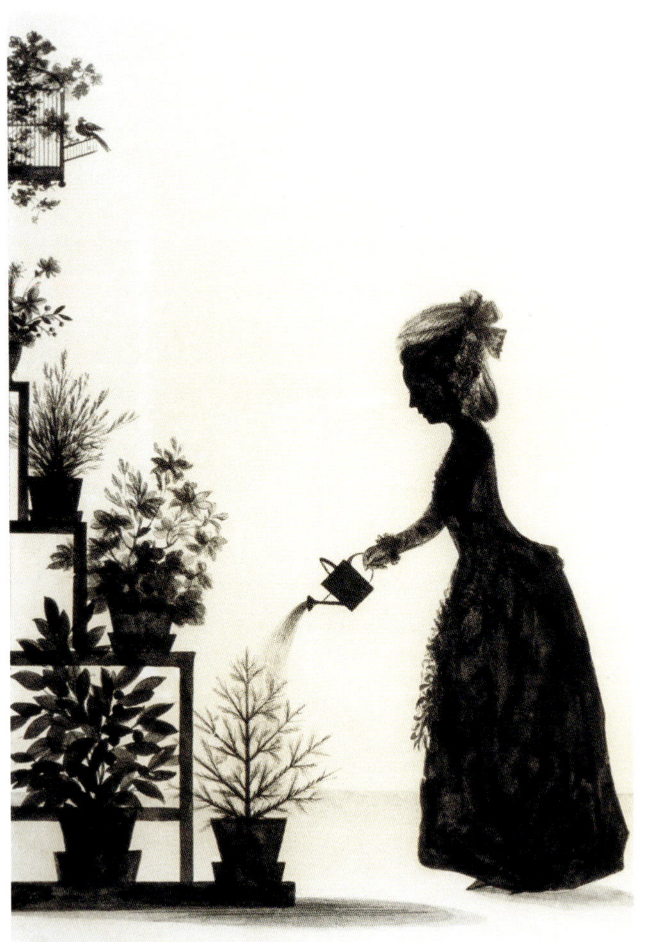

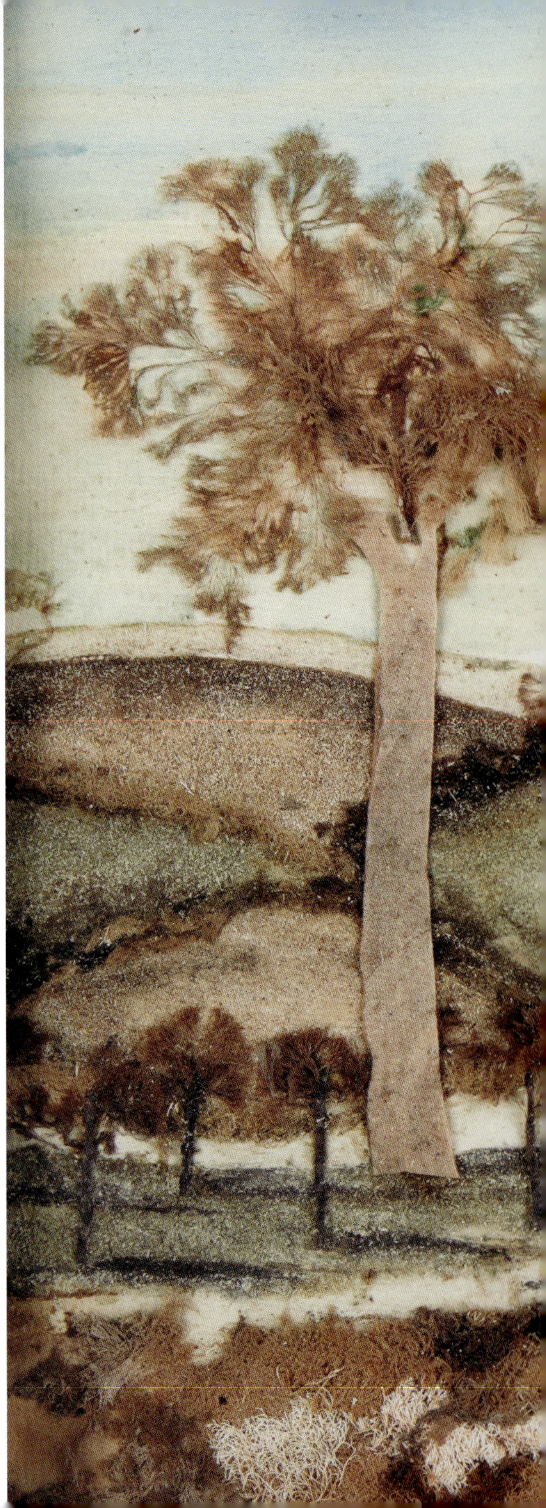

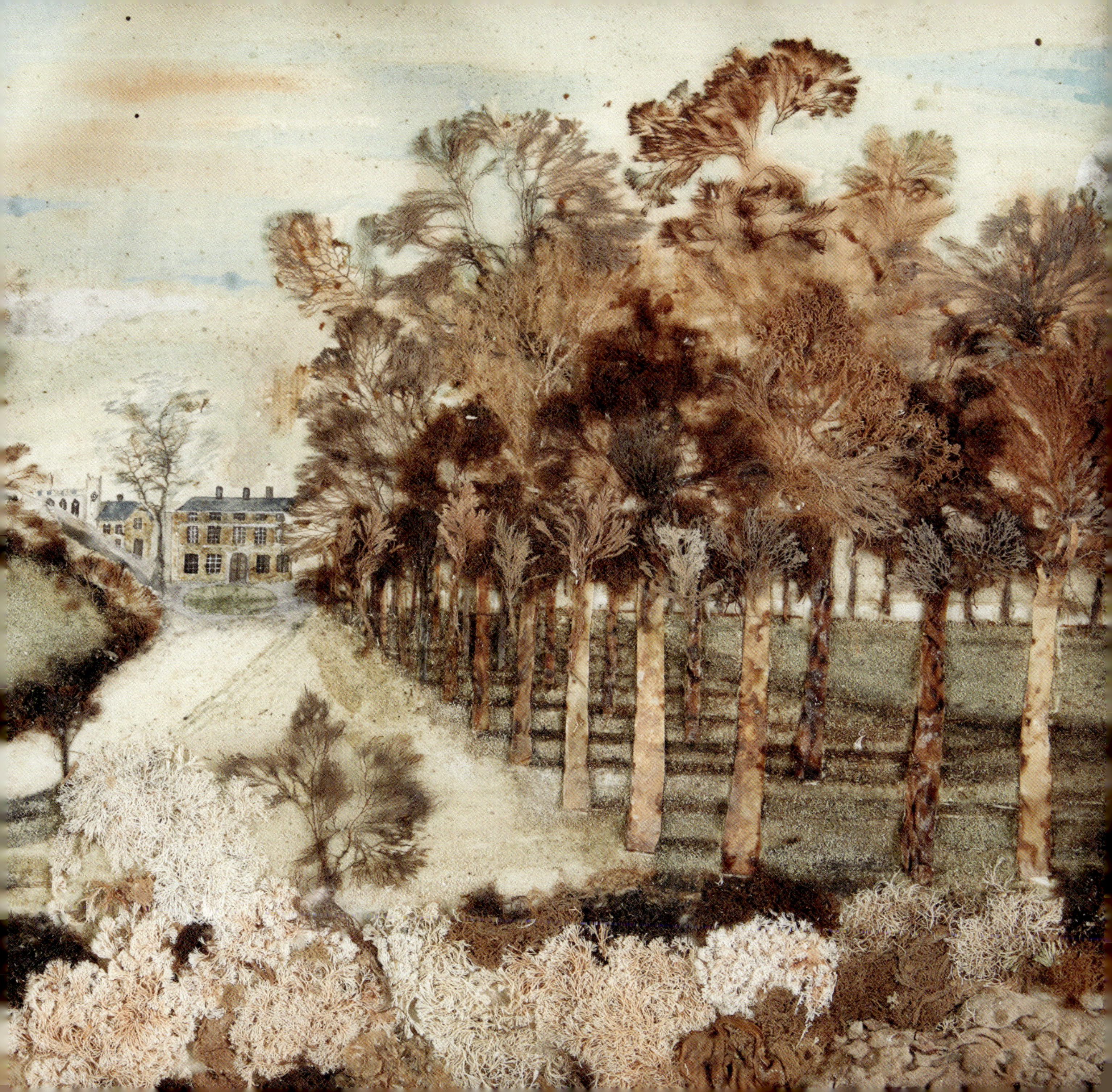

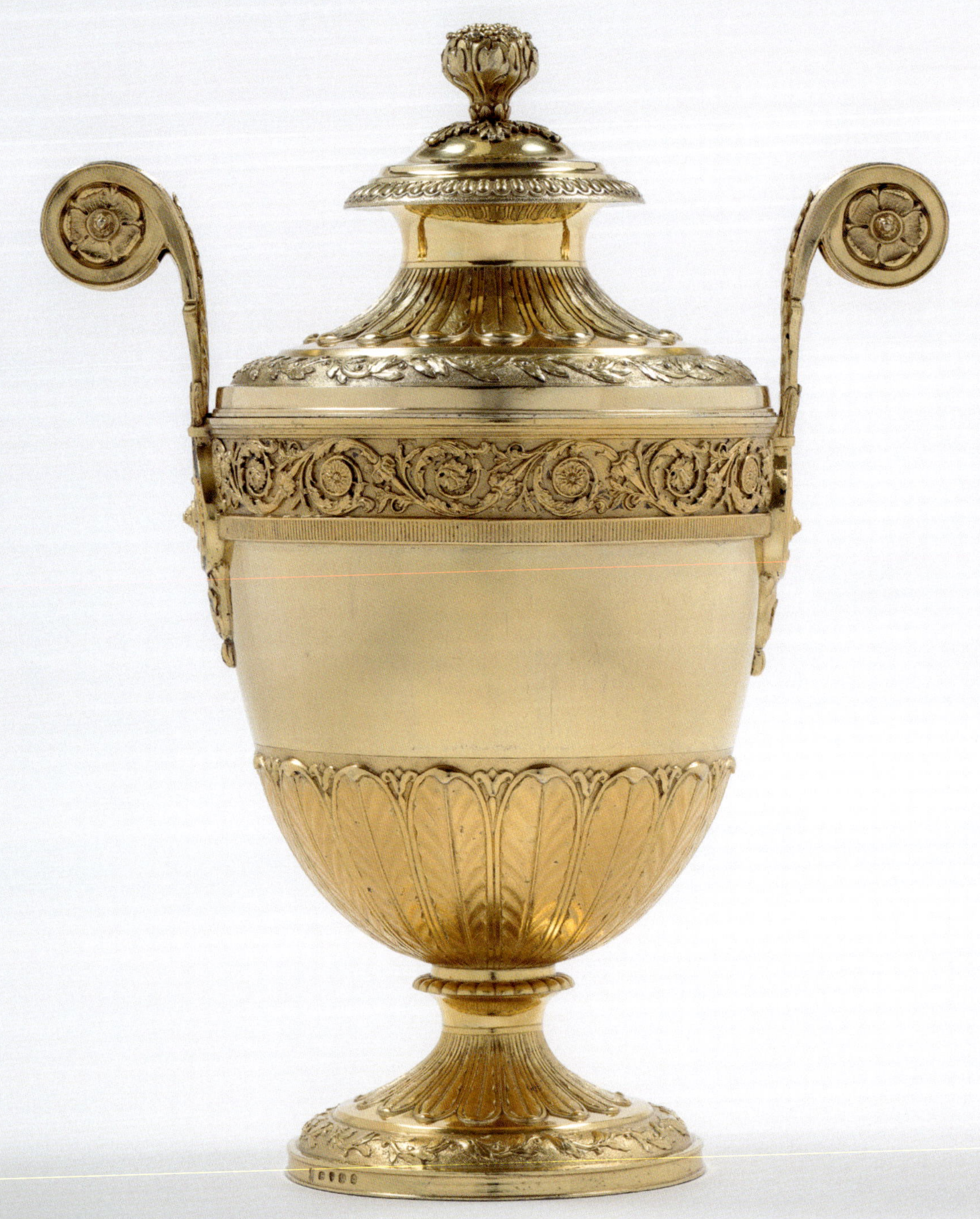

WOMEN AND THE WORLD

In the early 19th century Frances Talbot (page 101) and Mary Ellen Best (page 107) took the opportunity to travel into continental Europe with their brushes. Best, and many other women artists like her, occupied a place between 'amateur' and 'professional' practice – exhibiting and selling work, winning prizes, taking commissions, but unable to sustain these activities because of the competing demands of their home lives.

Despite her travels, much of Best's work was hyper-localised and focused on recording the minutiae of domestic life. Her self-portrait in the painting room of her York home (pages 108–9) is fascinating: despite her direct gaze, it is the room and blazing fire that are the focus of the image. She presents herself confidently as an artist, her works hang on the surrounding walls, but she is almost secondary to her own domestic environment, perhaps foretelling the tension between them that would arise later in her life.

Photography was an emerging innovation in the early 19th century, and Anna Atkins (page 112) and Constance Talbot (1811–80), of Lacock Abbey, Wiltshire, are among the earliest women photographers in the world. This new technology – offering a cheaper and quicker route to a 'selfie' – led to a decline in the popularity of traditional portrait

← Silver gilt cup and cover by Rebecca Emes (d.1829/30) and Edward Barnard (d.1855), 1811–12, 43 x 33.5 x 20cm, Osterley Park and House, London (NT 772326.1)

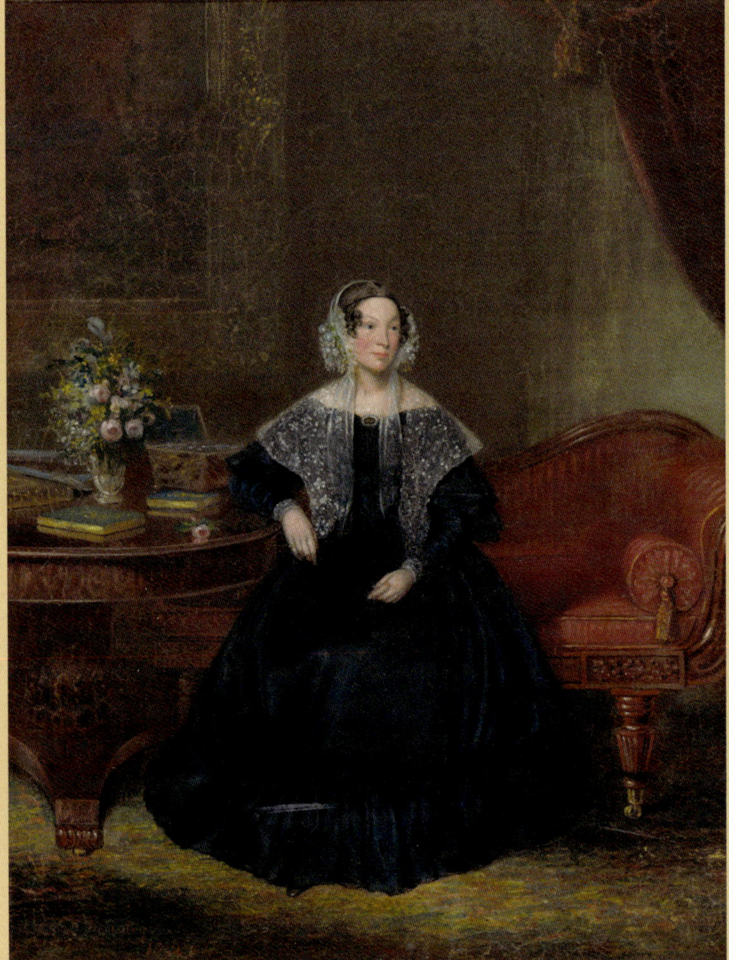

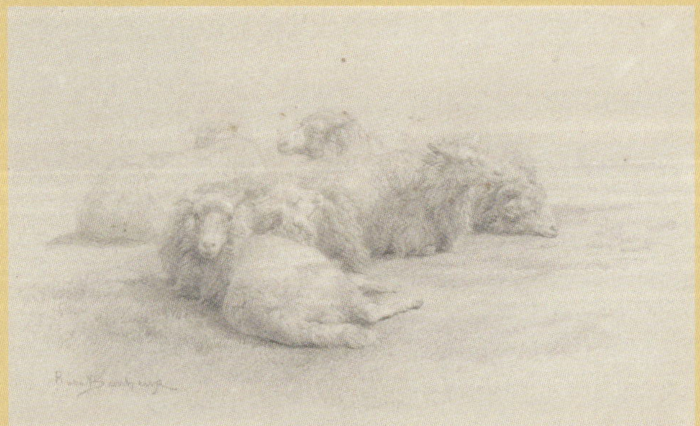

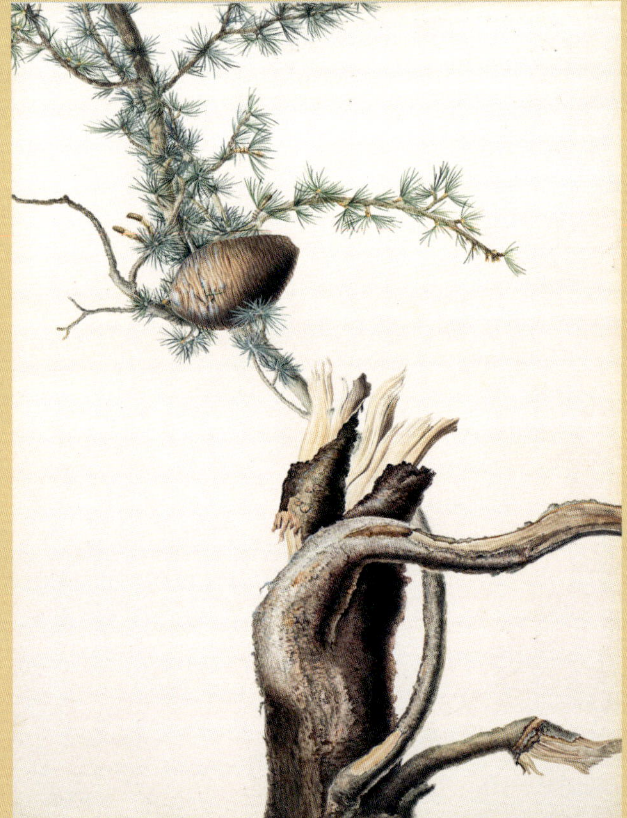

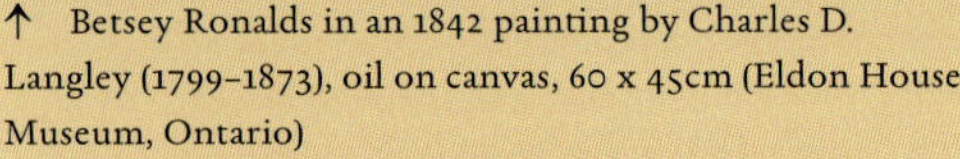

↑ Betsey Ronalds in an 1842 painting by Charles D. Langley (1799–1873), oil on canvas, 60 x 45cm (Eldon House Museum, Ontario)

↗ *Sheep Resting*, Rosa Bonheur (1822–99), undated, pencil on paper, 21 x 33cm, Cragside, Northumberland, transferred through the National Land Fund, 1967 (NT 1226526)

→ *A Fragment of the Ruin of an Old Cedar Tree Blown in Kensington Gardens, London*, Margaret Meen (1751–1834), c.1790–1810, watercolour on vellum, 56.4 x 42.6cm, The Vyne, Hampshire (NT 719474). Meen taught painting to Eliza Smith (later Chute), her sisters and niece.

miniatures, which were the bread and butter of artists specialising in this field, such as Sarah Biffin (page 114) and, earlier, Anne Mee (example on page 83). Like Biffin, botanical artist and teacher Margaret Meen (1751–1834, example opposite, below right) benefited from the stability and cachet attached to royal and noble patronage. She taught Queen Charlotte and her daughter to paint flowers and insects, and dedicated her 1790 journal, *Exotic Plants from the Gardens at Kew*, to the Queen. From 1770 to 1820 Meen was employed to document new plants being grown at the Royal Gardens at Kew, London, where plant collecting was inextricably linked to British colonial expansion. Meen's work forms an important record of the introduction to Britain of many new species, including the first dahlia, from Mexico. Kew also provided inspiration for artists such as Betsey Ronalds (page 104) and, later, Marianne North (1830–90), who established a public gallery in the gardens that still exists today, displaying more than 800 of her vivid botanical paintings.

The founding of the Society of Women Artists around 1855 offered further opportunities for women to exhibit and sell work. Elizabeth Thompson, Lady Butler (1846–1933), and the French artist Rosa Bonheur (1822–99) were early members. Both are known for their large realist canvases – Bonheur specialising in animals (opposite, top right) and Butler in military scenes, both traditionally 'male' subjects – and both women were critically acclaimed during their careers.

Rebecca Emes's business produced luxurious silver for a global market (page 98), taking advantage of the demand for British-made goods in the growing empire. Throughout the 19th century Mary Chawner (1792–1870) and her family were among the most successful specialist makers of silver flatware (mostly spoons, forks and servers). Many more women ran or worked in smaller workshops at this time, or might have been employed to undertake specific tasks, such as polishing or packing silver. The National Trust's collections include pieces marked by many women, including Elizabeth Morley, Hannah Northcote, Mary Ann Reilly, and Mary and Eliza Sumner. Frustratingly little is known about most of these women, however, beyond the objects they left behind.

Silver service

REBECCA EMES (d.1829/30)

Rebecca Emes was a partner in one of the largest manufacturing silversmiths of its day. Emes and Barnard's London workshop created pieces for its own aristocratic customers and also supplied major retailers, including the prestigious royal goldsmiths Rundell, Bridge & Rundell.

Following the death of her husband, John (1762–1808), like Louisa Courtauld and many other women before her, Emes took over his business. Her first mark was registered in 1808, jointly with William Emes, her husband's executor, probably to ease the process of arranging John's estate. A few months later she registered her first mark with her partner, Edward Barnard (d.1855), who was a reliable and known hand, having previously worked as foreman of the company for John. Together, they developed a highly successful business, supplying silver across Britain and overseas, including to the USA and India.

The range of products the firm created was impressive and meant it could capitalise on a market of wealthy buyers hungry for gleaming silver to adorn their homes. It also shifted cannily as styles and habits evolved, introducing new patterns and forms in response to consumer demand. Emes and Barnard produced tea and coffee sets; dining accoutrements for the fashionable table, such as cruets, tureens and toast racks; and more personal practical items, such as inkstands and chamber candlesticks. The towering centrepiece at Anglesey Abbey (opposite) – which appears to be lifted up on the backs of three winged lions – would have been a magnificent conversation piece at dessert, as well as providing light for those gathered around the table (and fruit to be taken from the bowl).

Some of Emes and Barnard's most spectacular commissions were presentation pieces. Racing cups formed an important element of this work and the cup at Osterley, the prize for the winner at the Chelmsford Races in 1813 (page 94), is an elegant example. RC

→ Silver gilt and glass centrepiece by Rebecca Emes and Edward Barnard, 1818–19, 66.5 x 30.5 x 28cm, Anglesey Abbey, Cambridgeshire (NT 516439)

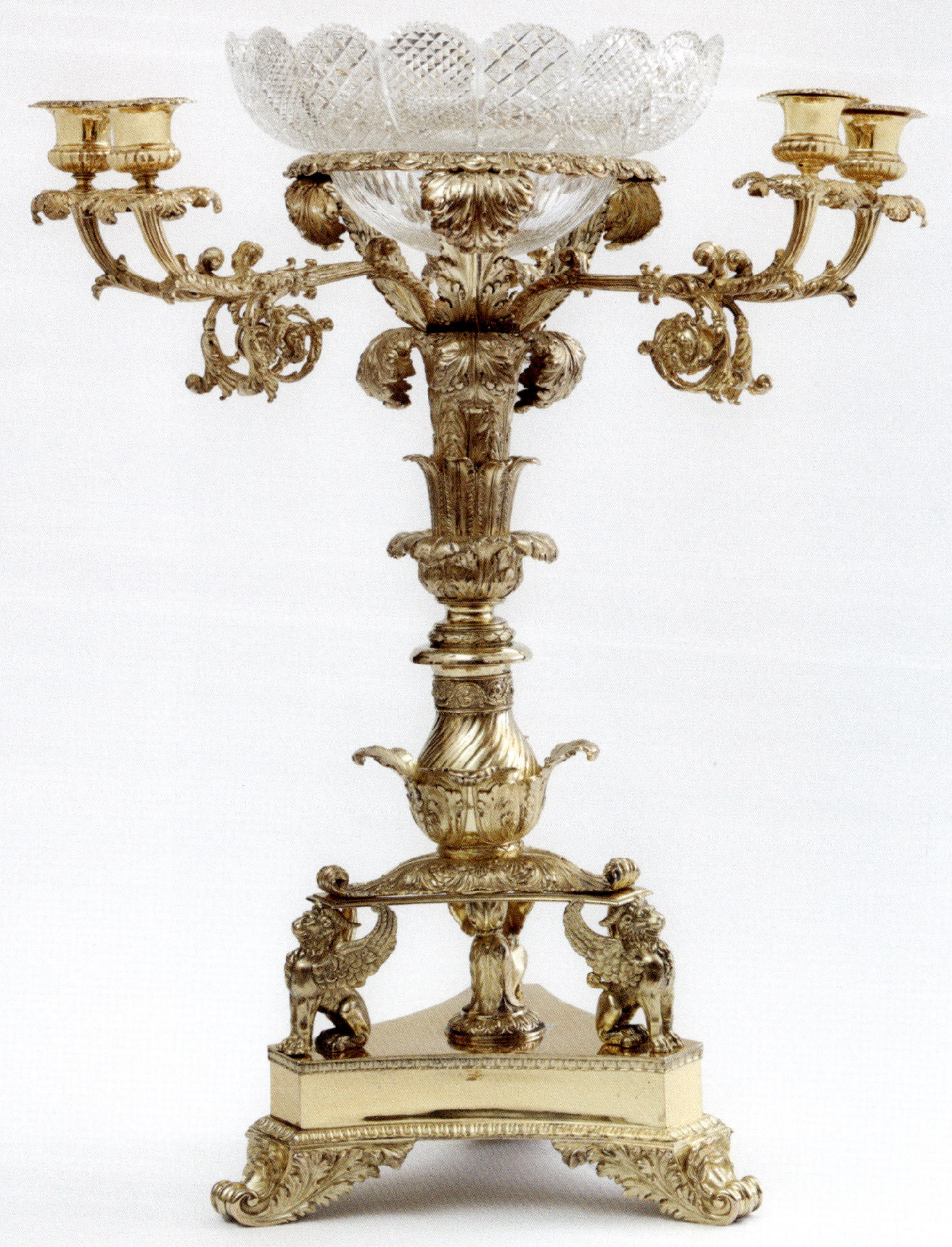

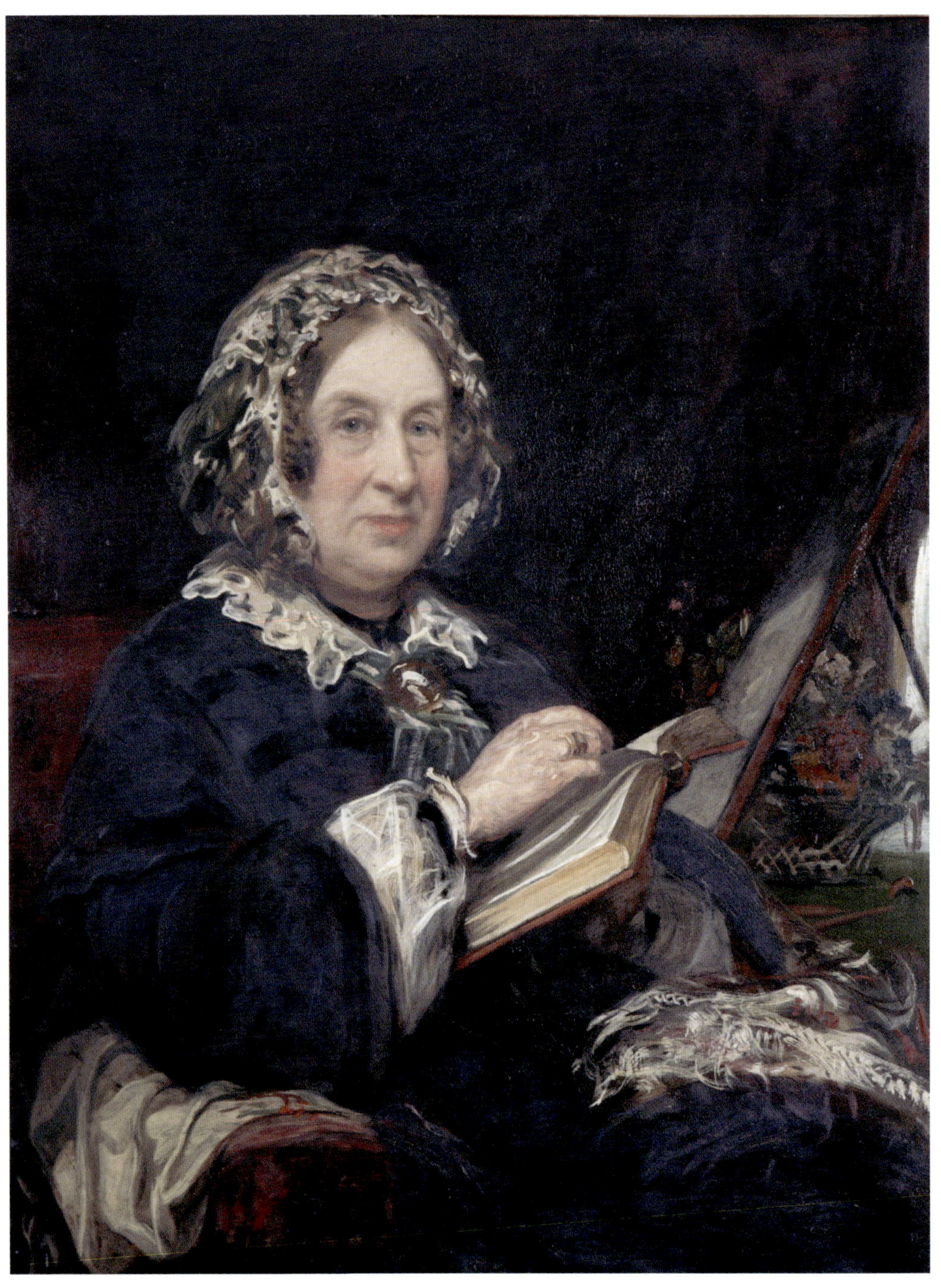

‘The product of her pencil’

FRANCES TALBOT (1782–1857)

← *Frances Talbot, Countess of Morley*, James Sant (1820–1916), c.1852, oil on canvas, 84.5 x 72cm, Saltram, Devon, ⁑ 1957 (NT 872271)

Frances Talbot, Countess of Morley, was a talented amateur artist, illustrator and novelist. A portrait of Talbot in later life (opposite) depicts her surrounded by these passions – she reads a book while a picture waits to be finished, or admired, on a table easel beside her.

Aged 16, Talbot was awarded a silver medal in ‘polite arts’ by the Society for the Encouragement of Arts, Manufactures and Commerce (later the Royal Society of Arts) for her painting of Raphael’s *Virgin and Child*. In the following years she was awarded the larger silver palette medal for a painting after Titian, and a further silver medal for a painting of a ‘Herb Girl from nature’. These subjects suggest that Talbot was experimenting with painting figures – although, as a woman, she would not have been permitted to attend life-drawing classes to develop this skill. That constraint might explain why, during the Peace of Amiens, she went to Paris to study for a few months with the artist François Gérard (1770–1837), who was celebrated for his portraits of French nobility. A large collection of Talbot’s watercolours is held at Saltram in Devon, many showing scenes of continental Europe, including examples copied from artists such as William Callow and David Roberts.

Talbot’s interest in wax modelling probably began following a visit to Saltram in 1813 by coloured-wax artist Samuel Percy (1750–1820). Talbot created a number of family portraits in this medium, including at least two copies of a tender image of her stepson, Henry Villiers Parker (1806–17), sculpted in 1814 before his tragic death, aged just 11 (overleaf).

Talbot’s obituary in *The Annual Register* for 1857 creates a picture of a vibrant woman of wit and good conversation, making special note of her literary and artistic work – ‘a woman of strong mind and considerable literary and artistic abilities … [she] has left behind her a numerous collection of paintings, the product of her pencil’. RC

↓ *Henry Villiers Parker, Viscount Boringdon*, Frances Talbot, Countess of Morley, 1814, framed wax relief portrait, 13cm (diameter), Osterley Park and House, London (NT 772581)
→ *The Piazza of St Mark's, Venice, with the two pillars from Acre*, Frances Talbot, Countess of Morley, 1830–57, watercolour on paper, 25 x 19.4cm, Saltram, Devon (NT 872202). Probably copied from an engraving by Edward John Roberts after an original work by Samuel Prout.

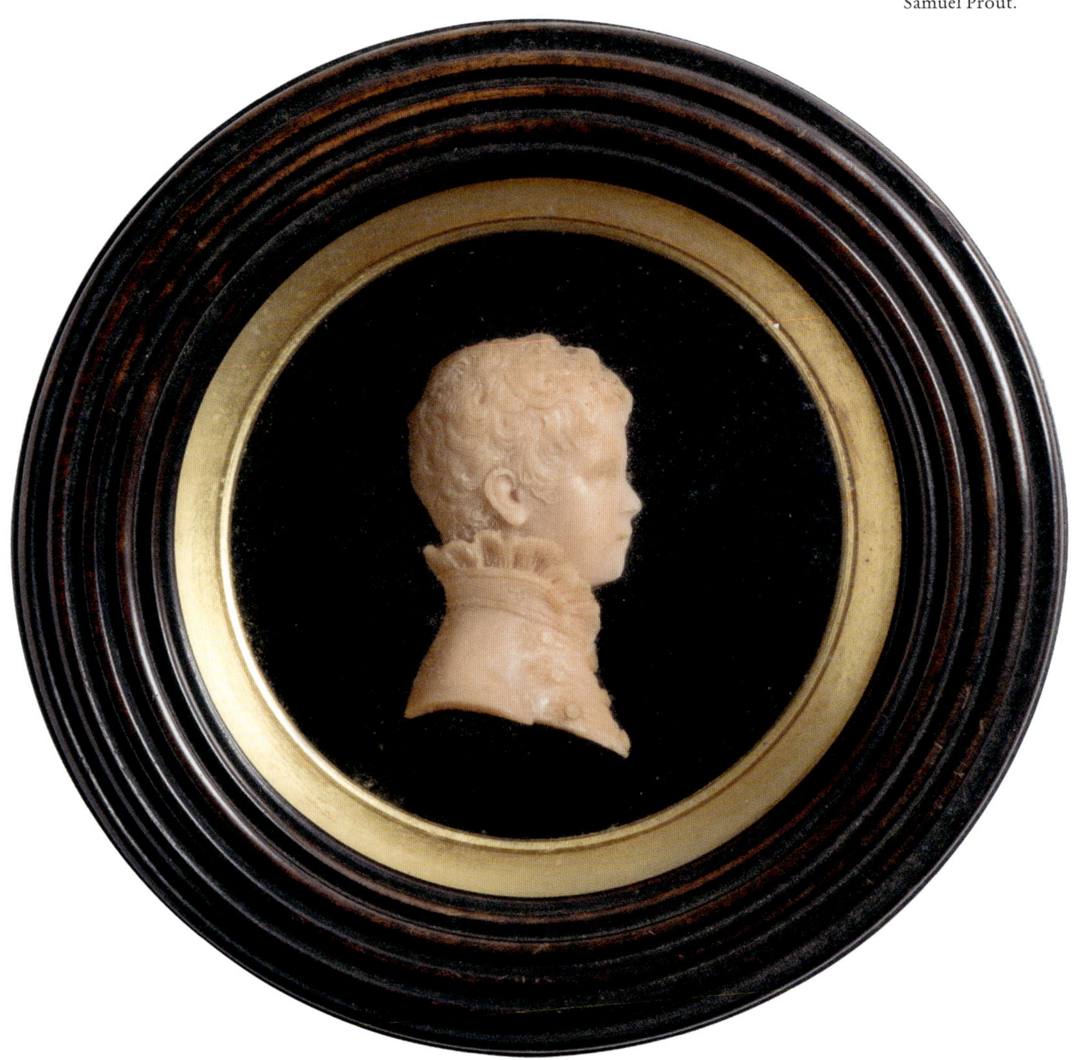

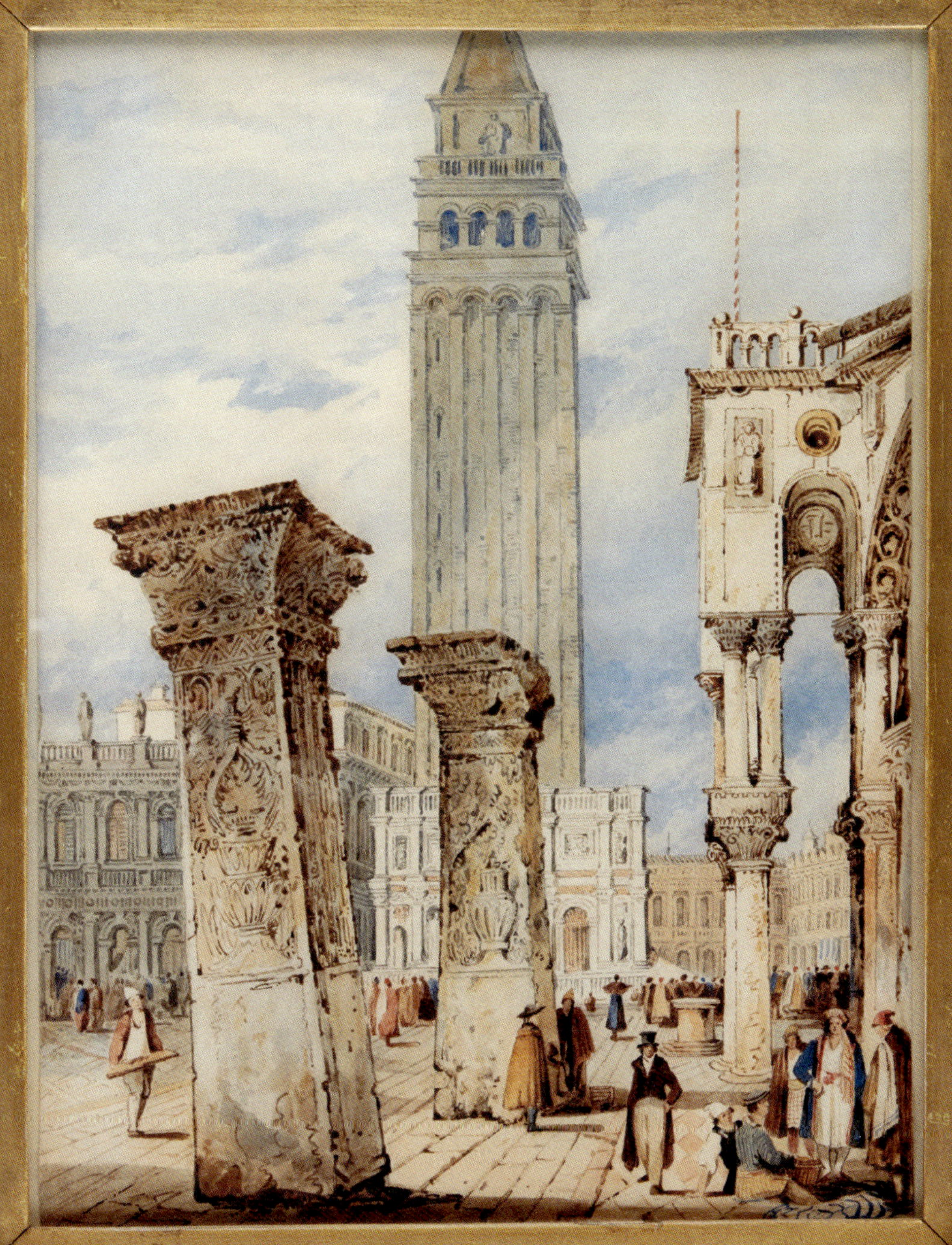

Drawn from nature

ELIZABETH RONALDS (1788–1854)

Elizabeth (Betsey) Ronalds is best known for the 179 mini-masterpieces she created for a book of 1831 celebrating apples. The Ronalds family had run a successful fruit nursery in Brentford, west London, for three generations. At its height it encompassed nearly 50 acres of land across Brentford, Isleworth, Little Ealing and East Bedfont. For almost 40 years it shared and exchanged plants with the Royal Botanic Gardens at Kew and the Horticultural Society of London's garden at Chiswick. The botanist Joseph Banks was rapidly acquiring specimens for Kew as a result of European colonial expansion and the plant collecting that followed in its wake.

The Ronalds' nursery supplied 110 'East India Seeds' to Kew in 1813. In 1788 Banks had placed extensive orders with the Ronalds' nursery for fruit, vegetable and ornamental plants and seeds for settlers in newly colonised Australia. Similar orders went to colonies in New Zealand, Tahiti, New York and the West Indies.

Betsey Ronalds was able to use these connections to draw and paint specimens in the important collections at Kew, furthering her own artistic practice and helping her family to identify new species for stocking the nursery. She painted watercolours to catalogue the fruits and flowers grown in the nursery, which helped to promote the business. The influential horticulturalist John Claudius Loudon (1783–1843) visited the family in 1829 and later described Ronalds' work in his publication *Gardener's Magazine* as 'a style surpassed by no artist whatever'.

Ronalds' most ambitious work was the body of wonderful hand-coloured lithographic engravings she produced for her father's book *Pyrus malus Brentfordiensis* (1831). This volume was a celebration of the 300 apple cultivars grown by the family, a specialism of the nursery. Her plates show the apples positioned mainly stem down in a grid formation – a technique promoted by Loudon – with the colours and textures of the skins rendered with remarkable accuracy to aid identification of the species. Each apple was accompanied by a short description of its qualities written by her father. The book cost five guineas with coloured plates, four guineas uncoloured. Ronalds also contributed several illustrations for Loudon's important, multi-volume botanical encyclopedia *Arboretum et fruticetum Britannicum* (1838). RC

→ Six varieties of apple in a hand-coloured lithograph by Betsey Ronalds, from Hugh Ronalds' book, *Pyrus malus Brentfordiensis: or, a Concise Description of Selected Apples* (Plate II), 1831, Calke Abbey, Derbyshire, ‡ 1985 (NT 3186031)

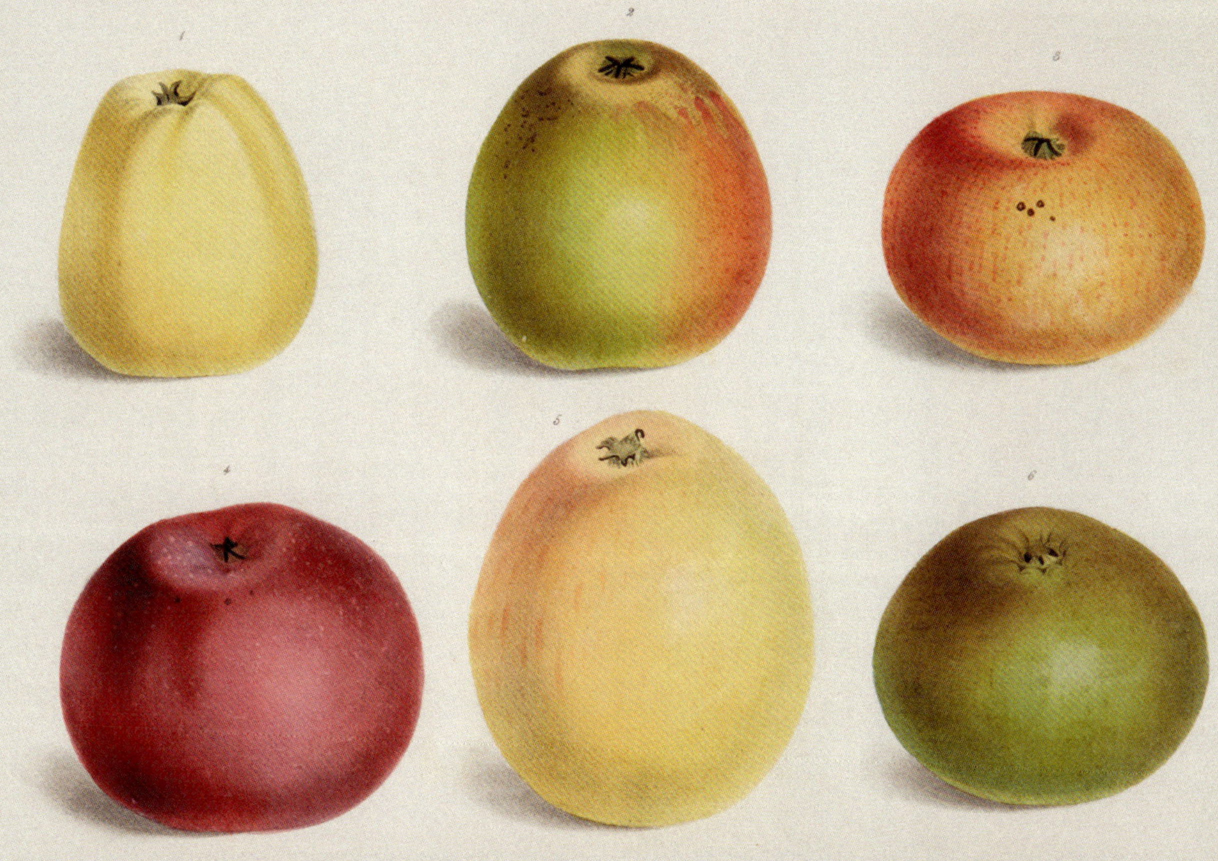

No. 1 Early Wax	No. 4 Sops of Wine
2 Browns Summer Beauty	5 Eve Apple
3 Thorli Pippin	6 Hicks' Fancy

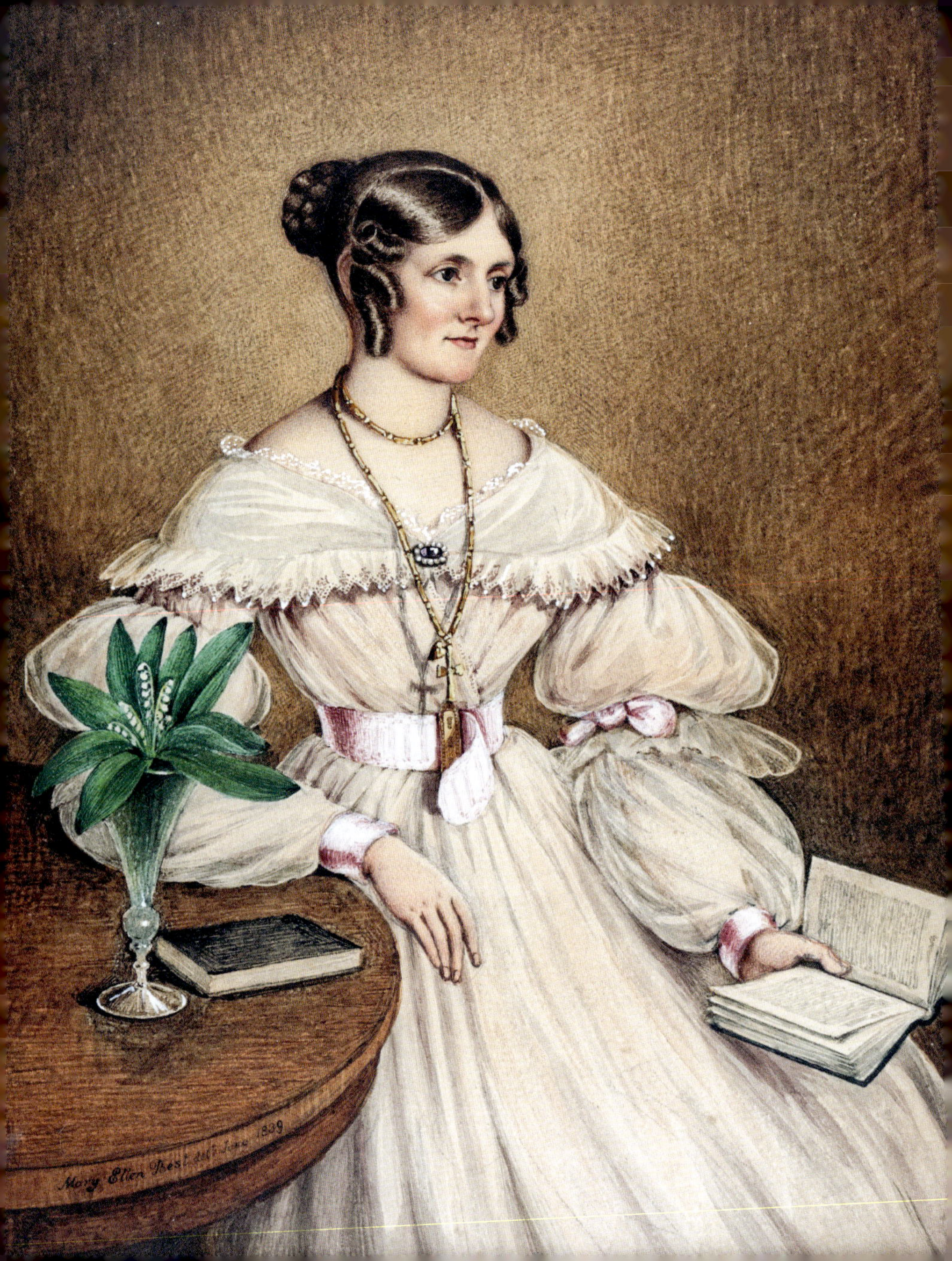
Mary Ellen Best
1839

Painting life in York

MARY ELLEN BEST (1809–91)

The paintings of Mary Ellen Best create a vivid picture of Victorian domestic life. Best recorded the people and places she knew, capturing the ordinary in extraordinary detail.

She was born in York and took lessons in drawing and painting as a child. Readying herself to practise as an artist, she sketched daily, read voraciously on the history of art and visited Yorkshire country houses, such as Fountains Hall, to study their collections. With her mother and a box of watercolours, Best travelled through the Netherlands and Germany (where she would eventually live) in the 1830s, visiting art galleries and museums, and picking up occasional portrait commissions along the way.

Best has been described as operating within the constraints placed upon her as a middle-class woman. Although she exhibited, sold and received prizes for her watercolours, and attracted many commissions, she did not take a studio (working instead from home), train apprentices, or display or advertise her work for sale. Despite being relatively prolific (she painted about 40 portraits per year), like many women artists she gradually stopped painting in her forties, following her marriage and the births of her children. The advent of photography might also have reduced the demand for the types of work that Best produced.

She is especially known for her portraits, often of friends and family in Yorkshire, and her remarkably detailed, documentary images of interiors – both considered acceptable subjects for women artists at the time. They are object- and pattern-rich: tables are laden with ceramics and glasses, wallpapers vibrate with colour, the grain of pine floor-boards catches in the sunlight, and ornaments are arranged neatly in their proper places. Most of Best's portrait sitters were women. She painted two generations of the Worsley family, including her good friend Rose (overleaf), in the late 1830s. RC

← *Frances Stovin*, Mary Ellen Best, 1839, watercolour on paper, 34 x 27cm, Ormesby Hall, North Yorkshire (NT 707927)

↓ *Rose Stovin*, Mary Ellen Best, 1837, watercolour on paper, 40 x 30.5cm, Ormesby Hall, North Yorkshire (NT 707934)
→ *The Artist at Work*, Mary Ellen Best, 1838–9, watercolour on paper, 25.7 x 36cm (York Museums Trust)

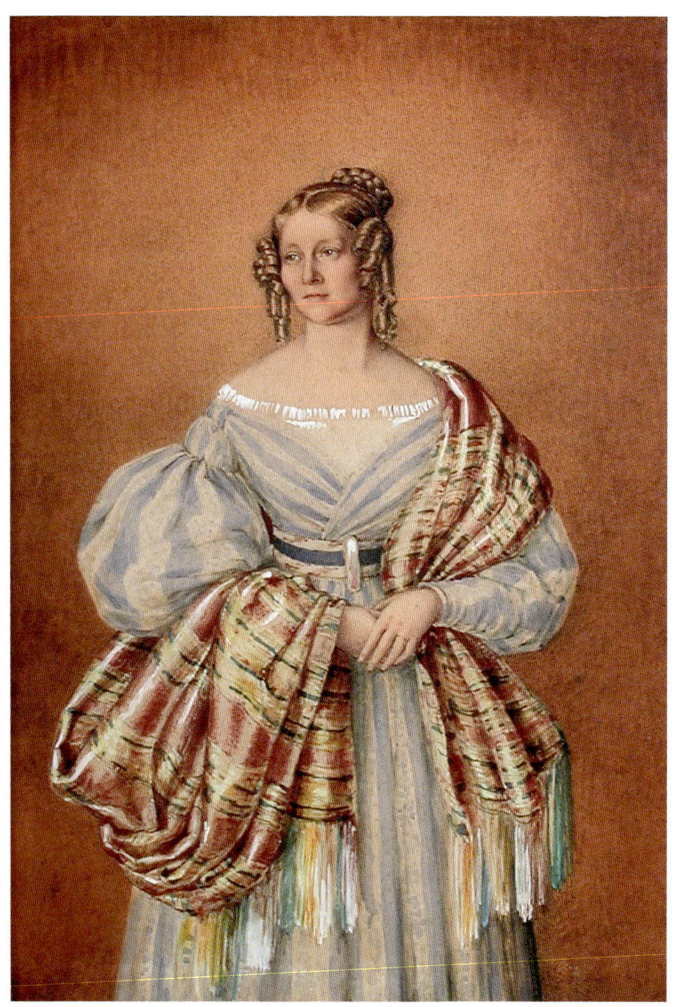

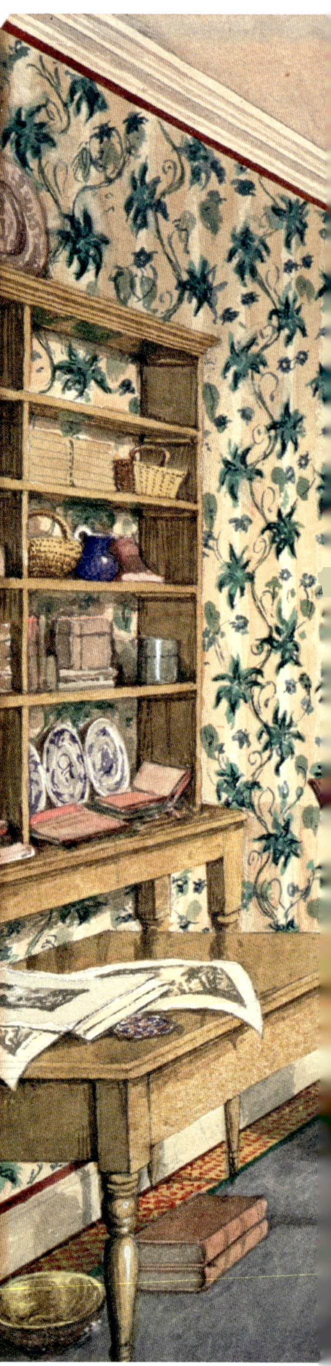

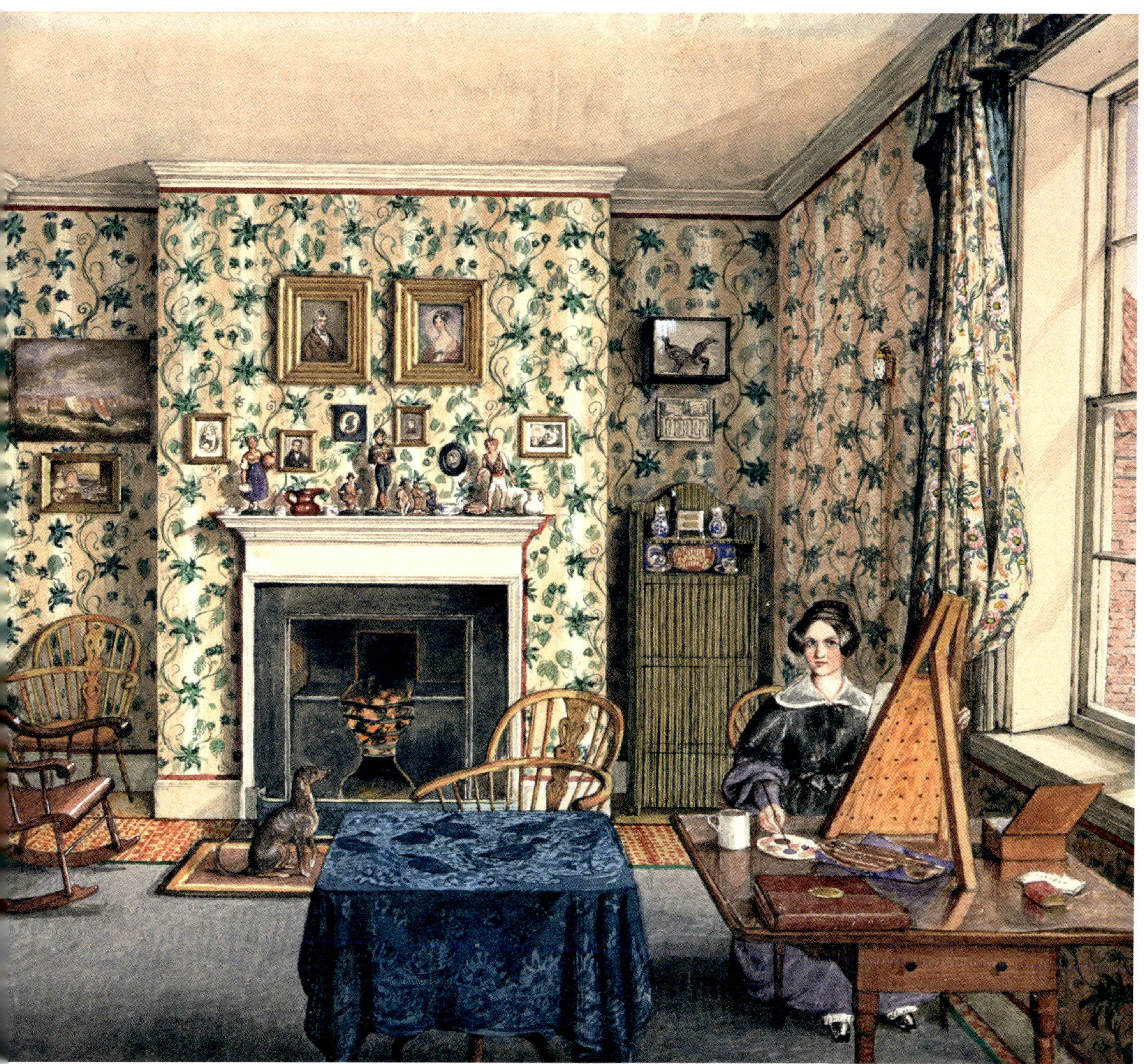

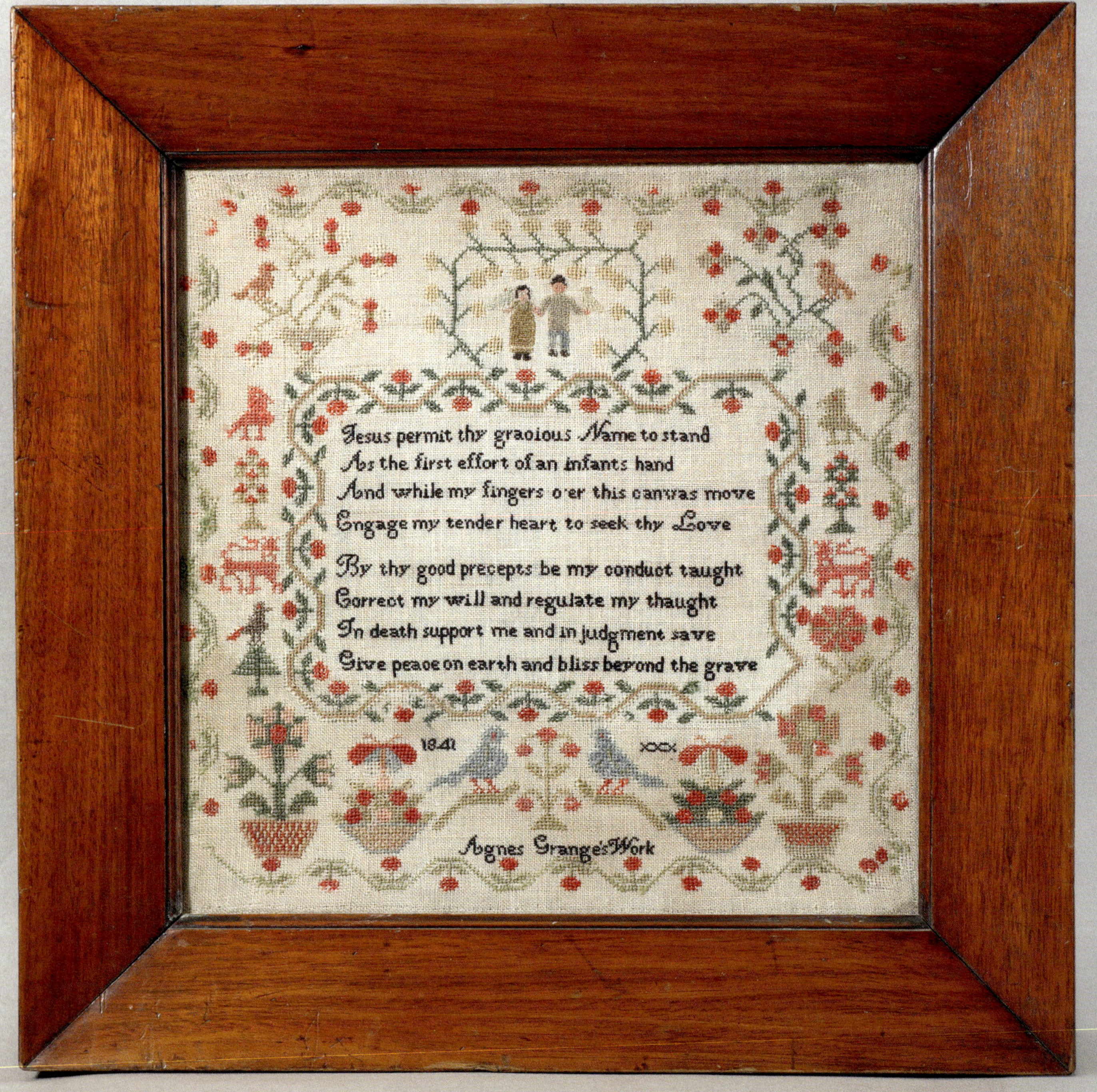
Jesus permit thy gracious Name to stand
As the first effort of an infants hand
And while my fingers o'er this canvas move
Engage my tender heart to seek thy Love
By thy good precepts be my conduct taught
Correct my will and regulate my thaught
In death support me and in judgment save
Give peace on earth and bliss beyond the grave
1841
Agnes Grange's Work

'While my fingers o'er this canvas move'

AGNES GRANGE (1828–95)

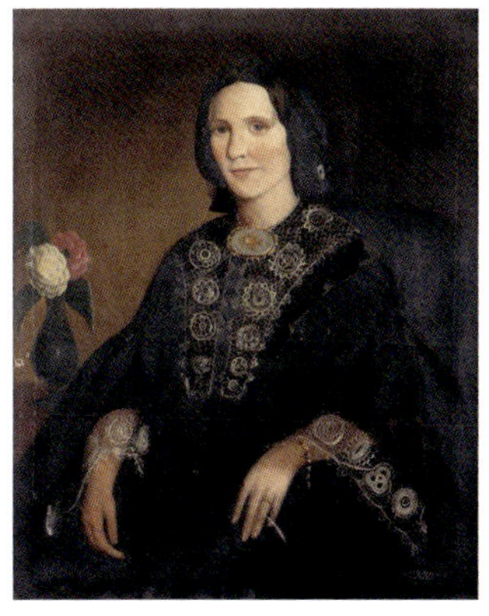

← Wool work sampler with religious embroidered verse and decoration by Agnes Grange, 1841, 35 x 35cm (sampler), East Riddlesden Hall, West Yorkshire (NT 201627)
↑ Portrait of Agnes Grange by an unknown artist, c.1850, oil on canvas (private collection). This portrait captures Agnes at the start of her married life in Liverpool.

This sampler by Agnes Grange is one of countless examples produced during the 19th century by girls from a wide range of social backgrounds. They frequently followed standard patterns and were demonstrations of the sewing skills that most women would be expected to employ throughout their lives. Many feature the verse picked out here, which explicitly connects Christian piety with the act of embroidery: 'And while my fingers o'er this canvas move/Engage my tender heart to seek Thy love.'

Such textiles often lose all connection with their creator, but here we know that Agnes was the youngest daughter of Areton and Anne Grange (née Slingsby), tenants at East Riddlesden Hall near Keighley in West Yorkshire. Agnes's mother was from a family of cattle farmers who rented pasture on the East Riddlesden estate, while her father was a bookkeeper who may have worked for the estate's absentee landlords. Agnes had been born in the hall in 1828.

In 1840 Agnes's world changed when her father rescued a man drowning in the local canal, only to die himself from an 'inflammation of the lungs' soon afterwards. The widowed Anne soon left East Riddlesden and moved in with her brothers around the time this sampler was being created by her teenage daughter. Perhaps in these stitches we see not only a formulaic act, but a rather more personal processing of grief and mourning.

The following year Anne would also die, leaving Agnes an orphan. In 1849 Agnes married Thomas Webster, a butcher and hide merchant from Liverpool, going on to raise a large family of her own. MC

Into the blue

ANNA ATKINS (1799–1871)

Anna Atkins is recognised today as the first person to publish a book illustrated with photographs – an achievement made possible by her pioneering application of the cyanotype process.

Atkins embedded scientific knowledge and artistic talent throughout her life and work, encouraged by her father, the chemist, mineralogist and natural scientist John George Children (1777–1852). Her contribution of 256 original drawings to illustrate his published translation of Jean-Baptiste Lamarck's *Genera of Shells* (1822–4) serves as an early example. Atkins nurtured a growing passion for botany, assembling significant botanical collections and joining the Botanical Society of London in 1839. Exposure to the groundbreaking inventions of Sir John Herschel (1792–1871) and William Henry Fox Talbot (1800–77) of Lacock Abbey led to her own innovative pursuits in the field of photography. She was quick to adopt Herschel's cyanotype process (announced in 1842) to make remarkable botanical photographs.

Brushing writing paper with a solution of iron salts to make it light sensitive, Atkins would lay a specimen and hand-written label directly on top, place them securely under glass in the sun for several minutes and finally wash in water. Her absorbing, delicate and camera-less studies of nature were rendered in negative form – shades of white against the alluring Prussian blues that permeate the paper.

Atkins gave the first part of her privately published book *Photographs of British Algae: Cyanotype Impressions* to the Royal Society in 1843. Hundreds more prints followed in instalments over the following decade. She later made this *Hedysarum* genus print (opposite), thought to have belonged to the now dispersed album *Cyanotypes of British and Foreign Flowering Plants and Ferns* (1854), which she created for her friend Anne Dixon. AS

→ *Hedysarum specimens*, Anna Atkins, 1854, cyanotype, 34.8 x 24.5cm, Lacock Abbey and Fox Talbot Museum, Wiltshire (NT 98244)

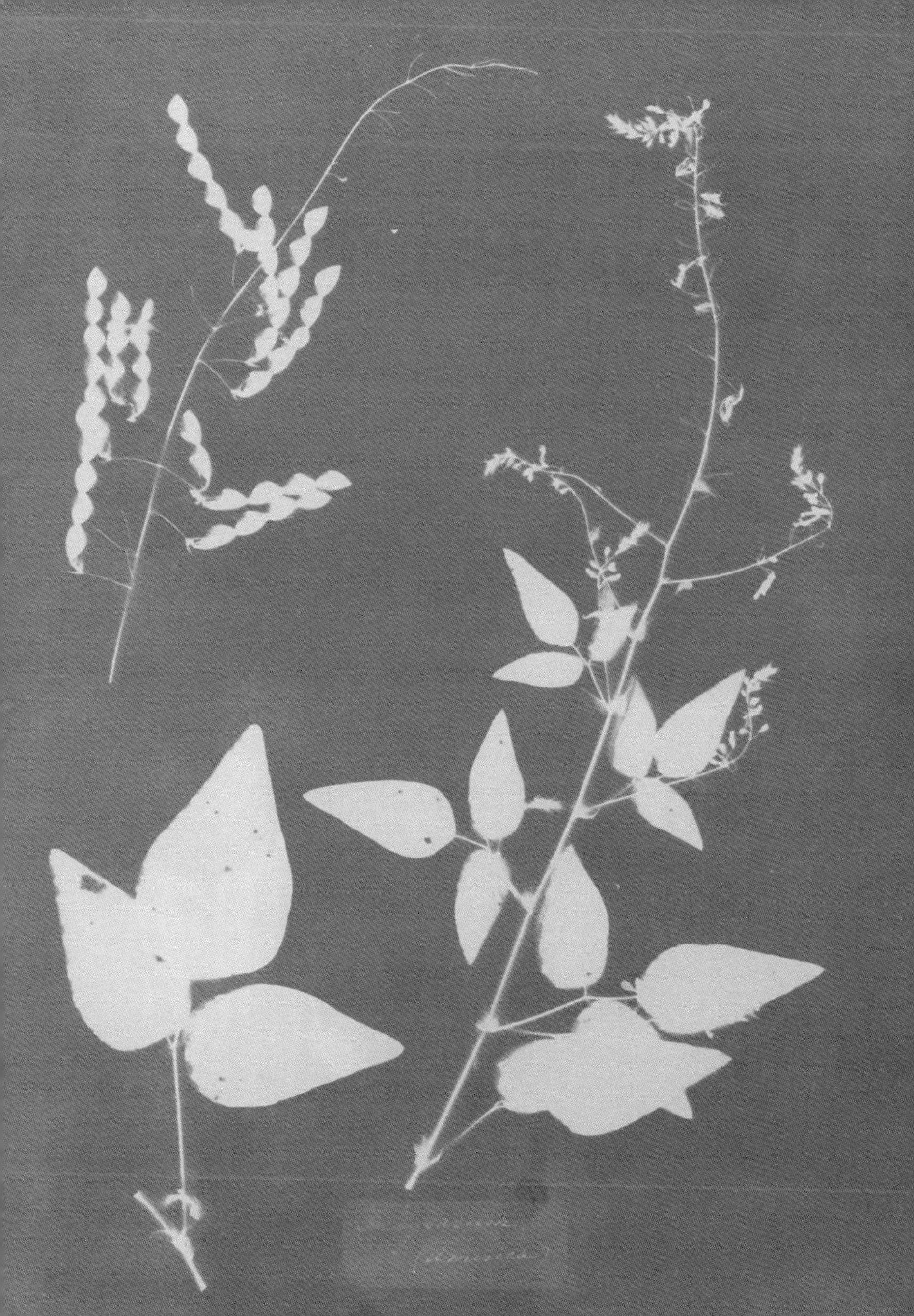

‘The famous Miss Beffin’

SARAH BIFFIN (OR BEFFIN) (1784–1850)

Sarah Biffin (or Beffin) was a celebrated disabled artist. She was born into a farming family in Somerset, where her creative life began at an early age. She taught herself to sew as a young child and became an accomplished dressmaker. Born without arms or legs, Biffin began painting lessons aged 20, using her mouth and shoulder to control the brush (as shown in the portrait, right). She left home soon afterwards and began touring the country with her teacher, Mr Dukes. Biffin demonstrated sewing and painting for paying audiences, who received a sample of her writing to take away.

This entrepreneurial spirit drove Biffin’s career and she experienced periods of considerable success. George Douglas, 16th Earl of Morton (1761–1827), became an important patron and introduced her to the miniature portrait artist William Marshall Craig (d.1827), who provided her with additional specialist training. Biffin moved between cities – including Brighton, Birmingham, Oxford and Cheltenham – undertaking commissions for clients, and offering lessons in lithography and miniature painting.

In 1821 Biffin established her own studio on the Strand in London and was working mostly to commission for wealthy clients, describing herself in a newspaper advertisement as ‘the famous Miss Beffin, miniature painter of London’. That same year, she exhibited four miniatures at the Royal Academy of Arts, received a silver medal from the Royal Society of Arts, and was appointed as miniaturist to Willem Frederick, Prince of Orange-Nassau (1772–1843). In 1830 she was appointed as miniaturist to Princess Augusta Sophia (1768–1840), daughter of King George III.

Following the death of the princess and a decline in the fashion for miniatures, Biffin struggled financially but did continue to work. She painted an affecting portrait of the Marchioness of Abercorn (opposite) while based on Mount Pleasant in Liverpool. A public appeal to raise money to guarantee her an annual income was led by the Rathbone family of philanthropists and the collector Joseph Mayer. Almost 30 years after her first showing, Biffin exhibited once more at the Royal Academy, a few short months before her death in 1850. RC

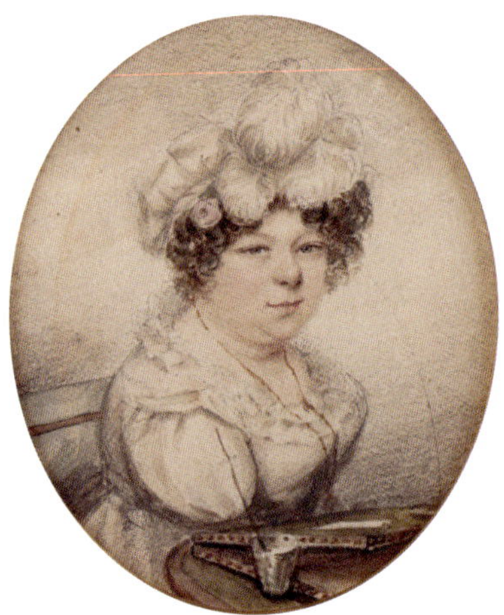

↑ Sarah Biffin (or Beffin) in what is thought to be a self-portrait, *c.*1825, watercolour and graphite, 10 x 10cm (National Portrait Gallery, London)
→ *The Marchioness of Abercorn at the Cottage of Industry*, Sarah Biffin, 1846–50, watercolour on card, 43 x 38cm, Llanerchaeron, Ceredigion (NT 461462)

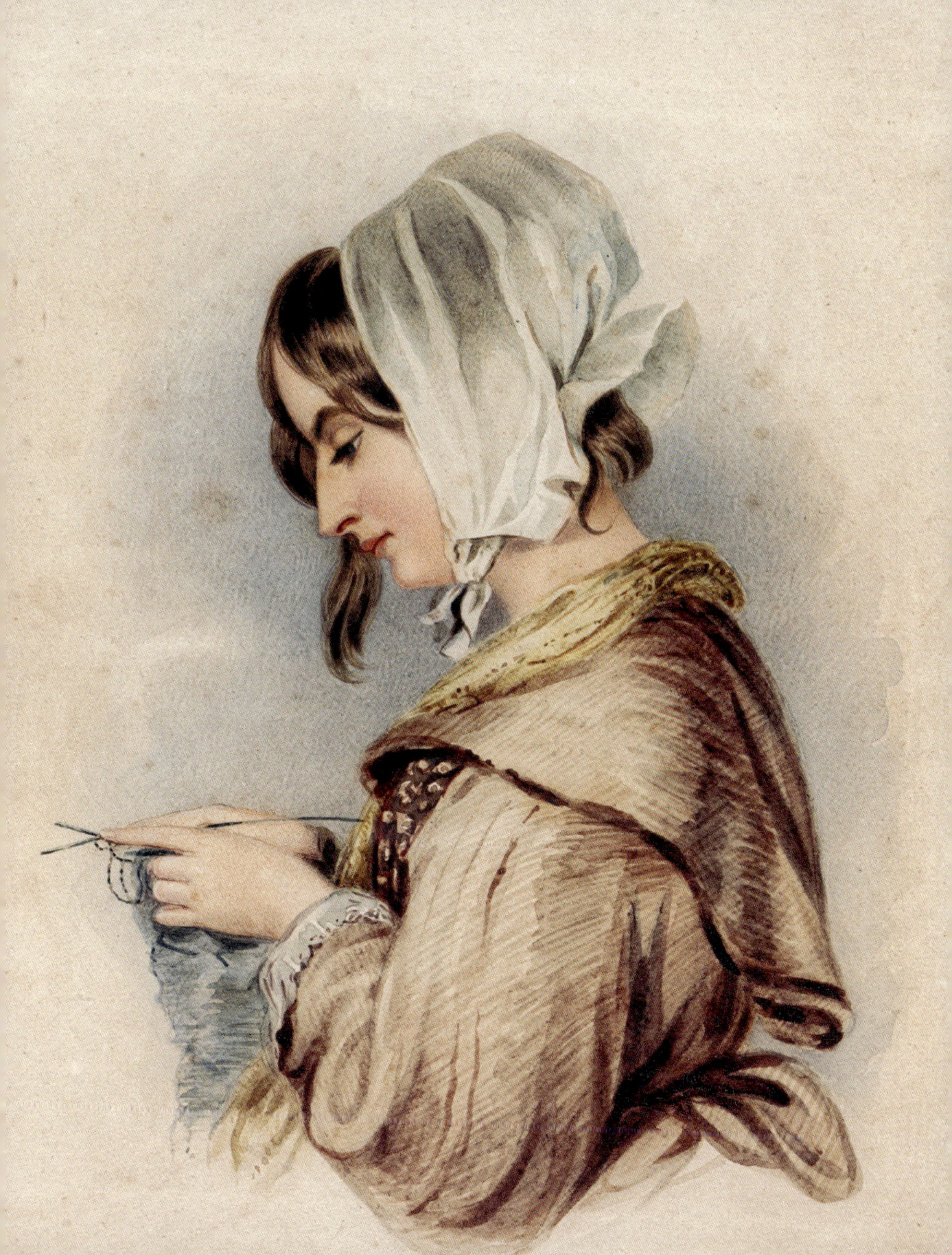

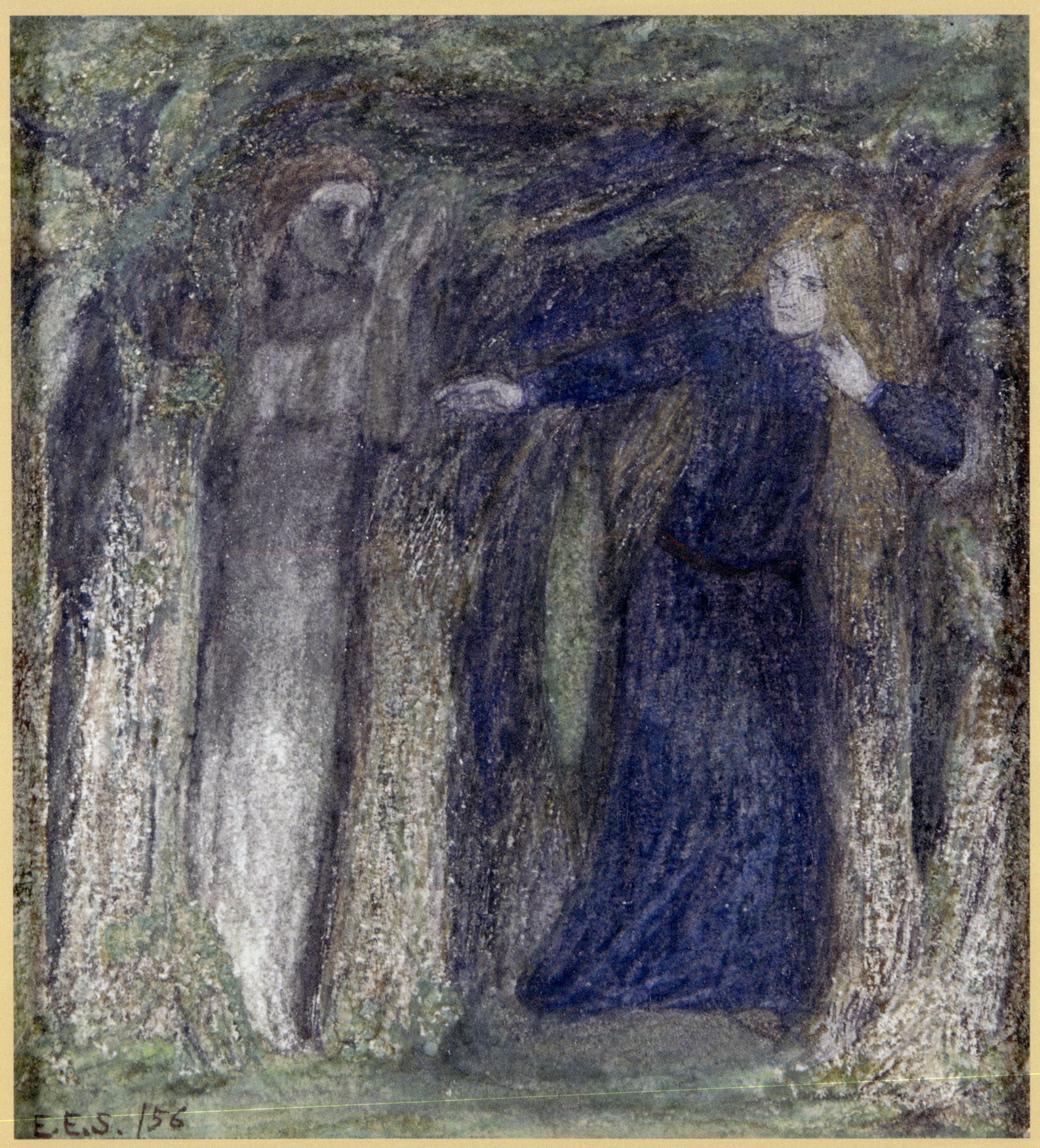
E.E.S. /56

MAKING THEIR WAY

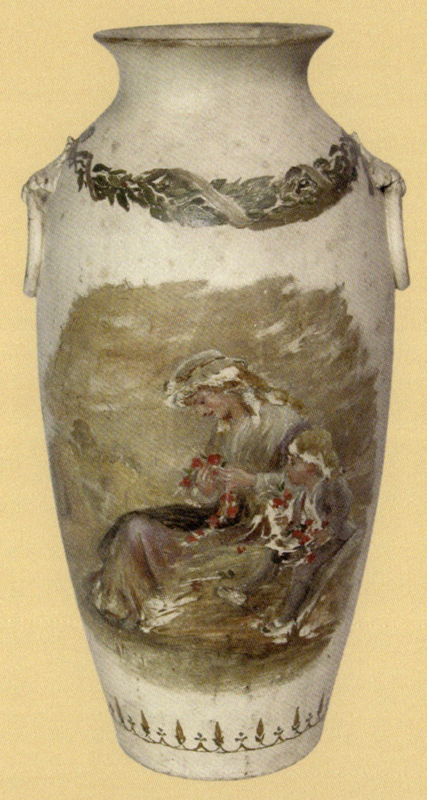

← *The Haunted Wood*, Elizabeth (Lizzie) Eleanor Siddal (1829–62), 1856, gouache on paper, 12 x 11cm, Wightwick Manor, West Midlands (NT 1287904). The National Trust holds an important group of works by Siddal at Wightwick.

↑ Vase painted by Laura Wilson Barker, *c.*1870, made by Minton, 1867, biscuit earthenware, 26.8 x 12cm, Smallhythe Place, Kent (NT 1117108.1)

Despite one of its champions, John Ruskin (1819–1900), declaring that there '[had] never been … a lady who could paint', the Pre-Raphaelite movement had women at its centre, as artists, poets and models.

Lizzie Siddal was from a working-class background, largely self-taught and resolutely determined to be an artist. She initially worked as a paid model for the Pre-Raphaelites and exhibited work just twice during her short life. She was the only woman included in the first Pre-Raphaelite exhibition, held in London in 1857 and organised by Ford Madox Brown (1821–93), which included *The Haunted Wood* (opposite). Pioneering photographer Julia Margaret Cameron captured soulful portraits inspired by the Pre-Raphaelite aesthetic, including of Marie Spartali Stillman and the Fraser-Tytler sisters (page 142).

Harriet Hosmer (page 128) was one of a group of American women sculptors who moved to Rome to pursue careers away from the restrictions placed on them in the US. Florence Claxton (1838–1920) petitioned for women to be admitted to the Royal Academy of Arts, a goal that was realised in 1860 (it would take more than 30 years more, however, for them to be admitted to its life-drawing classes). Her watercolour of 1860 (overleaf) satirises the ideas and key players of the Pre-Raphaelite movement. John Everett Millais (1829–96) is shown as Paris, handing the prize of a golden apple to the one of the Three Graces he finds most beautiful – a fiery-haired caricature of the Pre-Raphaelite ideal. The opening of the progressive Slade School of Fine Art in 1871, where all students could access life models, advanced women's art training (for those who could afford it), placing them on a more equal footing with their male peers. Early attendees included Kate Greenaway (1846–1901), best known for her children's book illustrations, Mary Seton Watts (page 142) and Evelyn De Morgan (page 145).

The influence in the 1880s of Arts and Crafts ideals, which recognised the social importance of the arts, led to new opportunities for women to participate in them, to excel in making and to earn a living. They trained and practised professionally at companies selling or producing 'artistic' goods, such as Liberty & Co., Morris & Co. and Della Robbia, or set up independent workshops. They shared their work publicly at exhibitions organised by, among others, the Arts and Crafts Exhibition Society. Alexander Fisher was a regular exhibitor and an important figure in the revival of enamelling, which was practised by many women artists including his pupil Ernestine Mills (1871–1959). Fisher's ethereal enamel portrait of Nina Cust (below right) is a wonderful example. Women such

↙ *The Choice of Paris: An Idyll*, Florence Anne Claxton (1838–1920), *c.*1860, watercolour and bodycolour, gum arabic and gold paint on paper laid down on panel, 29.2 x 38.1cm, Hinton Ampner, Hampshire (NT 1529624)

↓ *Nina Cust*, Alexander Fisher (1864–1936), 1898, painted enamel on copper in an iron and silver frame, 17.5 x 10.5cm, signed and dated: 'Alex Fisher 1898' and inscribed: 'NINA CVST', Belton House, Lincolnshire, purchased with a grant from the National Heritage Memorial Fund, 1984 (NT 435439)

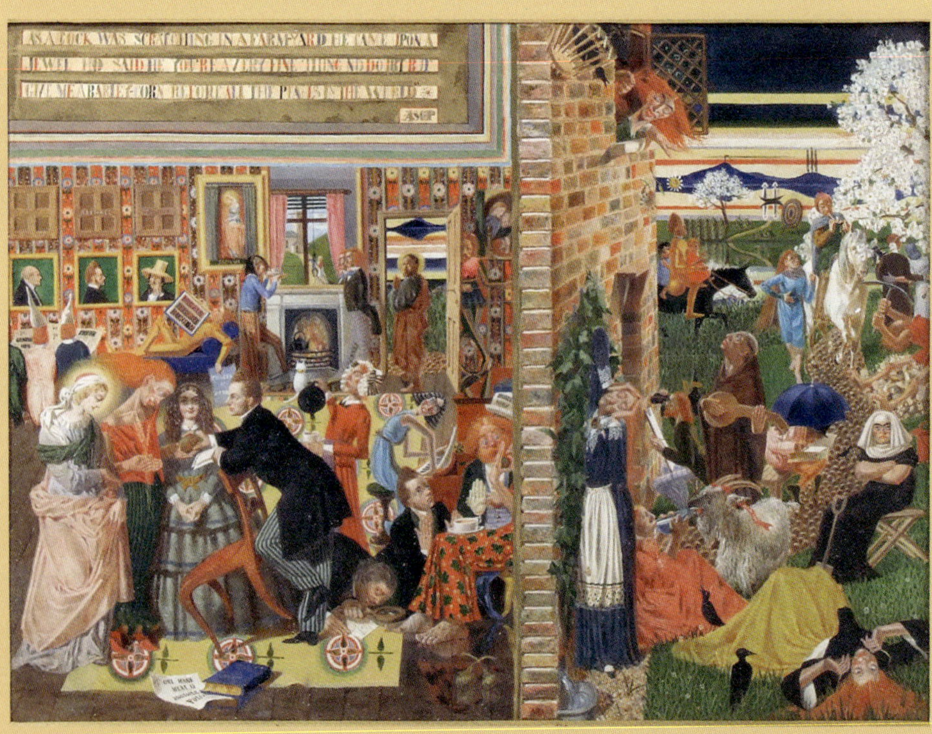

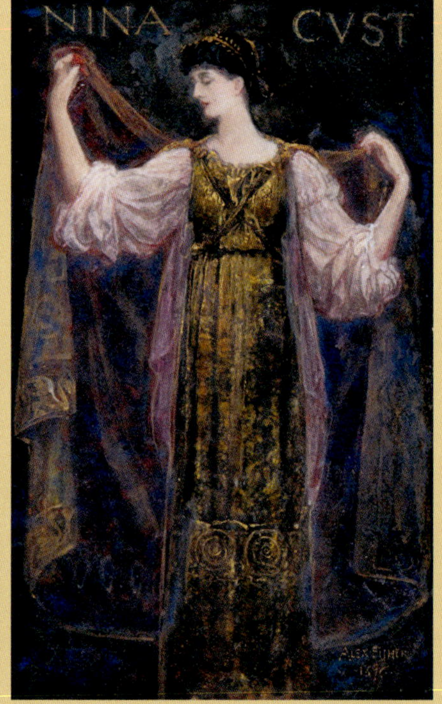

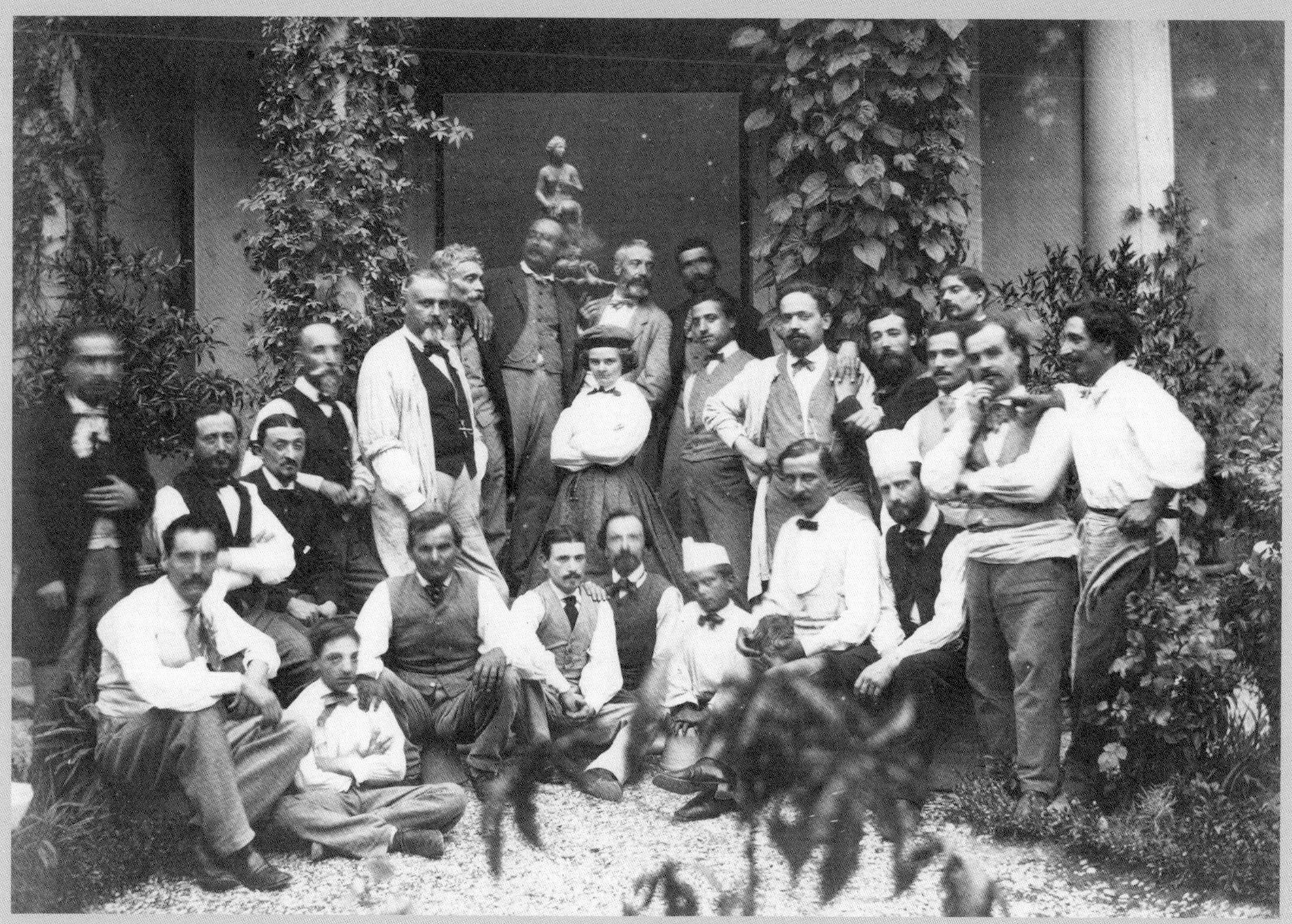

↑ Harriet Hosmer with her assistants and carvers in the courtyard of her studio, Rome, 1867 (Department of Image Collections, National Gallery of Art Library, Washington DC; image courtesy Library of Congress)

as the Garrett cousins (page 130) were also breaking into professions typically dominated by men, such as interior design and decoration.

Among the creative pastimes practised by women, 'china painting' exploded in popularity. Ceramic manufacturers took advantage by supplying blanks (unglazed pots) and ready-mixed pigments. The composer Laura Wilson Barker (1819–1905) painted a pair of vases with portraits of Kate and Ellen Terry on blanks made by Minton (page 117). A young Beatrix Potter (page 182) and her father also transferred images of rabbits (appropriately) from *Vere Foster's Drawing Copy-Books* onto tiles.

‘Miss Dixon loves her work’

ANNIE DIXON (1817–1901)

Annie Dixon was a prolific miniature portrait painter. A favourite of Queen Victoria, Dixon was commissioned to paint many royal portraits. Her talent (and moderate prices) ensured that she continued to work, despite competition following the introduction of photography.

Dixon was born in Horncastle, Lincolnshire, and was the eldest of seven children – their father was a corn merchant. In her 1876 book on women artists, Ellen Clayton notes that ‘family affairs rendered it necessary that, early in life, Miss Dixon should make her own way in the world’. She received some tuition in miniature painting from Magdalena Ross (1801–74), and by 1851 was working (probably hand-colouring photographs) at the studio of Mrs Ann Cooke (1796–1870) in Hull – thought to be one of the first commercial photography studios opened by a woman.

By 1859, when Dixon received her first royal portrait commission from Queen Victoria, she had established her reputation as a miniature portrait artist – more than 20 examples of her work are in the Royal Collection.

No doubt buoyed by her regal patron, Dixon built a noble and aristocratic clientele and enjoyed a long, highly productive career. She had a particular affinity for depicting children, and painted Adelbert Wellington Brownlow Cust, 3rd Earl Brownlow of Belton House, Lincolnshire, as a boy (page 122) and again as a young man, 14 years later. For over 30 years she also showed her best work at the annual Royal Academy exhibitions.

Clayton wrote, ‘Miss Dixon loves her work, finding in it her greatest pleasure, and seldom gives herself a holiday.’ This insatiable drive to paint meant Dixon continued to take commissions into her seventies, including a luminous portrait probably of Lady Collet (opposite), stopping only when her eyesight began to fail. RC

→ Portrait miniature possibly of Nina Emma Caroline Theobald, Lady Collet (1863–1922), Annie Dixon, 1891, watercolour on ivory, 8.9 x 6.6cm, Dunham Massey, Cheshire (NT 936727)

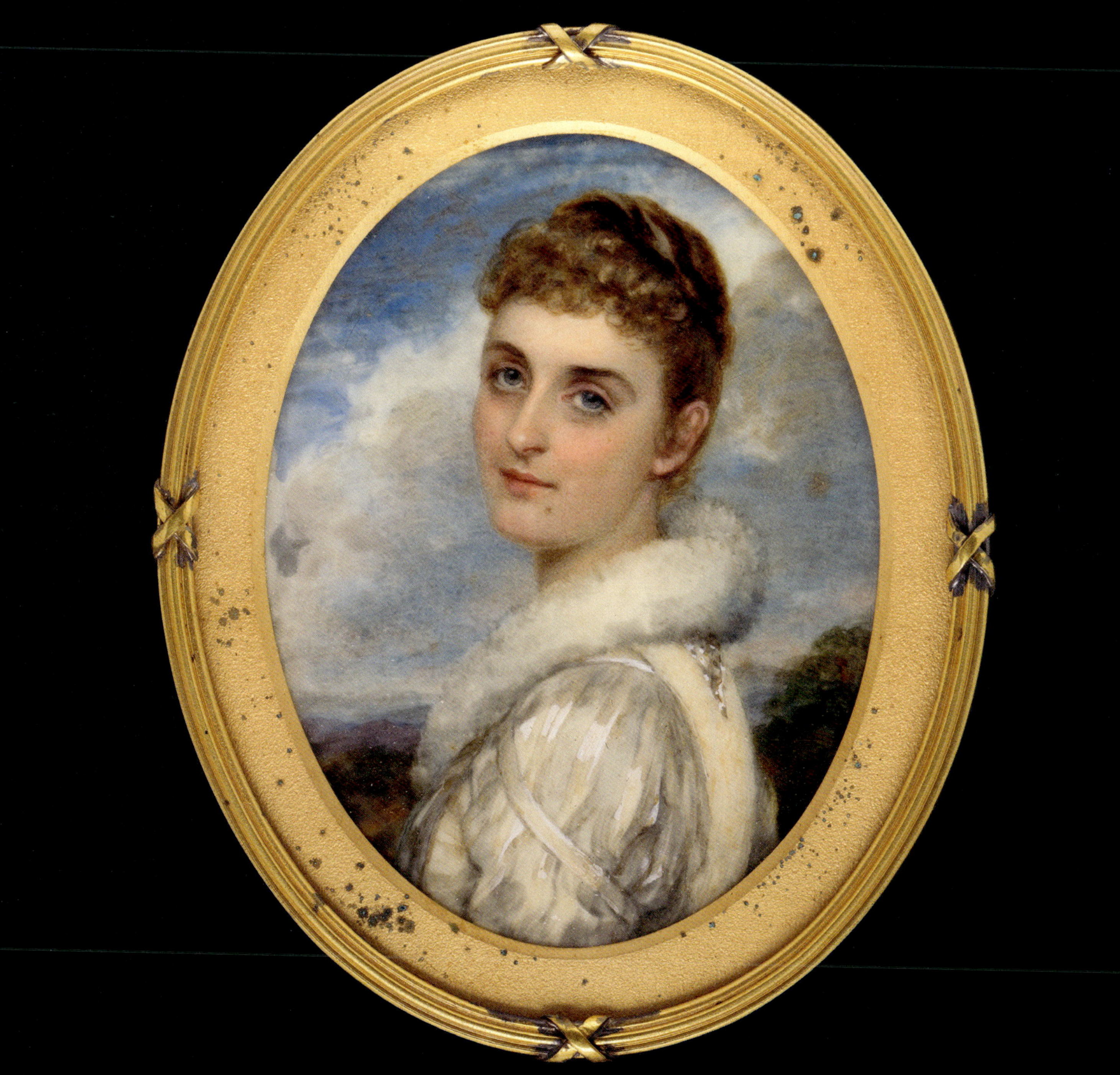

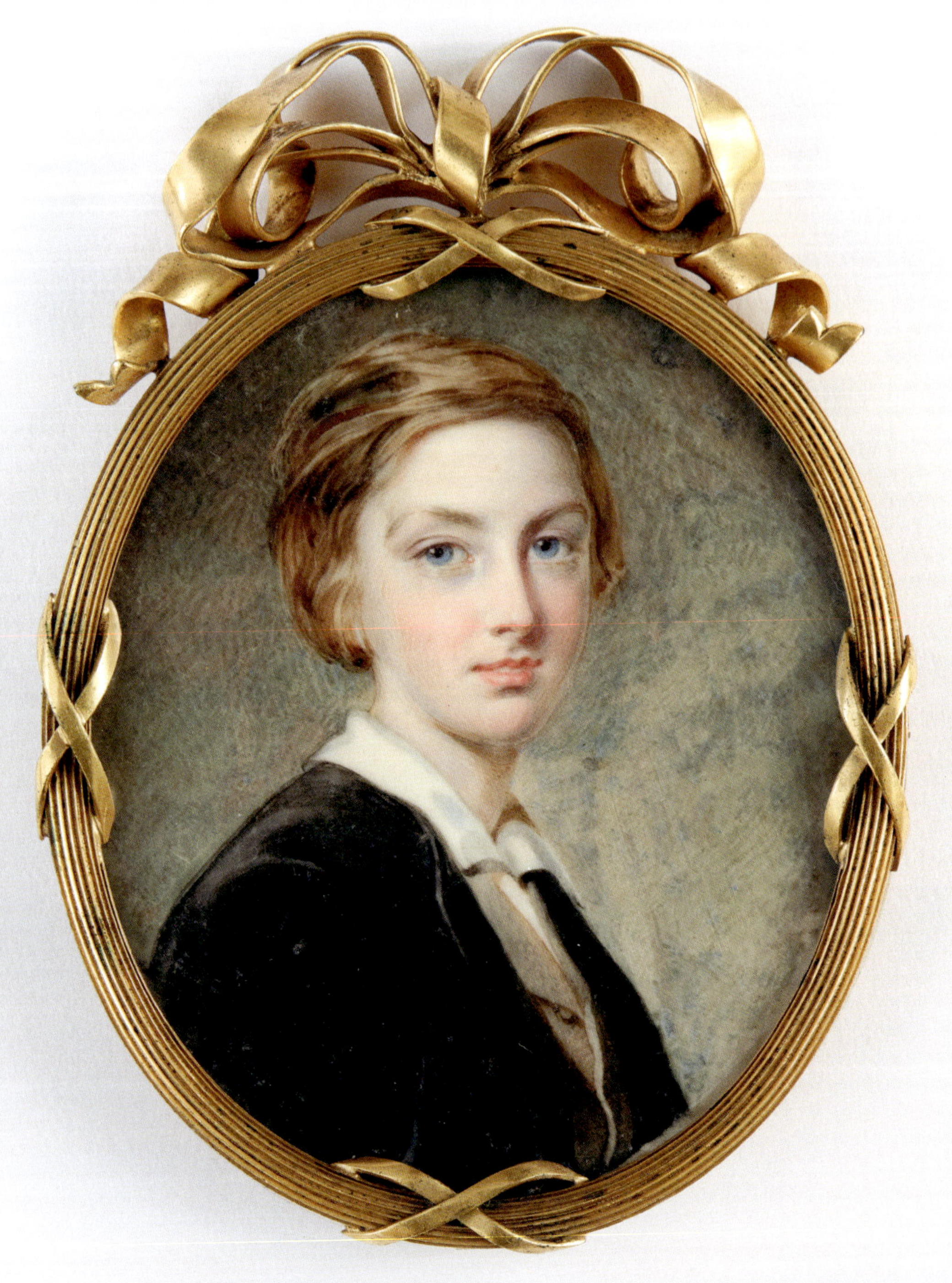

← *Adelbert Wellington Brownlow Cust, 3rd Earl Brownlow,* Annie Dixon, 1855, watercolour on ivory, 8cm (height), Belton House, Lincolnshire, purchased with a grant from the National Heritage Memorial Fund, 1984 (NT 435997)

↓ *Annie Dixon,* Louisa Anne Beresford, Marchioness of Waterford (1818–91), 1887, watercolour and pencil, 8.7 x 15cm (National Portrait Gallery, London)

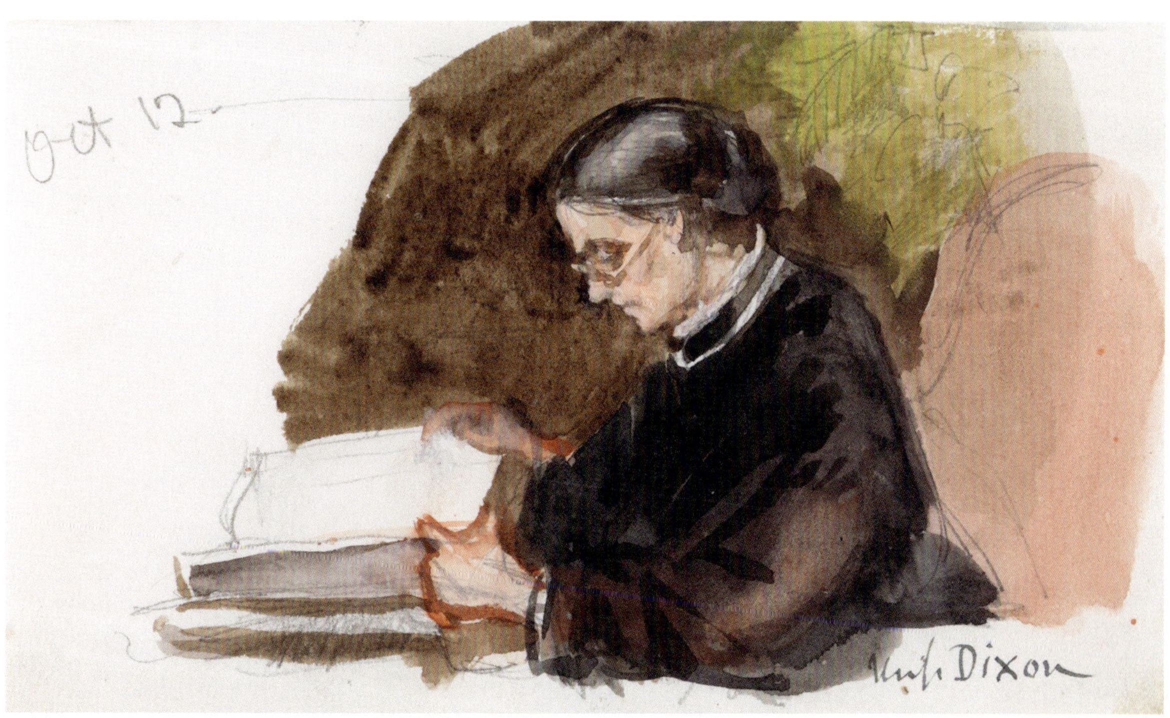

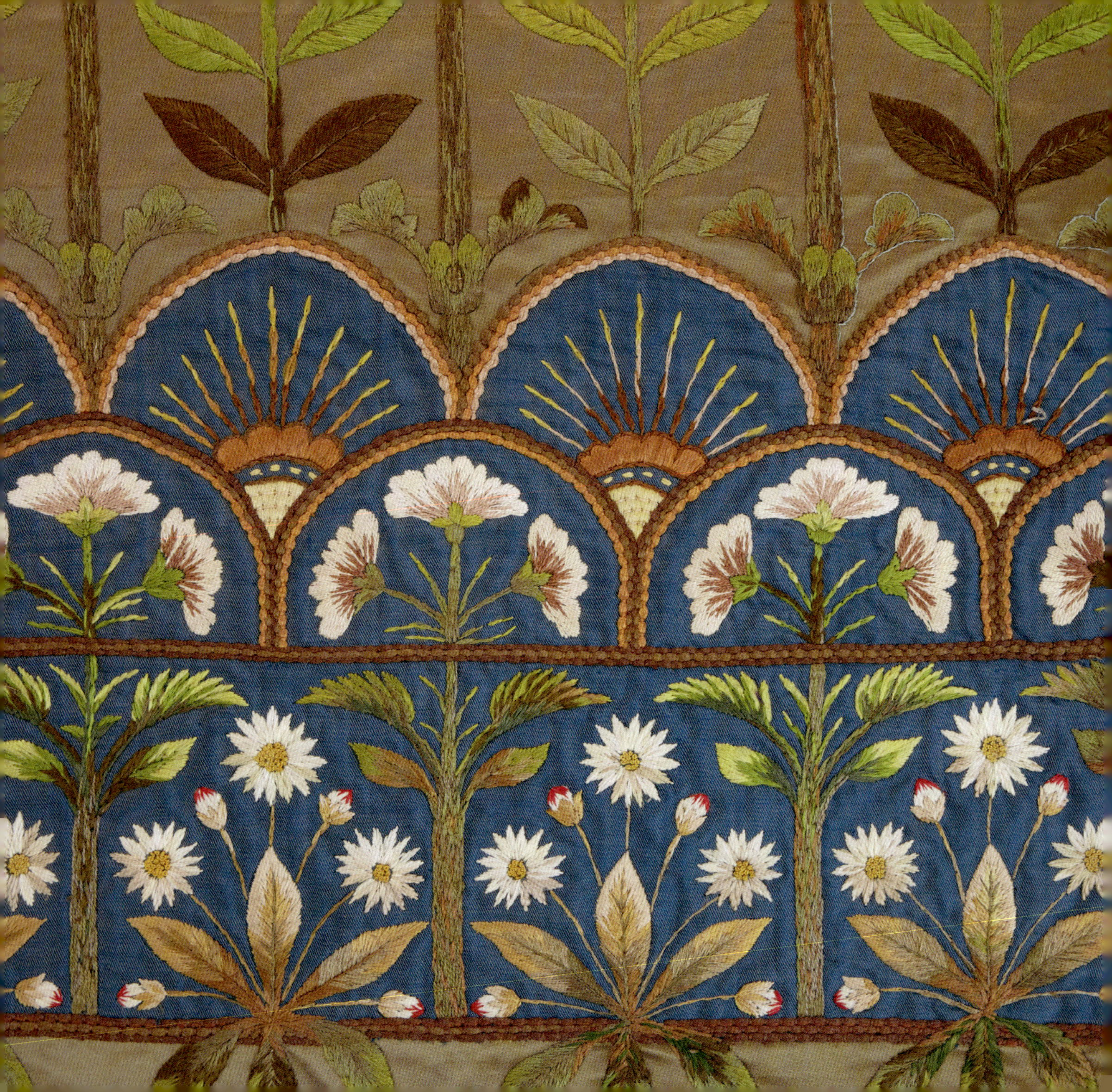

‘The ever new joy of creation’

LADY MARIAN COMPTON, VISCOUNTESS ALFORD (1817–88)

Lady Marian Alford believed that hand embroidery should be valued as an art form and deserved to be recognised as a skilled profession. These two principles led her, with Princess Christian of Schleswig-Holstein (1846–1923, daughter of Queen Victoria) and Lady Victoria Welby (1837–1912), to establish the School of Art Needlework (later the Royal School of Needlework) in London in 1872. An article in the *Art Journal* described Alford, its vice president, as ‘the life and soul of the school’.

Based above a bonnet shop on Sloane Street, it initially employed 20 women – all ‘reduced gentlewomen’ who needed to earn a living. Within three years the number of employees had grown five-fold and the school moved to new premises in South Kensington. The women were taught a broad range of needlework skills,

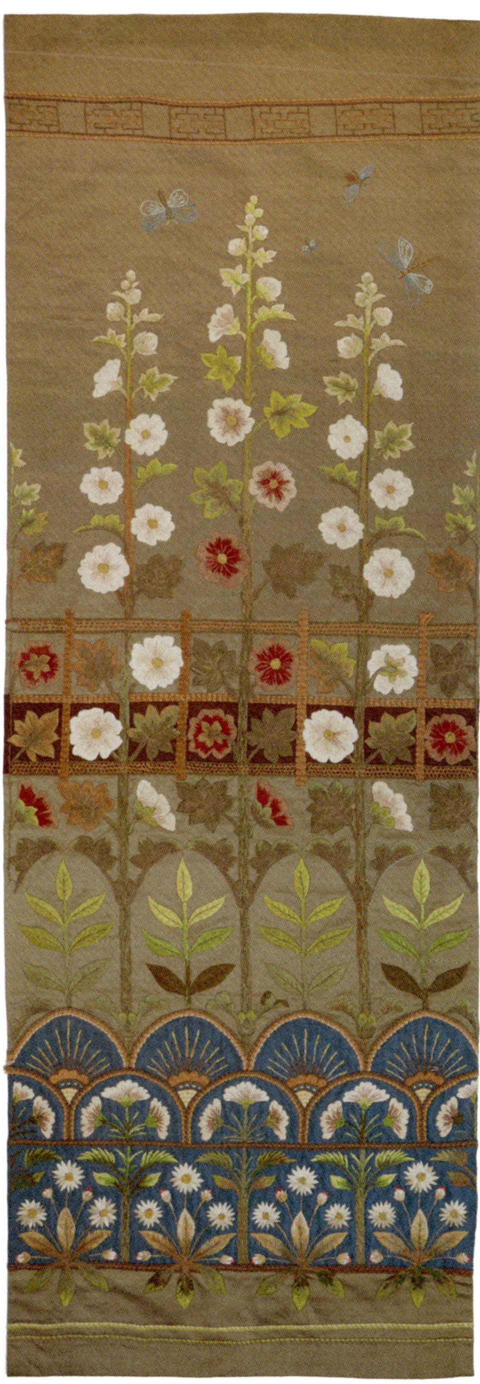

↔ Needlework panel depicting hollyhocks and daisies, Lady Marian Alford, c.1869–87, hand embroidered on satin ground, 146 x 49cm, Belton House, Lincolnshire, purchased with a grant from the National Heritage Memorial Fund, 1984 (NT 436967)

enabling them to work on commissions, exhibit work, undertake repairs to historic textiles and teach others.

In 1886 Alford published her influential historical and technical study *Needlework as Art*, which observed that '... millions have enjoyed the art of the needle for thousands of years, and it will continue to be a solace and a delight as long as the world lasts, for, like all art, it gives the ever new joy of creation'.

Alford was also a keen patron of artists, including Elisabet Ney (1833–1907), the first woman to study sculpture at Munich Academy of Art (Alford exchanged a piece of her celebrated embroidery for two of Ney's commissioned works). Alford had a long, close relationship with sculptor Harriet Hosmer (page 128) – Elizabeth Barrett Browning described Alford kneeling before the artist and placing a heart-shaped ruby and diamond ring on her finger, to Hosmer's delight.

Hosmer was commissioned to create the ambitious *Siren* fountain for Alford's Knightsbridge home, Alford House (opposite), which was built in 1869–71 by the architect Sir Matthew Digby Wyatt (1820–77). Alford designed the external ornamental ironwork and much of the interior decoration; an 1869 design for a curtain in crimson and gold, with sunflowers and thistles, is at Belton House, Lincolnshire. A beautiful set of monogrammed curtains, later adapted into bed hangings, may also have been created for Alford House. RC

↓ *Lady Marian Margaret Compton, Viscountess Alford*, Sir Francis Grant (1803–78), 1841, oil on canvas, 90.2 x 69.9cm, Belton House, Lincolnshire, purchased with a grant from the National Heritage Memorial Fund, 1984 (NT 435959)
→ Alford House in Knightsbridge captured by an unknown photographer, *c*.1870s (Victoria and Albert Museum, London)

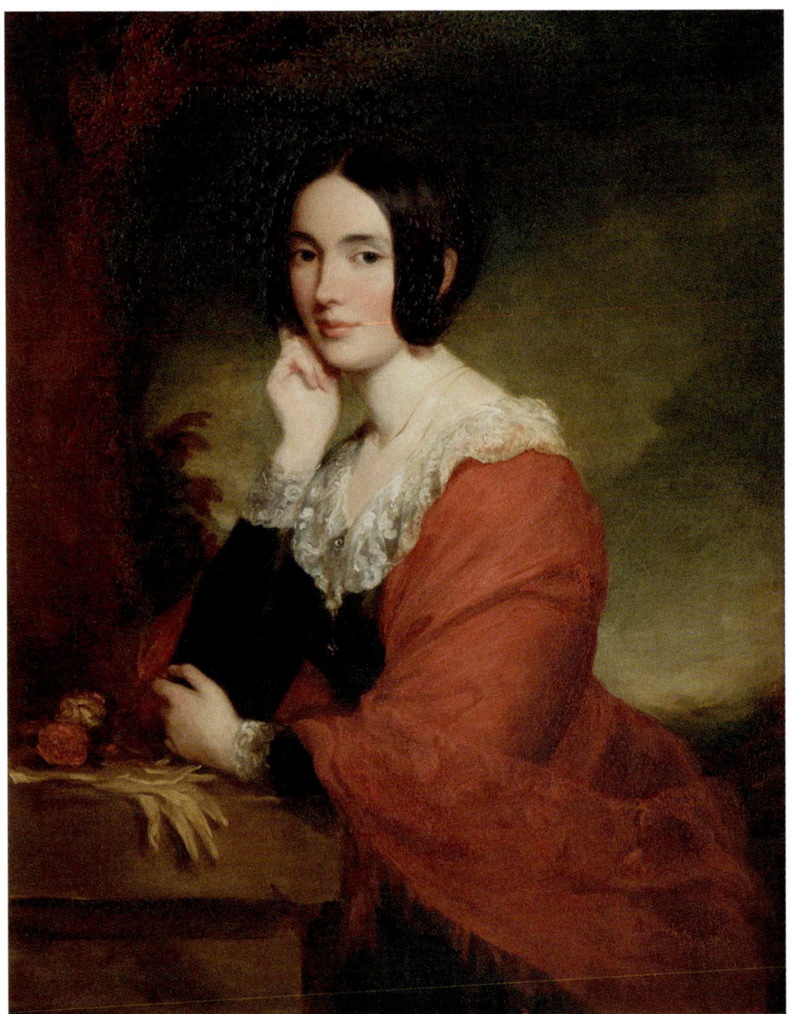

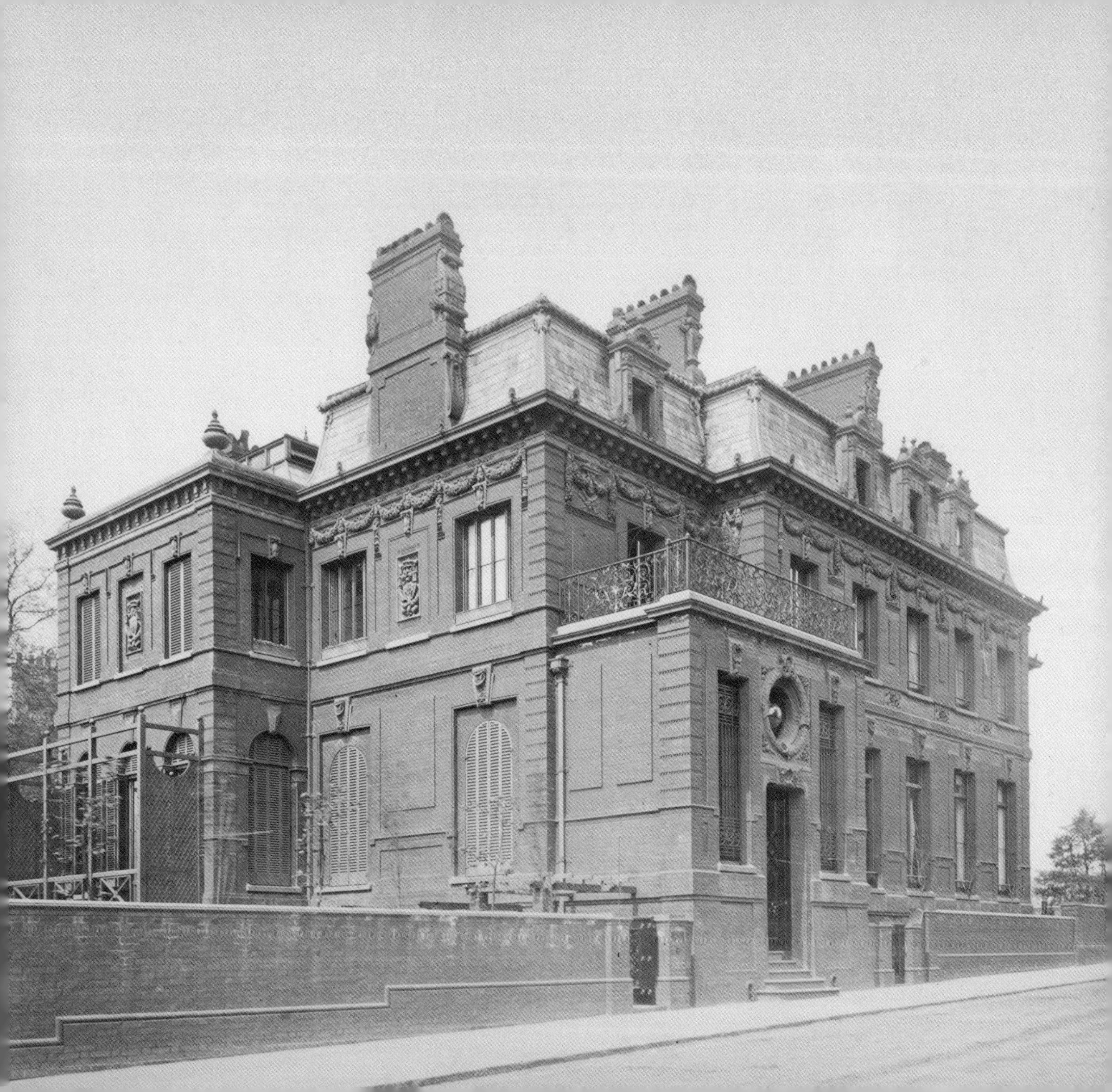

Outside the beaten path

HARRIET GOODHUE HOSMER (1830–1908)

'I honor every woman who has the strength enough to step outside the beaten path when she feels that her walk lies in another', wrote Harriet Goodhue Hosmer to a friend.

Born in the Boston, Massachusetts suburb of Watertown in 1830, Hosmer studied anatomy at an all-male medical school before sailing to Italy in 1852 in pursuit of a career as a sculptor. She was bound for Rome, a sculptural epicentre and cosmopolitan hub that had long made space for women on the cultural stage.

Hosmer trained with the Welsh Neo-classical sculptor John Gibson (1790–1866) before setting up her own workshop near the Piazza del Popolo (page 119). A ready supply of marble, artisan assistants and life models became available to her. 'I can learn more and do more here, in one year,' she said, 'than I could do in America in ten.'

She lived with the American actor Charlotte Cushman and Cushman's partners Matilda Hays and, later, the sculptor Emma Stebbins. Cushman modelled an emancipated way of life for Hosmer, who too was gay.

Yet public success – and financial security – depended on navigating the rules of Victorian feminine propriety. Hosmer was routinely compelled to defend her work, as critics were unable to believe it was her own, and to justify her marital status. A woman, she wrote, 'must either neglect her profession or her family, becoming neither a good wife and mother nor a good artist. My ambition is to become the latter, so I wage eternal feud with the consolidating knot.'

Working in the Neo-classical style, Hosmer cleverly expressed feminist ideas through her choice and characterisation of sculptural subjects derived from myth, history and literature. Her *Sleeping Faun* (opposite) is a playful response to antique sculptures and to the *Marble Faun*, a popular novel by fellow New Englander Nathaniel Hawthorne, published in 1860.

Hosmer opened her studio to the public and promoted her work with skilful panache. Within ten years of arriving in Rome she had become internationally famous, paving the way for other expatriate women sculptors seeking to make their name in continental Europe. ARW

→ *Sleeping Faun*, Harriet Goodhue Hosmer, after 1865, marble, 166 x 146 x 67cm, signed: 'H HOSMER FECIT ROMÆ', Anglesey Abbey, Cambridgeshire (NT 516616)

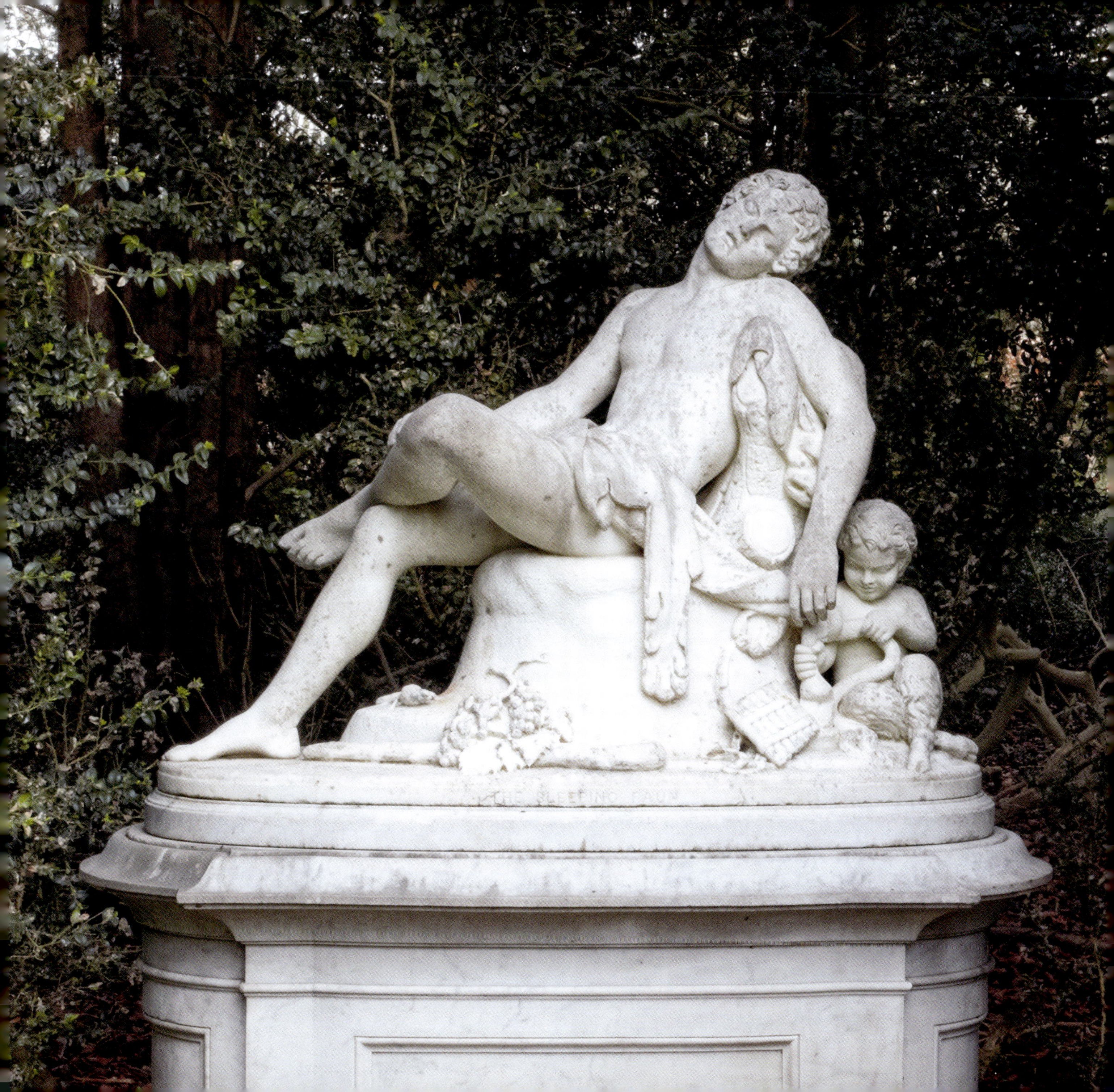
THE SLEEPING FAUN

Disruptive decorators

AGNES GARRETT (1845–1935) AND RHODA GARRETT (1841–82)

The cousins Agnes and Rhoda Garrett opened their interior decoration business from their London flat in the early 1870s. In doing so, they disrupted the field completely. Before the Garretts, interior decoration was a male-dominated business. Men designed and supplied wallpaper, furniture and textiles for the home. Women, put simply, did not.

The cousins were active suffrage campaigners and were passionate about improving the lives of fellow women. By carefully manipulating the well-established connection between the home, femininity and domesticity, they were able to position interior decoration as a new field of employment eminently suitable for women. But earning the sobriquet of Britain's first women interior decorators was no mean feat, and the cousins struggled to find a firm willing to offer them professional training. Fortunately, the Garretts were well-connected and cleverly exploited their network to build a clientele. Their work was well covered by the press, with celebrity clients including Hubert and Maude Parry, Lord Kelvin, Catherine Buckton, Ada Wellesley and Lady Dorothy Nevill. Unfortunately, interior decoration is ephemeral and little evidence of these commissions survives.

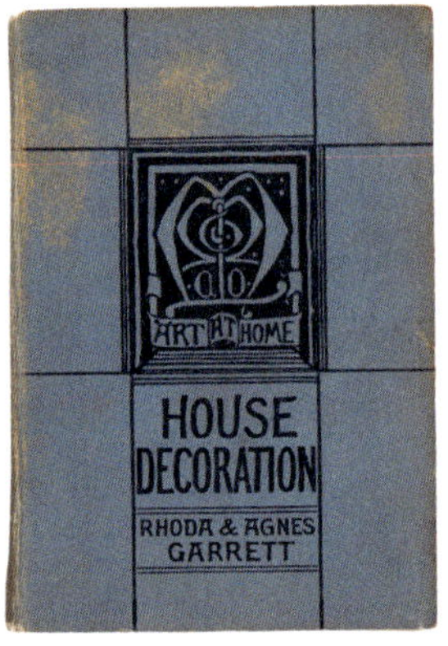

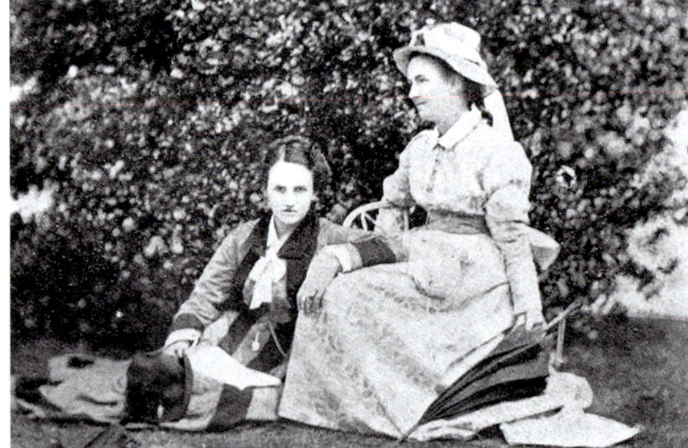

↖ *Suggestions for House Decoration*, the Garretts' influential 1876 book, which was part of Macmillan's 'Art at Home' series.
↑ Rhoda (left) and Agnes Garrett, undated (private collection)
→ View of a bedroom at Standen showing a daybed designed c.1880 by Agnes Garrett and Rhoda Garrett, mahogany, velvet, brass, 95 x 124.5 x 54cm, Standen, West Sussex (NT 1214057)

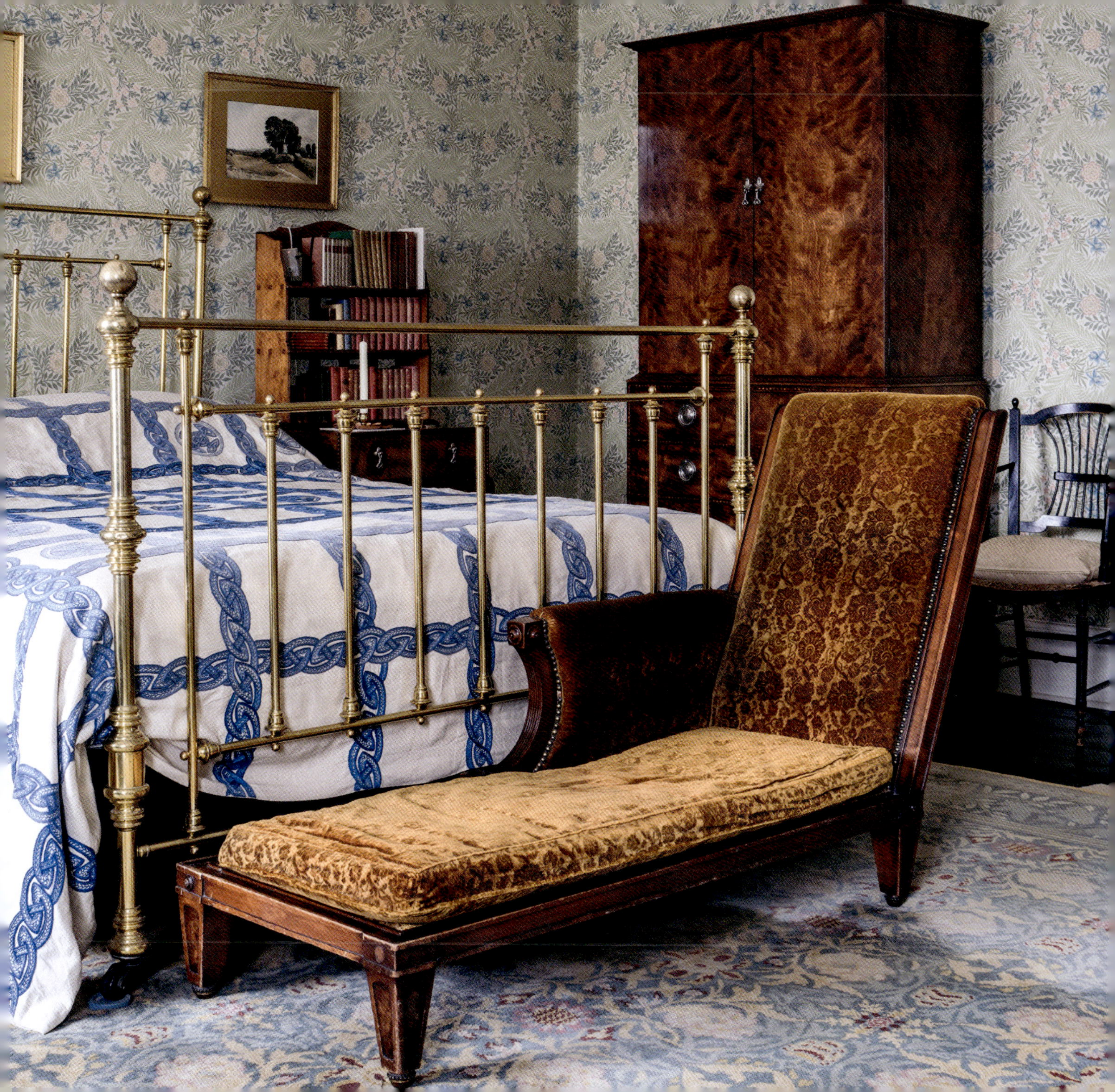

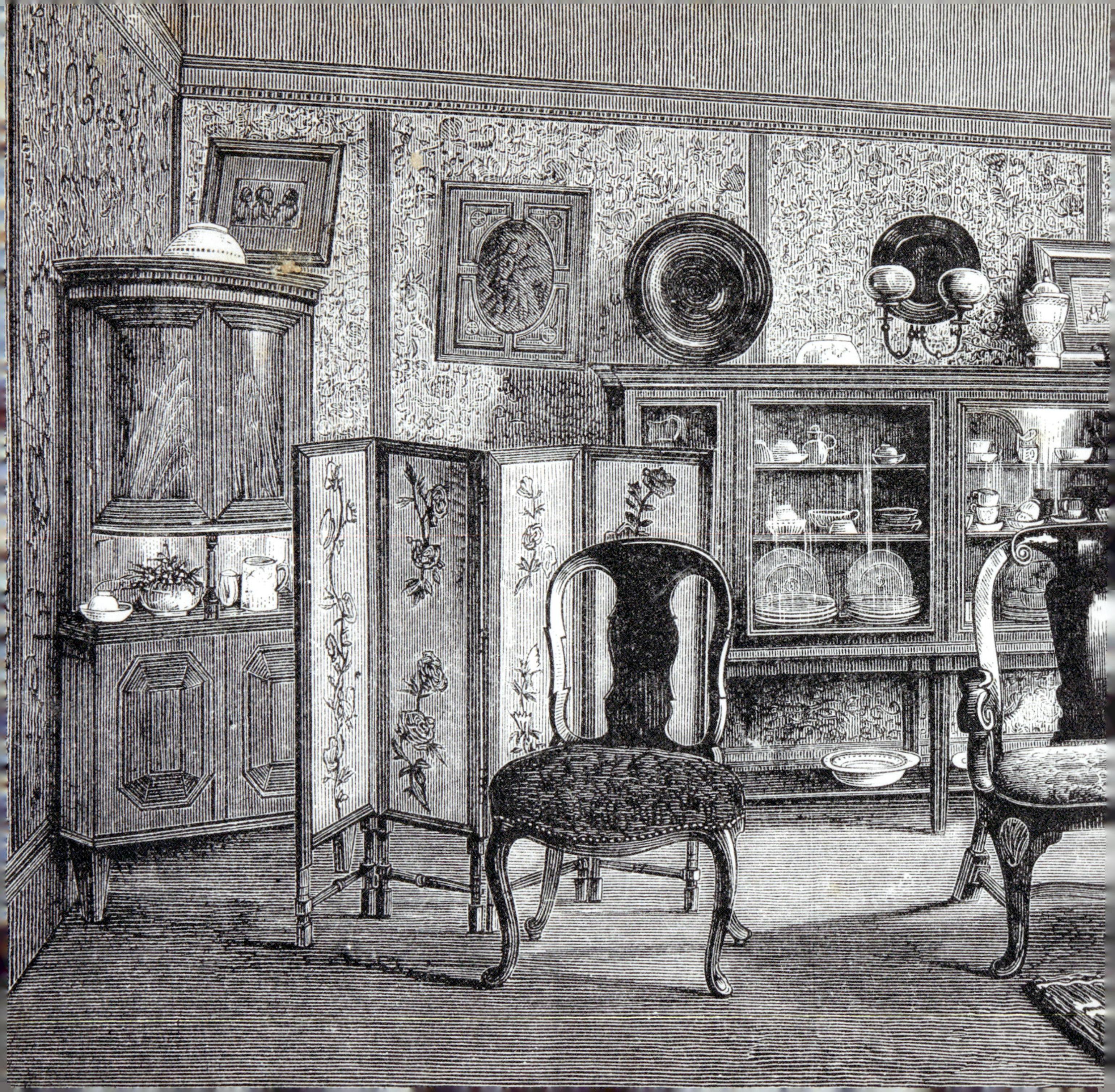

← 'View of Drawing Room' (detail) from *Suggestions for House Decoration in Painting, Woodwork and Furniture* by Agnes Garrett and Rhoda Garrett, 1876, Standen, West Sussex (NT 3177870)
→ Corner cupboard designed *c*.1880 by Agnes Garrett and Rhoda Garrett, walnut, mirror glass and brass, 158 x 87.5 x 62.5cm, Standen, West Sussex (NT 1213990)

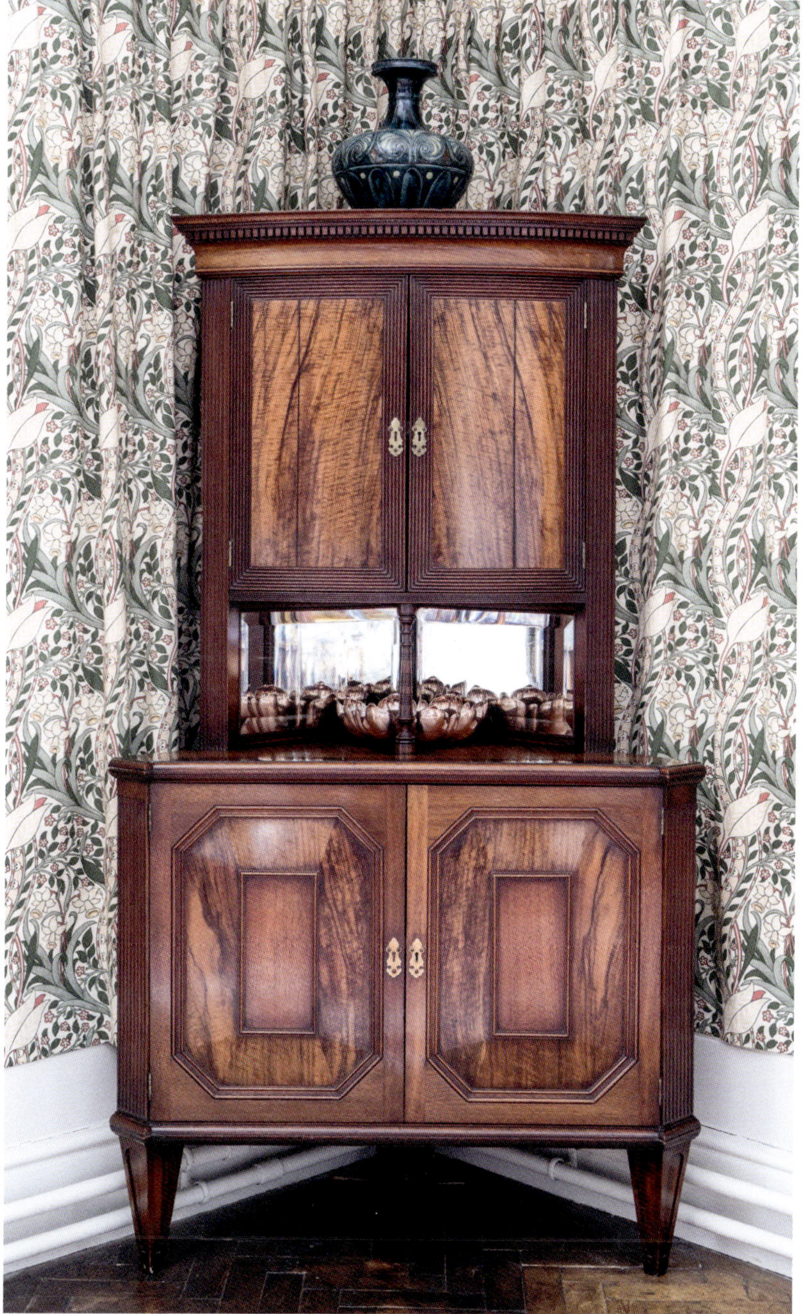

The collection at Standen of several pieces of Garrett furniture, probably one of their earliest commissions, is a remarkable exception. With their gracefully tapered legs and subtle historic references, the pieces showcase the cousins' signature Queen Anne style. Several were featured in the Garretts' 1876 book *Suggestions for House Decoration*. Aimed at the metropolitan middle classes, the manual offered advice on how to decorate tastefully on a limited budget, and firmly established the Garretts as tastemakers and experts.

Although Rhoda died young in 1882, Agnes continued in business until 1905. In doing so, she paved the way for future generations of women to make their mark on interiors around the UK. MG

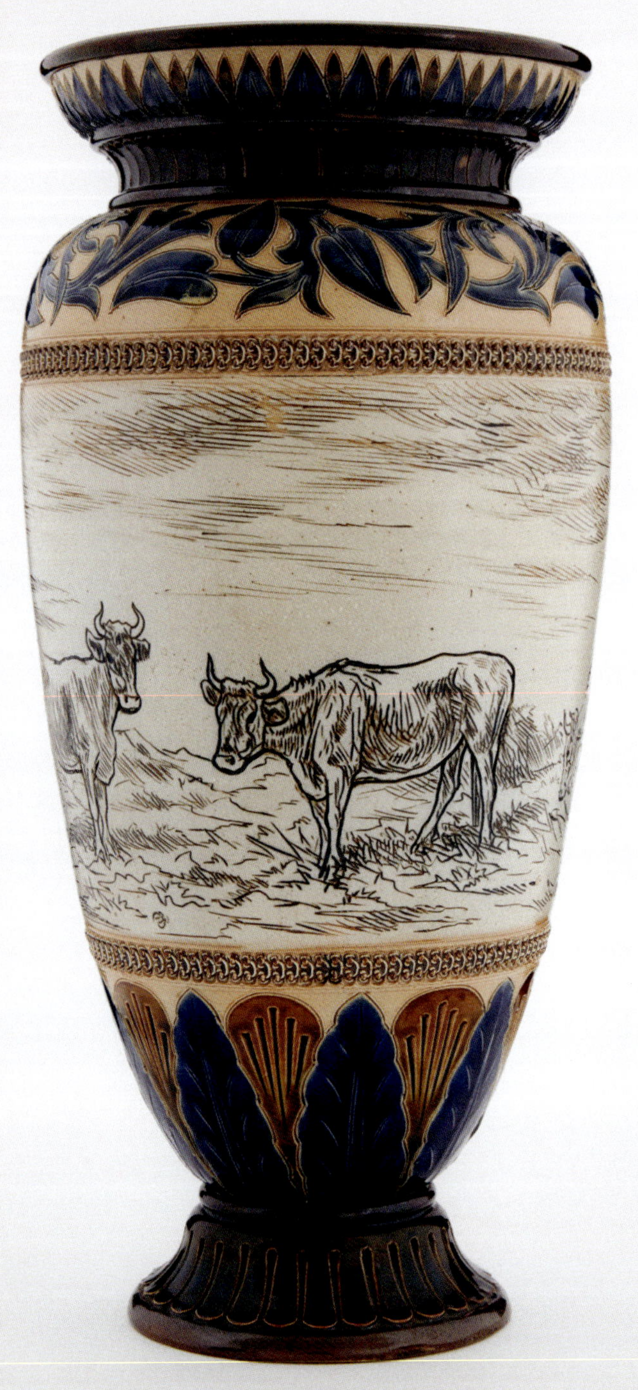

'Rare, even among artists of distinction'

HANNAH BARLOW (1851–1916)

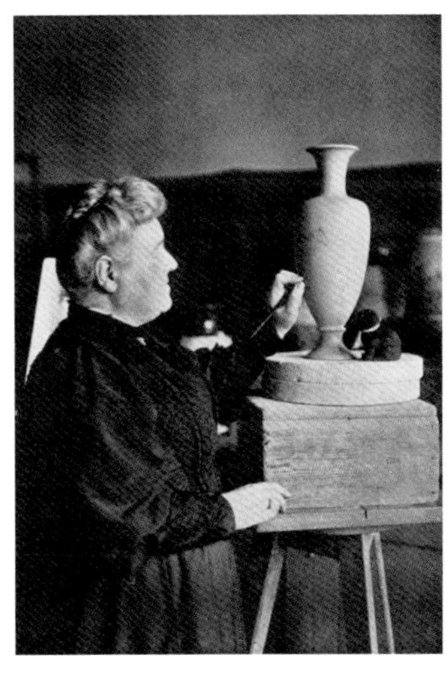

← Vase designed and decorated by Hannah Barlow and made by Doulton & Co. of Lambeth, 1883, stoneware with sgraffito and coloured glazes, 40 (height) x 18cm (diameter), Standen, West Sussex (NT 1213896)

↑ Hannah Barlow photographed for US magazine *The World's Work*, Vol. XVIII (June–November 1911)

Hannah Bolton Barlow introduced giraffes, sheep, horses and ducks to the shelves and cabinets of many Victorian homes. She was one of the most successful and distinctive ceramic artists at Doulton & Co.'s Lambeth Art Studio in London.

Barlow trained at the Lambeth School of Art and Design and briefly worked at Minton's art pottery in Kensington before joining Doulton in 1871. Her vision, talent and tenacity played a major part in Doulton's success.

Barlow specialised in sgraffito, in which a design is incised directly into the clay surface, often through a light-coloured slip. Her mastery of this challenging technique was described by the writer C. Lewis Hind as 'demanding a precision of touch rare, even among artists of distinction'. This is remarkable considering that in 1876 Barlow had lost the use of her (dominant) right hand. She wore hand splints for a few months and taught herself to use her left hand to execute her meticulous decoration. Although her right hand remained partly paralysed, she continued to pursue a long, successful career with the pottery. By the time she retired in 1913, she was head of the studio.

A large number of women worked at Doulton, principally decorating pieces designed by the studio artists. Barlow taught herself to throw vessels on a potter's wheel, so was a fully-fledged ceramic artist, designing forms as well as decoration. She is renowned for her spirited, economic depictions of animals, and took inspiration from the large menagerie of pets she kept at home, which included a tame fox and a Black Mountain sheep.

A true collaboration, this vase (opposite) was designed by Barlow and decorated with the assistance of her sister Lucy Anna Barlow (active 1882–5), as well as by Mary Aitken (active 1875–94) and Jenny F. Weekes (active from 1882). All three can be identified through their monograms, marked on the base. RC

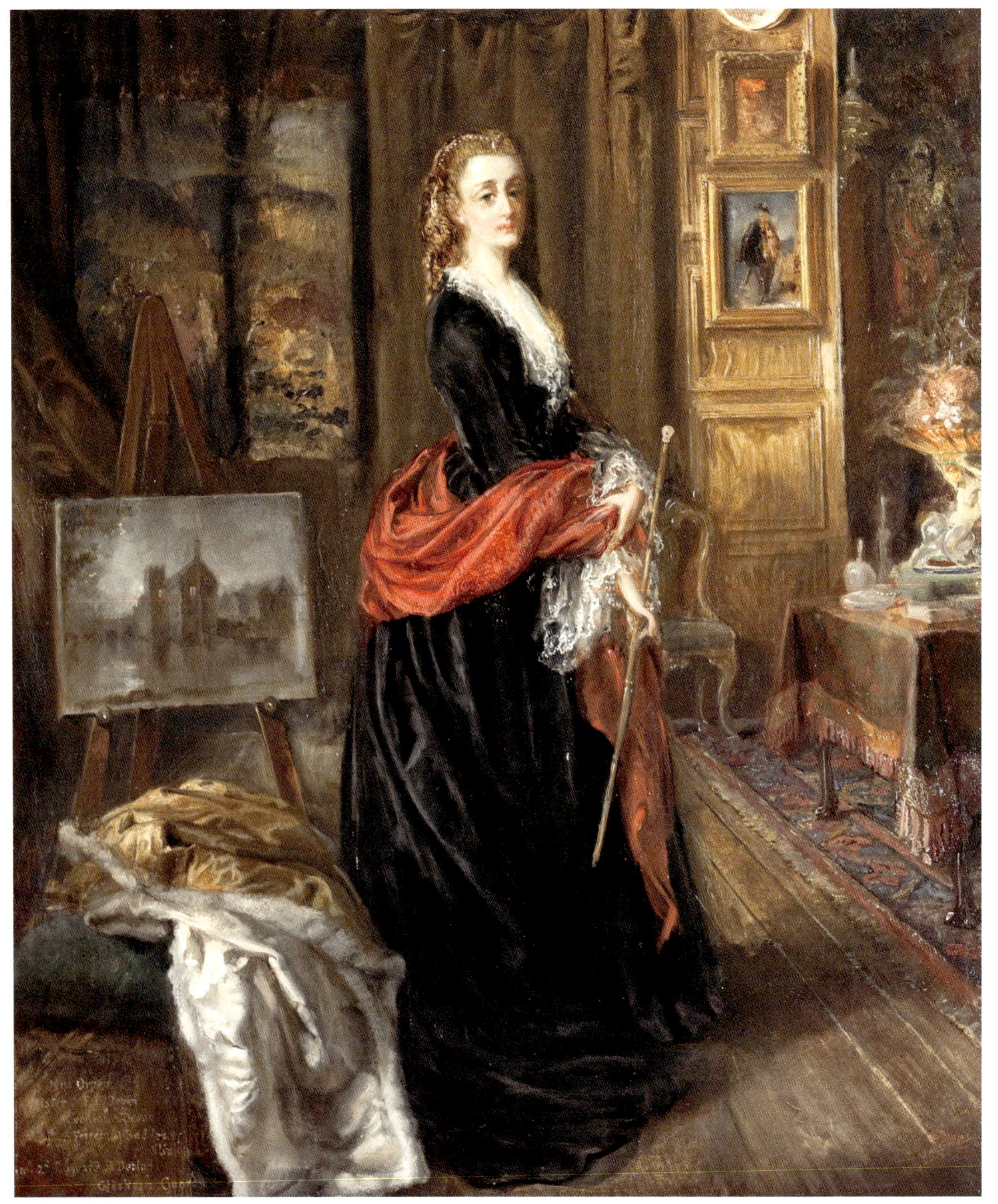

A life on canvas

REBECCA ORPEN (*c.*1830–1923)

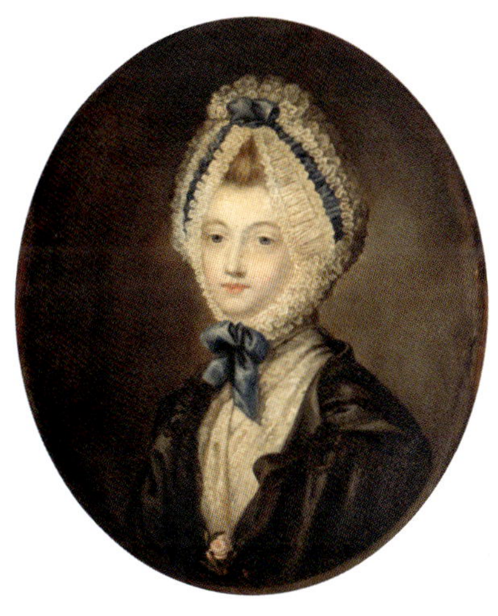

← *Self-portrait in Her Painting Room at Baddesley Clinton*, Rebecca Orpen, 1885–96, oil on canvas, 91.4 x 80cm, Baddesley Clinton, Warwickshire, National Land Fund, transferred to National Trust in 1980 (NT 343187)

↑ *Elizabeth Gunning, Duchess of Argyll and Hamilton*, Rebecca Orpen, after Katherine Read (1723–78), date unknown, oil on panel, 48.3 x 38.1cm, Baddesley Clinton, Warwickshire, National Land Fund, transferred to National Trust in 1980 (NT 343143)

Rebecca Dulcibella Orpen was a prolific and dedicated amateur painter. Her creative life allowed her to record her family lineage, honour the people and places that mattered to her, express her devotion to the Catholic faith, and create a sense of rich beauty in the interiors of her serene, moated home, Baddesley Clinton in Warwickshire.

Orpen was born in County Cork, Ireland. It is likely that she was given some instruction in painting by her aunt Lady Georgiana Chatterton (1806–76), an experienced oil painter with whom Rebecca lived for most of her life.

Orpen used oils, watercolours and pastels, and worked in a dress she had specially ordered ('a plain warm dress for painting in'), so she didn't need to worry about getting it dirty. A rare artist's dummy or lay figure – a life-sized posable model used in the absence of a live one – now in the collection at Packwood House, Warwickshire, may have originally belonged to her (NT 557908). Orpen and Lady Chatterton planned the refurbishment of the Chapel at Baddesley Clinton, collaborating to create ornate triptych paintings, with Orpen painting the reredos behind the altar and scenes from the Rosary inspired by Old Master paintings.

In the 1880s, as a way to refine her skills, Orpen was directly copying works at the National Gallery, London. Amateurs and professionals could apply to be a copyist at the Gallery for three months by sending the Keeper a written application and an example of their work. Orpen's copy of *Pietà* after Francesco Francia remains in the collection at Baddesley Clinton (NT 343202). A different copy work is her version of Katherine Read's pastel portrait of Elizabeth Gunning (left), made in about 1770 and later much reproduced in print.

An expressive self-portrait (opposite) shows Orpen presenting herself as an artist. She stands, mahlstick in hand, in her Painting Room at Baddesley Clinton, where she could take advantage of the light streaming in through the bay window. On the easel behind her is a view of her home from the north-east side, a view she returned to paint on several occasions. A portrait of her second husband, Edward Heneage Dering, hangs on the panelling to her left. RC

‘I try for beauty and harmony everywhere’

GERTRUDE JEKYLL (1843–1932)

Gertrude Jekyll is best known as an innovative garden designer and horticulturalist. However, she was also an influential writer on the practice and philosophy of gardening, and a multi-faceted artist and designer who mastered a range of traditional crafts, including embroidery, furniture inlay and decorative ironwork.

Jekyll attended the National School of Art (later the Royal College of Art) in South Kensington, and soon began exhibiting paintings and attracting a broad range of creative commissions. These included embroidered textiles, painted wall panels and wrought-iron gates for Alfred Waterhouse’s redevelopment of Eaton Hall in Cheshire, and other textiles for Sir Frederic Leighton (1830–96). In around 1913 Jekyll designed an embroidered banner for the Godalming Branch of the National Union of Women’s Suffrage Societies – in 1909 she was elected vice-president alongside her friend, Mary Seton Watts (page 142), who was president.

Jekyll’s horticultural interest began early in life and was heavily influenced by travel in the Mediterranean, where she collected specimens, sending them home to test their hardiness in the British climate. In her 1899 book *Wood and Garden* Jekyll described her naturalistic style of gardening as a form of landscape painting with living things: ‘I am strongly for treating garden and wooded ground in a pictorial way … I try for beauty and harmony everywhere, and especially for harmony of colour.’

Jekyll’s collaboration with the architect Sir Edwin Lutyens (1869–1944) produced many wonderful houses and gardens, their first major project together being her own home, Munstead Wood, Surrey. Here, Jekyll not only lived but conducted her garden design business, ran a commercial plant nursery, undertook planting

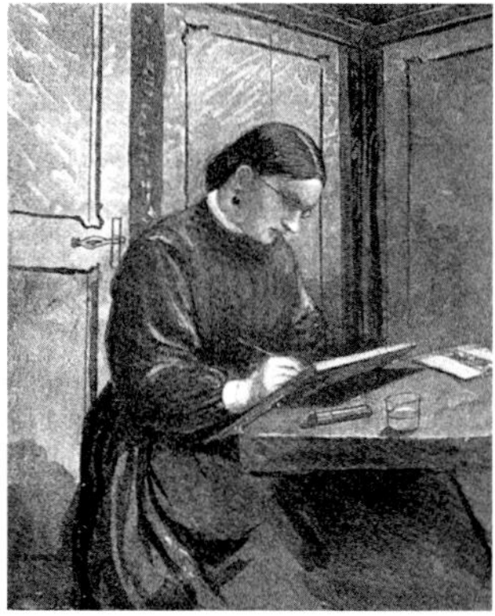

↑ Drawing of Gertrude Jekyll made by her friend Mary Severn Newton in 1863, while the pair were travelling through Greece and Turkey (later published in Francis Jekyll’s 1934 book, *Gertrude Jekyll: A Memoir*).
→ Munstead Wood, the house in Surrey designed by the architect Sir Edwin Lutyens for Gertrude Jekyll, his friend and collaborator.

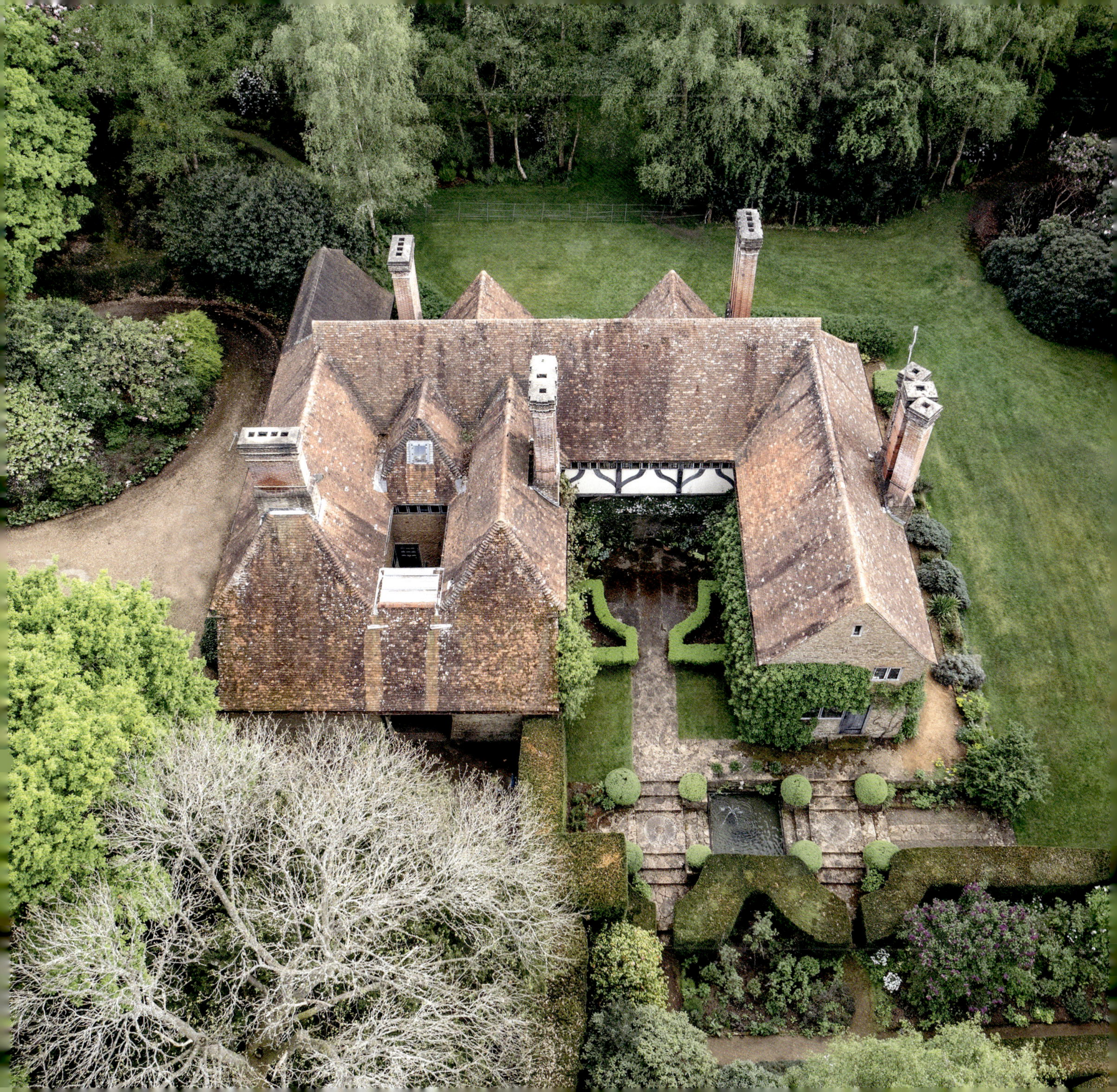

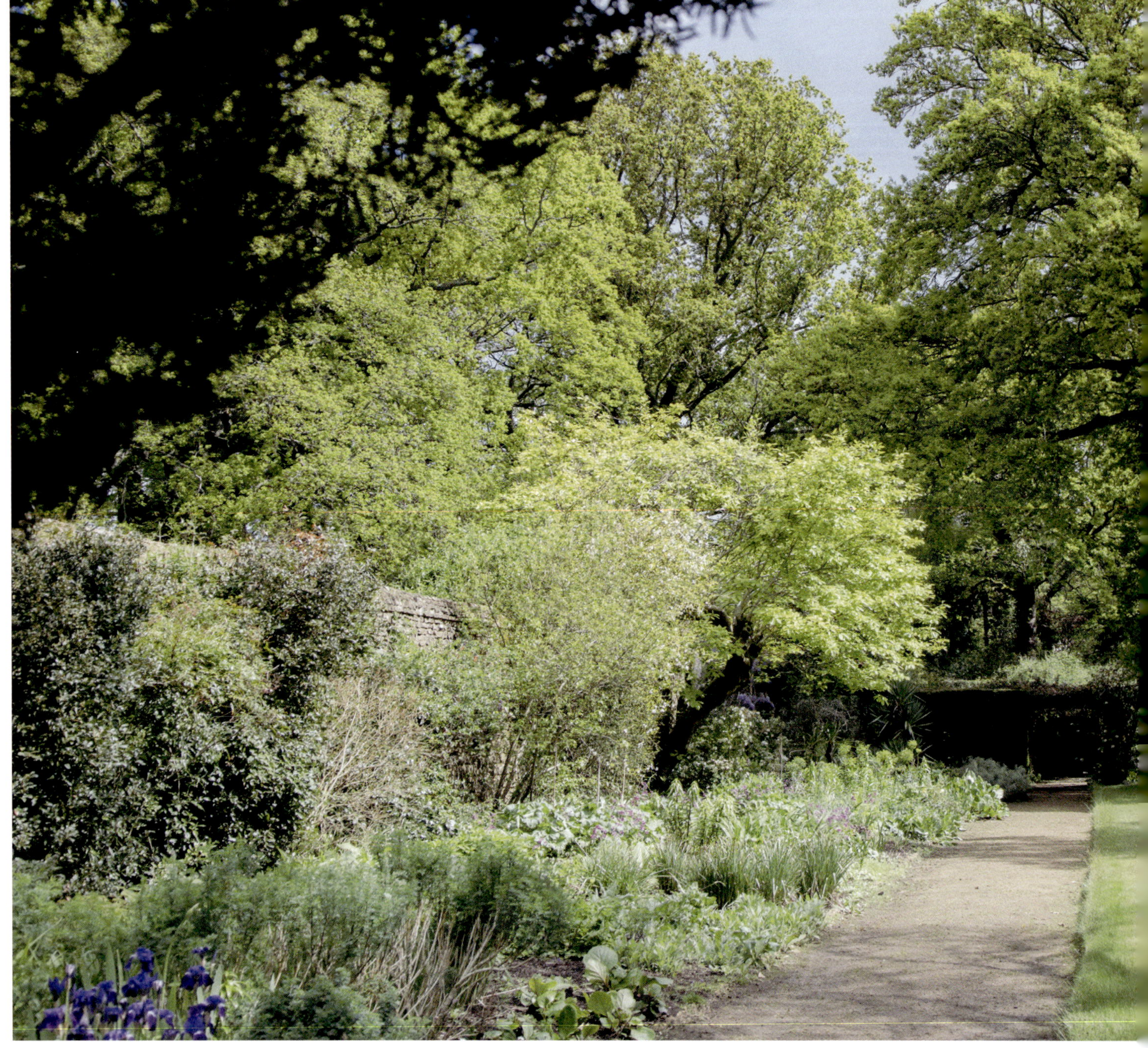

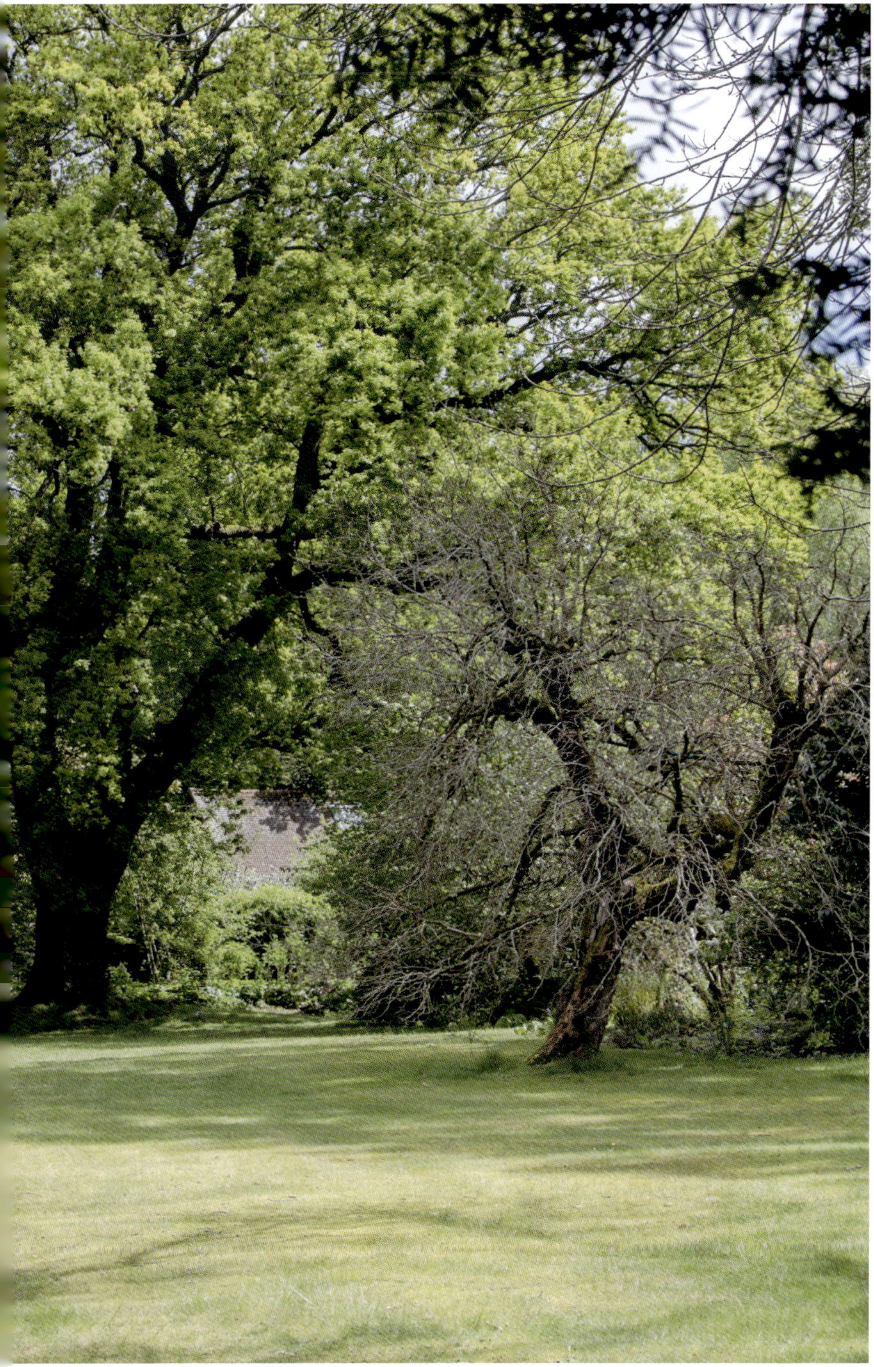

← The innovative Long Border at Munstead Wood, Gertrude Jekyll's house and garden in Surrey, which was the shop window for her horticultural business.
↓ Detail of a corner cupboard, oak with mother-of-pearl and ivory inlay depicting cornflowers, made by Gertrude Jekyll in around 1900, 26.2 x 50.9cm (panel), Munstead Wood, Surrey

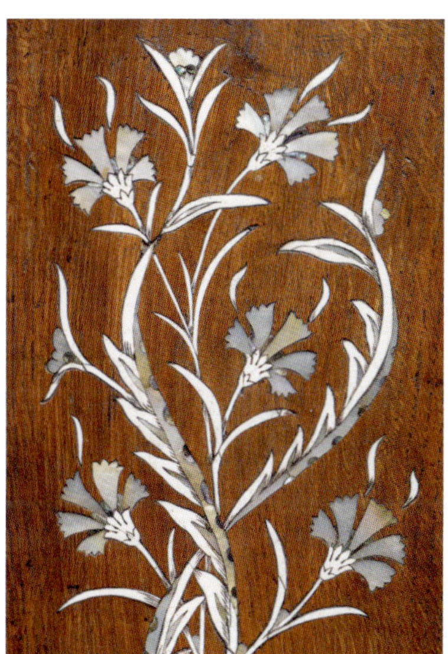

experiments and wrote prolifically. Her books, illustrated with her own photographs and drawings, include a guide to designing rock gardens, a garden book for children, and guides on plant species, such as lilies and roses. A number of Munstead Wood's interior features were designed and made by Jekyll – perhaps in her workshop at the property – including inlaid furniture (above), gesso overmantels and ironwork.

In 1897 Jekyll was awarded the Royal Horticultural Society's Victoria Medal of Honour, the highest accolade for horticulture. RC

The Arts and Crafts ideal

MARY SETON WATTS (1849–1938)

Mary Seton Watts was a visionary artist, designer and ceramicist. She was the creative force behind the Compton Pottery and the Watts Chapel, the latter renowned for its fabulous decorative interior. Watts was also actively involved in the suffrage movement.

Having trained at the Slade School of Art, she went on to study with sculptor Aimé-Jules Dalou (1838–1902), whose work in terracotta must have made a mark on his student. A substantial legacy from her father meant Watts was financially independent; she rented a studio in Pimlico, London, and began to teach clay modelling at a local boys' school. She was also a member of the Home Arts and Industries Association, which taught traditional crafts to ensure their survival and help overcome poverty in rural areas.

Watts married the artist George Frederic Watts (1817–1904) in 1886 and they built a home together – Limnerslease in Compton, Surrey. Mary designed its gesso ceilings and other decorative features. By 1899 she had founded the Compton Pottery – part business, part social and educational enterprise – later

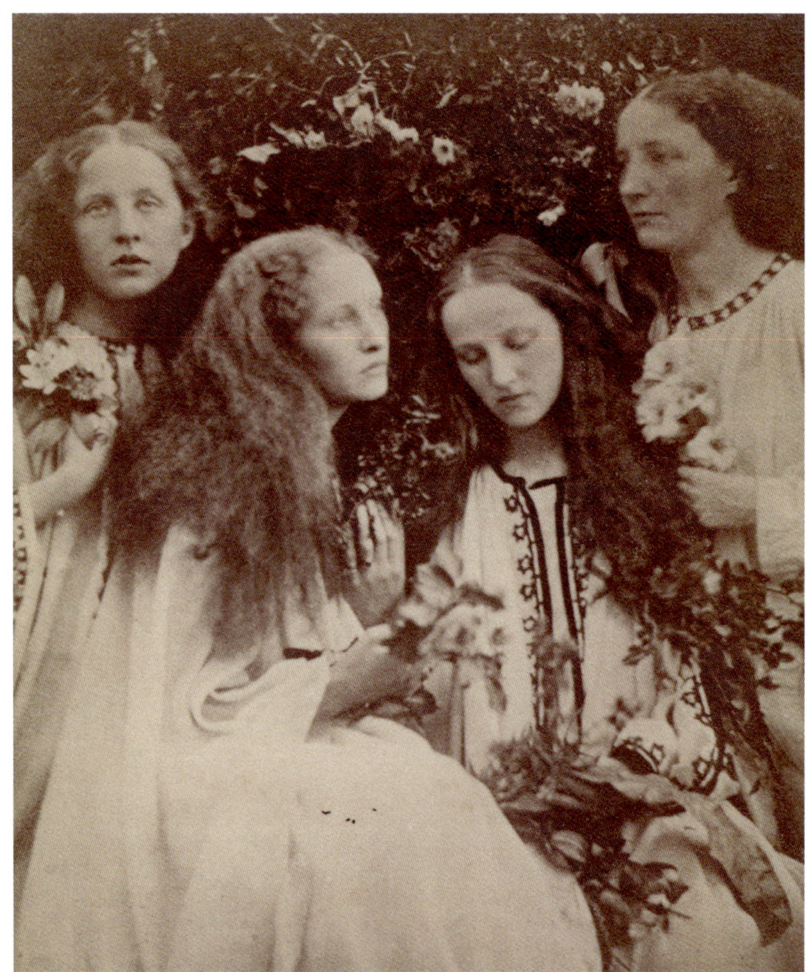

↙ *The Rosebud Garden of Girls*, Julia Margaret Cameron (1815–79), 1868, albumen carte de visite on gold-edged mount. Mary (second from right) poses with her sisters Nelly, Christiana and Ethel Fraser-Tytler.
→ Figure of *St Margaret* (originally holding a reliquary, now lost), *c.*1904–36, Compton Pottery, earthenware with cold-painted decoration, 30.5cm (height), Fenton House, London (NT 1448988)

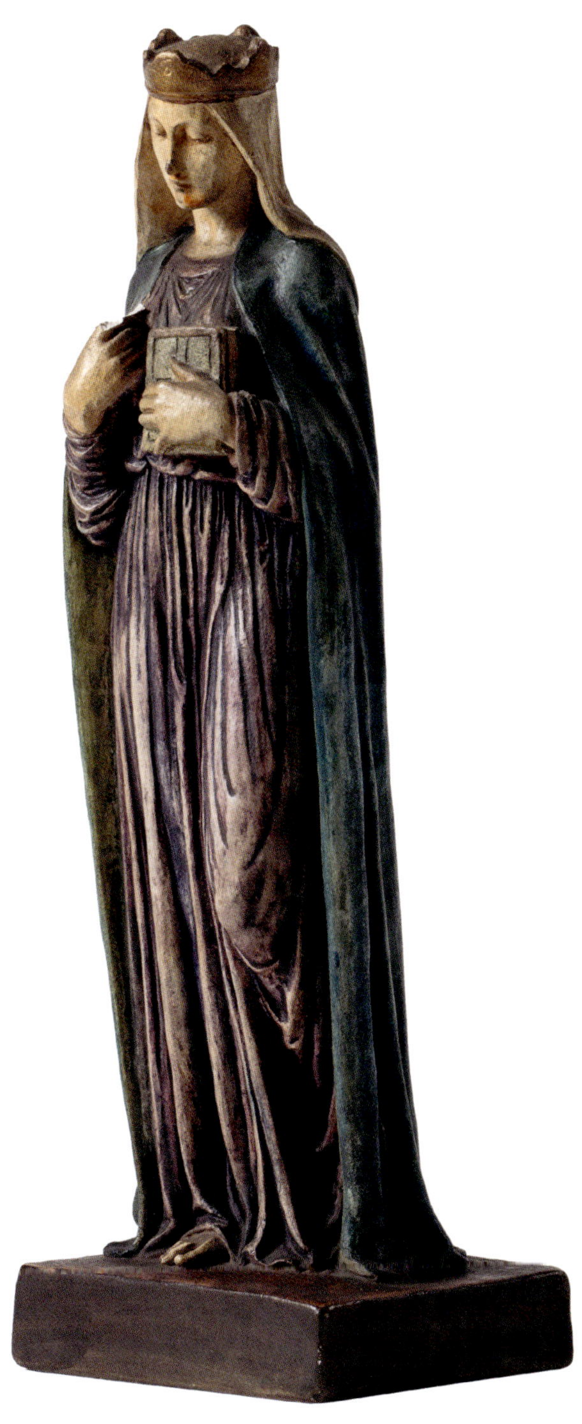

known as the Potters' Arts Guild. Its first products were terracotta garden ornaments sold through Liberty & Co., made using red terracotta clay from a seam on the property, and gravestones – all designed by Watts. A range of small decorative items, including boxes, figures and vases were made using fine clay brought in from Dorset, and sold in the Pottery showroom. They were hand-painted using an egg- and ammonia-based medium, then waxed or varnished, but not glazed, which meant that the coloured surfaces were susceptible to flaking, especially if washed. The pottery continued to operate until the 1950s.

Another major achievement was the design and building of the Watts Cemetery Chapel. Watts led this work, which took almost a decade to complete and was undertaken in collaboration with villagers she had trained to model in terracotta. The building is adorned with their complex architectural reliefs incorporating Celtic and Art Nouveau imagery, the interiors covered with experimental gesso relief panels painted in jewel-like colours. RC

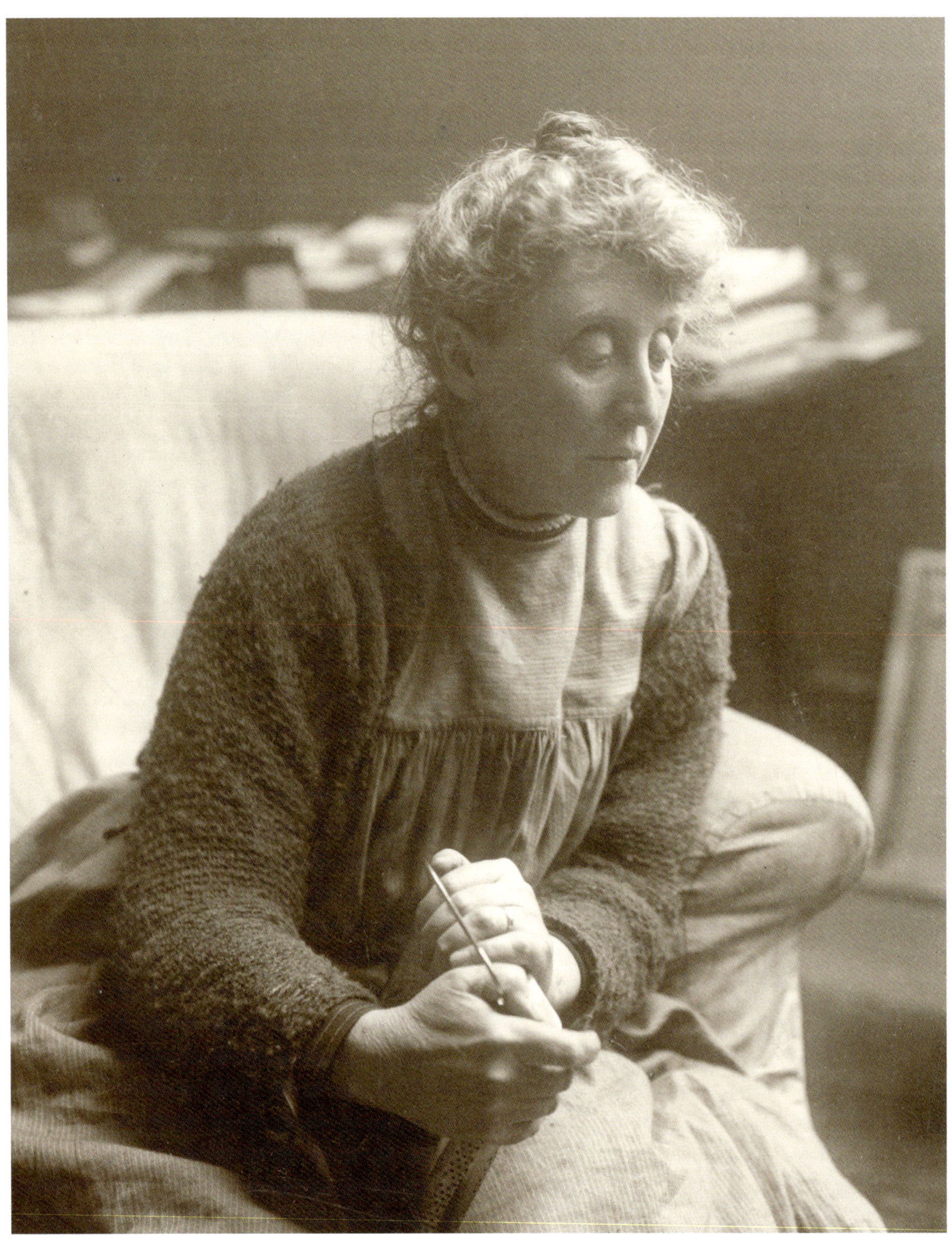

Sunflowers and symbolism

EVELYN DE MORGAN (1855–1919)

← Evelyn De Morgan, captured c.1890 by an unknown photographer

In 1873, at the young age of 17 and despite her parents' opposition, Mary Evelyn Pickering (later De Morgan) was one of the first women to enrol at the recently established Slade School of Art in London. This was one of the few schools at which women could access life models (at least, before 5pm) – both female nudes and partially draped males – which had long been a foundational part of a state education in art for men but was radically new for women.

Pickering flourished at the Slade, winning prizes for her life drawing, receiving the prestigious Slade Scholarship and spending time in Italy studying the work of Renaissance masters. Adopting her gender-ambiguous middle name so that her work would be judged on its merit alone, from 1876 Evelyn began to exhibit and sell her paintings to critical acclaim. In 1886 she married potter William De Morgan, supporting his art pottery business through the sales of her work.

Evelyn De Morgan was part of the later Pre-Raphaelite circle, which included many women artists. She is considered a pioneer of the allegorical female nude and her paintings often centre on the female body. Her early works are history paintings – drawing on biblical, literary or mythological sources, these were considered the most prestigious subjects for an artist and reflect her professional ambition. Her 1885 pastel study for a later oil painting, *Clytie with Sunflowers* (overleaf), is a fine example. Clytie stands nude, rooted in a patch of sunflowers, grieving the loss of the love of Helios, the god of the sun. Her arms are raised in a protective pose, as she turns away from Helios's rays.

De Morgan's later works explored ideas around spirituality and were also profoundly impacted by the events of the First World War. *The Mourners* (overleaf) is one a group of symbolic, pacifist paintings that directly respond to the conflict, which De Morgan exhibited at her studio in 1916 to raise funds for the Red Cross and the Italian Croce Rossa. RC

↓ *Clytie with Sunflowers* (study), Evelyn De Morgan, 1885, pastel on paper, 104.1 x 44.5cm, signed: 'EP', Wightwick Manor, West Midlands (NT 1288980)
→ *The Mourners*, Evelyn De Morgan, *c.*1915, oil on canvas, 60.3 x 89.5cm, signed: 'EDeM', Wightwick Manor, West Midlands (NT 1288978)

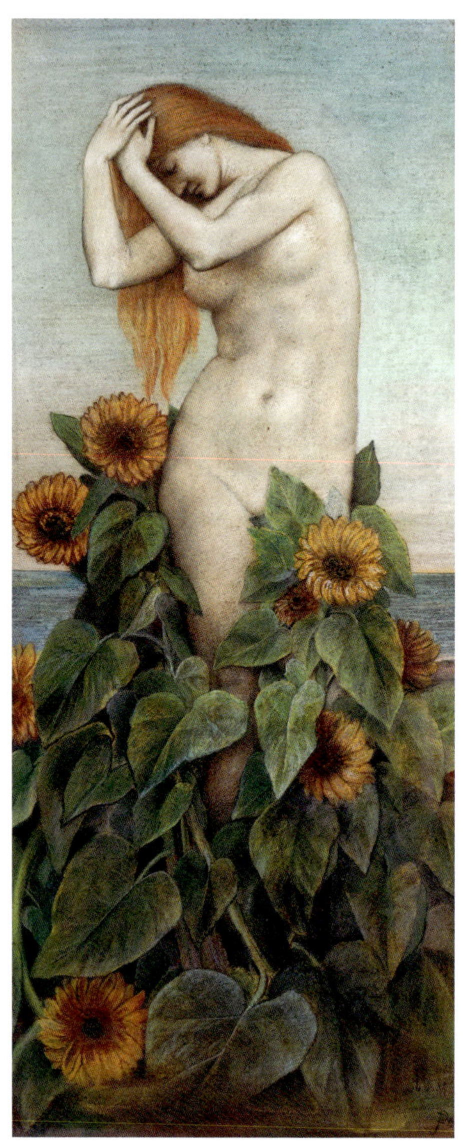

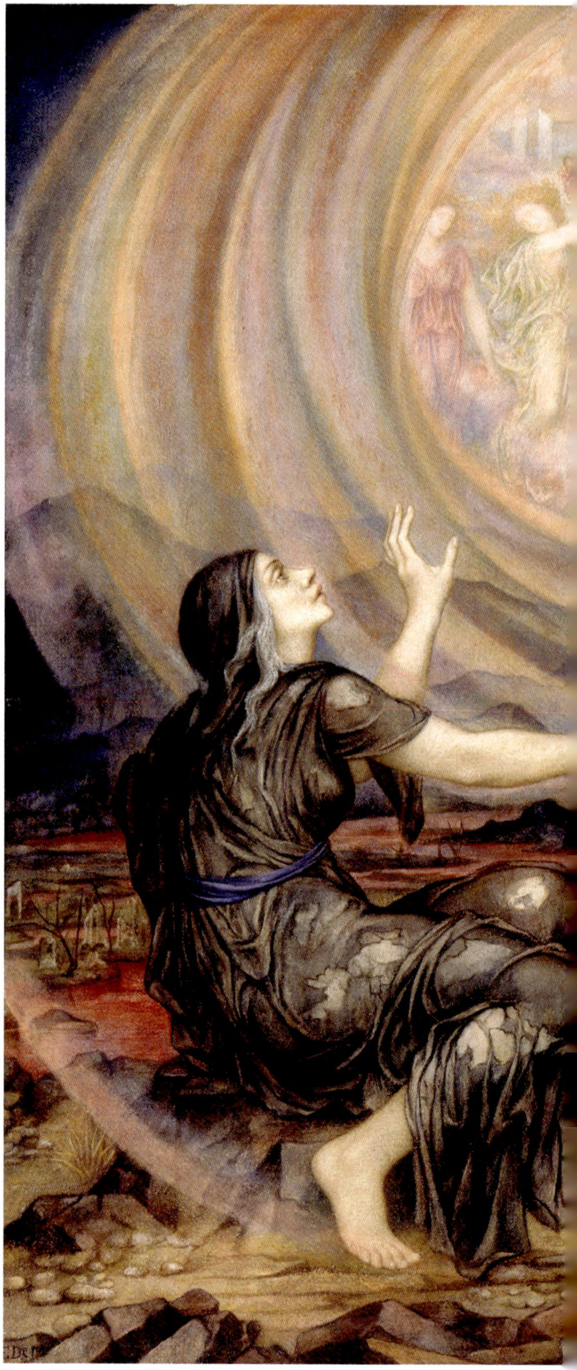

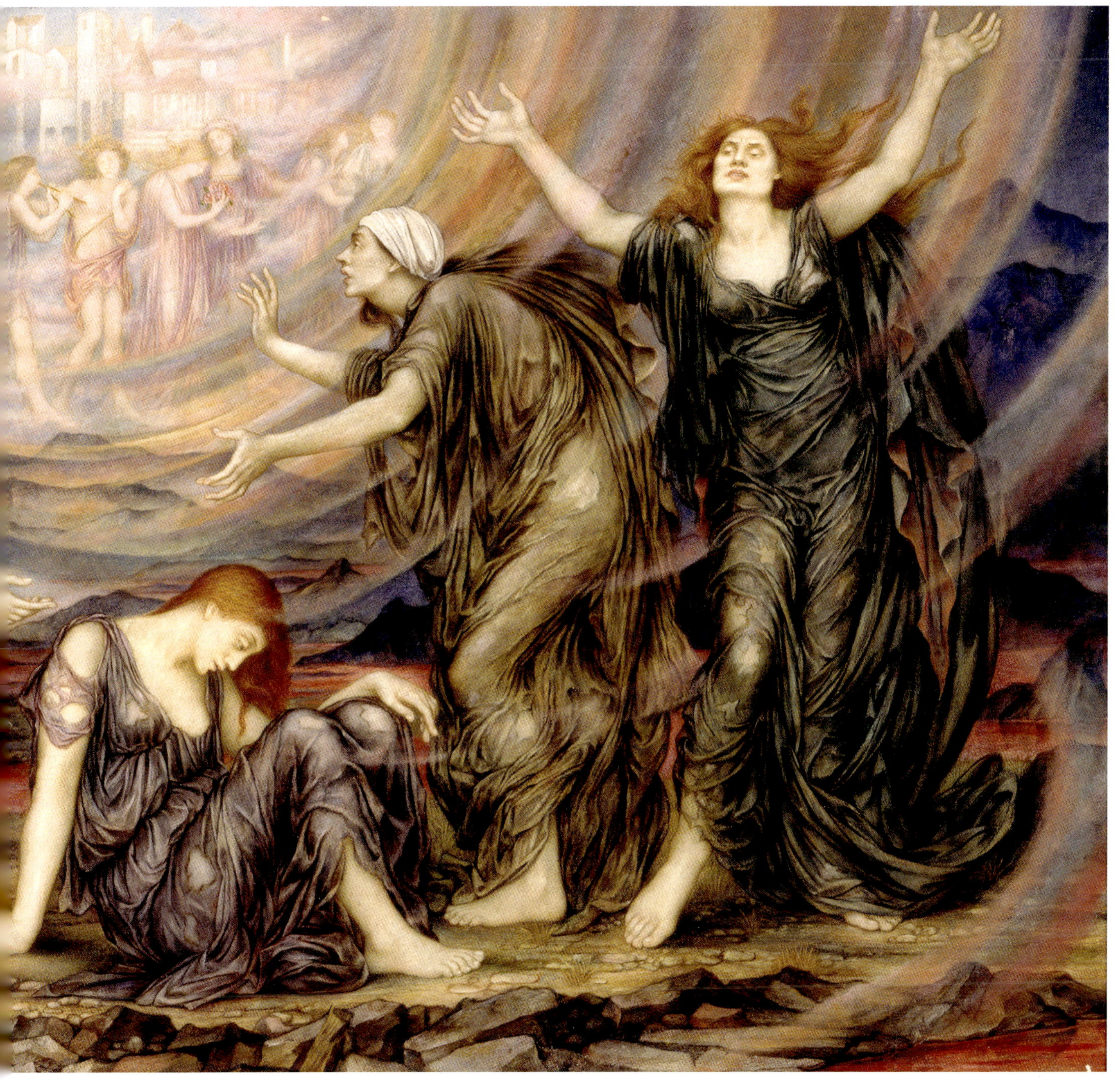

Model, muse and artist

MARIE SPARTALI STILLMAN (1844–1927)

‘I stayed at Kelmscott for ten days and felt quite shut out of the busy world in that beautiful walled garden.’ Marie Spartali Stillman was Jane Morris’s ‘dear friend’ who ‘paints quietly in the garden, making pretty portraits’. Using her favourite medium of watercolour, her series depicting Kelmscott Manor (page 150) – William Morris’s ‘heaven on earth’ – included a gift to Morris, now at Wightwick Manor, West Midlands.

Born into the close-knit Anglo-Greek community in London, Spartali Stillman’s cosmopolitan upbringing brought her into contact with Pre-Raphaelite patrons and artists. From 1865 she studied with Ford Madox Brown alongside his daughters, Lucy and Catherine. She was also in demand as a model, sitting for her childhood friend the sculptor Maria Cassavetti (later Zambaco),

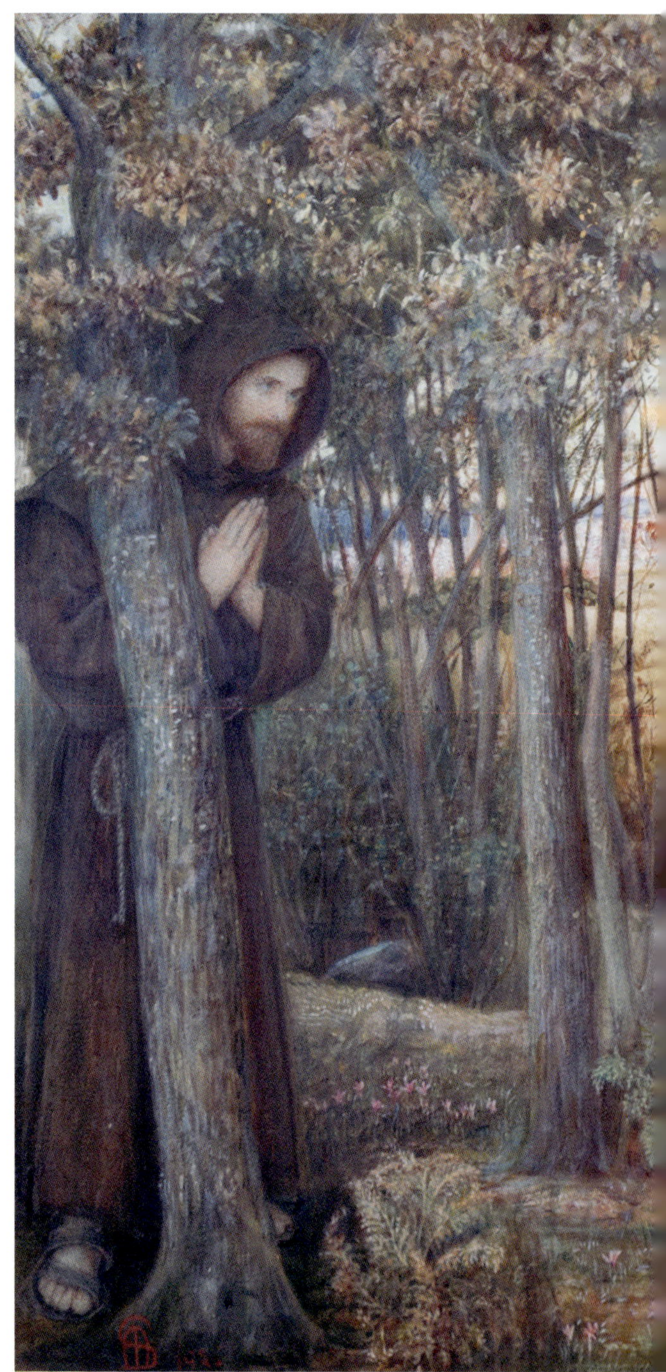

→ *How the Virgin Mary Came to Brother Conrad of Offida and Laid Her Son in His Arms*, Marie Spartali Stillman, 1892, watercolour, body-colour and gold paint on paper, 98.5 x 68.2cm, Wightwick Manor, West Midlands (NT 1287919)

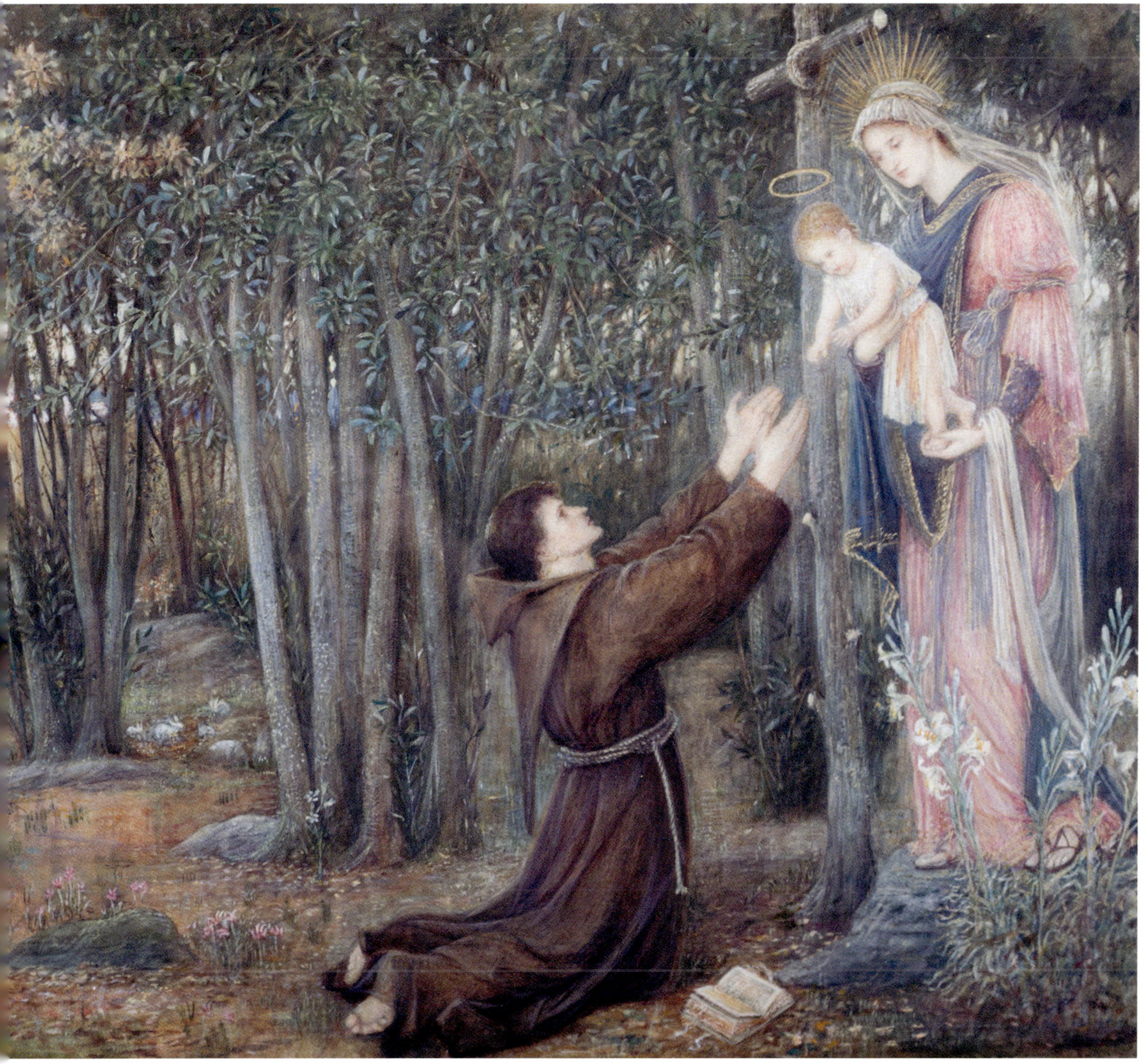

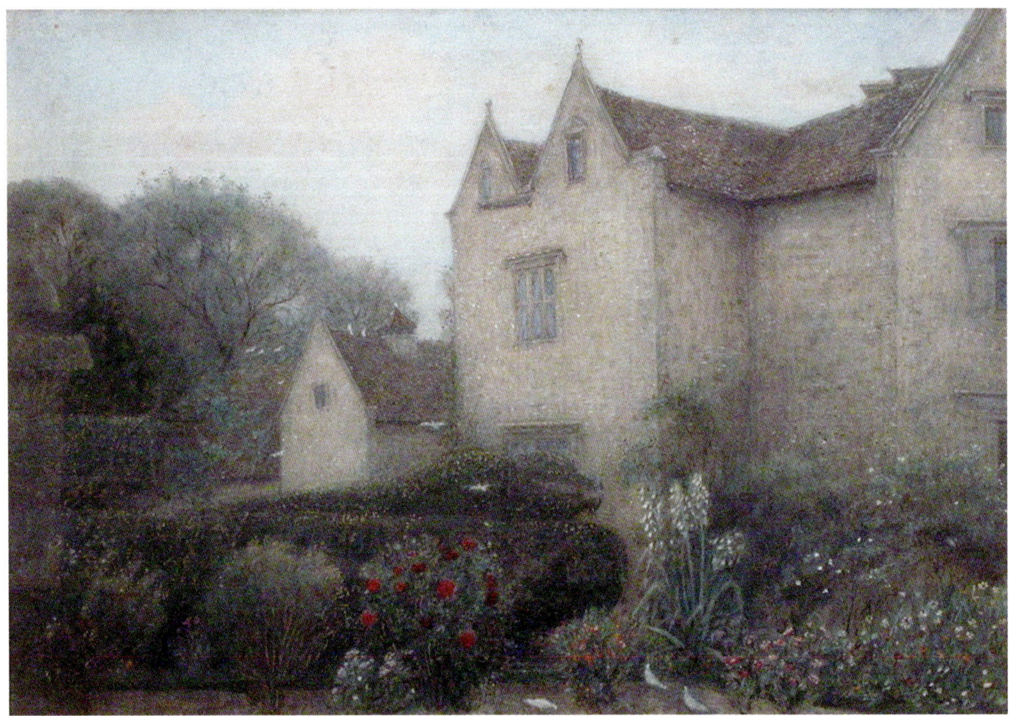

← *Kelmscott Manor*, Marie Spartali Stillman, undated, watercolour on paper, 52.8 x 66.8cm, Wightwick Manor, West Midlands (NT 1287932)
→ *Marie Spartali Stillman*, Maria Zambaco (1843–1914), 1886, alloy medal, 13.6cm (diameter) (British Museum, London)

and the photographer Julia Margaret Cameron (1815–79).

After her marriage to William Stillman in 1871, the family lived an itinerant life in England, the USA and Italy. In Florence the artist was part of the Anglo-American community that included John Singer Sargent and Vernon Lee, and she was included in Ellen Clayton's *English Female Artists* (1876). In 1893 she wrote from Rome to her artist daughter Effie: 'I have found several charming subjects which I hope will sell for a few ££ by and bye [sic]'.

The lives of saints provided subjects for a number of Spartali Stillman's works – in the example shown here (pages 148–9) her husband was used as the model for Brother Peter, standing to the left. Edward Burne-Jones commented on her working sketch for Friar Conrad's vision: '... I don't know how it could go wrong anywhere'. The view through the trees was influenced by Bellini's *The Assassination of St Peter Martyr* (1505–7), and features in a number of her other works.

Spartali Stillman produced 170 known works over a 60-year career, exhibiting in the UK and the USA. The largest public collection of her work is held at Delaware Art Museum, Wilmington. AMS

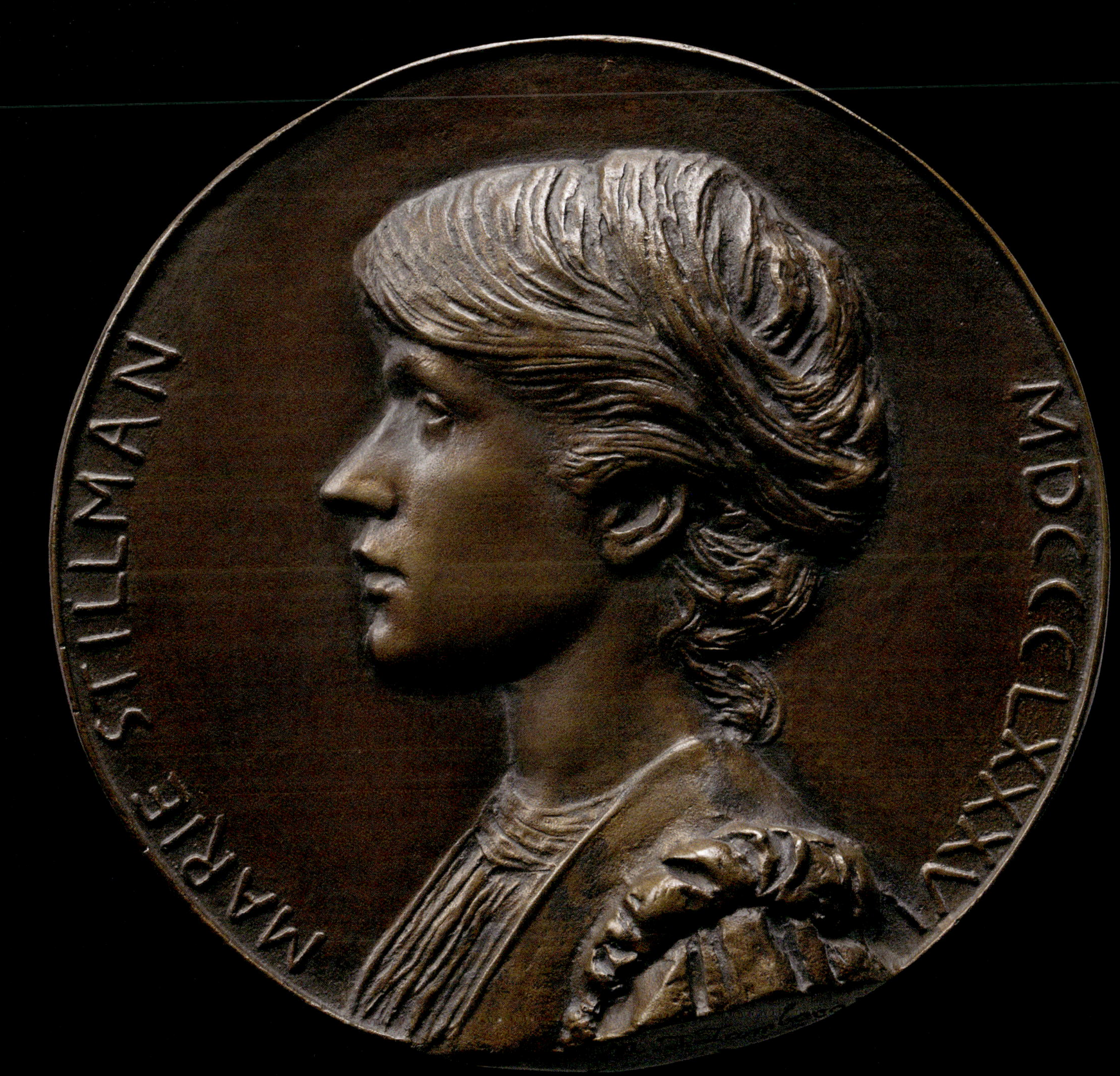
MARIE STILLMAN
MDCCCLXXXVI

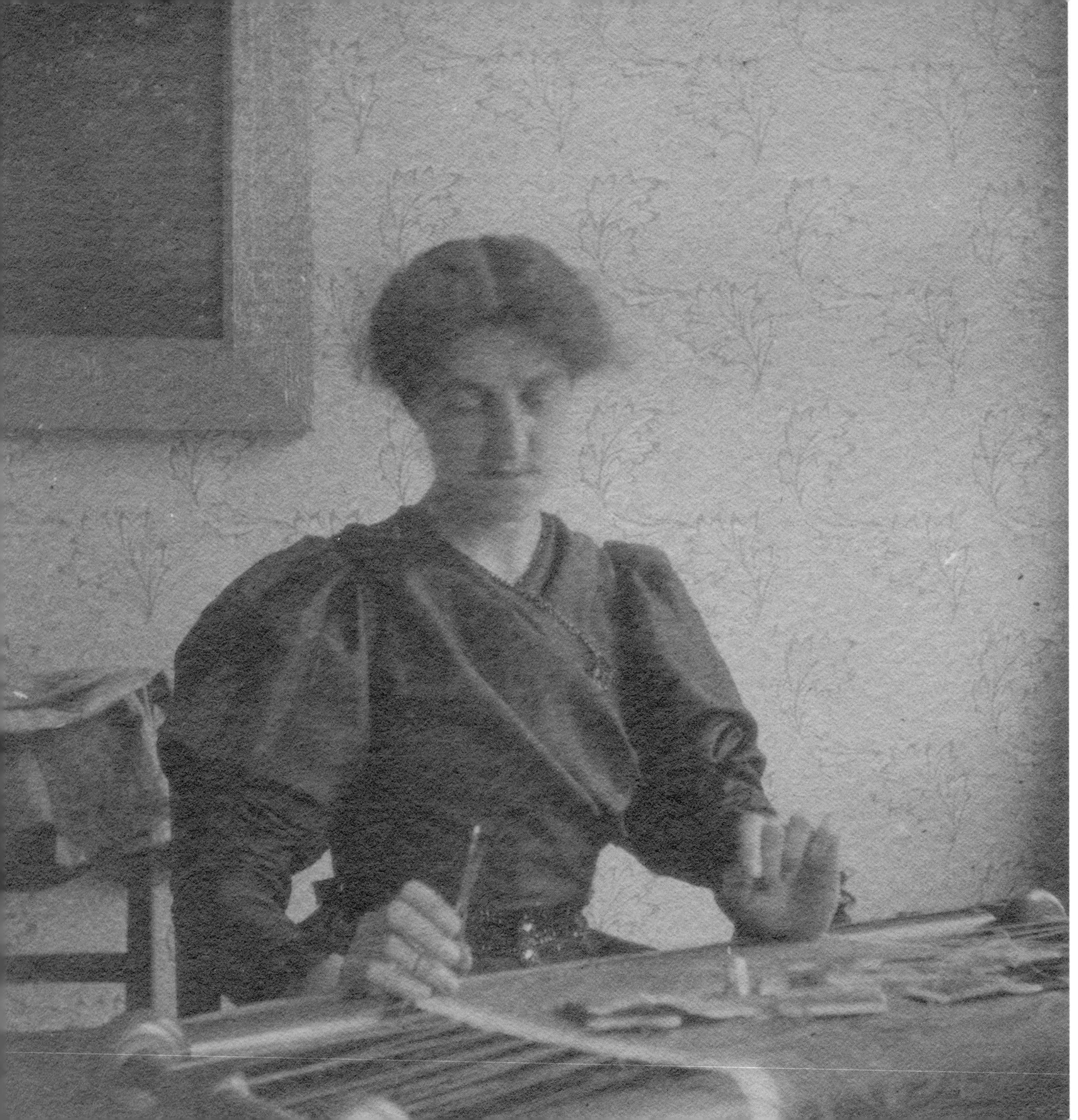

‘Embroidery deserves to be taken seriously’

MAY MORRIS (1862–1938)

In her 1893 book *Decorative Needlework*, May Morris wrote that ‘a belief in the power of beauty is a wholesome thing, and I make no apology for preaching it by the way. As an art, therefore, that should help to decorate home life very largely, and public life too … embroidery deserves to be taken seriously.’

Morris is best known for her work as a designer and maker of embroidery, but she excelled in many areas during her long career. Her principles were in accord with those of the Arts and Crafts movement, which valued traditional hand methods of manufacture over mechanisation, respecting the integrity of materials, taking inspiration from nature and avoiding excessive decorative embellishment. Morris became a central figure in the Arts & Crafts Exhibition Society, showing her work regularly and contributing to publications.

She chose to specialise in embroidery as a student at the National Art Training School (later the Royal College of Art) in South Kensington. In 1885, aged 23, she took over the management of the embroidery division of her family’s business, Morris & Co., which she ran successfully for 11 years. Morris also taught embroidery at several art schools and studied, wrote and lectured in Britain and the USA on historical embroidery techniques – her particular passion – and on other aspects of the decorative arts. Her love of tradition is evident in a pair of dress sleeves in the collection at Wightwick Manor, West Midlands (page 155); their spiralling stems and delicate flowers are inspired by 16th- and 17th-century embroidery. Morris also designed three wallpapers for Morris & Co., including one of its most successful papers, *Honeysuckle* (overleaf), and designed and created many wonderful pieces of jewellery as an independent maker.

In response to the exclusion of women from the Art Workers’ Guild (which did not admit women members until 1964),

← May Morris working on an embroidery, unknown photographer, early 1890s (National Portrait Gallery, London)

Morris founded the Women's Guild of Arts in 1907. This society provided support, inspiration and camaraderie for women working independently in a wide variety of creative practices. Its first chair was Mary Seton Watts (page 142).

Morris lived at Kelmscott Manor, Oxfordshire, with Mary Lobb (1878–1939), with whom she had an enduring relationship. Morris's impact on the Arts and Crafts movement and her ongoing legacy cannot be overstated. RC

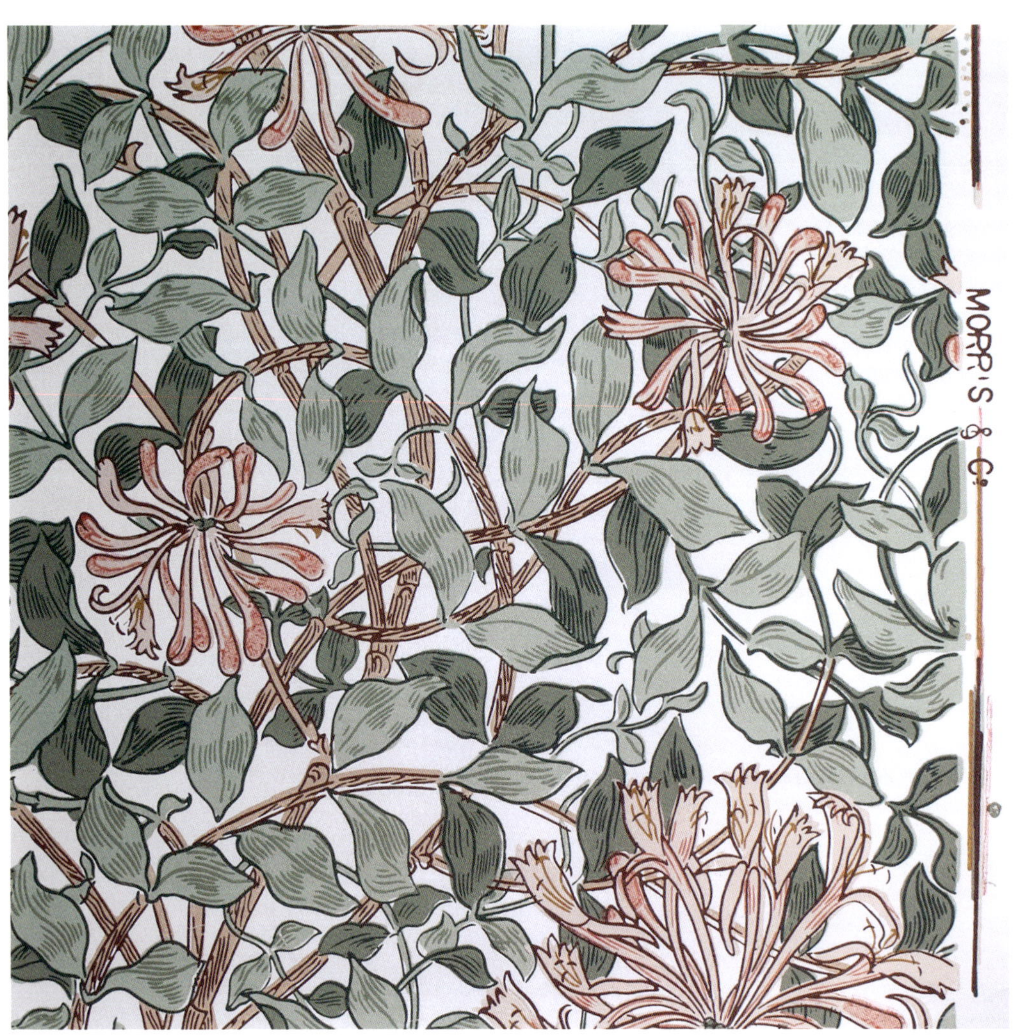

← Sample of block-printed wall-paper, *Honeysuckle*, designed by May Morris, originally manufactured by Jeffrey & Co., *c.*1883 (later reprint), Wightwick Manor, West Midlands (NT 1290767)

→ A pair of dress sleeves designed and embroidered by May Morris, *c.*1890, coloured silks on linen, worked in chain stitch, 62 (length) x 29cm, Wightwick Manor, West Midlands (NT 1289314)

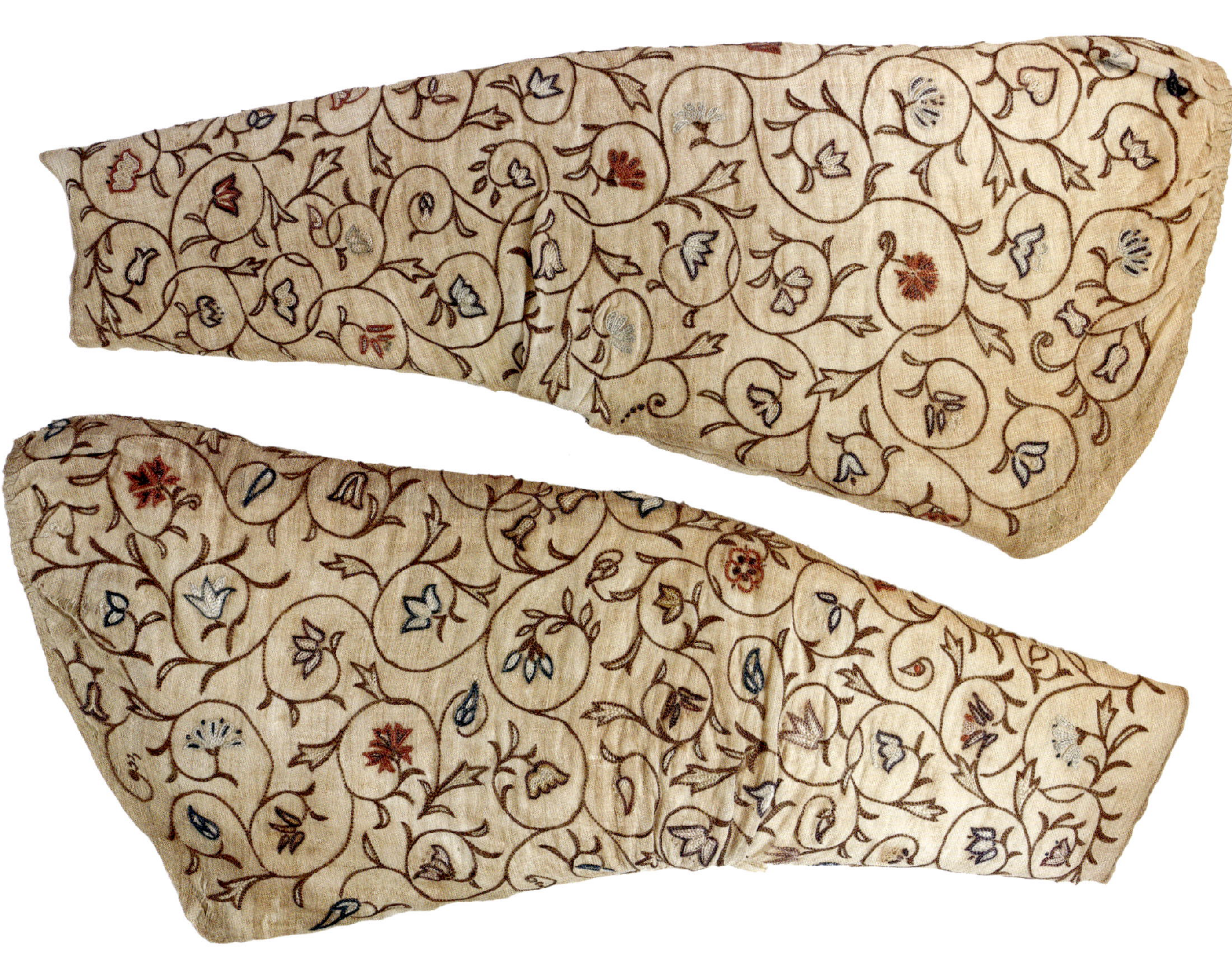

‘A very gentle soul’

WINIFRED HOPE THOMSON (1864–1944)

Writing to a friend while living in Paris, Winifred Hope Thomson remarked, ‘my brush is still an enemy to be struggled against instead of a willing and active servant’.

Thomson was writing in the 1880s during the formative years of her artistic career, while studying in France under Jean-Jacques Henner and Carolus Duran. Despite her misgivings, she had already enjoyed significant success at home in England. She studied at the National Art Training School in South Kensington and was the first woman to be awarded a gold medal in the national competition open to all students at government art schools. The *South London Press* reported that, ‘as there are some 280 schools it may easily be calculated that Miss Thomson defeated a tremendously large number of competitors … many thousands of drawings were sent in in competition’. Winifred was born in Edinburgh in 1864, the third of four children born to Robert and Clara Thomson. Throughout much of her adult life she lived with her brother Courtauld, either in London or at Dorneywood in Buckinghamshire.

Although current research is yet to identify the sitter in Thomson’s most remarkable portrait of a woman known as ‘Mammy Liza’ (opposite), she became renowned for her portrait miniatures of wealthy society figures, which were exhibited in Paris and London.

In later years Thomson went on to write cookery columns for *The Times* and published a book, *Someone to Dinner – Chef Cooking for Little Kitchens*, in 1935. Throughout her life Thomson turned her hand to a number of different disciplines, from illustration and portraiture to needlework and photography, and on her death was described by her brother as ‘a very gentle soul of outstanding intellect and a wide range of artistic gifts’. BA

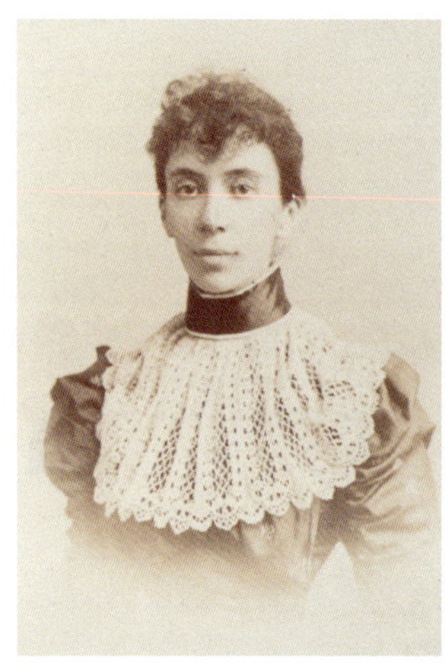

↑ Winifred Hope Thomson, unknown photographer (The Bodleian Libraries, University of Oxford)
→ *Portrait of a woman, known as Mammy Liza*, Winifred Hope Thomson, c.1890–1910, oil on canvas, 36.8 x 27.9cm, Dorneywood, Buckinghamshire (NT 1507745)

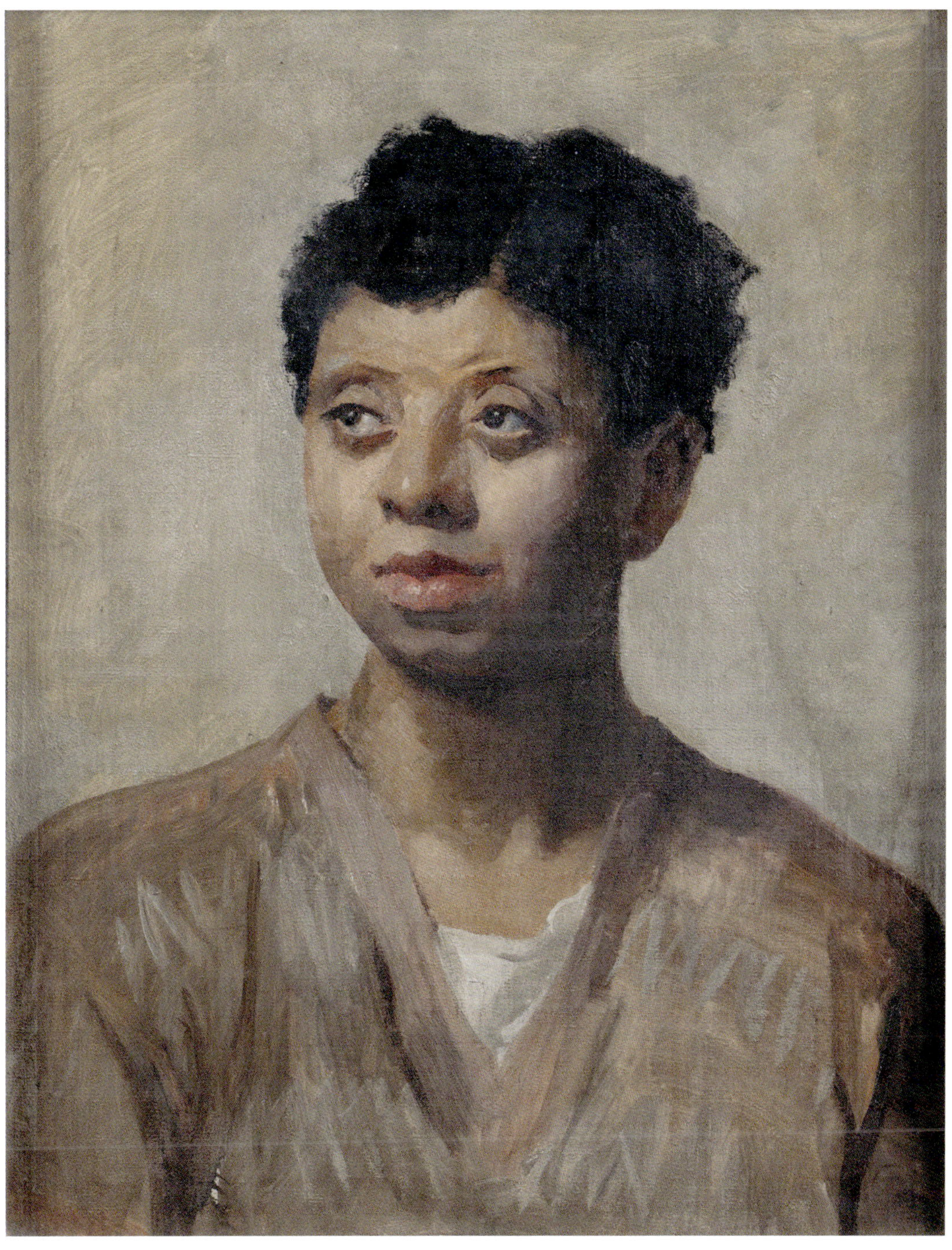

Universal woman

EMMELINE CUST (1867–1955)

Born Emmeline Welby-Gregory, 'Nina' Cust was a writer, editor, translator, poet and sculptor. She was descended from a line of intellectual women – her mother, Victoria, published extensively on the philosophy of language, while her grandmother Emmeline was a famous travel writer and poet.

Cust is now recognised as one of the great creative women of Belton House, Lincolnshire. But this was not always the case. The troubled circumstances of her marriage to Belton's heir, Harry Cust (1861–1917), once dominated her narrative – an example of how women's histories can become skewed or diminished.

Some, but probably not all, of Nina Cust's sculpture is known today. Signed portrait busts in plaster, marble and metal exist at Belton, and in its church there is a monumental marble effigy of Harry – staggering in its scale and emotional weight. Cust was herself the subject of portraits by the Arts and Crafts enamellist Alexander Fisher (page 118), and by the Symbolist painters George Frederic Watts and John Collier. Contemporary accounts speak of her artistic interests and aesthetic sensibility. She was twice depicted by the sculptor Sir Alfred Gilbert, his portrait of her exhibited at the Royal Academy in 1900.

Amateur (non-professional) sculpture was practised by women in Nina's social circle. Associated with an elite cultural group known as the 'Souls', it may have been through the influence of fellow Soul and exhibited artist Violet Manners, Duchess of Rutland (1856–1937), that she took up sculpture. Sir Alfred Gilbert, who was supported by Manners, may also have given her sculpture lessons. Indeed, Gilbert's bust of Nina (Ackland Museum, Chapel Hill) and her self-portrait (opposite) share clear similarities.

Nina Cust continued to sculpt well into the 20th century, exhibiting a bust of her niece Joan at the Royal Academy in 1906. In addition to practising sculpture, she published books and academic articles, and was the first to translate into English the French philologist Michel Bréal's landmark book *Semantics: Studies in the Science of Meaning* (1900). ARW

→ *Self-portrait*, Emmeline 'Nina' Welby-Gregory, Mrs Henry Cockayne-Cust, *c.*1894–1900, plaster, 74 x 48 x 39cm, Belton House, Lincolnshire, purchased with a grant from the National Heritage Memorial Fund, 1984 (NT 436834)

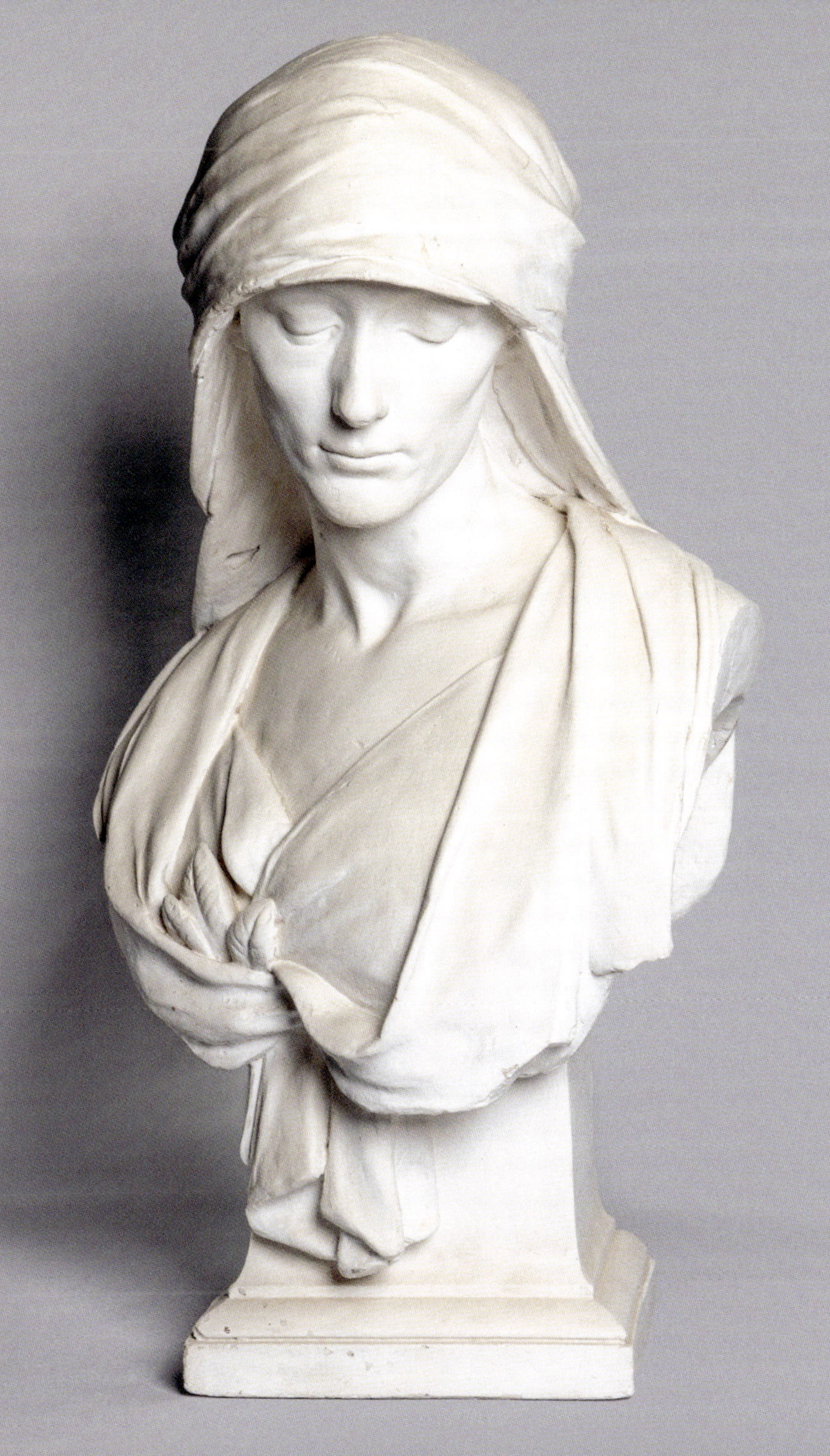

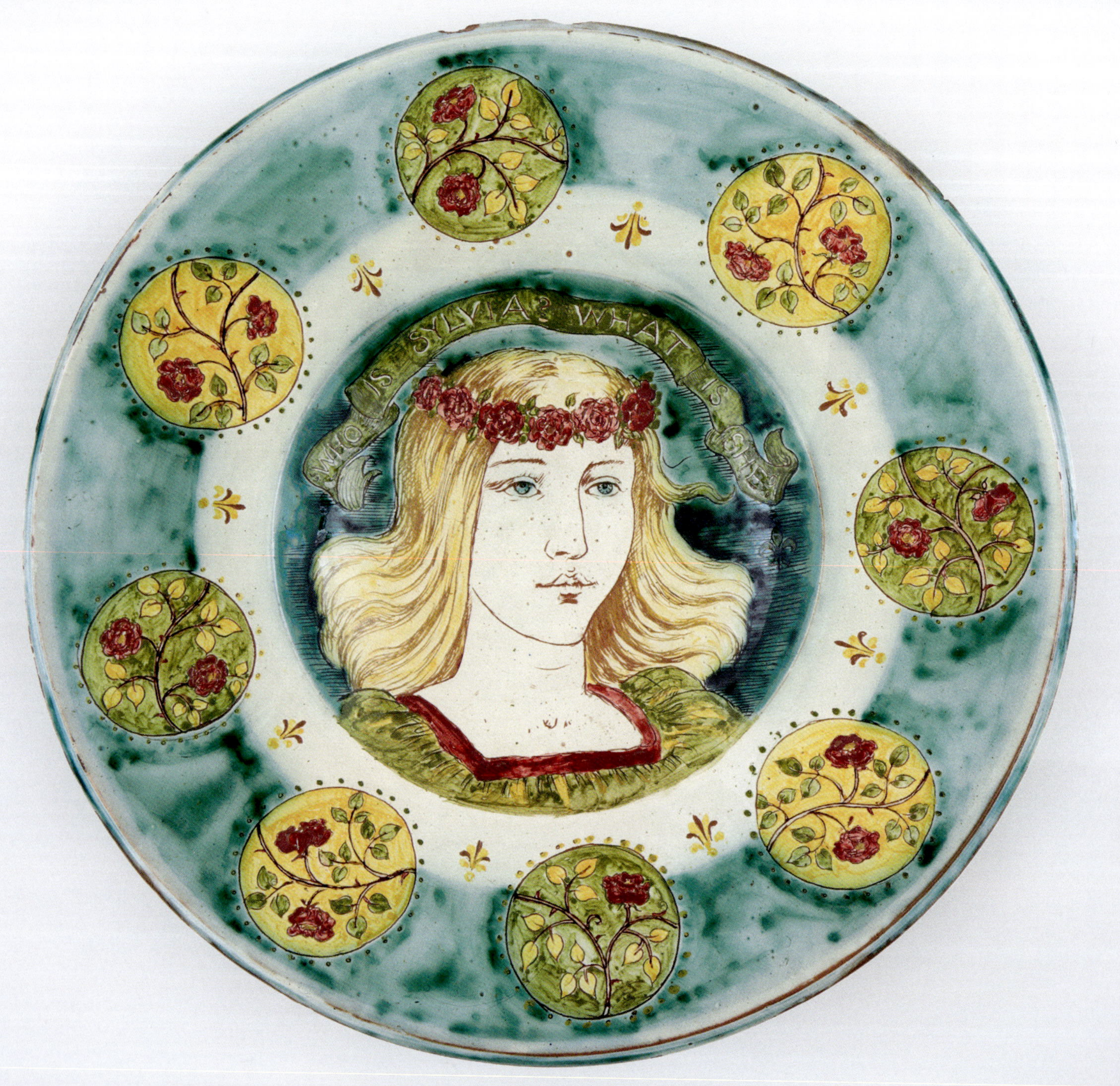
WHO IS SYLVIA? WHAT IS SHE?

‘A woman of independent ways’

CASSANDRA ANNIE WALKER (1875–1936)

← Plaque decorated by Cassandra Annie Walker and designed by Harold Rathbone, Della Robbia Pottery, Birkenhead, 1896, earthenware with sgraffito and coloured glazes, 47cm (diameter), Standen, West Sussex (NT 1213669)

Cassandra Annie Walker grew up in Liverpool and worked at the short-lived Della Robbia Pottery in Birkenhead, which operated from 1894 to 1906. Taking its name and inspiration from the maiolica (tin-glazed earthenware) masterpieces of Italian Renaissance sculptor Luca della Robbia (*c*.1400–82), the studio was established according to Arts and Crafts principles, aspiring to use local labour and materials, and to create works entirely by hand. The Della Robbia Pottery employed many women as designers and decorators, and Walker's work is among its very finest and most progressive.

While working at Della Robbia, Walker attended Liverpool School of Architecture and Applied Art, and won a scholarship from the Liverpool Corporation to study at Westminster School of Art. She described her profession as ‘pottery designer’ and was entrusted with a number of important commissions for Della Robbia.

Walker was particularly interested in architectural ceramics, and exhibited several wall panels and reliefs at Liverpool's Walker Art Gallery, attracting critical praise in contemporary art publications such as *The Studio*. Walker is remembered as ‘a woman of independent ways and behaviour’, who often wore a flowing, Arab-style cloak while walking around Liverpool.

Walker had an affinity for figurative work and attended evening life classes as part of her training in 1901–2. This is shown to beautiful effect in her striking depiction of Sylvia from Shakespeare's *Two Gentlemen of Verona* on a wall plaque (opposite) decorated by her to a design by the pottery's manager, Harold Rathbone (1858–1929). The inscription ‘Who is Sylvia? What is She?’ is taken from a song in the fourth act of the play, which ends ‘To her let us garlands bring’, inspiring her floral crown and the roundels of roses that encircle her. Walker's precise sgraffito lines cut through the pale white slip to the red clay beneath, giving an illustrative, expressive quality to Sylvia's face. The pale ground colour, flattened perspective and scroll are inspired by 16th-century Italian maiolica *Belle Donne* portrait plates. RC

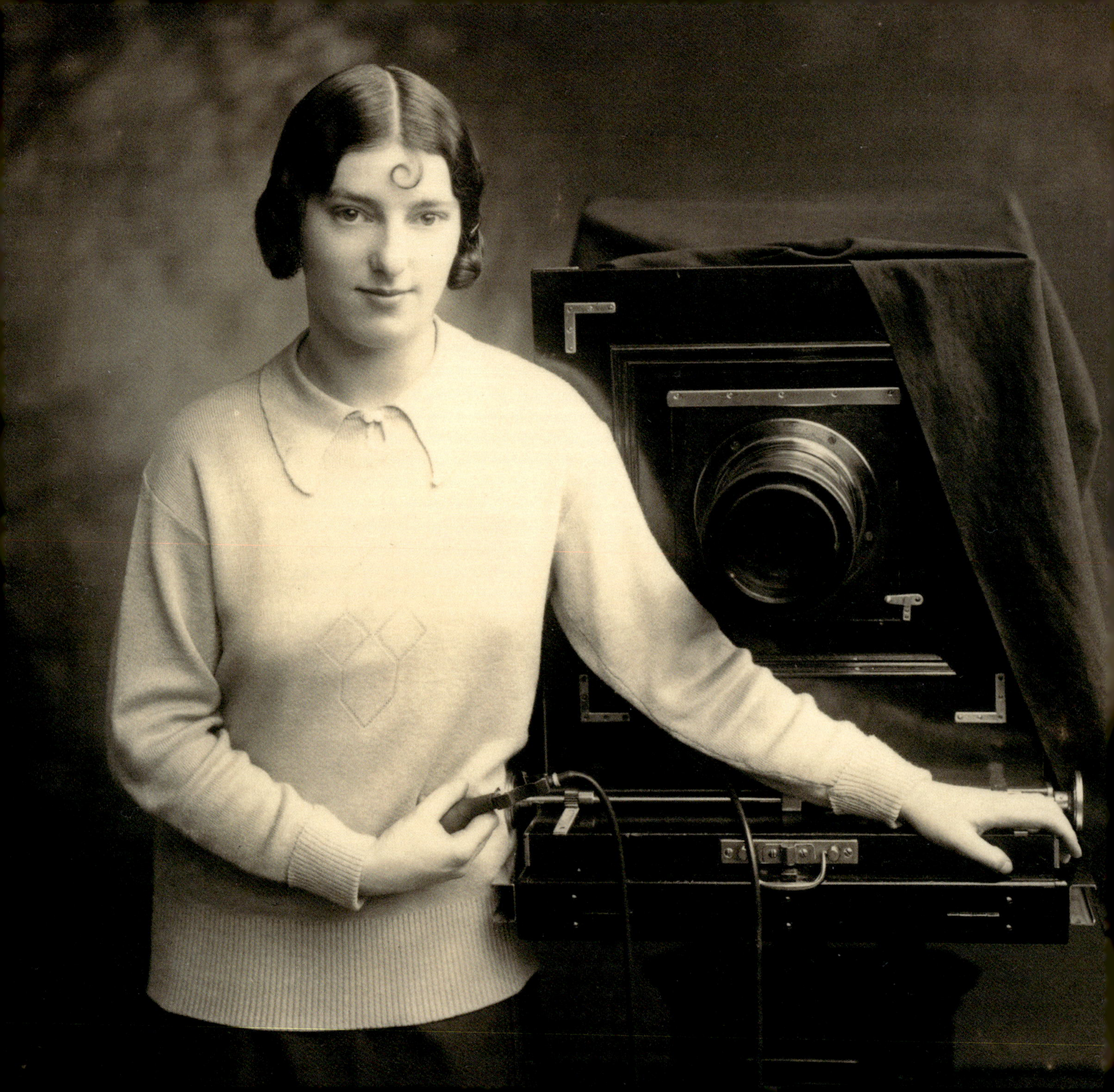

MODERN WOMEN

In 1907, frustrated at the refusal of the Art Workers' Guild to admit women members, May Morris (page 153) and her mother, Jane, an embroiderer, were among the founders of the Women's Guild of Arts in London. Its aim was to champion the right of women art workers to be considered as seriously as their male peers and to be afforded the same opportunities.

In line with the principles and values of the Arts and Crafts movement, and with a desire to elevate the profile of the applied arts, the new guild organised lectures, occasional exhibitions and demonstrations. Many of the women featured in these pages were members – Mary Seton Watts (page 142), Pamela Colman Smith (page 170), Evelyn De Morgan (page 145), Agnes Garrett (page 130), Louise Powell (page 176) and Marie Spartali Stillman (page 148). So too was aristocratic sculptor Lady Feodora Gleichen (1861–1922), who had trained at her father's sculpture studio in St James's Palace, before attending the Slade School of Art. Gleichen was posthumously among the first women admitted to the Royal British Society of Sculptors, with a prize for women sculptors established in her name.

In the early 20th century the campaign for women's suffrage had started to gather real momentum and many artists and designers supported the cause. Some were members of groups campaigning for enfranchisement, such as the Artists' Suffrage League or the Suffrage

← Portrait of Margaret Mills (later Hardman) by the Ritchie studio, *c.*1929, gelatin silver print, 16 x 14cm (print), The Hardmans' House, Liverpool (NT 974233)

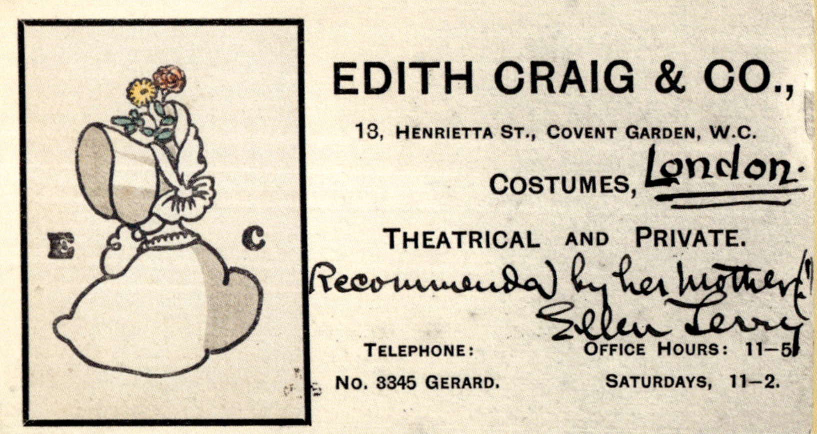

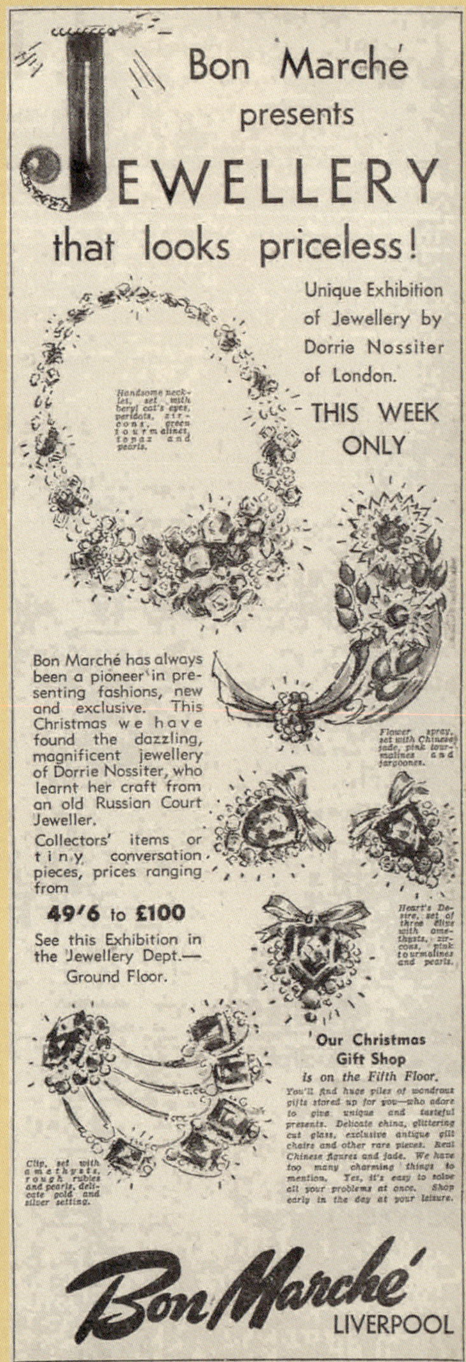

Atelier, which included Edith Craig (page 173) as a member. Dressmaker and artist Amy Kotzé (page 179) was one of many creative women in London advertising their businesses in suffrage publications such as *Votes for Women* and donating work to raise funds for the cause. The power of subverting the feminine stitch seems to have had a particular resonance in the movement, with women such as Gertrude Jekyll (page 138) designing or embroidering banners for marches, or Kotzé offering dresses embroidered in the colours of the cause. One of the most potent material remnants of the campaign is the 'Suffragette Handkerchief' embroidered with the names of more than 60 women from the Women's Social and Political Union. Made largely in 1912 during periods of incarceration at Holloway prison for militant activism, it includes the stitched signature of Welsh sculptor Edith Downing (1857–1931), who was subjected to brutal force-feeding. Remarkable photographs by press photographer Christina Broom (1862–1939; pages 180–1) are an invaluable and evocative record of the campaign for the vote, which was not fully realised until 1928.

Despite the economic and social challenges exacerbated by the devastation of war, many women established and succeeded in the business of design during the first half of the 20th century. In the Staffordshire potteries, Daisy Makeig-Jones (1881–1945) was one of the women designing for Wedgwood at this time, creating intricate, glistening designs for its 'Fairyland Lustre' range. Susie Cooper

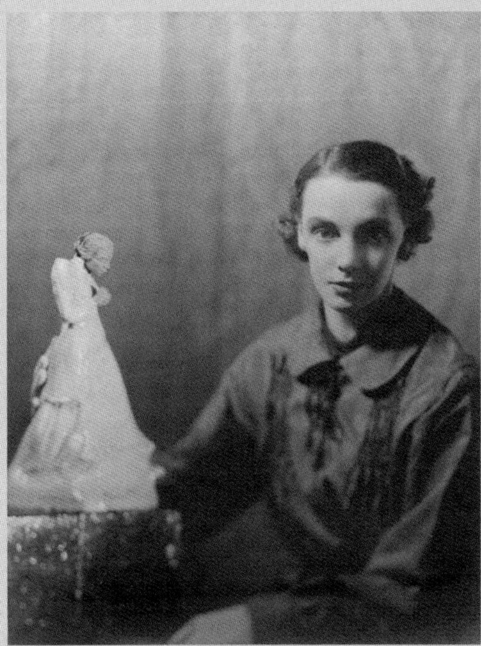

↞ Business card for Edith Craig & Co., *c.*1902–3 (NT 1124049)
← Advertisement for the upmarket Bon Marché department store in Liverpool featuring the jewellery of Dorrie Nossiter (page 218), *Liverpool Daily Post*, 18 November 1941
↑ Susie Cooper in a 1938 photograph by Cleo Cottrell (National Portrait Gallery, London)

(page 214) and Clarice Cliff (1899–1972) both embraced Modernism, taking stylistic cues from European abstraction and embracing Art Deco. Women also played an important role in documenting life during the Second World War, including painter and illustrator Evelyn Dunbar (1906–60), who was the only full-time, salaried woman employed by the War Artists' Advisory Committee, recording life on the Home Front, and photographer Lee Miller (1907–77) – best known for her sublime surrealist images. Liverpool-based Margaret Hardman (page 188) has recently gained increased recognition for her work as a photographer, capturing dramatic portraits, landscapes and urban scenes in the mid-20th century.

A number of women represented in the National Trust's collections played key roles in the development of aspects of Modernism in Britain and Europe during the early 20th century, including Eileen Agar (page 209), Rita Kernn-Larsen (1904–98), Sonia Delaunay (1885–1979), Marion Dorn (page 196), Vanessa Bell (page 200) and Mary Fedden (1915–2012). This was also an exciting time in the development of the studio pottery movement, in which Norah Braden (1901–2001) and Katherine Pleydell-Bouverie (1895–1985) were important early figures. Both trained at the Central School of Arts and Crafts (now Central St Martins) in London, and later worked with Bernard Leach in St Ives, Cornwall. Pieces by them are in the collection at Greenway, Devon. In the 1920s Pleydell-Bouverie established a pottery at her family's estate in Coleshill, Oxfordshire (now owned by the National Trust), working for a time with Braden, then her partner. She used clay from the estate and gathered wood and foliage for ash glazing.

During the 1920s and 1930s both artists exhibited in London galleries to critical acclaim and had pieces acquired by the Victoria and Albert Museum, London. Pleydell-Bouverie later gave a substantial body of work (including pieces by Braden) to the foundational collections of the Crafts Study Centre, which preserves and celebrates the best of British craft.

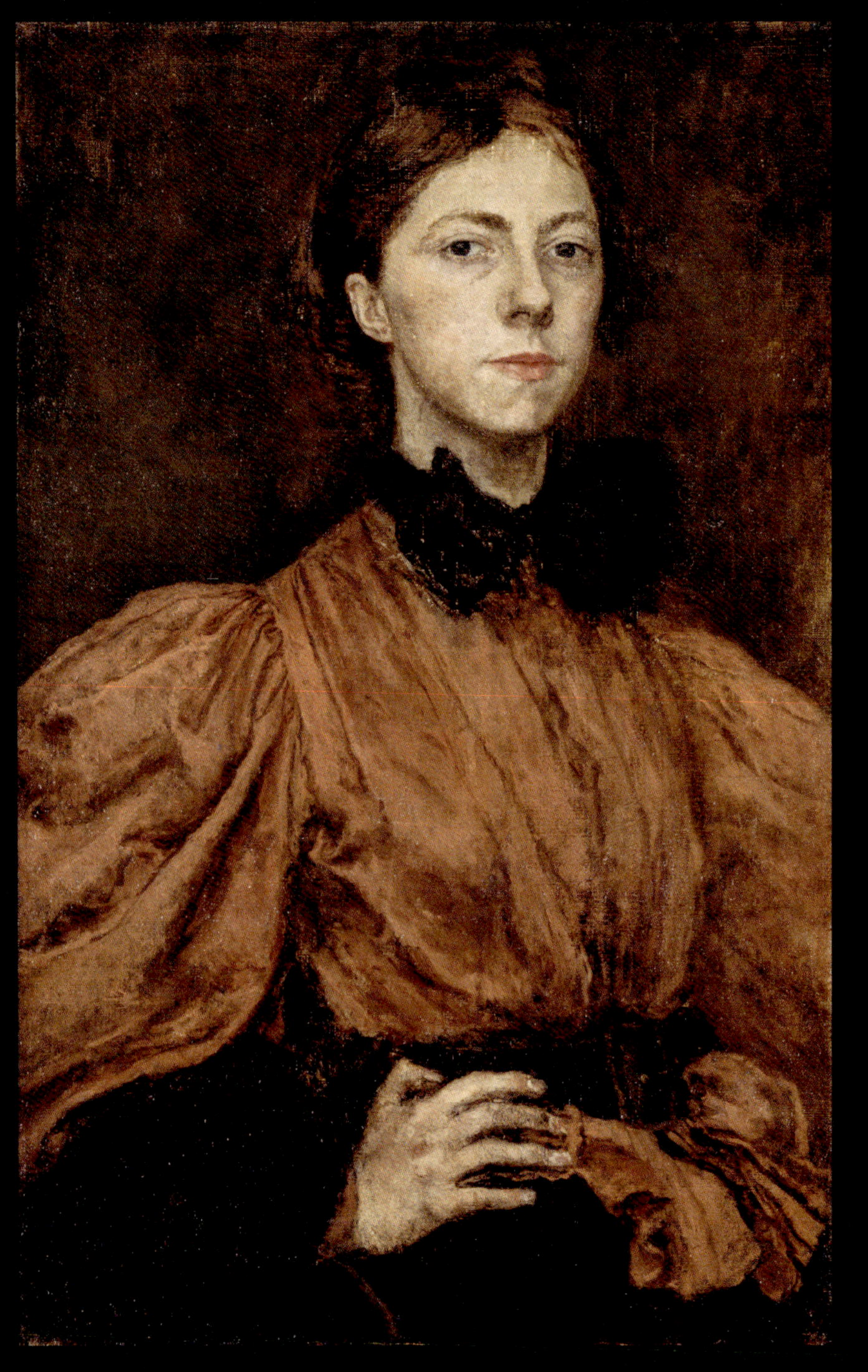

A star pupil

GWEN JOHN (1867–1939)

← *Self-portrait*, Gwen John, *c.*1900, oil on canvas, 61 x 37.8cm (National Portrait Gallery, London)

'I am quite in my work now & think of nothing else … Every day is the same. I like this life very much,' wrote Gwen John in a letter to the collector John Quinn in March 1922.

Welsh by birth, Gwen John made her first visit to Paris in 1898, at a time when it was the crucible of modern European painting. Her training at James Abbott McNeill Whistler's Académie Julian led directly to two of her great self-portraits (National Portrait Gallery and Tate), the latter acquired by her Slade School of Art tutor Professor Fred Brown. Women were given unprecedented access to the life room at the Slade, where Gwen John studied in 1895–8, winning two prizes – a certificate for figure drawing and, in her final year, the Melville Nettleship Prize for Figure Composition.

The portrait by Augustus John of his sister in a fashionable cape (page 168) illustrates how style-conscious she was. Augustus greatly admired his sister's work, predicting that, 'fifty years from now I shall be known as the brother of Gwen John'.

Gwen returned to Paris in the winter of 1903 and lived there and in nearby Meudon until her death in 1939. Her Parisian circle of women friends included several Slade-trained artists. She was influenced by the work of her contemporaries and kept notebooks in which she wrote about their works. Her paintings of interiors, sometimes empty or occupied by a lone female figure, can be seen as part of wider developments in contemporary art.

'At the moment I am doing some things which I see in the woods and the meadows and the roads around Meudon', John wrote in 1927. The gouache of Meudon (page 169), an area that she came to know well, illustrates her interest in landscape and townscape, and was a place she also painted at night, recalling the nocturnes of her early tutor, Whistler. AMS

↙ *Portrait of Gwen John*, Augustus John (1878–1961), late 1890s, ink and wash on paper, 29 x 20cm (mount), Mottisfont, Hampshire (NT 769753)
→ *View of House from Window*, Gwen John, 1920–30, gouache and pencil on paper, 29 x 20cm (mount), Mottisfont, Hampshire (NT 769752)

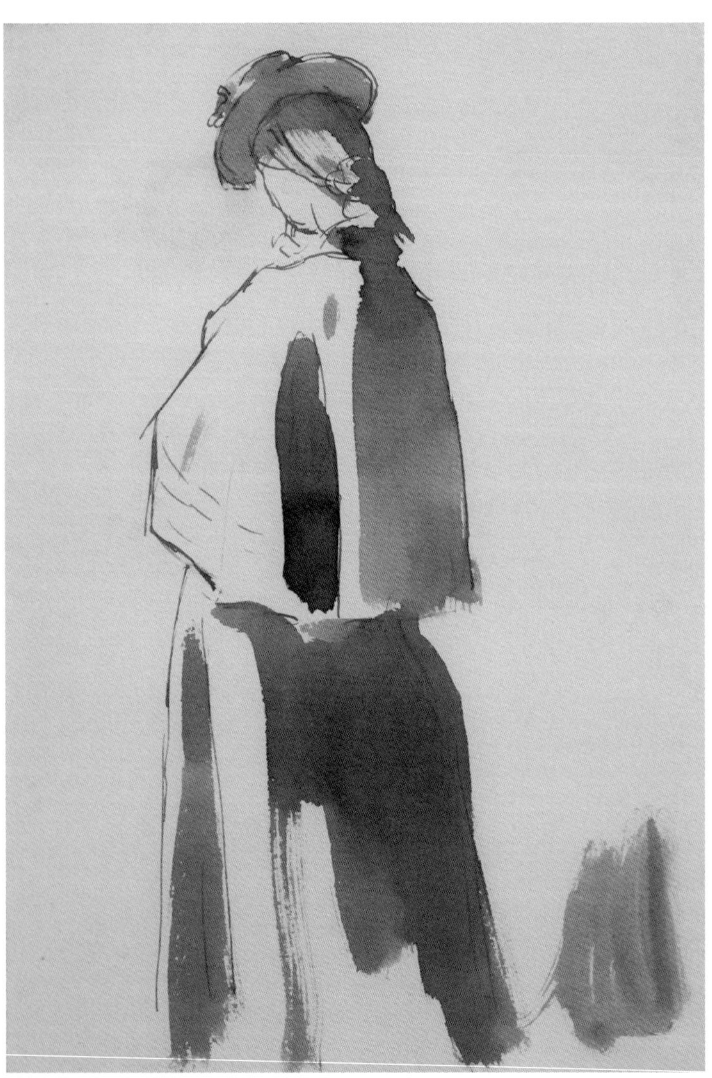

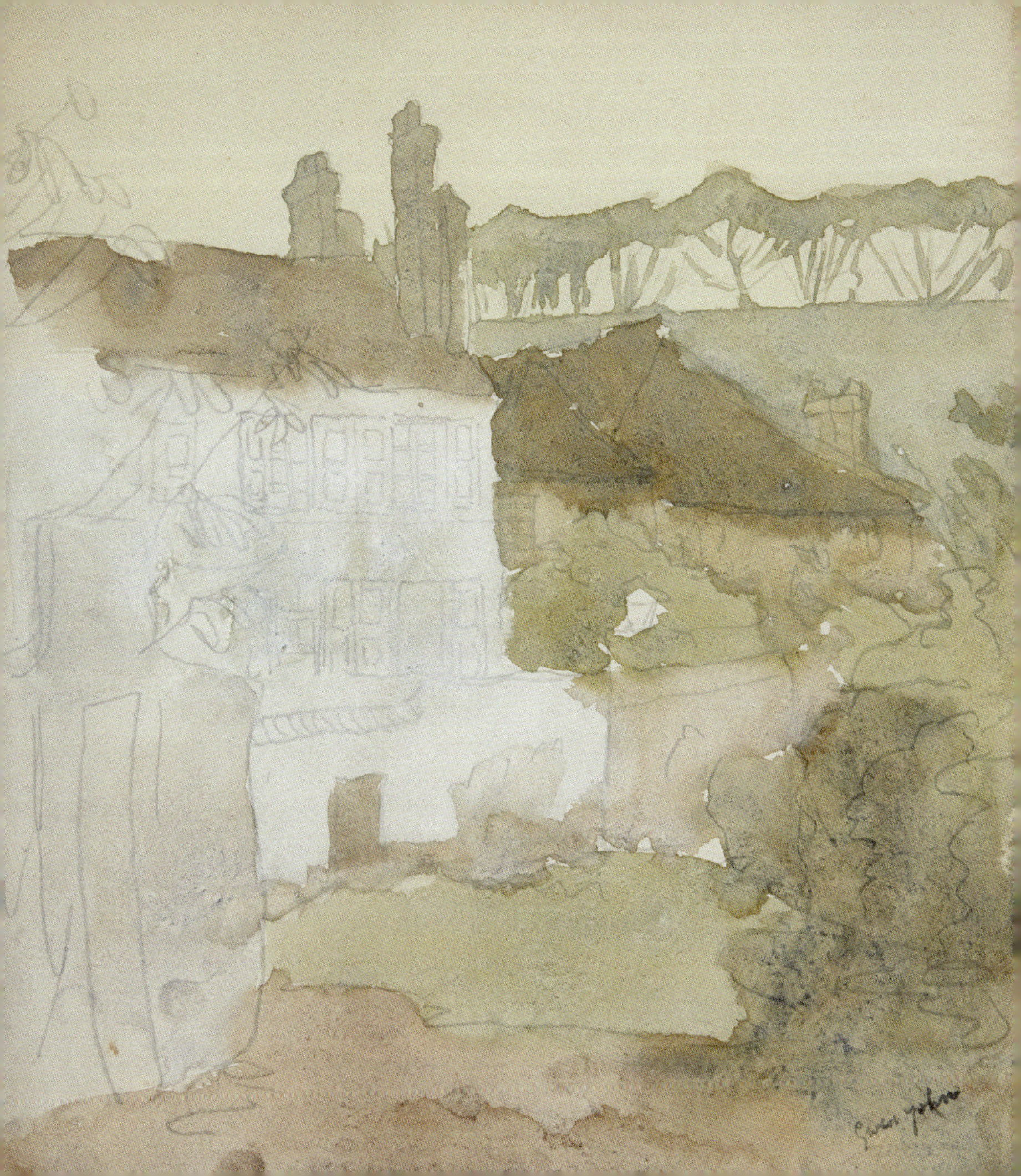
Gwen John

‘Strange and vivid individuality’

PAMELA COLMAN SMITH (1877–1951)

Pamela (Pixie) Colman Smith was an artist, illustrator and occultist. She is best known for her writings on Jamaican folklore and her illustrations for the Rider-Waite-Smith tarot deck, the most widely used in the world. Born in London, Colman Smith and her family lived in Manchester, Jamaica and Brooklyn. Aged 15, she enrolled at the Pratt Institute in New York, but her mother’s death and her own ill health meant that she left before completing her studies.

She returned to England and became part of the Lyceum Theatre company, working on costume and set designs. It was led by Ellen Terry (1847–1928), who gave Pixie her nickname, Henry Irving (1838–1905) and Bram Stoker (1847–1912). In 1901 she joined the Golden Dawn, a fashionable occult group, where she met the poet Arthur E. Waite, who commissioned her to illustrate a tarot deck. Its popularity was in a large part due to her designs. In 1904 she established the *Green Sheaf Press*, which mainly published work by women writers, including her own 1905 collection of Jamaican folk tales, *Chim-Chim Stories*. She also illustrated Terry’s book *The Russian Ballet* in 1913.

Colman Smith was described in a 1912 article as possessing a ‘strange and vivid individuality’. She was probably biracial and queer, and it has been argued that she humoured, or even embraced, the marginalised position in which others placed her. By frequently depicting herself in Japanese costume (page 2), she played into the speculation surrounding her cultural background.

Colman Smith experienced a form of synaesthesia that meant she could see music, and she created paintings of these visions. They captured the interest of influential avant-garde New York gallerist Alfred Stieglitz (1864–1946), who held several exhibitions of her work – the first by a non-photographer to be shown at his Photo-Secession Gallery.

The collection at Smallhythe Place, Kent, includes many works by Colman Smith, particularly hand-coloured prints made from her original drawings that feature Ellen Terry (opposite). There are also personal items, presumably given as gifts to Terry, including a hand-illustrated book of verse, *Ellen Peg’s Merry Book of Joys*, and other handmade objects, such as this joyful mermaid doll (right). RC

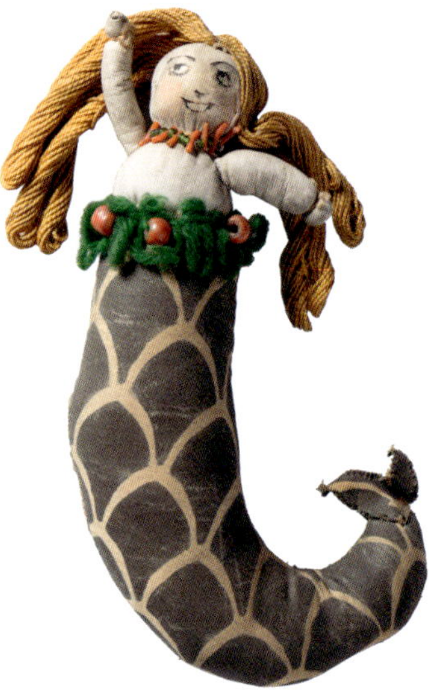

↑ Mermaid doll made by Pamela Colman Smith, *c.*1900, textile, 22 x 13.5 x 4.5cm, Smallhythe Place, Kent (NT 1119033)

→ *Dame Ellen Terry as Mistress Page in the Merry Wives of Windsor*, Pamela Colman Smith, 1902, hand-coloured print, 31.5 x 24cm, Smallhythe Place, Kent (NT 1118414)

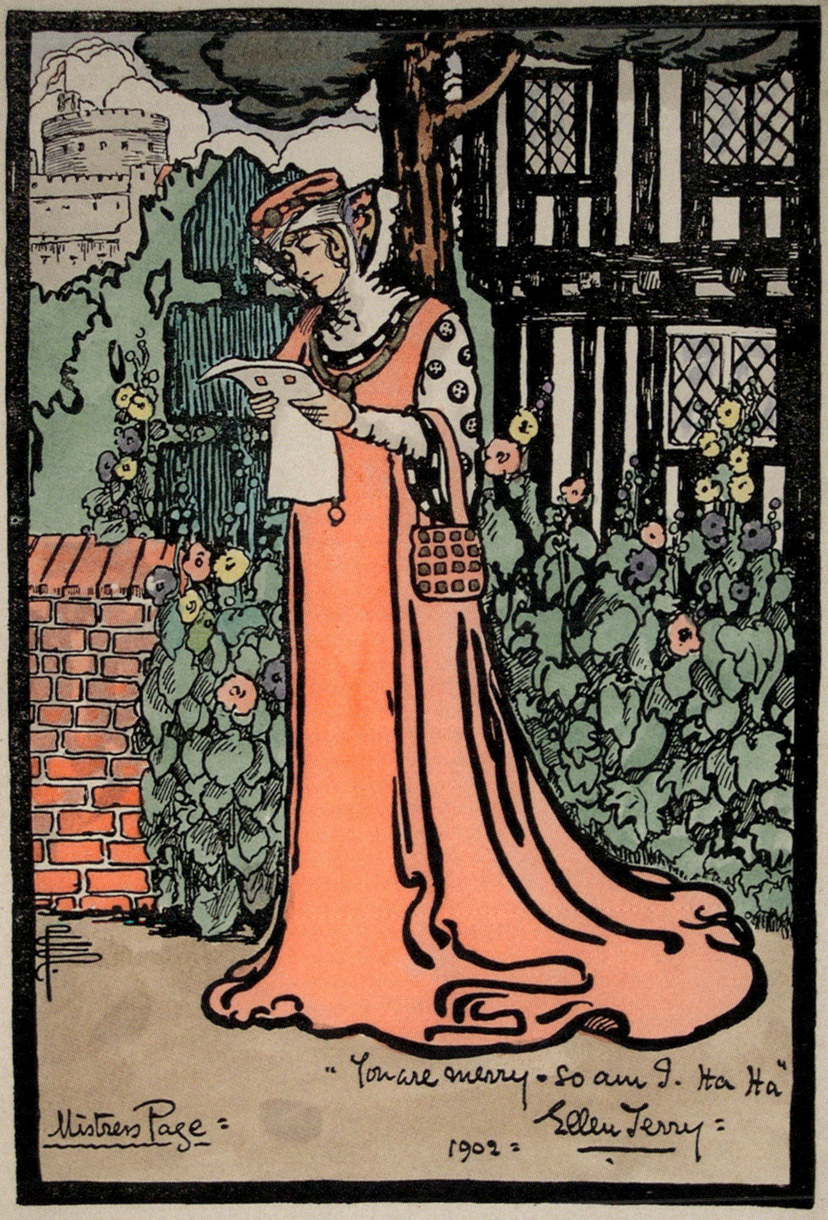
"You are merry - so am I. Ha Ha"
Mistress Page =
1902 =
Ellen Terry =

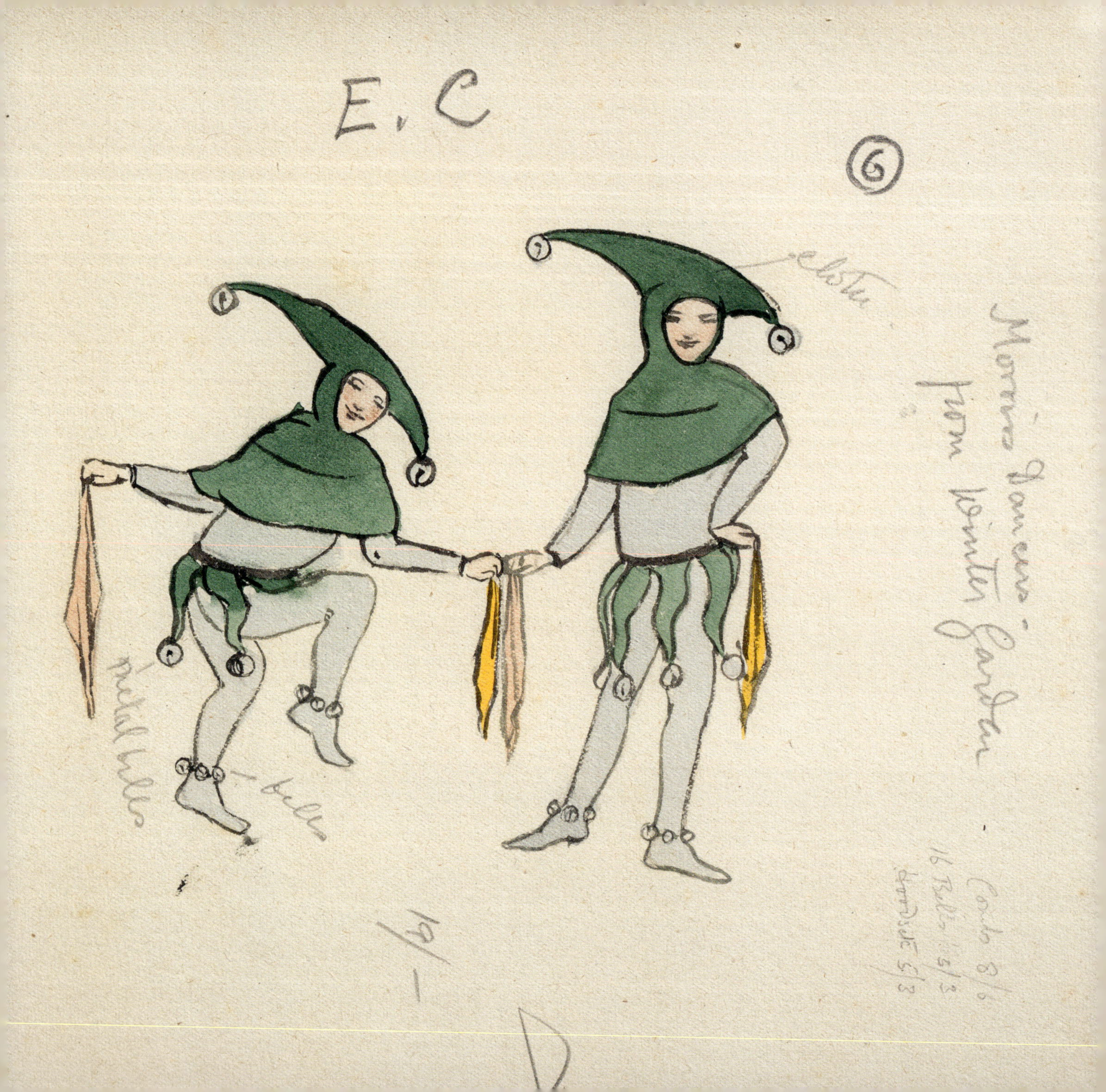

E. C

⑥

Morris dancers - from Winter Garden

elastic

bells

Cards 8/6
16 Bells 5/3

19/-

A life on the stage

EDITH CRAIG (1869–1947)

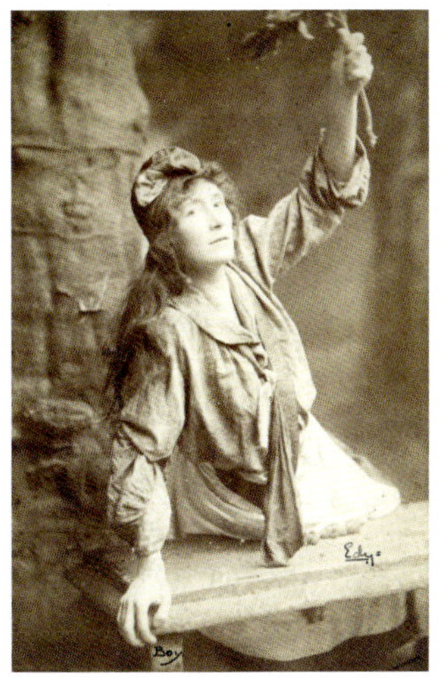

← Designs for costumes for morris dancers from the Middlesbrough Winter Garden, for the Mount Grace pageant, Edith Craig, *c.*1925–7, Smallhythe Place, Kent (NT 1124050)
↑ Edith Craig in Henry Irving's 1899 production of *Robespierre*, for which she also designed the costumes, Smallhythe Place, Kent (NT 1122771)

As the daughter of one of the most famous and celebrated actresses in the world, Edith (Edy) Craig was surely destined for a life on (or behind) the stage.

Craig was a theatre director, producer, costume designer and actor who defied many conventions. She designed costumes for and performed with the Lyceum Theatre company, including on its tours to the USA in 1895 and 1907. In 1899 she was commissioned by Henry Irving to design the costumes for his production of *Robespierre*. Inspired by this experience – and with the financial support of her mother, the actress Ellen Terry (1847–1928) – Craig established her own theatrical costume atelier, Edith Craig & Co., in Covent Garden. From 1902 to 1903 she collaborated with her friend Pamela Colman Smith (page 170) to design sets for plays by William Butler Yeats and John Millington Synge at the Imperial Theatre in London.

Craig was active in the women's suffrage movement and worked for the Actresses' Franchise League, which campaigned for the right to vote by staging propaganda plays and selling suffrage literature. Craig directed and starred as Rosa Bonheur in *A Pageant of Great Women*, a pro-suffrage play written by Cicely Hamilton (1872–1952). In 1911 she founded the Pioneer Players, which became internationally respected for its promotion of the work of women in the theatre. Craig later directed plays for the Everyman Theatre in London and was appointed art director at Leeds Art Theatre. She also gained a national reputation for her pageant productions, including at Mount Grace Priory in North Yorkshire (1927) and the Jubilee Pageant at Tenterden (1935), close to her home in Kent.

Craig lived in a long-term polyamorous relationship with the writer Christopher Marie St John (1871–1960) and the artist Clare (Tony) Atwood (1866–1962). After her mother died in 1928, she converted a barn in the grounds of her idyllic Kent home, Smallhythe Place, into a theatre and directed memorial performances on the anniversary of Terry's death. RC

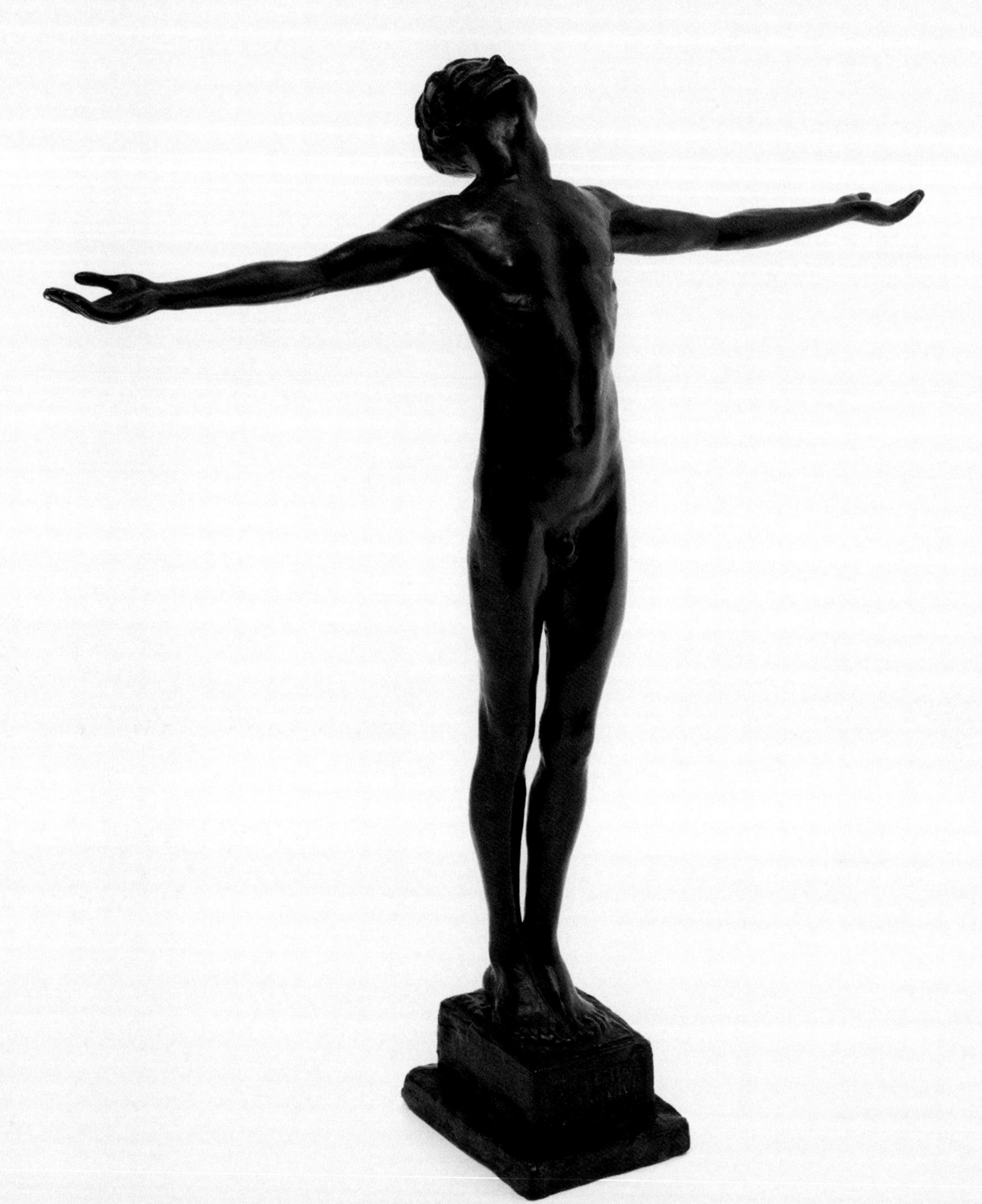

‘An artist first’

KATHLEEN SCOTT (1878–1947)

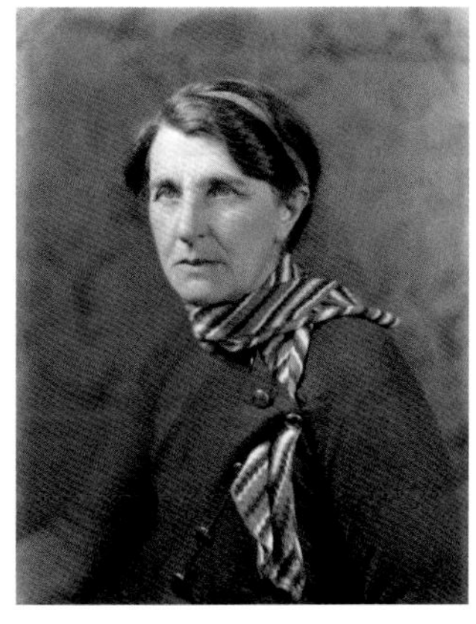

← *These had most to give*, Kathleen Scott, 1922–3, bronze, 45.4 x 39.8cm, signed and inscribed: ‘THESE HAD / MOST TO GIVE / 1914–1918’, Anglesey Abbey, Cambridgeshire (NT 515080)
↑ Kathleen Scott photographed by Bassano Ltd in 1934 (National Portrait Gallery, London)

In 1934 Kathleen Scott was described as ‘one of the greatest woman sculptors of her time’. Three years later, as part of its ‘World of Women’ series, the BBC dedicated its first-ever television programme on sculpture to her.

The creator of 220 recorded works, Scott was as prolific as she was prominent – famed and framed, if not typecast, as the stoic widow of the Antarctic explorer Robert Falcon Scott (1868–1912).

Born Kathleen Bruce, she trained at the Slade School of Art (1900–2) before moving to Paris. Her diaries recount six exciting years in the city. She lived with the designer Eileen Gray and knew Auguste Rodin. Back in London, Scott’s sculpted portraits of friends in the public eye built her name and reputation.

Periodically, Scott paused sculpture in favour of humanitarian work. She went to Macedonia on a child-relief mission and during the First World War assisted the ambulance service and made electric coils for a machine-gun factory. In the aftermath of war, she was a modeller for a pioneering facial reconstruction and plastic-surgery unit. ‘These men without noses are very beautiful’, she observed in her diary, ‘like antique marbles’.

These had most to give (opposite) was one of her best works. Conceived as a war memorial – the ‘outstretched hands and the upturned head’ were, she said, ‘expressive of sacrifice’ and the war’s ‘holocaust of youth’. The final, large-scale statue was erected in a new context, as a monument to those killed on the British Antarctic Expedition of 1911–12 (Scott Polar Research Institute, Cambridge).

Kathleen Scott did not readily accept the label ‘woman sculptor’ – ‘I don’t believe in them’, she once wrote. Reflecting on what it meant to be a sculptor (of any gender), she counselled: ‘There is much climbing about on ladders and scaffolds, with heavy weights to lift and mallets to swing.’ But for the willing, the reward is ‘the most grateful, generous, and abundant of professions’. ARW

The art of ceramics

LOUISE POWELL (1882–1956)

Ada Louise Powell was a talented painter, calligrapher and embroiderer. She is best known for the intricate, hand-painted ceramics she produced as an independent artist working with pottery manufacturer Josiah Wedgwood & Sons.

Powell was from a creative family and ceramics were in her blood. Her grandfather Emile Lessore (1805–76) trained at the Sèvres porcelain manufactory in France, before moving to England and joining Minton, later becoming a design consultant for Wedgwood. Her father, Jules, and her sister Elaine Thérèse also painted Wedgwood ceramics.

Powell trained in calligraphy and illumination at the Central School of Arts and Crafts in London. An important early commission was the remarkable work she undertook to complete an unfinished illuminated manuscript translation of Virgil's *Aeneid* by William Morris (1834–96). The expression, line control, rich level of detail and use of jewel-like colour that she learned through her training translated beautifully into ceramic painting.

Following her marriage to Alfred Powell (1865–1960), Louise began to focus on ceramics. From their studio in Red Lion Square, London, the Powells designed and decorated Wedgwood blanks (undecorated pots), which were sent back to the company factory in Etruria, Stoke-on-Trent, to be fired and sold, often through the London retailer and glassmakers James Powell & Sons.

The Powells regularly visited Wedgwood, where they studied the historic pattern books and trained the factory's decorators in hand-painting on earthenware (at the time, ceramics were decorated mostly by printing). The Powells' relationship with Wedgwood lasted for 40 years and their work firmly re-established the company's reputation for artistry and traditional craftsmanship. Many of the artists they nurtured, such as Millicent Taplin and Star Wedgwood, went on to enjoy long and distinguished careers in the Potteries.

The Powells were good friends with George Bernard Shaw and his wife, Charlotte; a personalised lustre-decorated beaker in the collection at Shaw's Corner (opposite) must have been created by Louise as a personal commission or gift. A photograph of Shaw's desk shows the beaker behind his inkstand, filled with pens and pencils. Charlotte also owned a washstand painted by Louise Powell. RC

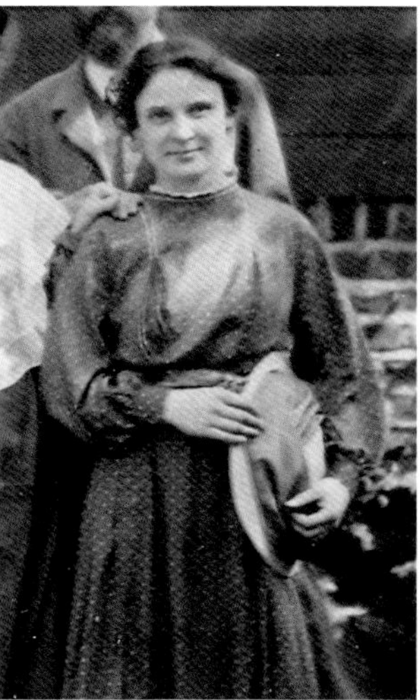

↑ Photograph (detail) of Louise Powell around 1907 (V&A Wedgwood Collection Archives, Stoke-on-Trent)
→ Beaker hand-painted in 1925 by Louise Powell for George Bernard Shaw, earthenware decorated with coloured glazes, lustre and enamels, 9.2 (height) x 7cm (diameter), Shaw's Corner, Hertfordshire (NT 1274575)

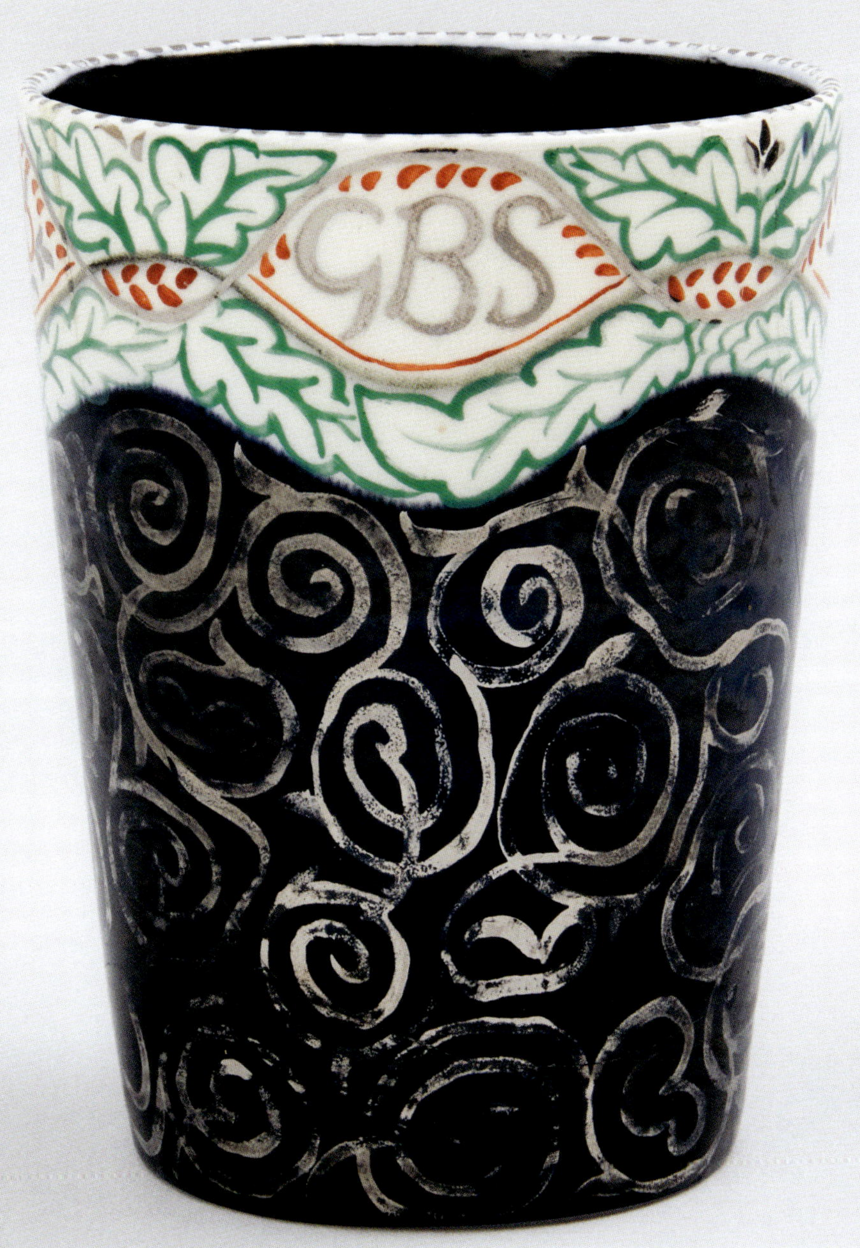
GBS

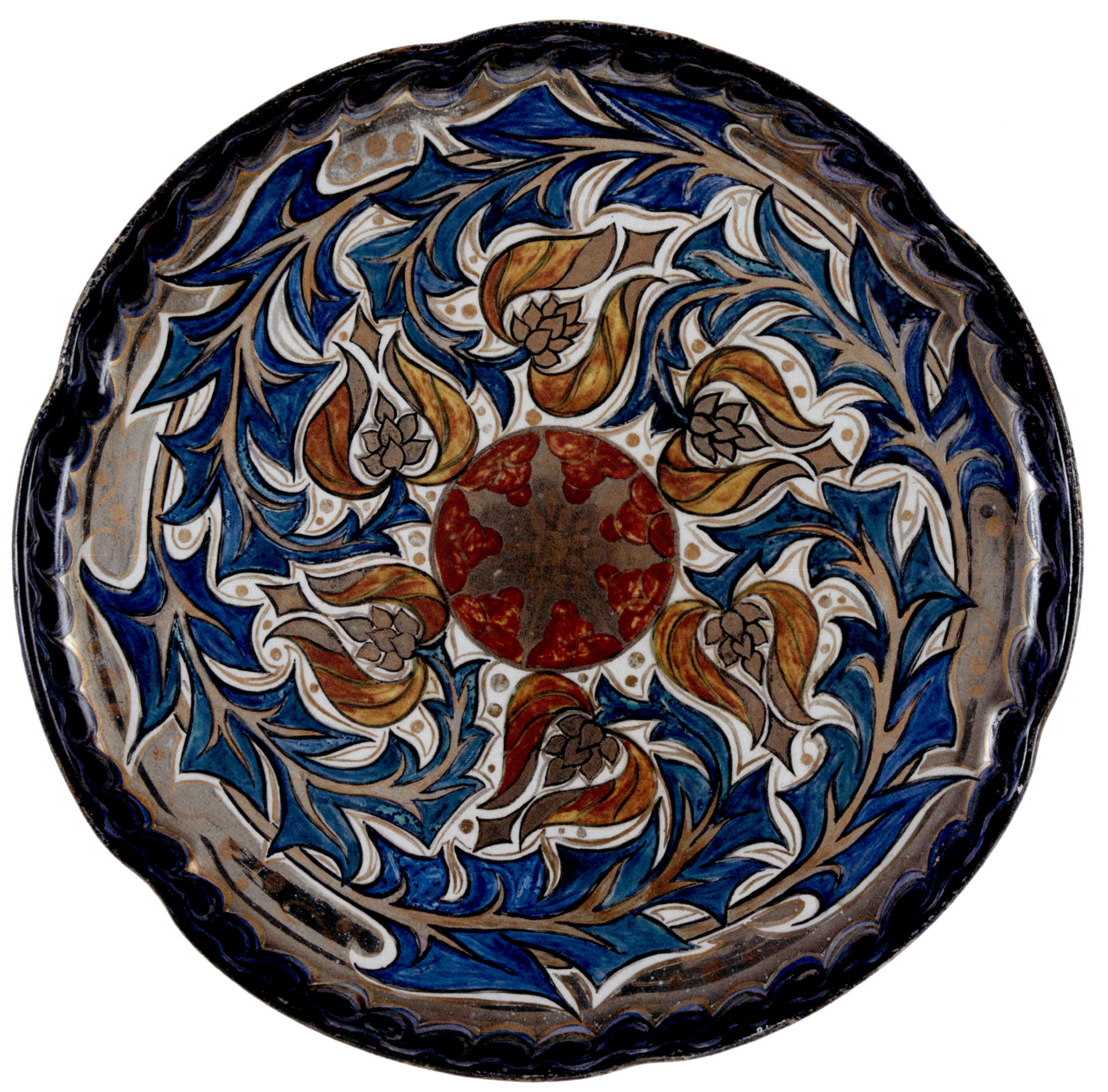

‘Artistic without doubt’

AMY KOTZÉ (1884–1976)

Amy Kotzé was a remarkably creative and enterprising woman. Her political and social beliefs were interwoven with her professional life as a dressmaker, artist, designer, decorator and businesswoman. Despite her prolific creativity, very few objects can be definitively attributed to her today; a wonderful dish at Nuffield Place in Oxfordshire (opposite), marked on the underside with her initials, is a rare exception.

Kotzé was born in South Africa and moved to London as a child. She began her working life at Liberty & Co. around 1907, designing and producing embroidery. Kotzé made herself a loose-fitting dress inspired by Liberty’s artistic clothing that attracted such admiration from friends that she soon realised she had a potential business venture on her hands. In 1908 she started advertising her own artistic dressmaking business, aimed at professional women, in the suffragette newspaper *Votes for Women*. She is shown proudly wearing her ‘Worker’s Dress’ in its first advertisement.

Kotzé was a member of the Conservative and Unionist Women’s Franchise Association, a suffrage organisation established in 1903 that was open to members of the Conservative and Unionist Party, which supported limited rather than universal suffrage to ‘duly qualified’ women. Kotzé offered embroidered embellishments in the colours of the cause – purple, green and white. She is said to have been commissioned to make a dress for Emmeline Pankhurst (1858–1928) to match a necklace bought for her by members of the Women’s Social and Political Union to mark her release from prison. Kotzé also sold garments to fundraise for the Women’s Social and Political Union at its 1909 Women’s Exhibition, and donated millinery to the 1913 Suffrage Summer Festival in South Kensington.

Kotzé was taught ceramic painting and metalworking by John Pearson (1859–1930). She also worked with feathers and in leather, making shoes and decorative objects, and as an interior decorator.

← Earthenware dish with lustre decoration by Amy Kotzé, 1923, 36cm (diameter), Nuffield Place, Oxfordshire (NT 1652555)

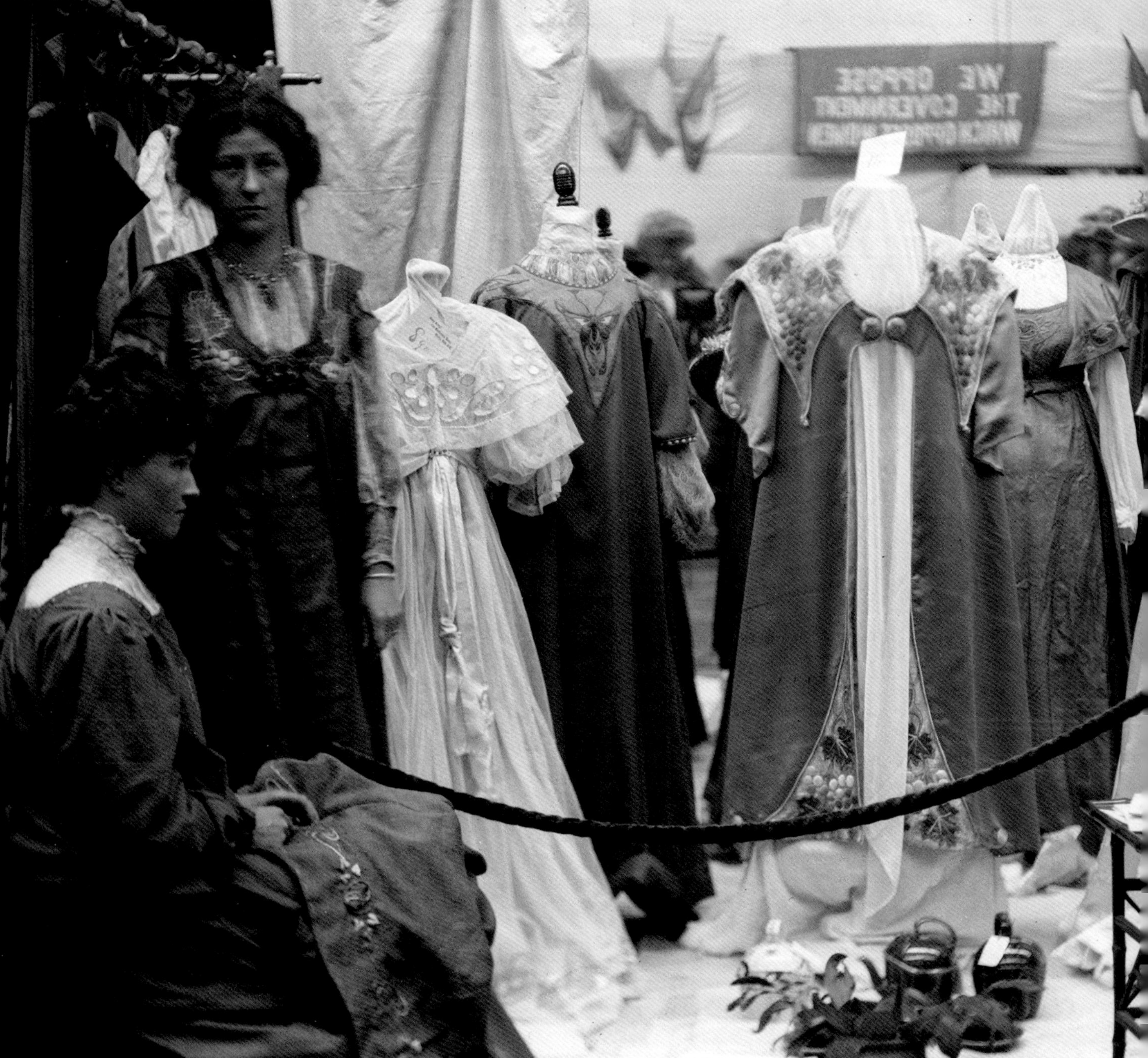
WE OPPOSE
THE GOVERNMENT

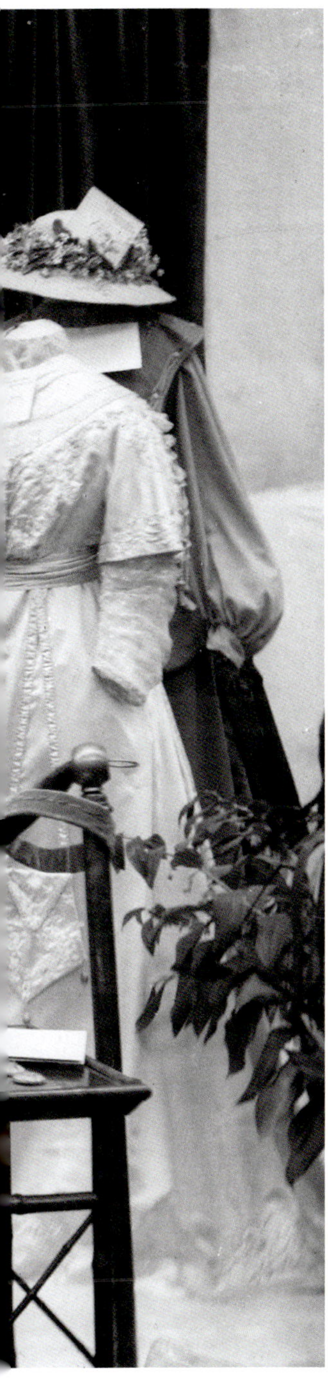

← Photograph of Amy and Louie Kotzé on Amy's dress stall at The Women's Exhibition, Knightsbridge, taken by Christina Broom (1862–1939) in 1909. Broom and her tripod camera can be seen reflected in the mirror at the back of the stall. (Museum of London)

→ Day dress in the style of Amy Kotzé, *c.*1908, napped wool flannel with hand embroidery, 140cm (length), Killerton, Devon (NT 1363253)

She established her Little Gallery, with a dressmaking workshop above, at Great Marlborough Street in London, where she also exhibited the work of artists including sculptor Henri Gaudier-Brzeska (1891–1915) and furniture-maker Arthur Romney Green (1872–1945). A 1914 review of an exhibition at the gallery describes Kotzé's garments as 'artistic without doubt', also noting the 'hand-wrought pottery, silver, and hand-woven materials of all kinds' on display. From 1923 Kotzé and her sister Louie (1873–1975) ran The Joy Shop on Avery Row, Mayfair, selling hand-crafted work and antiques.

One of Kotzé's most ambitious projects was a commission in 1932 to decorate the town centre of Stratford-upon-Avon with festoons of waxed-paper flowers to celebrate the opening of the Shakespeare Memorial Theatre. RC

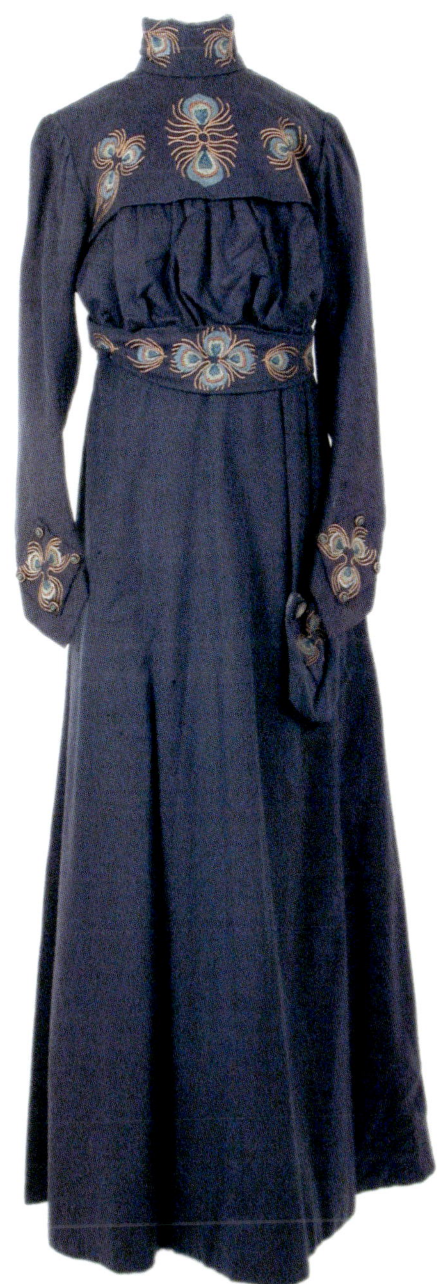

Stories and 'side-shows'

BEATRIX POTTER (1866–1943)

Beatrix Potter is one of the world's most loved children's authors and illustrators. She collaborated with many manufacturers to create merchandise for the characters brought to life in her 'Little Books'. Working with her publisher, Frederick Warne & Co., Potter's product lines (or 'side-shows', as she called them) ranged from board games and wallpaper, to figurines and handkerchiefs.

Letters between Warne and Potter indicate that she was closely involved in the development of her merchandise and was protective of her intellectual property. She expected her product lines to be of the highest quality, but also to reflect the spirit of her original creations.

In 1922 the Stoke-on-Trent manufacturer Grimwades Ltd began to produce children's tea-sets decorated with her characters, including Peter Rabbit, Squirrel Nutkin and Tom Kitten. It was not an easy relationship. The agreement had originally been signed in 1917, but labour and material shortages caused by the

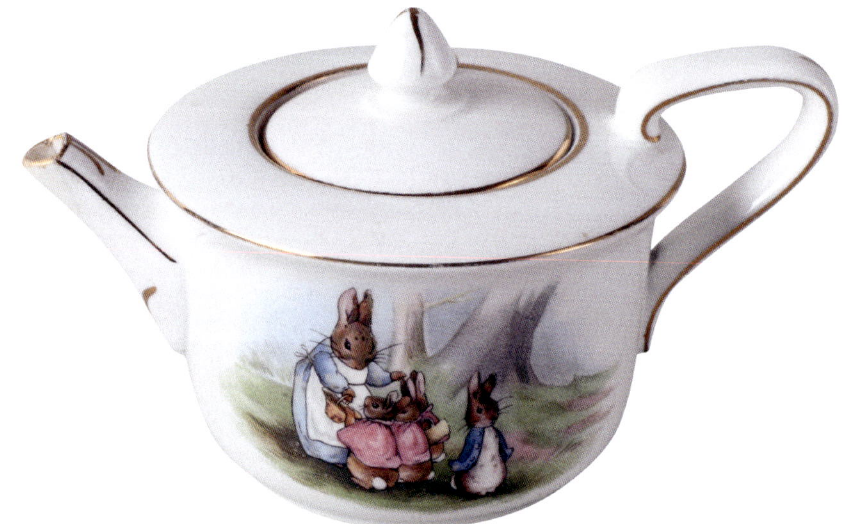

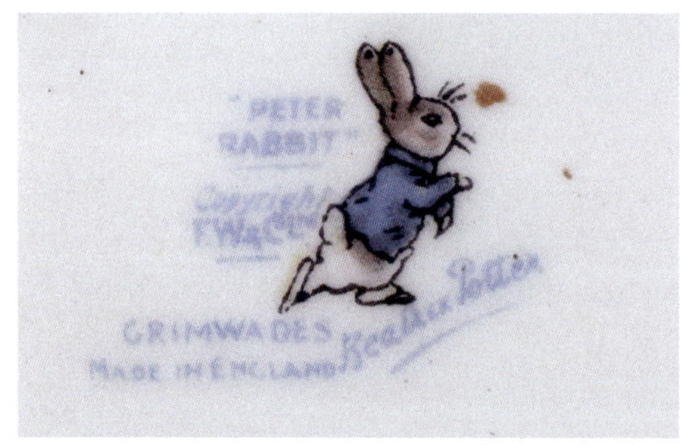

↑ Teapot produced by Grimwades Ltd of Stoke-on-Trent, 1922–4, bone china with lithographic transfer, 9 x 11.5 x 15.5cm, Hill Top, Cumbria (NT 641501)
← Detail of the factory mark on the teapot, showing Potter's signature
→ Beatrix Potter photographed in 1913 by Charles G.Y. King, Hill Top, Cumbria (NT 242332) (detail)

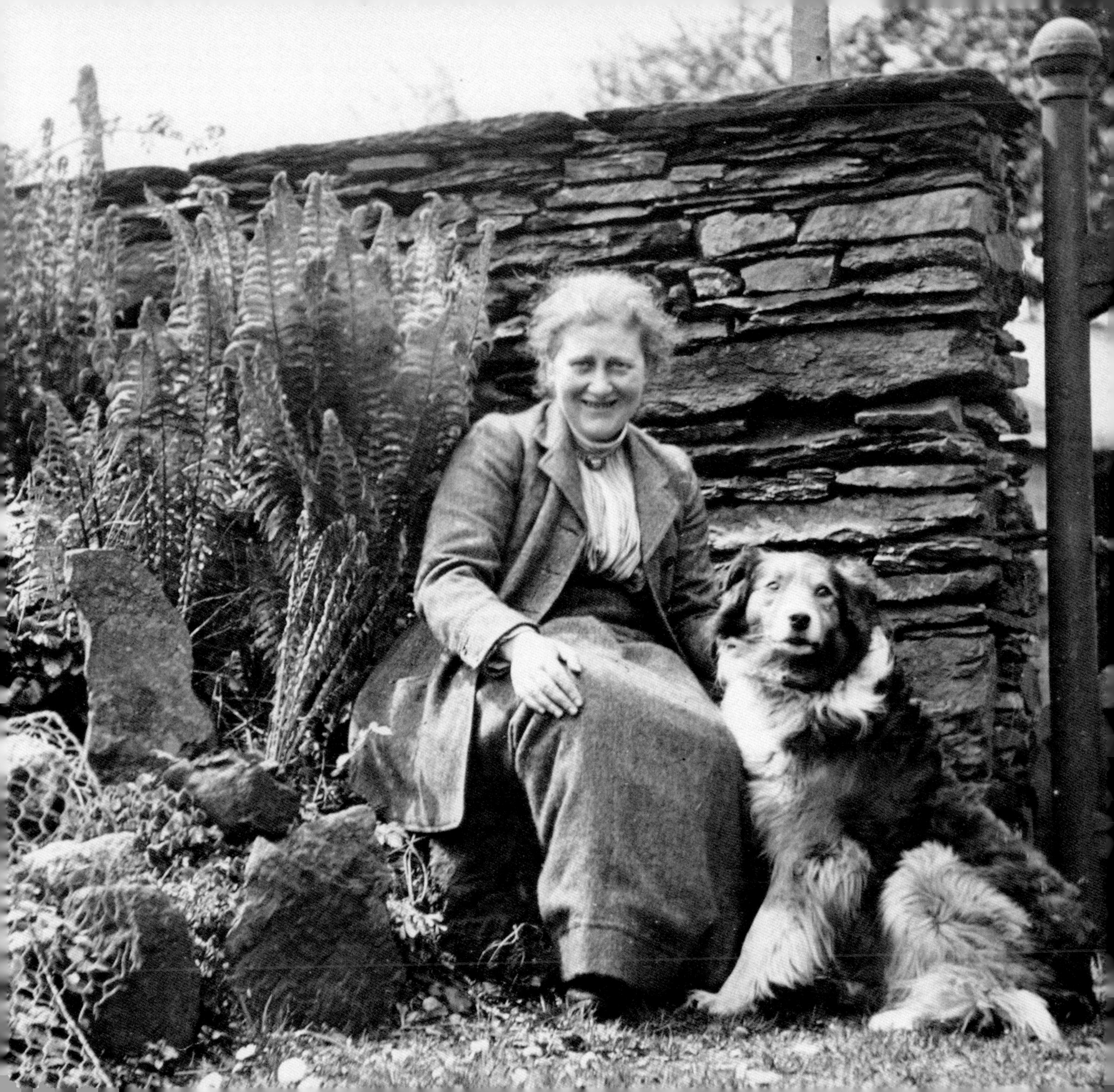

→ 'Peter Rabbit's Race Game', one of a wide variety of product lines or 'side-shows' that Potter developed with her publisher, Frederick Warne & Co., Beatrix Potter Gallery, Cumbria (NT 641987)

First World War resulted in long delays. Potter was frustrated, particularly given the constant threat of unofficial merchandise entering the market. In 1921 she wrote to Warne, 'It is provoking that Grimwade [sic] does not get out the authorised tea service and stop the gap. There is no doubt the ware would sell.' While she was broadly happy with the quality of the pieces, sales were initially disappointing, partly as Grimwades' representatives had been unable to get the stock into china shops, leaving Warne to sell the majority of sets through its own trade contacts.

The prominent mark incorporating Potter's full signature (page 182) is a little unusual for the 1920s, when designers were not usually named by ceramic manufacturers. However, this period saw an increasing number of women ceramic designers recognised clearly for the first time, with marks bearing their full names appearing on the underside of pieces. RC

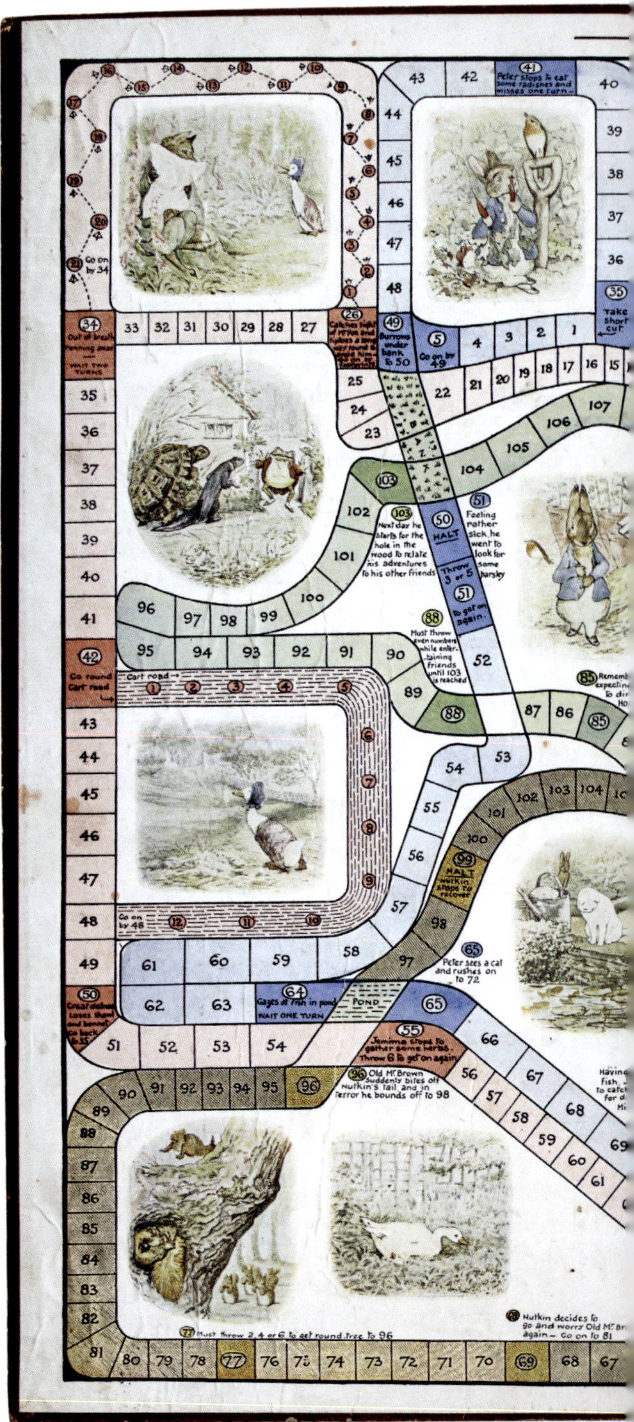

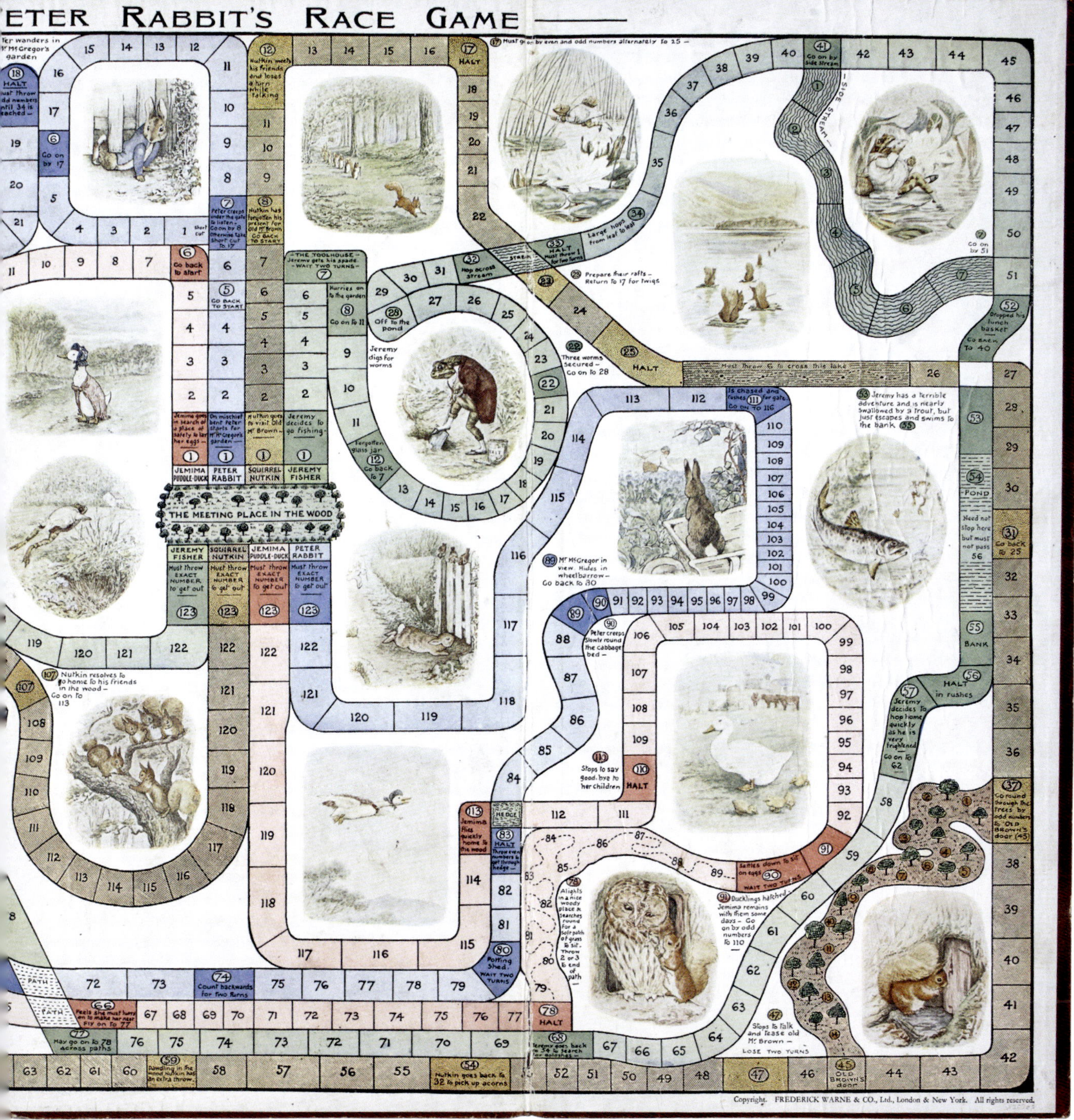

ETER RABBIT'S RACE GAME
Must go by even and odd numbers alternately to 25 –
Nutkin meets his friends and loses a turn while talking
Go on by 17
HALT
Peter creeps under the gate to listen – Go on by 8 otherwise take short cut to 17
Short cut
Nutkin has forgotten his present for Old Mr Brown. Go back to start
Go back to start
Go back to start
THE TOOLHOUSE – Jeremy gets his spade – WAIT TWO TURNS –
Hurries on to the garden
Go on to 11
Off to the pond
Hop across stream
Jeremy digs for worms
Forgotten glass jar Go back to 7
Large hops from leaf to leaf
STREAM
HALT must throw 1 for two turns
Prepare their rafts – Return to 17 for twigs
Three worms secured – Go on to 28
HALT
Must throw 6 to cross the lake
Go on by side stream
SIDE STREAM
Go on by 51
Dropped his lunch basket Go back to 40
Is chased and rushes for gate. Go on to 116
Jeremy has a terrible adventure and is nearly swallowed by a trout, but just escapes and swims to the bank
Jemima goes in search of a place of safety to lay her eggs –
On mischief bent Peter starts for Mr McGregor's garden –
Nutkin goes to visit Old Mr Brown –
Jeremy decides to go fishing –
JEMIMA PUDDLE-DUCK
PETER RABBIT
SQUIRREL NUTKIN
JEREMY FISHER
THE MEETING PLACE IN THE WOOD
JEREMY FISHER
SQUIRREL NUTKIN
JEMIMA PUDDLE-DUCK
PETER RABBIT
Must throw EXACT NUMBER to get out
Must throw EXACT NUMBER to get out
Must throw EXACT NUMBER to get out
Must throw EXACT NUMBER to get out
POND
Need not stop here but must not pass 56
Go back to 25
BANK
HALT in rushes
Jeremy decides to hop home quickly as he is very frightened Go on to 62
Mr McGregor in view. Hides in wheelbarrow – Go back to 80
Peter creeps slowly round the cabbage bed –
Nutkin resolves to go home to his friends in the wood – Go on to 113
Stops to say good-bye to her children
HALT
HEDGE
Jemima flies quickly home to the wood
HALT Throw even numbers to get through hedge –
Alights in a nice woody place & searches round for a soft path of grass & sits. Throw 2 or 3 to end of path
Settles down to sit on eggs
WAIT TWO TURNS
Ducklings hatched – Jemima remains with them some days – Go on by odd numbers to 110
Go round through the trees by odd numbers to "OLD BROWN'S door (45)
Potting Shed. WAIT TWO TURNS
Count backwards for two turns
PATH
PATH
Feels she must hurry on to make her nest Fly on to 77
HALT
May go on to 78 across paths
Dawdling in the wood Nutkin has an extra throw.
Nutkin goes back to 32 to pick up acorns
Stops to talk and tease old Mr Brown – LOSE TWO TURNS
OLD BROWN'S door

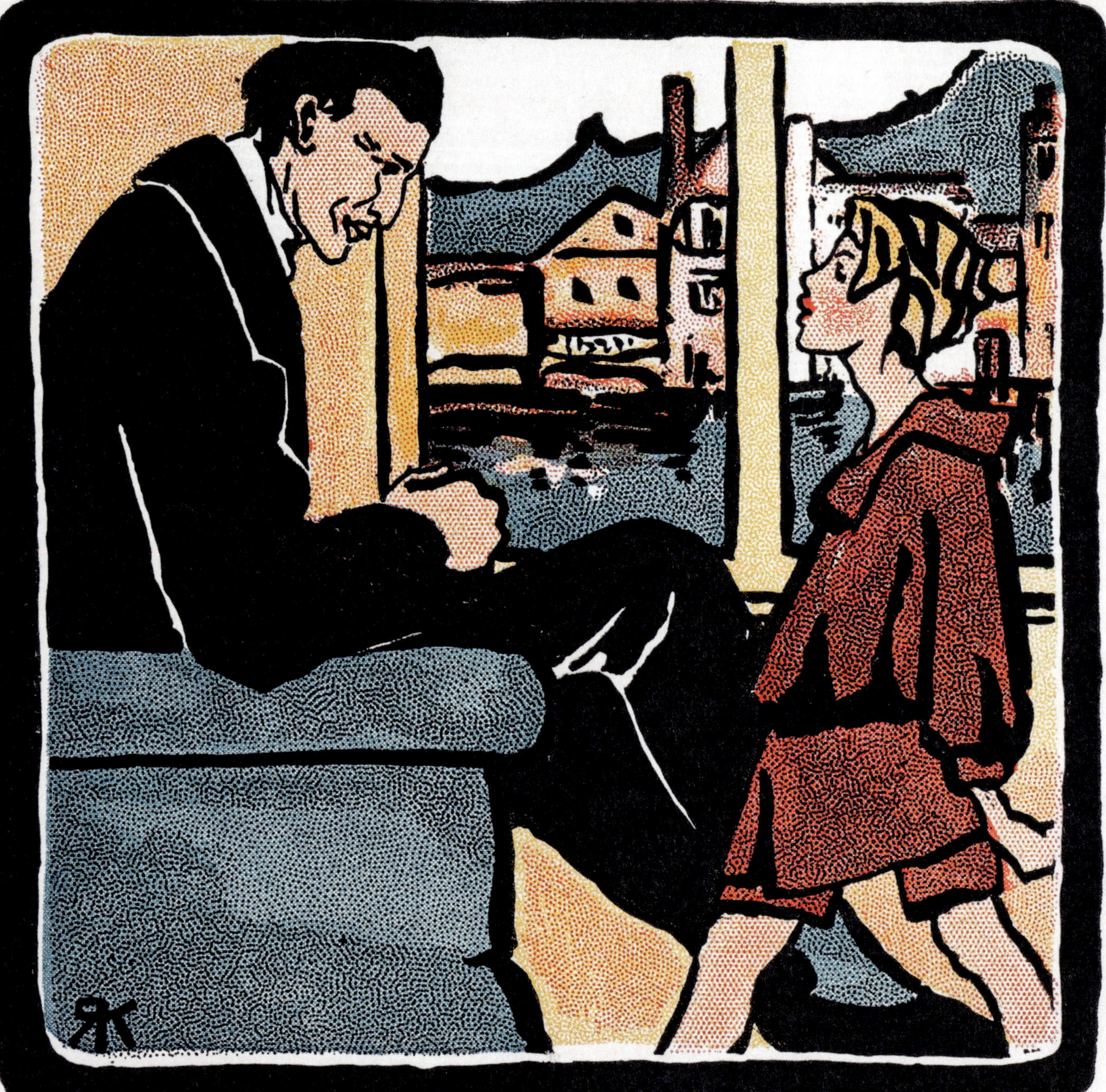

A creative life

RUTH PENNYMAN (1893–1983)

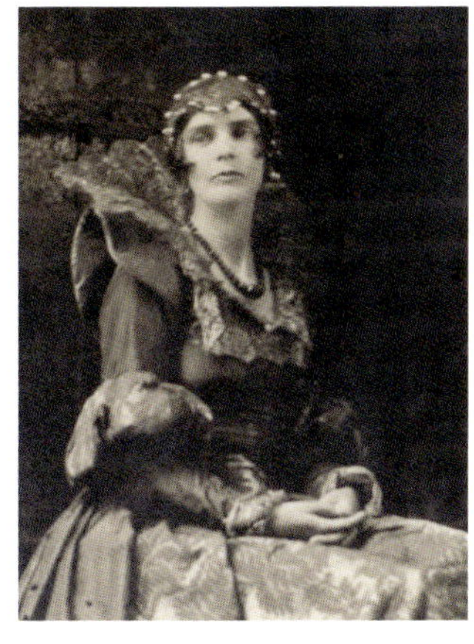

← Illustrated page by Ruth Pennyman from *The Binks Book*, 1921, The Chelsea Publishing Company, from a copy presented in 1925 to Jim Pennyman, whom Ruth married the following year, 19 x 25cm, Ormesby, Hall, North Yorkshire (NT 3224839)
↑ Photograph (detail) of Ruth Pennyman in theatre costume, *c.*1920, unknown photographer, Ormesby Hall, North Yorkshire (NT 710163)

Ruth Pennyman (née Knight) is still remembered in Teesside for her socialism and work in regional theatre. However, despite the many designs she created for her dramatic productions, including backdrops, costumes and publicity posters, her visual artwork and designs (examples of which are at Ormesby Hall, North Yorkshire) have been largely forgotten.

At a time when half the students at art college were women, Pennyman entered St John's Wood Art School in 1914. Her studies were interrupted by her time as a nurse during the First World War and were not completed until 1921. Living in Chelsea, she met many other artists and found work illustrating books for The Chelsea Publishing Company.

She provided illustrations for nursery rhymes and children's books, including her own story *The Binks Book*, which recounts the adventures of a boy called Binks, who lives with his artist father in Chelsea. Many of Pennyman's early drawings suggest that she was influenced by illustrators such as Walter Crane and the Arts and Crafts movement's fascination with medieval art, but comparisons can also be made with contemporary groups of artists in the 1920s, such as those in Bloomsbury and Camden.

By the time Ruth married James Beaumont Worsley Pennyman (1883–1961) in 1926, she seems to have stopped working as an illustrator. The owner of The Chelsea Publishing Company, Edith Place, visited Ormesby Hall only once, in 1927 – perhaps to encourage Pennyman to continue providing illustrations for her, but it was not to be. Pennyman continued to sketch privately and as part of the Cleveland Sketching Club for most of her life, but does not seem to have sold any work after this. Her influence can be seen in the establishment of Boosbeck Industries, a furniture business the Pennymans set up to alleviate the suffering of out-of-work miners in Cleveland in the 1930s. JW

Through her own lens

MARGARET HARDMAN (1909–70)

The photographic accomplishments of Margaret Hardman (née Mills) are increasingly appreciated, as are her energy and acumen in running a busy photographic business – the Burrell and Hardman studio in Liverpool.

Ethel Margaret Mills's ambitions in the field of photography started at school, where she was recommended to the photographer Edward Chambré Hardman (1898–1988), becoming his studio assistant in 1926. She quickly bolstered her technical and creative skills before moving to Paisley, Scotland, in 1929 to join John Douglas Ritchie's photographic studio, where a portrait of her standing next to a large plate camera (page 162) was taken. Her employee reference from Chambré described her in glowing terms as 'energetic, most intelligent and versatile', and remarked that 'we are very sorry to lose her'.

Margaret's relationship with Chambré blossomed despite the distance; united in their mutual passion for photography, they married in 1932. As the vivacious driving force behind their studio's operations, Margaret attentively engaged their clients and mainly female staff. One former employee later likened her to 'a flamenco dancer ... her temperament as fiery and flamboyant'. Margaret's astute, perfectionist eye pored over each stage of production, from the darkroom to retouching, and was directed with equal rigour at her own photography.

Miss Joan Sealby, later Mrs Doyle, worked for the Hardmans for seven years, developing negatives and sometimes printing. She turned model for this evocative post-war portrait by Margaret (opposite), which typifies her use of bold angles and composition to create a sense of drama.

Margaret's impressive rural and urban landscape photographs, in which she often focused on light and shadow, were cited by her husband, Chambré, as highly influential on his own pursuit of the genre. He frequently acknowledged Margaret's quiet observations, such as the shadow spilling over the doorstep of a building in Llandeilo, Carmarthenshire (page 190), or her 'cleverly seen' capture of the skating rink at a Swiss monastery (page 191), composed using a Voigtländer camera. Margaret submitted several of her prints to competitions, and exhibited in the UK and USA. AS

→ *No Bird Sang*, Margaret Hardman, 1948, gelatin silver print, 29 x 34cm (print), The Hardmans' House, Liverpool (NT 974232)

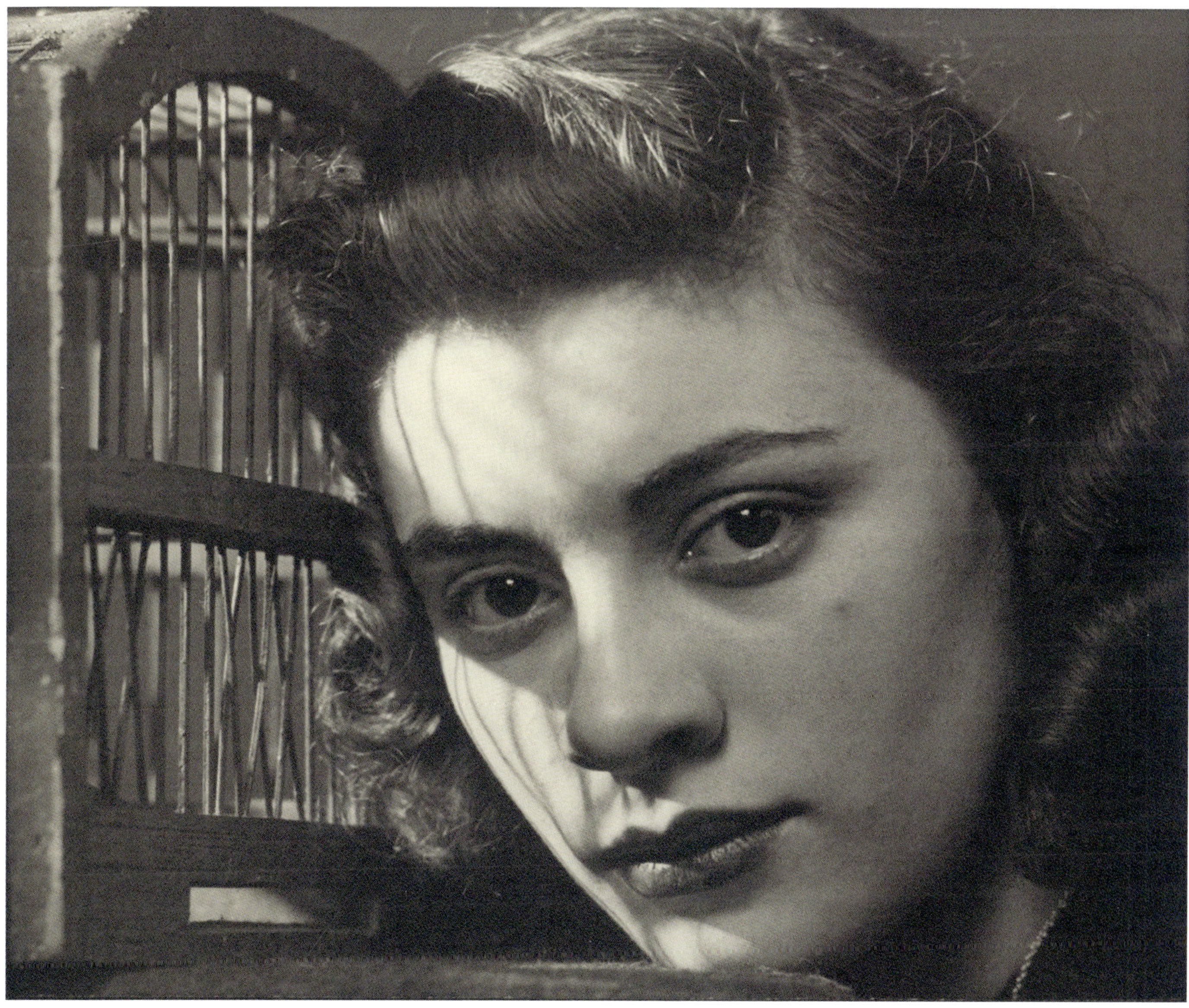

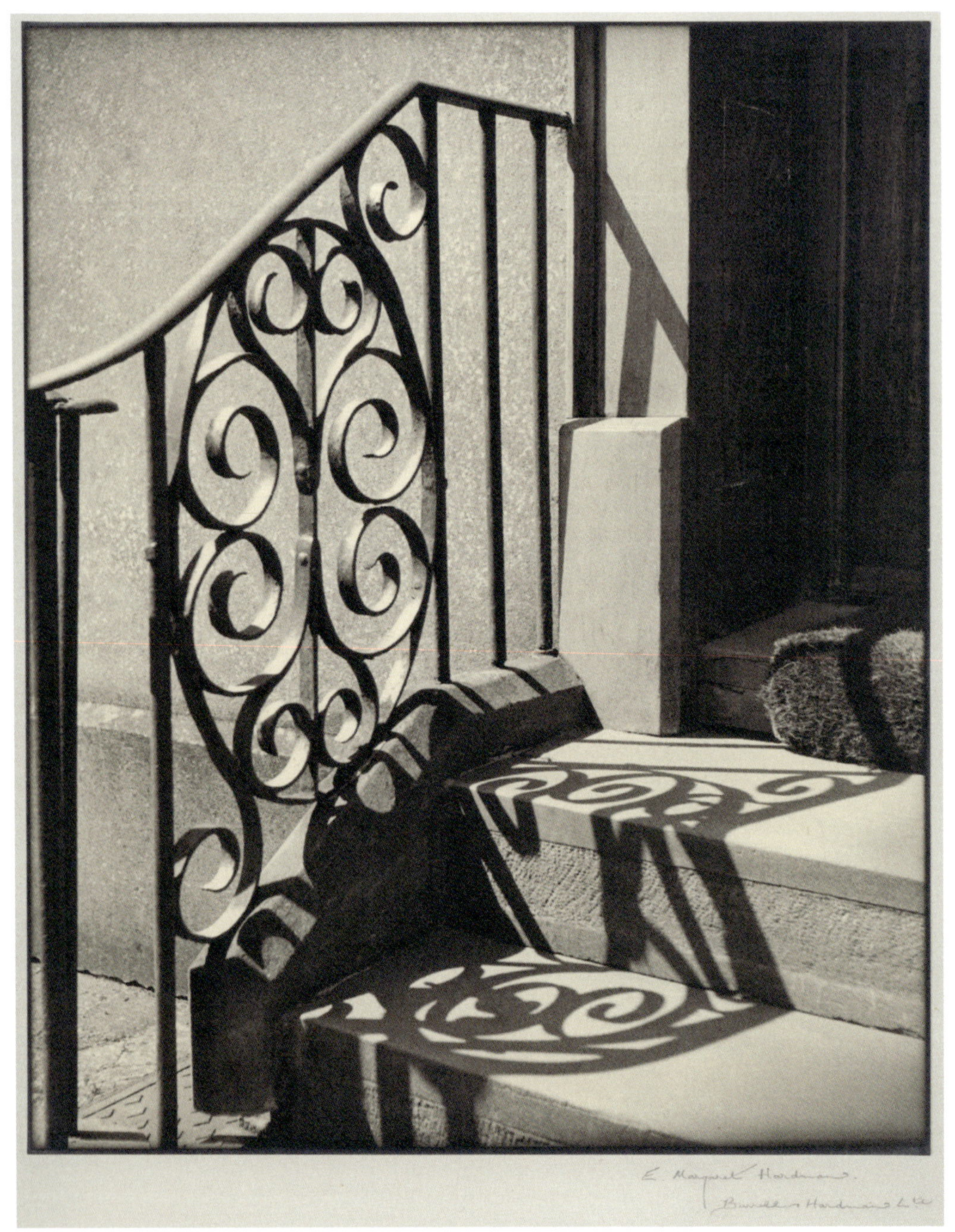

← *Georgian Handrail*, Margaret Hardman, *c.*1930s, gelatin silver print, 50.7 x 40.5cm (mounted), The Hardmans' House, Liverpool (NT 974382). Edward Chambré Hardman wrote of this image: 'Observed and photographed by my late wife in Llandeilo, Carmarthenshire. She also made the print. The image was taken using a Rolleiflex camera.'

↓ *Monks on Skates*, Margaret Hardman, 1932, gelatin silver print, 40.5 x 50.7cm (print), The Hardmans' House, Liverpool (NT 974384)

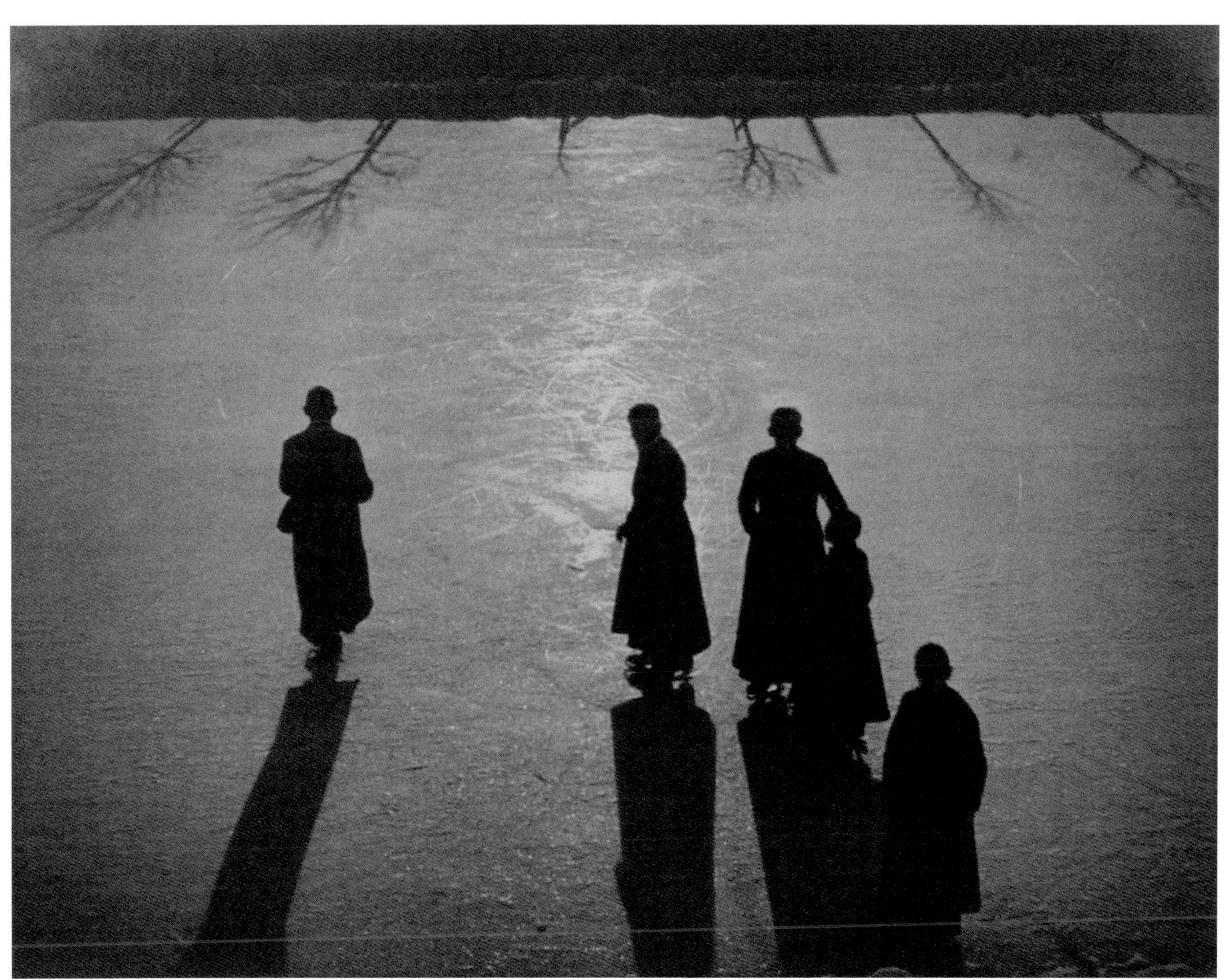

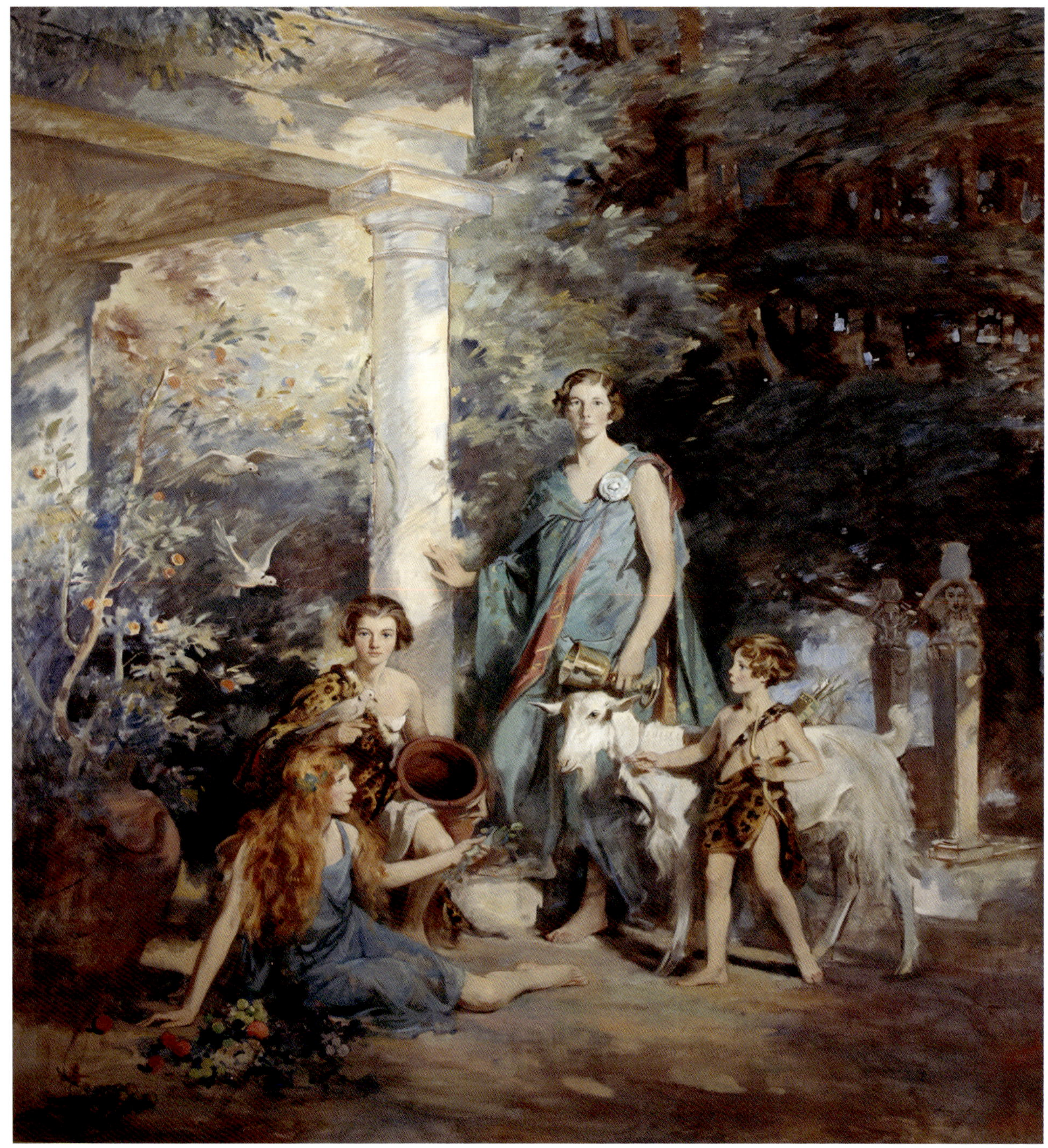

‘Dignity, space and restfulness’

EDITH CHAPLIN, MARCHIONESS OF LONDONDERRY (1878–1959)

The gardens created by Edith, Lady Londonderry, at Mount Stewart are among the most precociously playful cared for by the National Trust. Where else might you see a concrete dodo or an orangutan sitting happily on a classical column?

Describing her gardens in 1935, Lady Londonderry wrote: ‘they are planned on the Italian style, but on much less grandiose lines, suited to modern ideas and possibilities, yet they convey an impression of dignity, space and restfulness, three things that all designers of gardens must strive for’.

Lady Londonderry bought many new plants every year, with rare and heavily scented types being favoured, so her gardens were in a constant state of development. Today the gardens continue to evolve, albeit while using her personal gardening diaries as a guide and staying true to the ‘Londonderry style’.

Lady Londonderry laid out the gardens at Mount Stewart in the 1920s and 1930s. They are an assemblage of compartments, each with a distinctive style and narrative, infused with her varied passions and interests. A permeating influence is Celtic folklore, evident in the mythological references in the Shamrock Garden and *Tír na nÓg* burial ground. The group of influential friends she brought together from 1915 as the ‘Ark Club’ are celebrated in sculptures by Thomas Beattie (*c.*1866–1948) on the Dodo Terrace (pages 194–5). Each member took on the form of an animal or mythological character (Winston Churchill was ‘Winnie the Warlock’) and, at its centre, Lady Londonderry was Circe the Sorceress, a role she embodies in an allegorical painting by Edmond Brock (opposite).

This sense of playfulness and creativity also extended to the house, with its many grand but welcoming rooms transformed by Lady Londonderry. She designed new interiors in which recently acquired antiques joined family treasures, using light and texture to dramatic effect. Her bold use of contrasting colour, fine damasks and velvets, and satin sheen paints brought life to her interiors. Window openings connected her creations – indoor and out – so they could be enjoyed together. RC

← *Circe and the Sirens*, Edmond Brock (1882–1952), 1925, oil on canvas, 327.7 x 274.3cm, Mount Stewart, County Down (NT 1220965)

↓ An intimate double portrait in a gold Cartier cigarette case, commissioned as a gift from Lady Edith to her husband, Charles Vane-Tempest-Stewart, 7th Marquess of Londonderry; Beatrice Wainwright (active 1908–60), 1915, watercolour on ivory, 2.5 x 12.5 x 10.5cm, Mount Stewart, County Down (NT 1656323)
→ The Dodo Terrace at the entrance to the Italian Garden, Mount Stewart, County Down

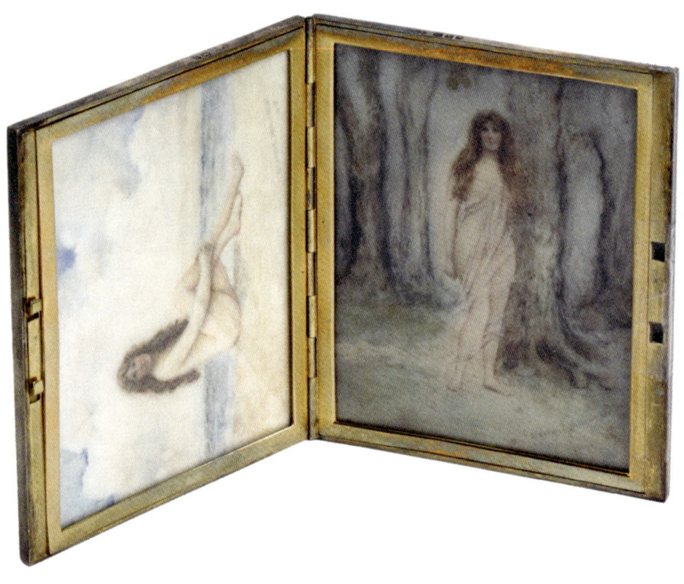

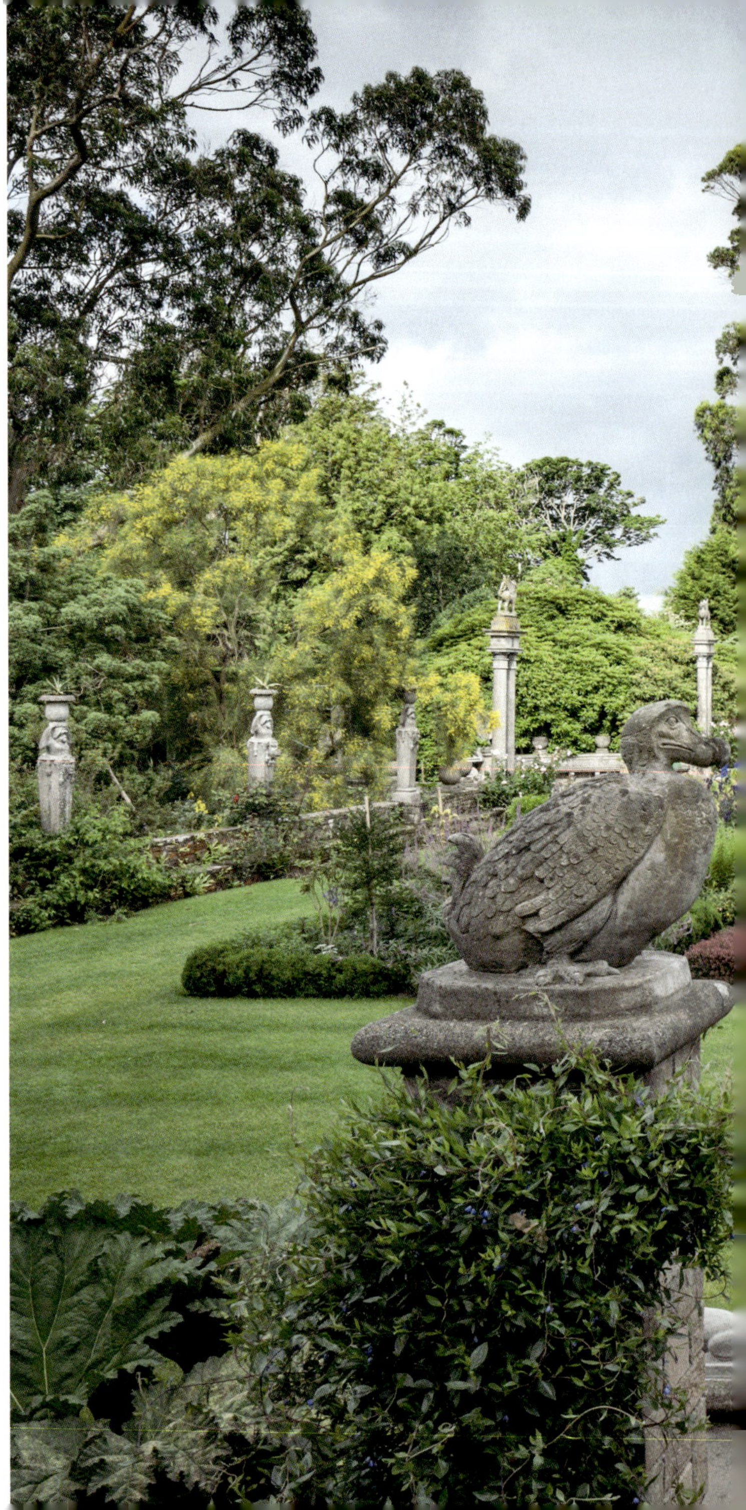

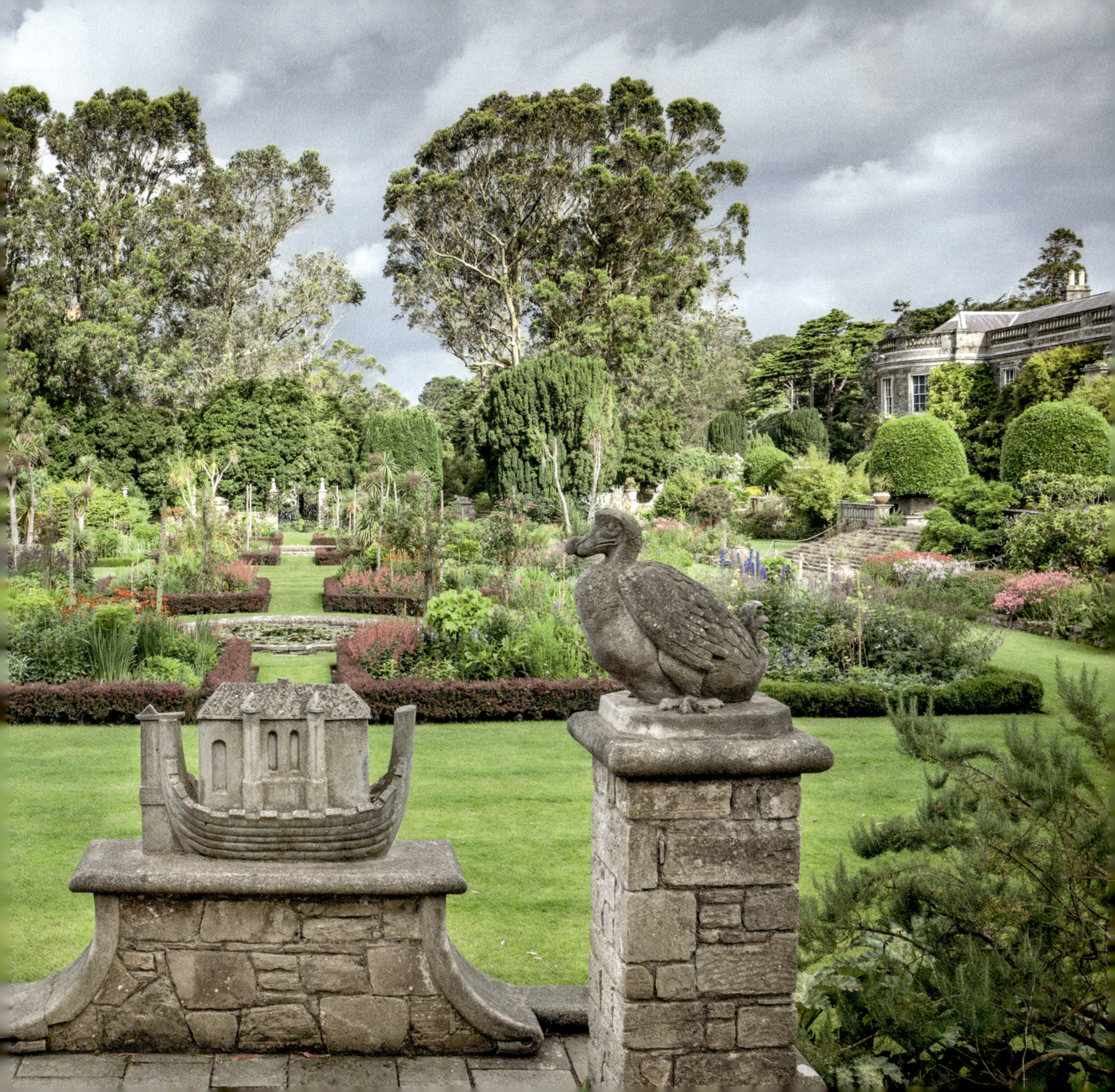

‘The architect of floors’

MARION DORN (1896–1964)

Marion Dorn trained at Stanford University, California, and moved to London in 1923. She quickly became recognised as one of the leading modern textile designers in Britain.

Dorn is best known for her luxuriously textured, hand-knotted ‘sculpted’ rugs and carpets, many of which were produced with the Wilton Royal Carpet Factory. By the 1930s Dorn had produced over 100 mostly abstract designs for Wilton. Each was marketed as a limited-edition work of art, leading to her being described in a 1932 article in *The Architectural Review* as ‘the architect of floors’.

In addition to working with manufacturers and exhibiting her work alongside other artists, Dorn received many important private commissions through her design consultancy. She created carpets and textiles for modern, fashionable interiors at Eltham Palace, as well as for the Cunard White Star cruise line. Rupert D’Oyly Carte was Chair of the Savoy Group, his family company, and commissioned extensive ranges of carpets and rugs from Dorn for the Savoy, Berkeley and Claridge’s hotels. The pieces by Dorn at Coleton Fishacre in Devon are among very few original furnishings owned by the D’Oyly Cartes still remaining at his country house.

Dorn also collaborated with architects and designers to produce innovative

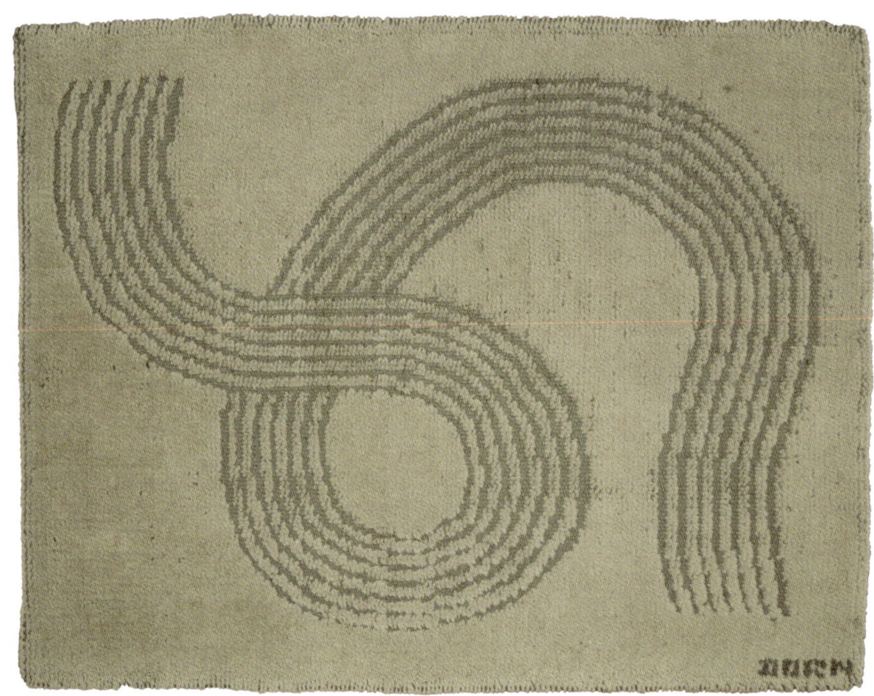

↑ Carpet designed by Marion Dorn, probably made by Wilton Royal Carpet Factory, *c.*1930, knotted and woven wool, Coleton Fishacre, Devon (NT 1502509)
→ Marion Dorn photographed by Carl Van Vechten in 1936 (Beinecke Rare Book and Manuscript Library, Yale University Library)

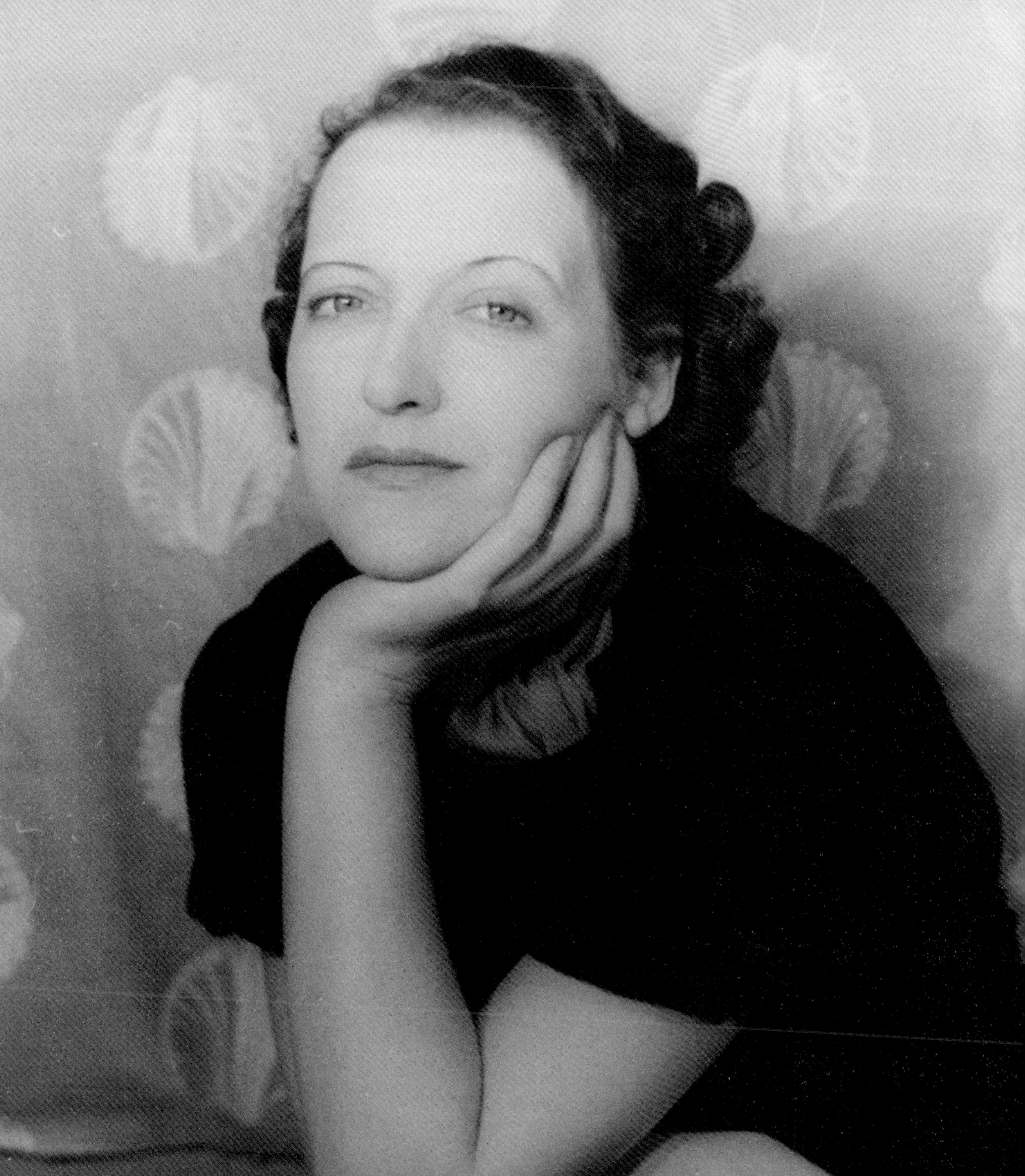

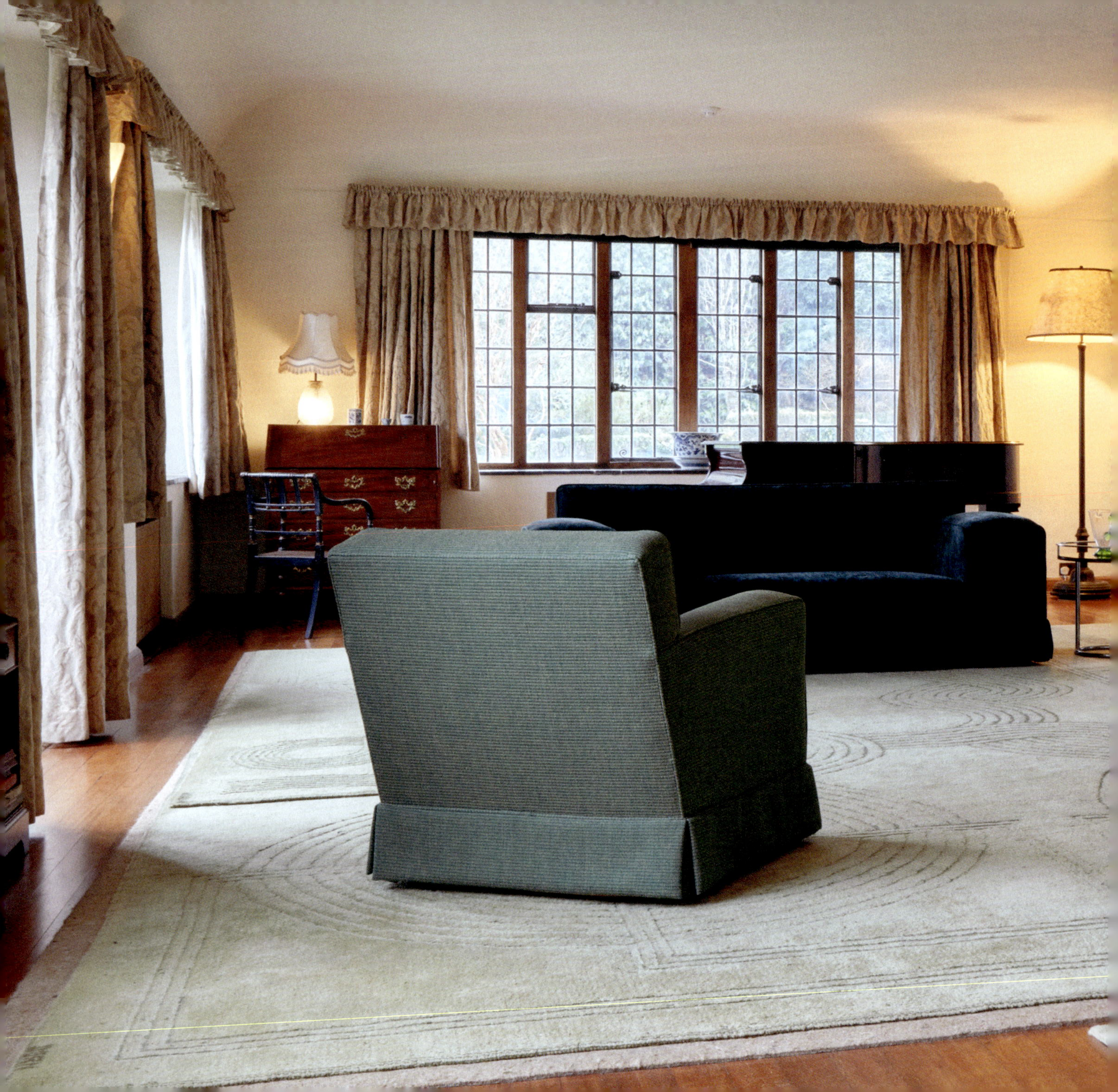

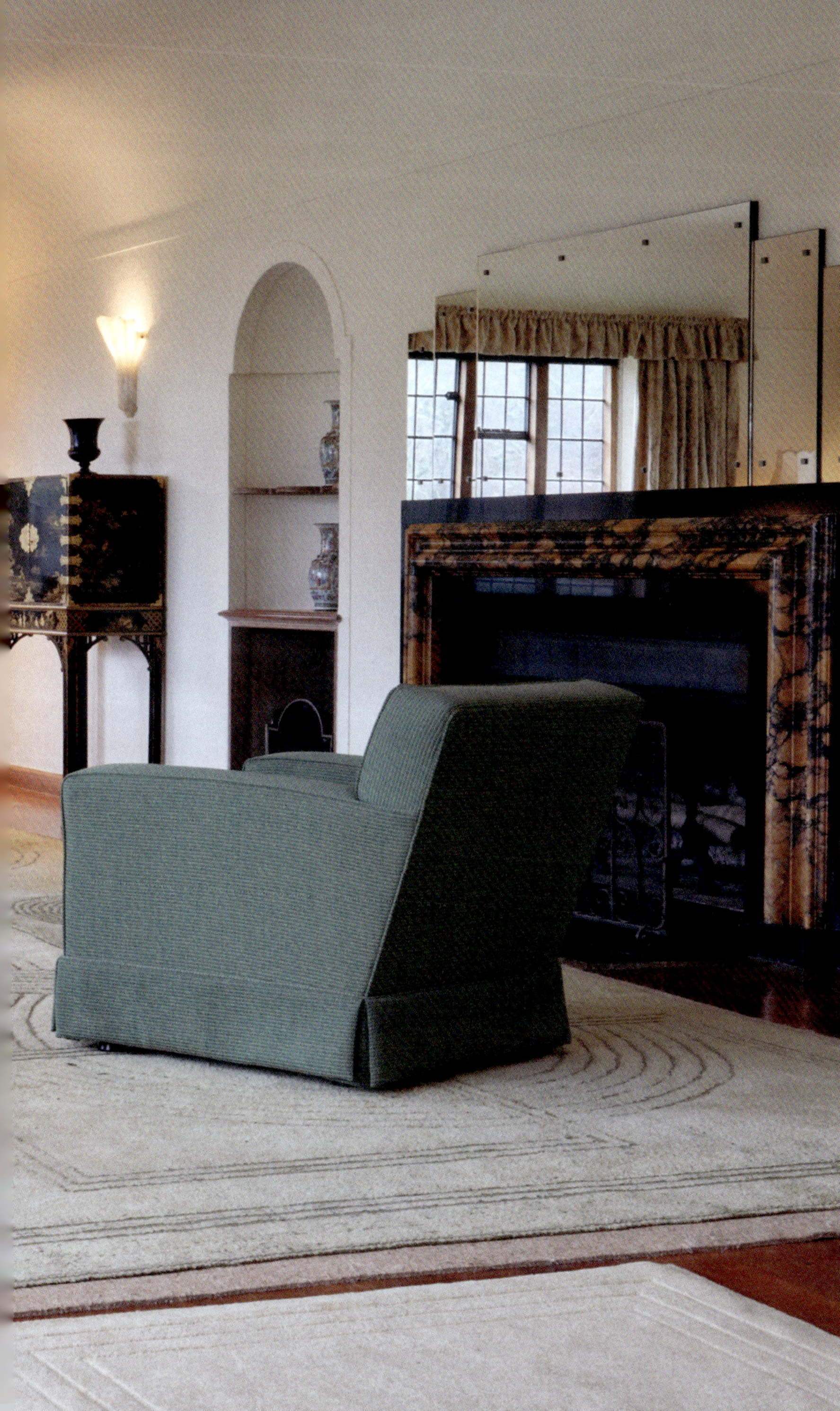

← Carpet designed by Marion Dorn, probably made by Wilton Royal Carpet Factory, c.1930, knotted and woven wool, Coleton Fishacre, Devon (NT 1502509)

interior schemes, including a carpet for the critically acclaimed 'all white' room created by Syrie Maugham (1879–1955) at her home in Chelsea. In 1937 Dorn was commissioned to produce seating upholstery designs for the London Passenger Transport Board.

Dorn returned to the USA in 1940 and continued to work privately and with manufacturers. One major project, in 1960, was the production of carpets for the Diplomatic Reception Room at the White House, Washington DC. In 1957, in recognition of her outstanding contribution to textile design, Dorn was awarded an honorary fellowship of the British Society of Industrial Artists.

As well as her sculpted carpets, Dorn designed theatre costumes and sets, wall hangings and wallpaper, embroidery, furnishing fabric and scarves. RC

A multifaceted artist

VANESSA BELL (1879–1961)

Vanessa Bell was a key figure in the circle of radical artists and intellectuals known as the Bloomsbury Group. She was a director of the progressive but short-lived Omega Workshops, established by Roger Fry (1886–1934). Aimed at breaking down boundaries between the fine and decorative arts, it opened in 1913 and sold textiles, furniture and household accessories designed and made by Bloomsbury artists.

Monk's House, East Sussex, is home to many of Bell's varied creations, commissioned or acquired by her sister Virginia Woolf (1882–1941). They include paintings – a striking portrait of Woolf among them – but also patterns for embroidery, textiles, hand-painted fireplace tiles, furniture and other objects. Some of the collections reflect other interiors that Bell created in collaboration with her partner, Duncan Grant (1885–1978), most famously and immersively at their East Sussex farmhouse, Charleston.

Bell designed the covers for most of Woolf's books, published through the Hogarth Press. She also decorated ceramics, painting blanks by Wedgwood and others modelled by Phyllis Keyes (1881–1968), often with the same loose brushwork and bold use of colour that characterise her oil paintings. In 1934 Bell produced two designs for Harrods' *Modern Art for the Table* project. This ambitious (although commercially unsuccessful) project brought together contemporary artists with ceramic and glass manufacturers, with the ambition to elevate the quality of industrial design and 'improve public taste'. Of Bell's 'Fitzroy' pattern, gleaming with purple lustre but rather complex in its design, critic Noel Carrington wrote that 'the sketchy drawing could be produced by transfer [printing], otherwise it seems less suitable for quantity production'.

Another remarkable commission was *The Famous Women Service*, made by Bell and Grant for the art historian Kenneth Clark (1903–83), now in the collection of the Charleston Trust. The 50 Wedgwood plates are painted with portraits of 'women in different capacities', from Elizabeth I to the Queen of Sheba. RC

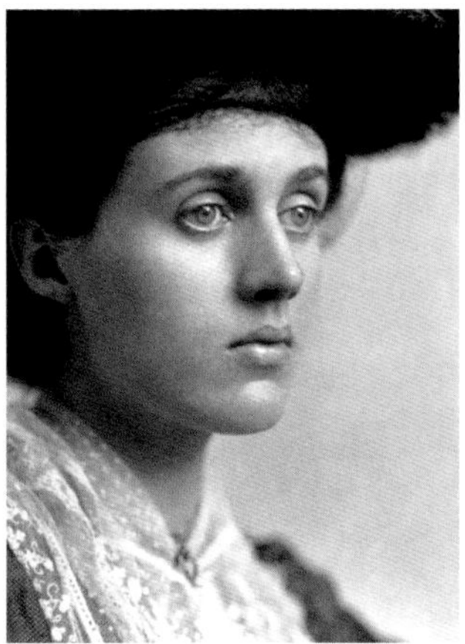

↑ Vanessa Bell photographed by George Charles Beresford in 1907
→ *Flowers*, Vanessa Bell, 1951, oil on canvas, 33 x 23cm, Mottisfont, Hampshire, presented by Derek Hill through The National Art Collections Fund (Art Fund), 1996 (NT 769776)

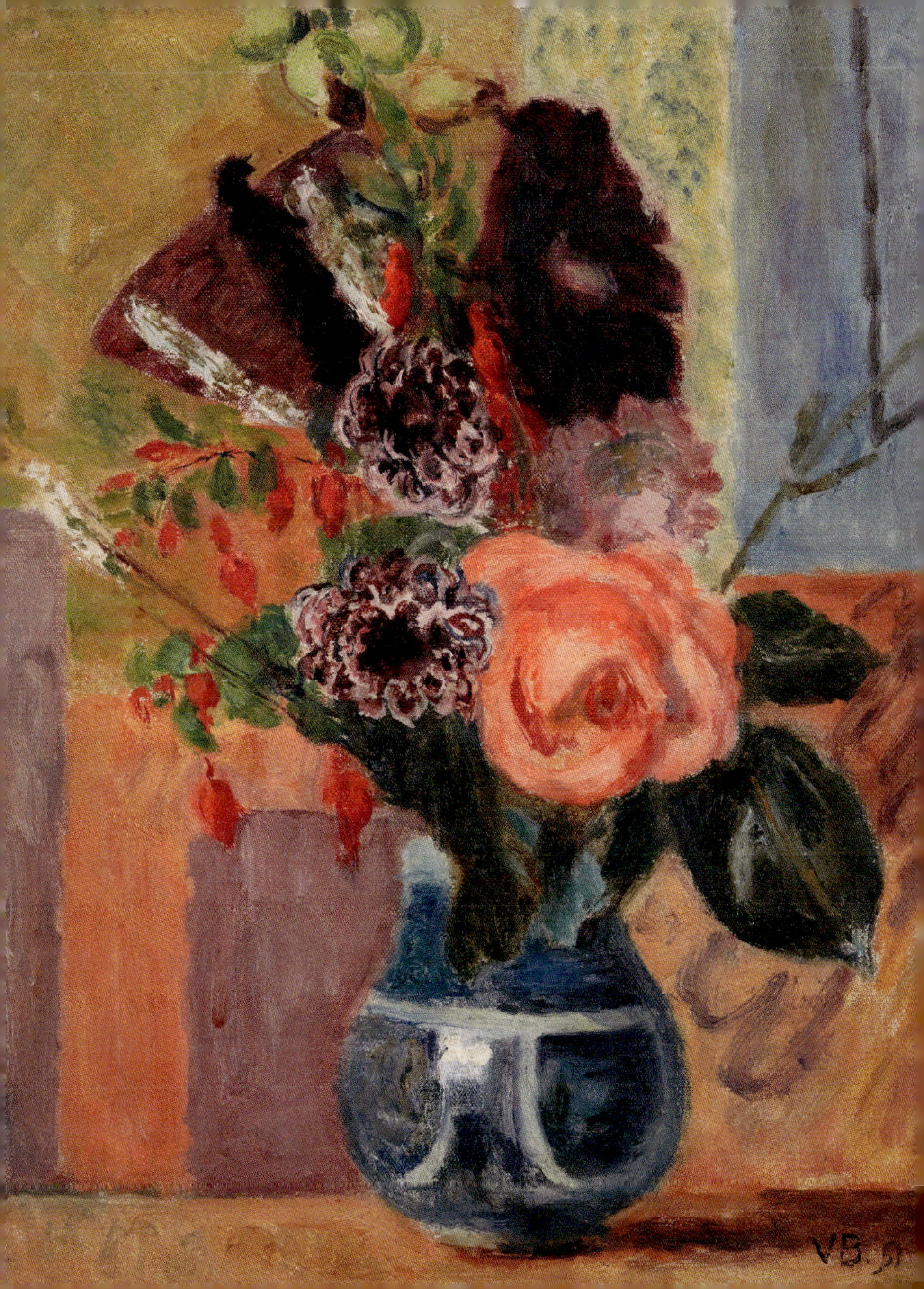

↓ Teapot designed by Vanessa Bell and made by E. Brain & Co. (Foley China), Fenton, Stoke-on-Trent, *c.*1934, bone china decorated with the 'Fitzroy' pattern, hand-coloured with purple lustre and overglaze enamels, 11.6 x 23cm, Monk's House, East Sussex (NT 768091)

→ Chair painted by Vanessa Bell and Duncan Grant, *c.*1930, beech and cane with modern upholstery, 101 x 58.5 x 54cm, Monk's House, East Sussex (NT 768175). This is one of four chairs with a matching table, made around 1930 for Virginia and Leonard Woolf's home at Tavistock Square in London.

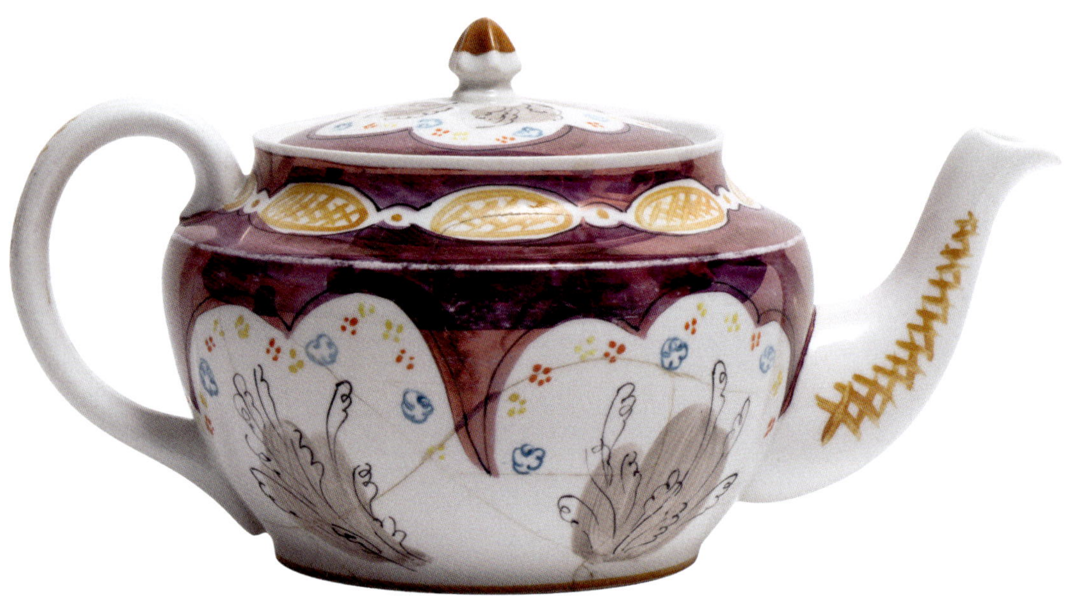

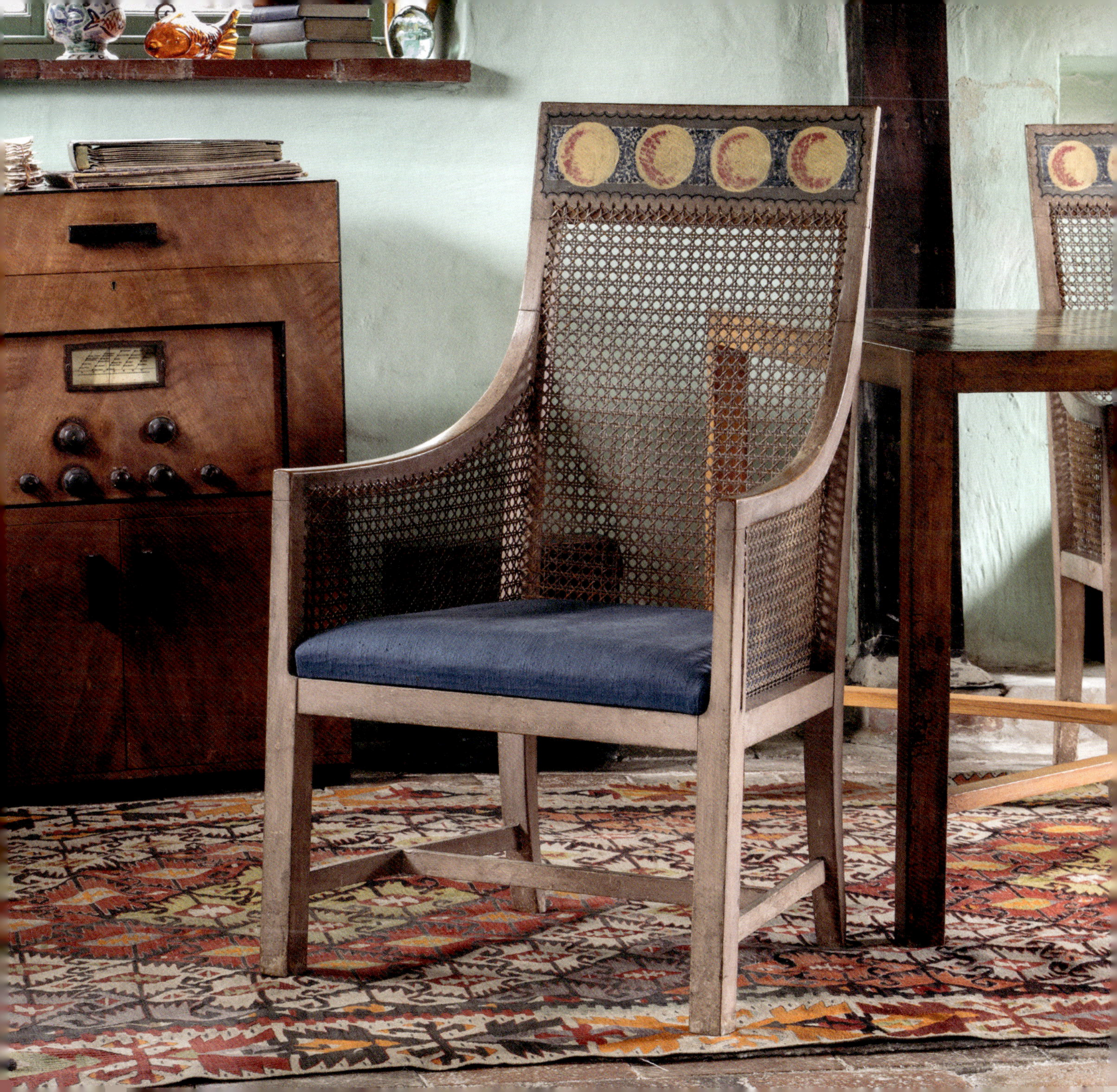

A career of firsts

LAURA KNIGHT (1877–1970)

'I am thankful to have known the tasks and struggles of common life, joy and despair like any other mortal. I am just a hard-working woman who longs to pierce the mystery of form and colour.'

These powerful lines appear in Laura Knight's second autobiography, *The Magic of a Line*, published to coincide with her large retrospective exhibition (the first of its kind for a woman) at the Royal Academy of Arts in 1965. During the course of an extraordinarily productive career spanning over seven decades, Knight was one of the most distinguished artists of her day. She portrayed a diverse range of sitters, from staff and patients at a racially segregated hospital in Baltimore in the USA, and members of the Women's Auxiliary Air Force, to subjects from the worlds of the circus, ballet and theatre. On seeing his finished portrait, an astonished George Bernard Shaw told Knight that she made him appear to be a sincere man, 'when all my life I have been an actor'. During the Second World War, under commission from the War Artists' Advisory Committee chaired by the art

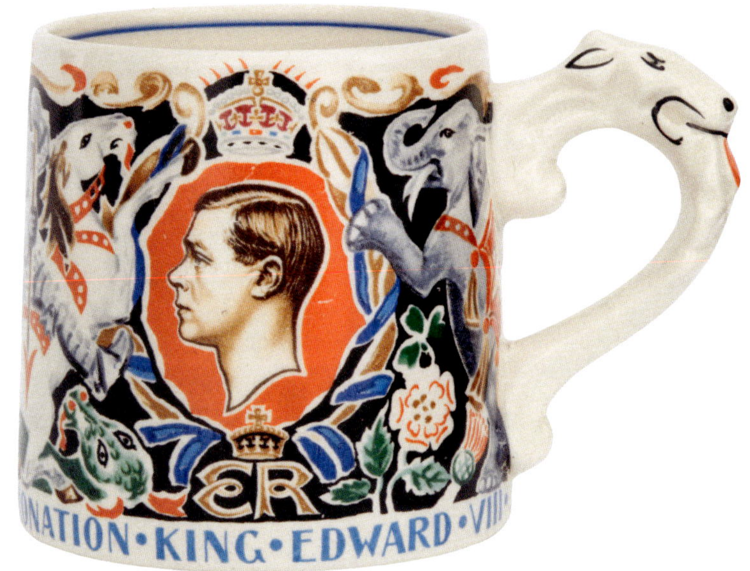

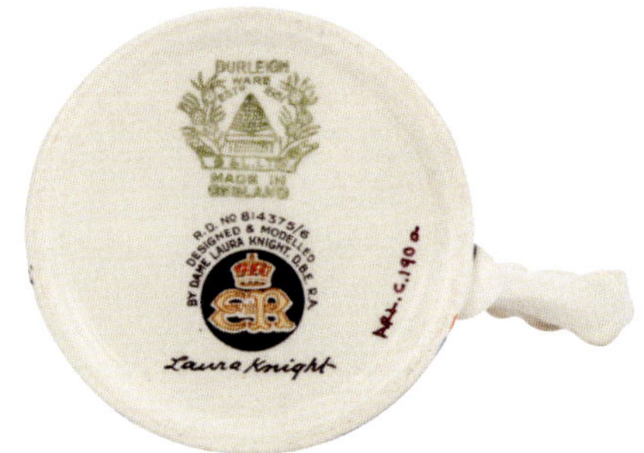

↑ Mug designed by Laura Knight and manufactured by Burgess & Leigh Ltd of Stoke-on-Trent, *c.*1937, transfer printed earthenware, 8cm (height), Arlington Court, Devon (NT 985467.1)
← Factory marks on the base of the mug
→ Laura Knight (detail), Bassano Ltd, 1936 (National Portrait Gallery, London)

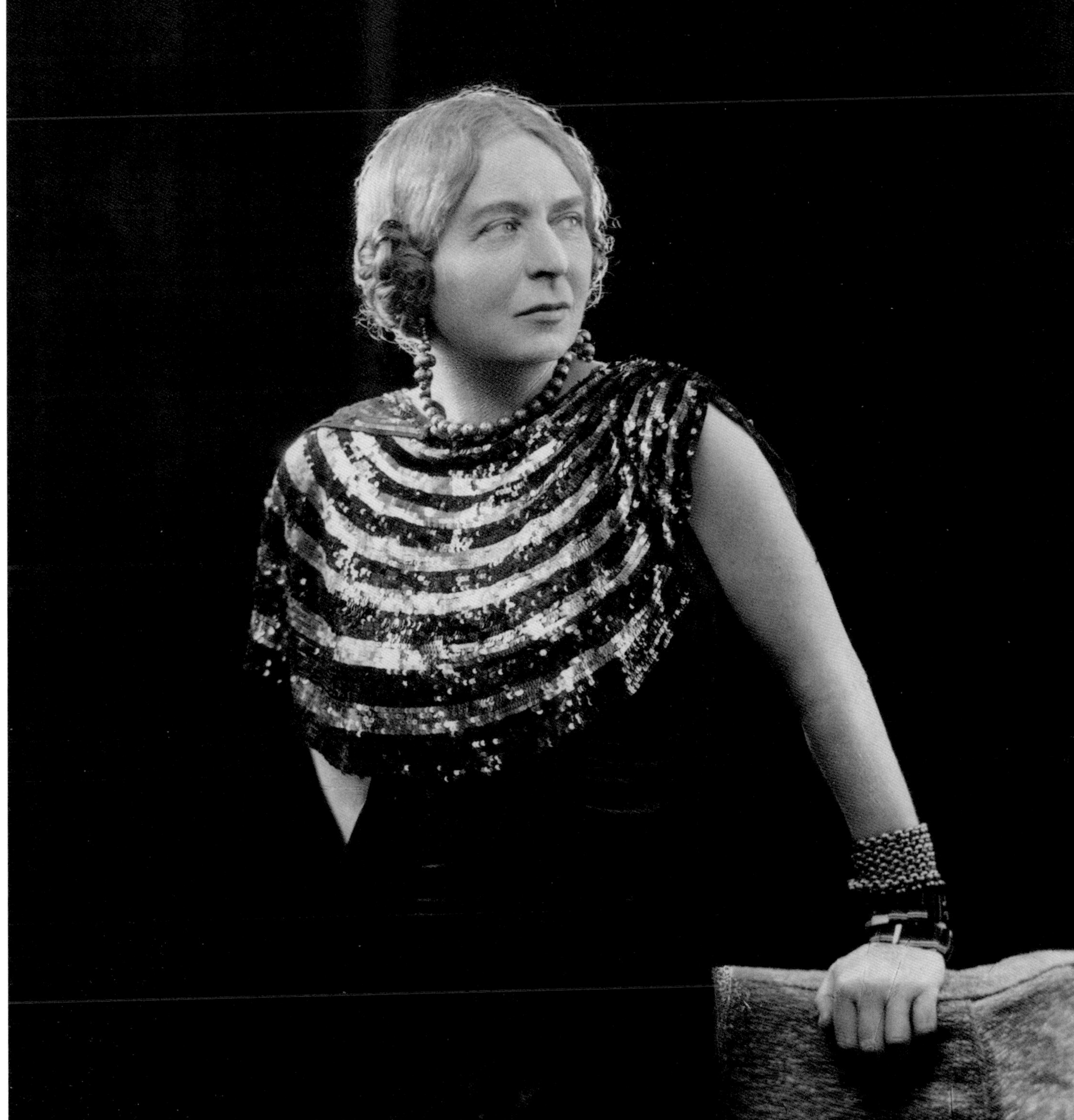

↓ *Getting Dressed*, Laura Knight, 1917, black and coloured chalk on paper, 34.8 x 24.8cm, Fenton House, London (NT 1449144)
→ *First Night in the Stalls*, Laura Knight, *c.*1932, pencil and watercolour on paper, 39.7 x 28.6cm, Shaw's Corner, Hertfordshire (NT 1275267)

historian Sir Kenneth Clark (1903–83), she often argued that she should be better remunerated.

Educated at a time when studying life-drawing was the preserve of male artists, Laura Knight overturned the social restrictions of the day by establishing her own life studio. Hers was a career of firsts: the first woman artist to be made a Dame of the British Empire in 1929, and in 1936 the first woman elected to full membership of the Royal Academy since founding members Angelica Kauffman (page 66) and Mary Moser in 1768.

Throughout Knight's professional career she worked in a wide variety of media. In the 1930s she was commissioned to design commemorative ceramics, including a mug for Burgess & Leigh Ltd to celebrate the coronation of Edward VIII (page 204). The same year, Wedgwood's Etruria factory commissioned her to produce a loving cup, the design later adapted for the coronation of George VI. Instead of using more traditional tropes of royalty, she portrays a circus elephant – symbolising the British Empire – opposite St George and the Dragon.

Towards the end of her long life she stated, 'my inner self continues to say even today – go on, keep on trying something different'. AMS

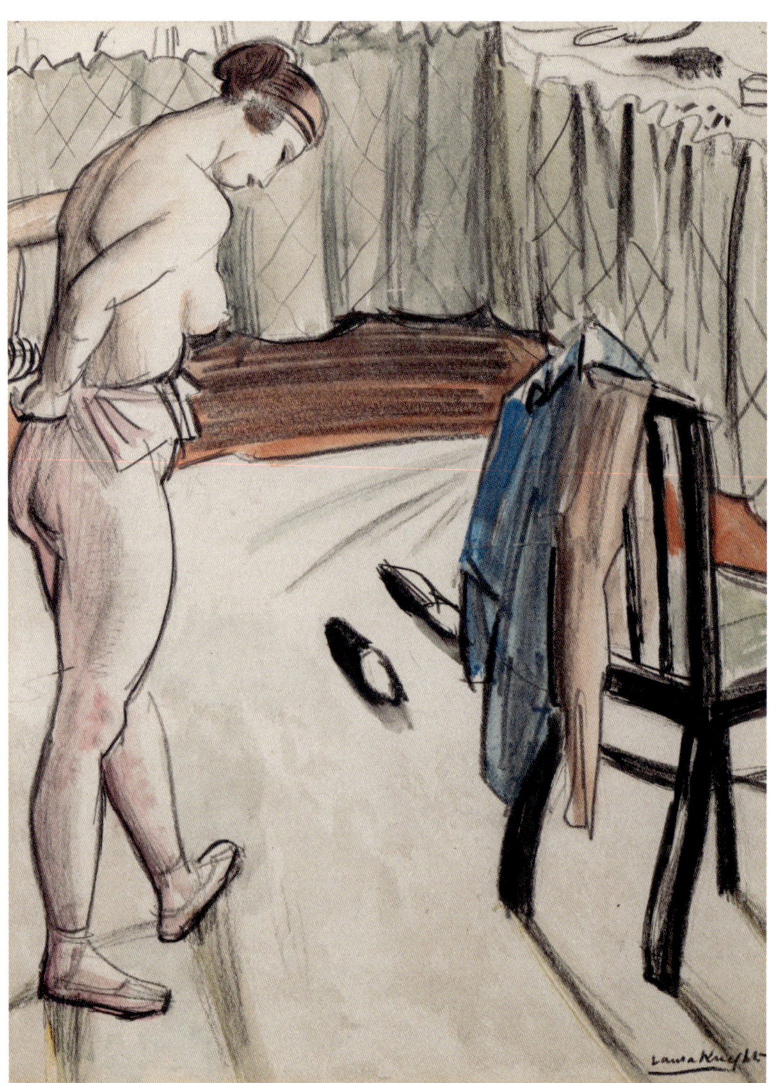

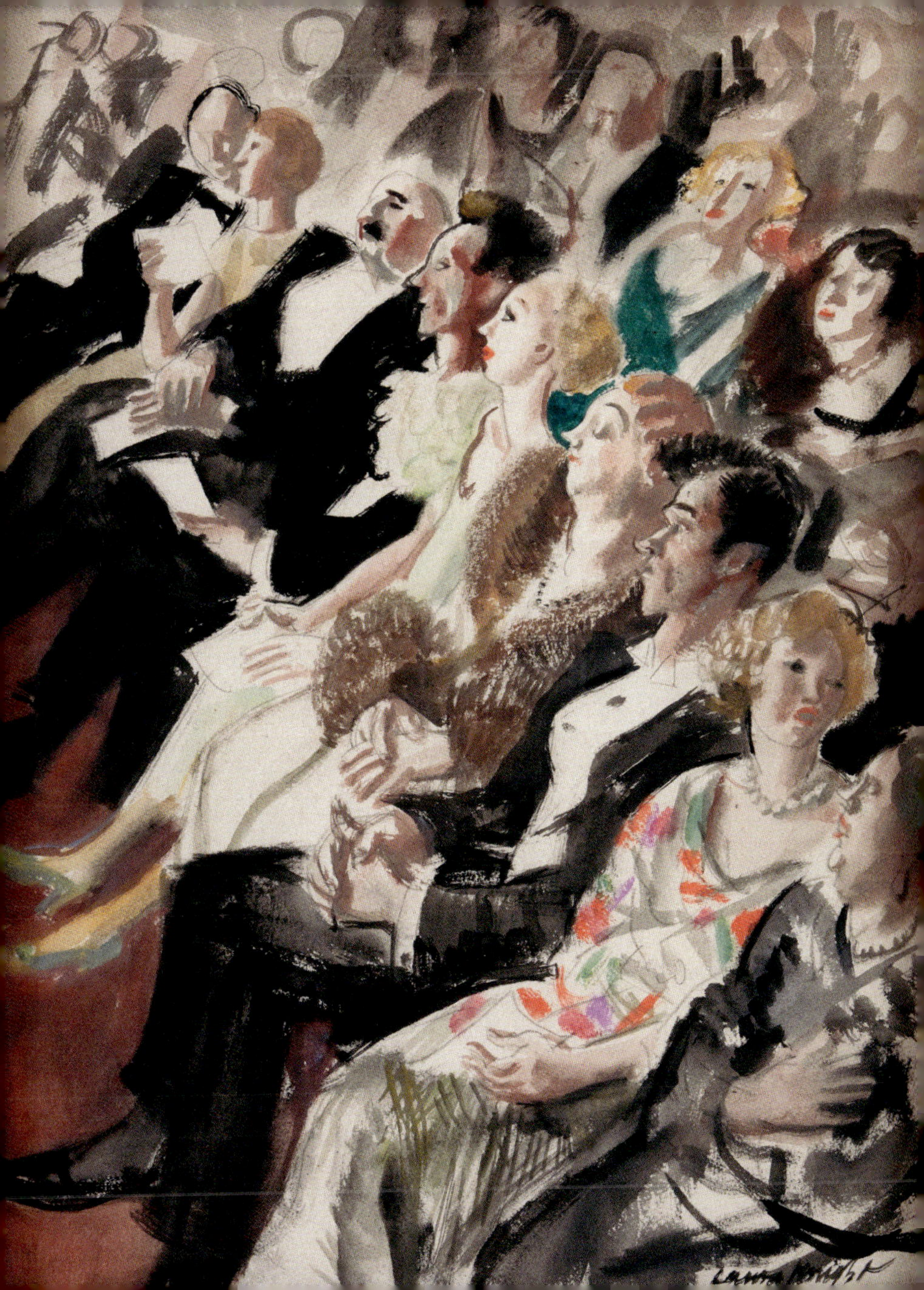

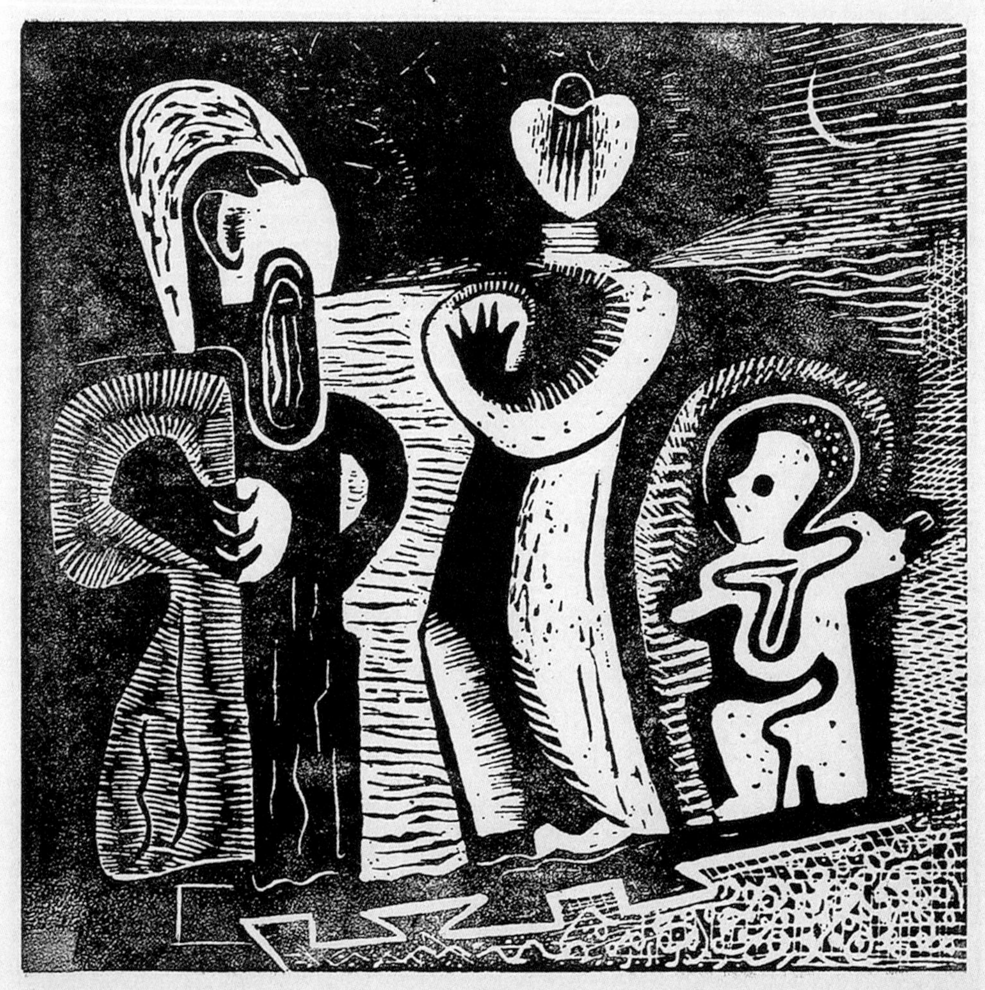

publ: 'The Island'. Eileen Agar: Surrealist design 1930.

Reluctant surrealist

EILEEN AGAR (1899–1991)

'One day I was an artist exploring highly personal combinations of form and content, and the next I was calmly informed I was a Surrealist!' Eileen Agar remembered a visit to her studio by Herbert Read and Roland Penrose that led to her being labelled a Surrealist and her inclusion – one of only a few women artists – in the International Surrealist Exhibition of 1936. Throughout her 70-year career, Agar brought together the anarchic tendencies of Surrealism and the abstract qualities of Cubism. Her practice moved seamlessly from drawing, painting and collage to sculpture and photography, drawing on classical art, ancient mythologies and the natural world.

Born in Argentina, Agar travelled to England as a young child, studying first under Lucy Kemp-Welch, who instructed her to 'always have something to do with art', then at Leon Underwood's Brook Green School of Art, and later the Slade School of Fine Art. During the 1920s, Agar forged her creative vision in Paris, a crucible of the intellectual avant-garde, where her circle included André Breton, Man Ray and Lee Miller.

Agar and her husband Joseph Bard founded *The Island* journal, 'dedicated to the plastic arts, poetry and the imagination'. *Family Trio* (opposite) featured in the September 1931 issue, during the time Agar was building her 'womb magic' theory. She wrote that 'the importance of the unconscious in all forms of Literature and Art establishes the dominance of a feminine order over the classical and more masculine order'. The piece is composed of three figures – one representing ancient patriarchy, the central floating feminine form straddling land and sea, and the embryonic child forming in the sea under a crescent moon.

Agar was a keen photographer and she made a series of photographs of Ursula and Ernö Goldfinger in their new home, 2 Willow Road, London (Tate collection). She showed three paintings alongside Ernö Goldfinger in the Surrealist section of the Artists International Association exhibition, held in 1937, and her work was included in the *Aid to Russia* exhibition curated by Ursula Goldfinger at Willow Road.

Agar was elected a Royal Academician in 1990 and published her autobiography, *A Look at My Life* (1988), when she was nearly 90. A copy resides in the book collection at 2 Willow Road. AMS

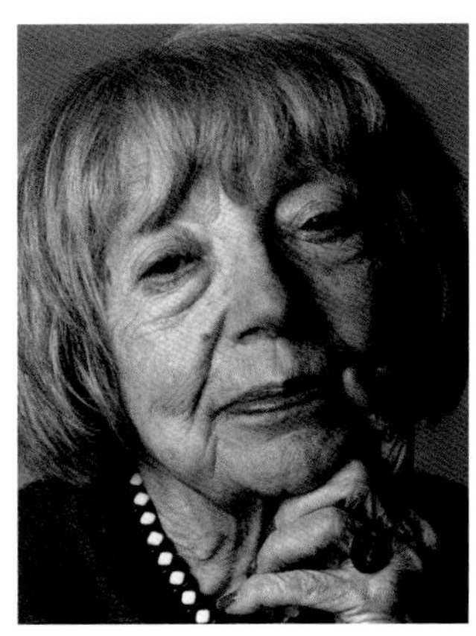

← *Family Trio*, Eileen Agar, 1930, woodcut on paper, 41 x 27cm, Dudmaston, Shropshire (NT 813721)
↑ Eileen Agar photographed by Trevor Leighton in 1988 (National Portrait Gallery, London)

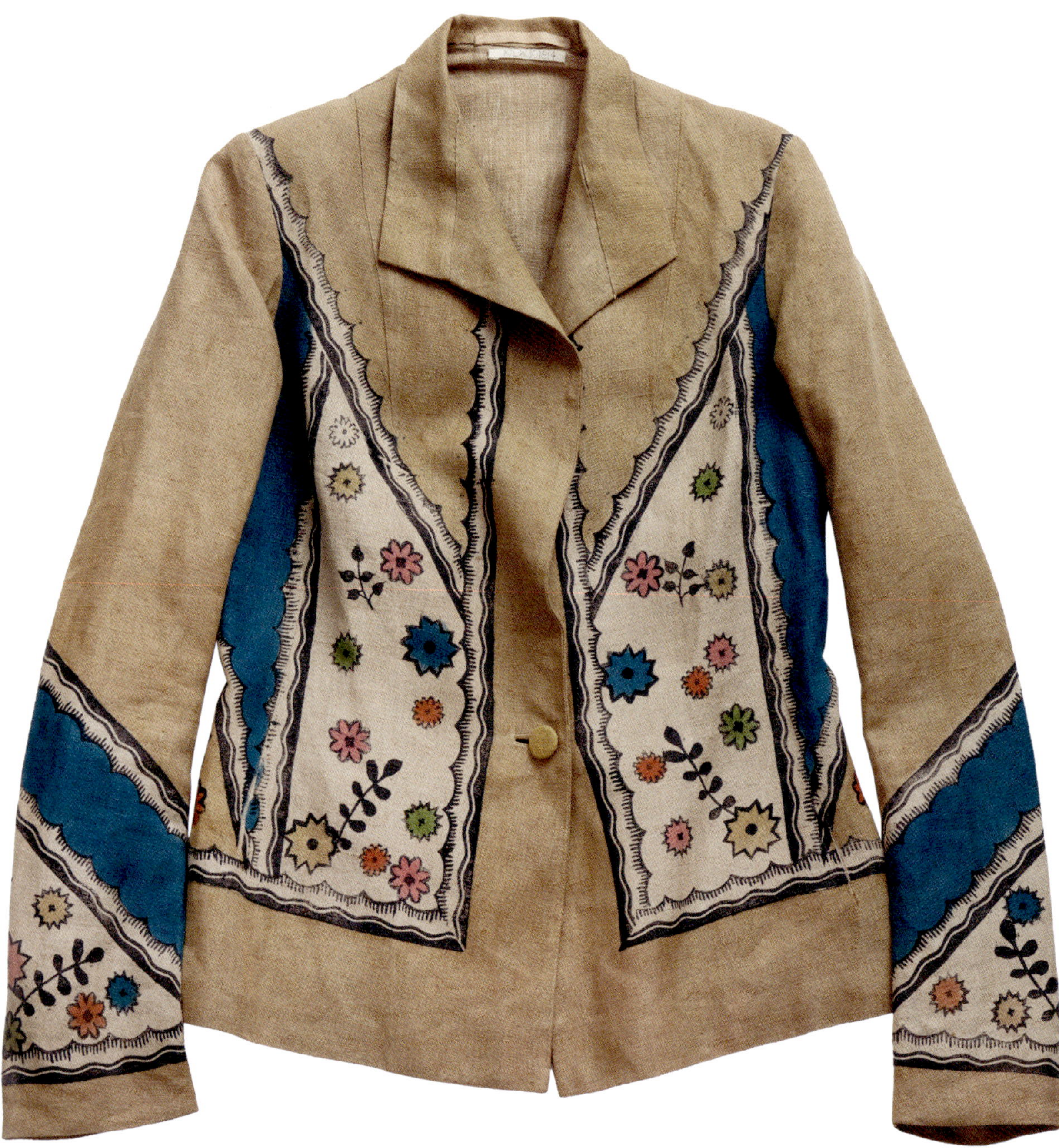

Artistic textiles

JOYCE CLISSOLD (1905–82)

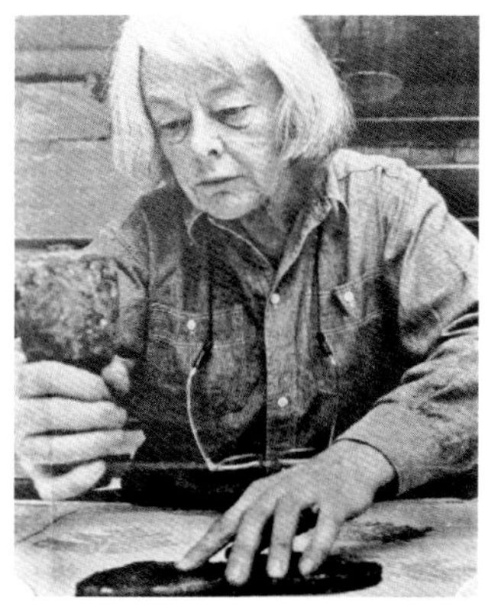

← Jacket designed by Joyce Clissold and made by Footprints, possibly 1930s–40s with some later alteration, hand-dyed linen, hand-block printed in the 'Persian Garden' pattern, 62cm (length), Killerton, Devon (NT 1367118)
↑ Rare undated photograph of Joyce Clissold at work, printing on fabric with a traditional hand block

Joyce Clissold was a student at the Central School of Arts and Crafts in London, where she studied wood-engraving, lino-cutting and printing. She began working at the Footprints textile-printing workshop while still a student. Established in Hammersmith in 1925 by Celandine Kennington, Gwen Pike and Elspeth Little, the workshop built a reputation for innovative dress and furnishing fabric designs, mostly designed and made by young female art students and sold at Little's shop, Modern Textiles.

In 1929 Clissold took over the running of the workshop and became responsible for its artistic output. She created all of the designs and cut the printing blocks, and her staff – as many as 50 local working-class women – mixed dyes and printed the fabrics. Wages were paid according to skill and length of service, and everyone was taught on the job, progressing through increasingly specialised tasks as their knowledge and experience grew.

Under Clissold, Footprints created unique, hand-produced textiles and finished garments designed to appeal to 'the wealthy bohemian'. True to its artistic foundations, pieces produced by Footprints were regularly included in exhibitions, including the annual Arts and Crafts Exhibition Society show at Burlington House and at the Mansard Gallery in Heal's department store, which showcased cutting-edge modern art and interior design.

In 1933 Clissold moved the workshop to the ground floor of her home in Brentford. While no doubt convenient in many ways, it was not a conventional set-up – side-by-side baths were used for dying fabrics in a bathroom and the smell of chemicals permeated the whole house. Clissold opened two shops in central London around this time, ideally placed for reaching well-heeled customers – the first in New Bond Street, the other on Knightsbridge. Each shop included a dressmaking workshop above and a

→ Detail of the back of a jacket designed by Joyce Clissold and made by Footprints (page 210), possibly 1930s–40s with some later alteration, hand-dyed linen, hand-block printed in the 'Persian Garden' pattern, 62cm (length), Killerton, Devon (NT 1367118)

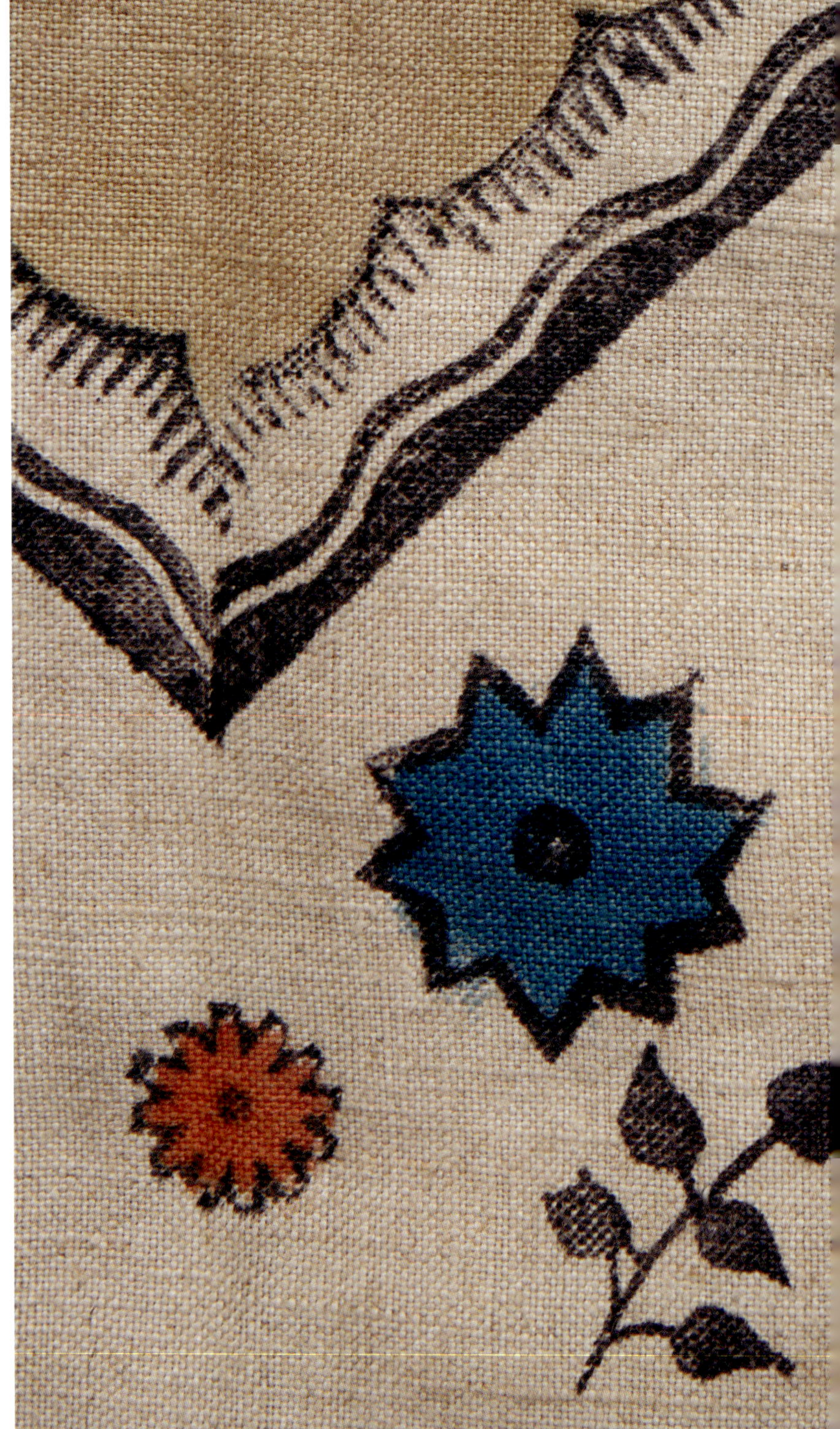

fabric showroom, where clients such as singer-actors Gracie Fields and Yvonne Arnaud could browse the luxurious array of printed and painted silks, linens, velvets and satins, and select their favourite design. There was also a space for choosing the style of garment to be made up, taking measurements and undertaking fittings with the in-house dressmaker, Madame Blanche.

The Footprints shops closed in 1940, as supplies and labour were diverted to the war effort. Clissold taught textile design at the Central School from 1936 to 1940 and after the war continued to run Footprints, albeit at a much-reduced scale, for the rest of her life. RC

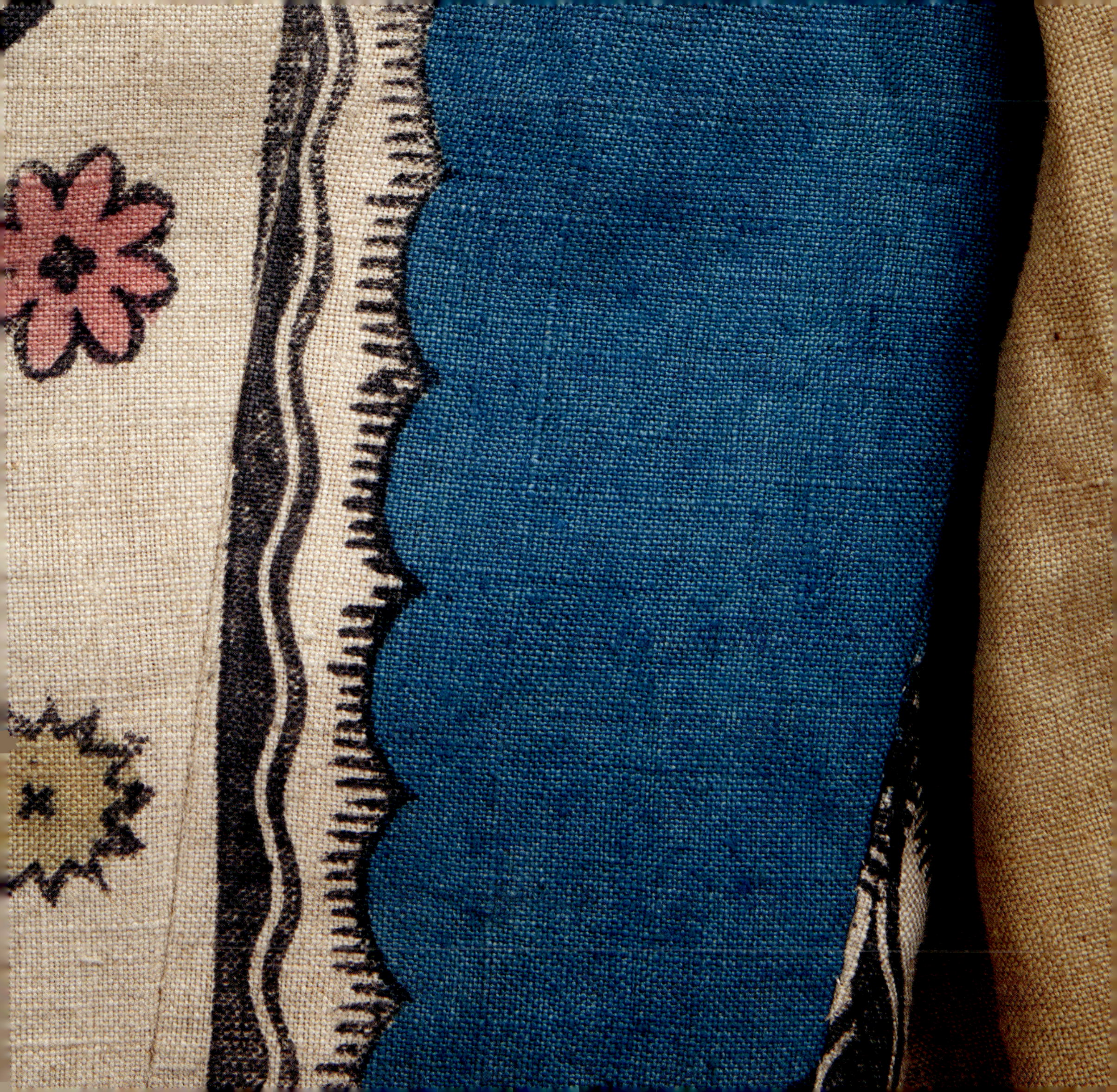

‘Of the modern school of thought’

SUSIE COOPER (1902–95)

Susie Cooper was an extraordinary leader in an industry dominated by men. During a career spanning seven decades, she created ceramics that were renowned for their elegance, affordability and utility.

Cooper was born in Staffordshire and attended evening classes at the Burslem School of Art as a teenager. Her teacher was pottery-industry stalwart Gordon Forsyth (1879–1952), who arranged a placement for her at the progressive decorating firm A.E. Gray & Co., where he worked as a freelancer. Cooper was appointed as a designer and decorated the ‘Gloria Lustre’ range (opposite and page 4), much of which was designed by Forsyth. The company received a Gold Medal for the ware at the 1925 Exposition Internationale des Arts Décoratifs et Industriels Modernes in Paris – the event that launched Art Deco into the world.

Aged 27, Cooper established her own business at the Crown Works in 1929. This gave her full creative control over the design process, enabling her to consider both surface decoration and shape. It was a risky decision at a time of economic instability, but one that was ultimately very successful. In 1932 the *Pottery Gazette and Trade Review* remarked that ‘Miss Susie Cooper … is a gifted, creative artist of the modern school of thought, one who reveals in her work a lovely imagination combined with a unique capacity to achieve the maximum degree of effectiveness in pottery decoration by recourse to the simplest modes of expression.’

Cooper’s ceramics were stylish but affordable. She understood changing consumer tastes and developed a progressive but restrained approach to design that coordinated perfectly with the modern interiors of the suburban middle classes, her typical customers. She made use of innovative techniques for the decoration of her pieces, including ceramic crayons, aerographing (spraying colour onto a pot) and lithographic printing, as well as traditional techniques such as hand-painting and sgraffito

→ Bowl from the ‘Gloria Lustre’ range by A.E. Gray & Co. Ltd of Staffordshire, *c.*1923–5, earthenware with lustre decoration, 11.3 (height) x 25.4cm (diameter), Tyntesfield, North Somerset, purchased from the estate of the late Lord Wraxall with the assistance of the National Heritage Memorial Fund and donations from members and supporters, 2002 (NT 28277)

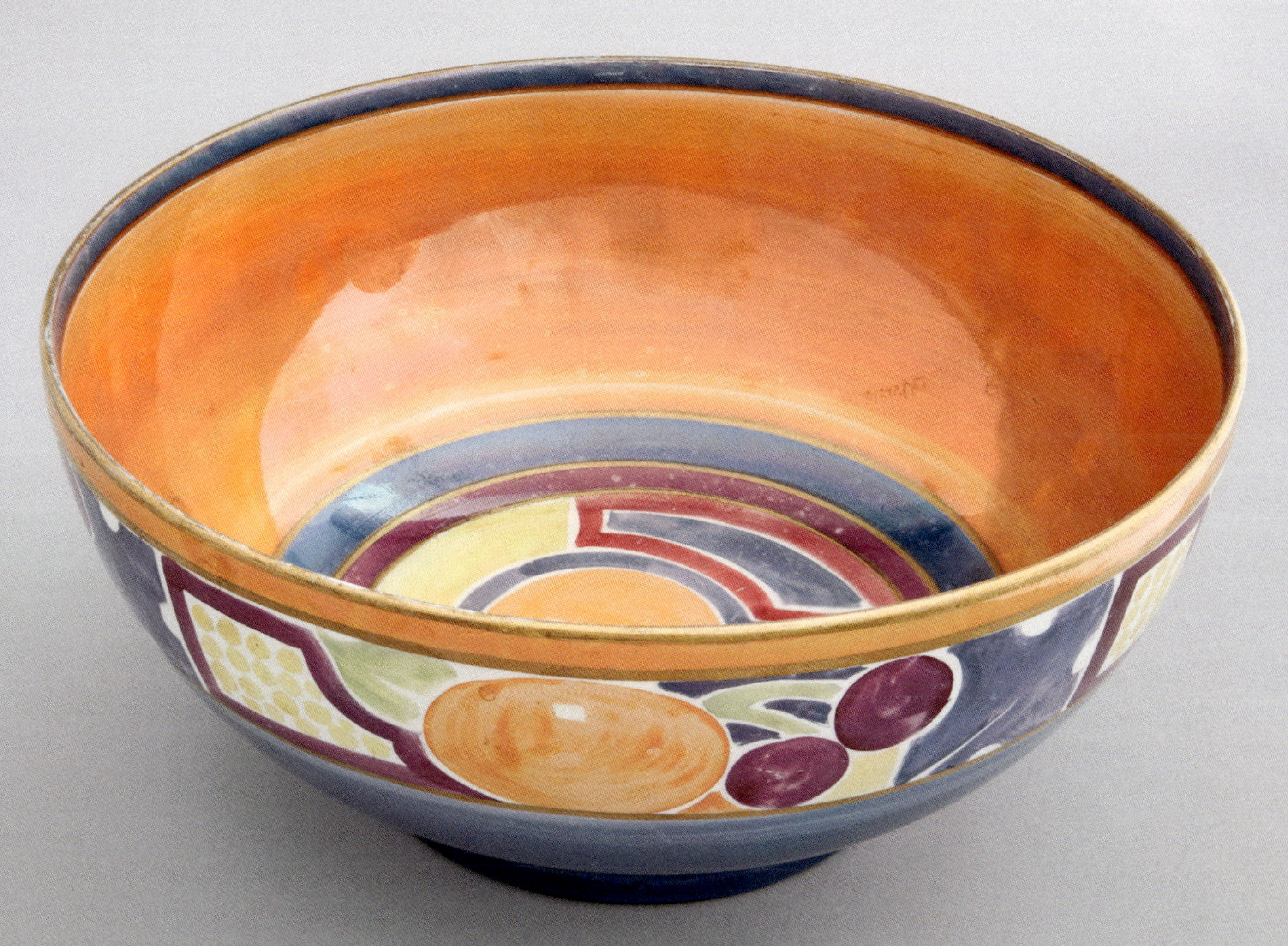

(incising a design into the clay surface). As a measure of her success, Cooper was awarded the title of Royal Designer for Industry in 1940. She was the only woman from the Potteries to have achieved this distinction.

Cooper's business was absorbed into the Wedgwood Group in 1966. She continued to produce cutting-edge designs, with influences ranging from Op Art to ancient Egypt. Her 'Corn Poppy' design was one of Wedgwood's best sellers during the 1980s. Her remarkable career was celebrated in a retrospective exhibition at the Victoria and Albert Museum, London, in 1987. RC

↙ Plate from the 'Dresden Spray' range by Crown Works of Staffordshire, designed 1935, bone china with lithographic print designed by Susie Cooper, 17.5cm (diameter), Wightwick Manor, West Midlands (NT 1288770)

↓ Detail of Susie Cooper's backstamp, Wightwick Manor, West Midlands (NT 1288770)

→ Jam pot and cover by Crown Works of Staffordshire, designed 1957, bone china with lithographic print in the 'Black Fruit' pattern designed by Susie Cooper, 9.5 x 9cm (diameter), Tyntesfield, North Somerset, purchased from the estate of the late Lord Wraxall with the assistance of the National Heritage Memorial Fund and donations from members and supporters, 2002 (NT 21564)

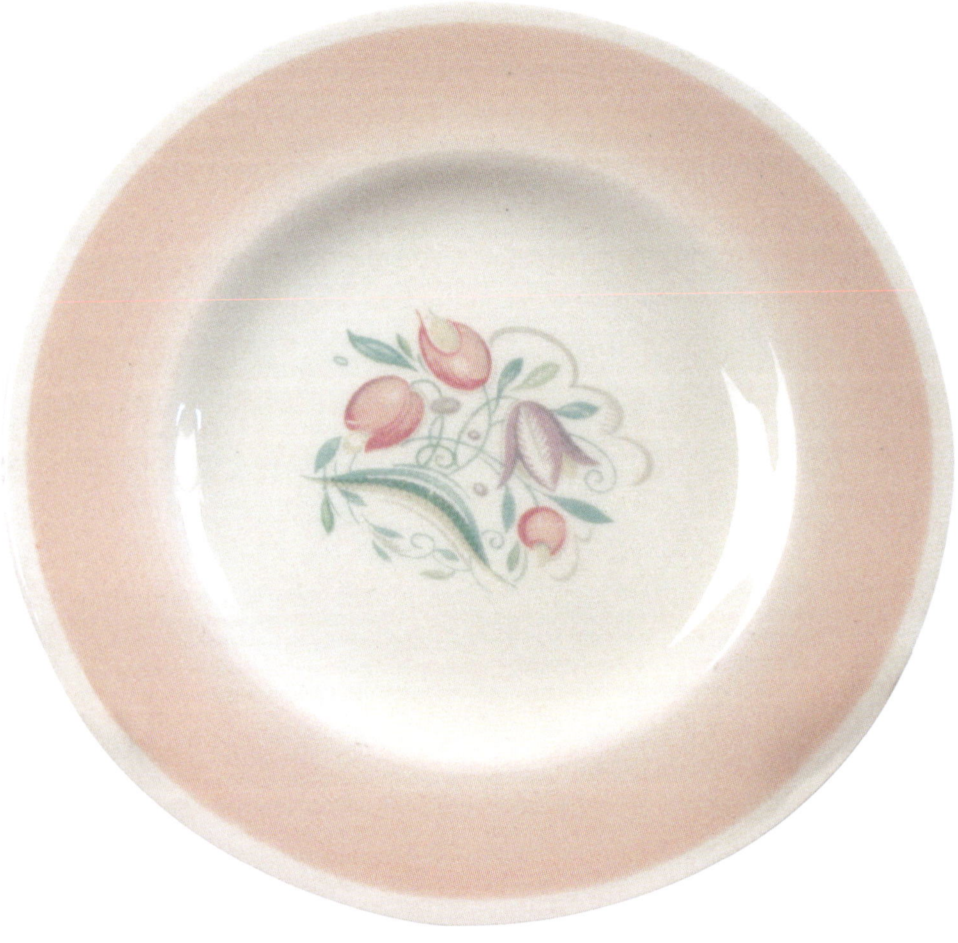

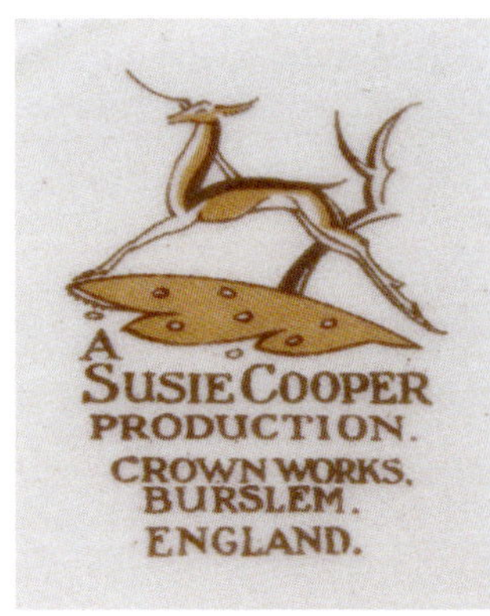

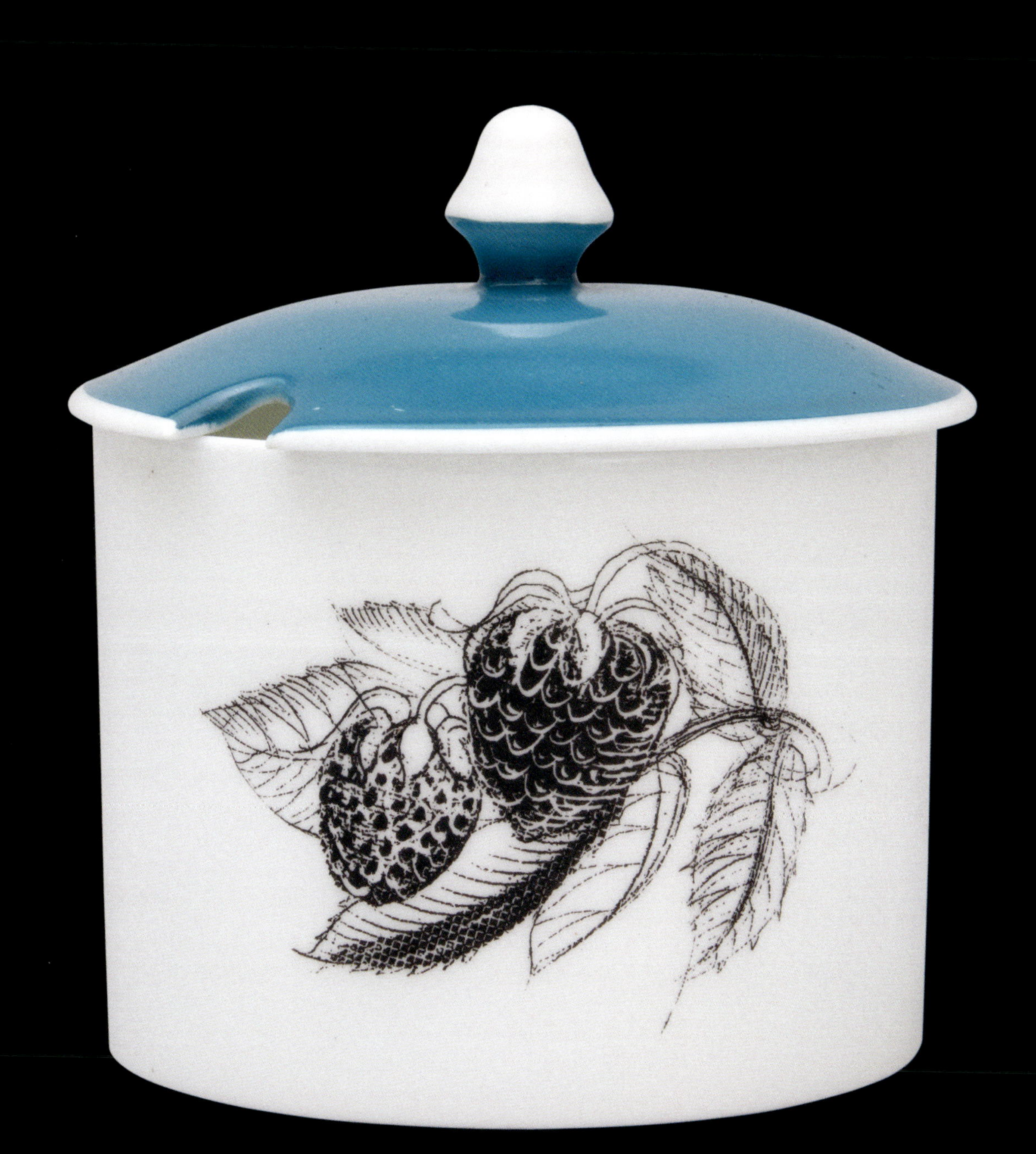

Harmonious colour

DOROTHY NOSSITER (1893–1977)

Dorothy (Dorrie) Nossiter was a respected maker and designer of jewellery working in the late Arts and Crafts tradition. She was born in Birmingham – a centre for excellence in jewellery – and from 1910 attended its Municipal School of Art. By 1929 she was based in London.

Nossiter's jewellery is rarely marked or signed (there was no legal requirement to hallmark jewellery at this time), so the attribution of her work can be difficult. Her pieces are characterised by densely clustered settings of precious and semi-precious gems in vibrant and soft colour tones (sometimes described as 'massed colour schemes'). The small, naturalistic gold grape and vine leaf motifs seen on this heavily jewelled cross pendant (opposite) often feature in her work. Nossiter made pendants, brooches, rings, dress clips and earrings – all intended to harmonise with fashionable clothing and to be suitable for day or evening wear.

Throughout her career Nossiter worked with the King brothers, who created the intricate silver and gold settings needed for her pieces. Although some designs do survive, a 1937 review of an exhibition of her work describes her working in a spontaneous way – 'she never draws a design, but works it out by playing with the gems she has chosen'.

Nossiter regularly exhibited her work, which helped to establish her reputation and even attracted royal clients – her work was reportedly owned by Queen Mary and the Princess Royal. Her jewellery was regularly included in annual shows such as the Applied Arts and Handicrafts Exhibition in London, as well as at independent galleries including The Spinning Wheel in Stratford-upon-Avon and The Craft House in Reigate. She also featured in a series of group exhibitions showcasing contemporary women artists held at Walker's Galleries on New Bond Street, London, between 1935 and 1939. In 1941 she showed a collection at the upmarket Bon Marché department store in Liverpool. An advertisement (page 164) shows the broad price range of Nossiter's work – pieces cost between 49 shillings and £100 ('collector's items or tiny conversation pieces'), roughly equivalent today to £100–£4,000.

Very unusually, Nossiter gave many of her jewels titles – from the elegant *Quiet Evening* to a multi-strand pearl and sapphire necklace that was evocatively named *She Done Him Wrong*. RC

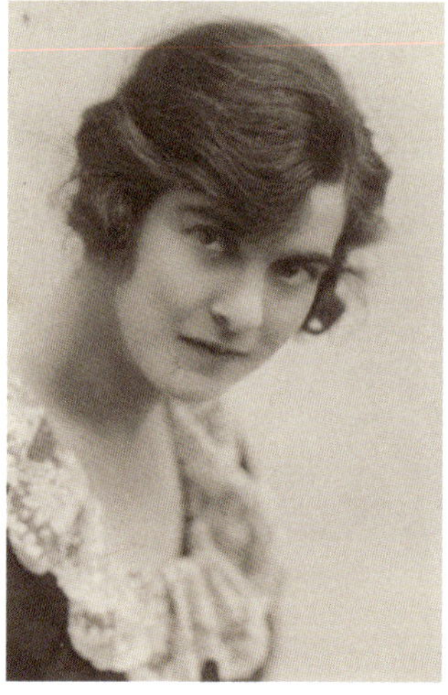

↑ Dorrie Nossiter, unknown photographer, late 1920s
→ Cross attributed to Dorrie Nossiter, *c.*1935, silver and gold set with zircon, chrysoprase, sapphire and pearl, 11.7 x 6.7cm, Anglesey Abbey, Cambridgeshire (NT 517244)

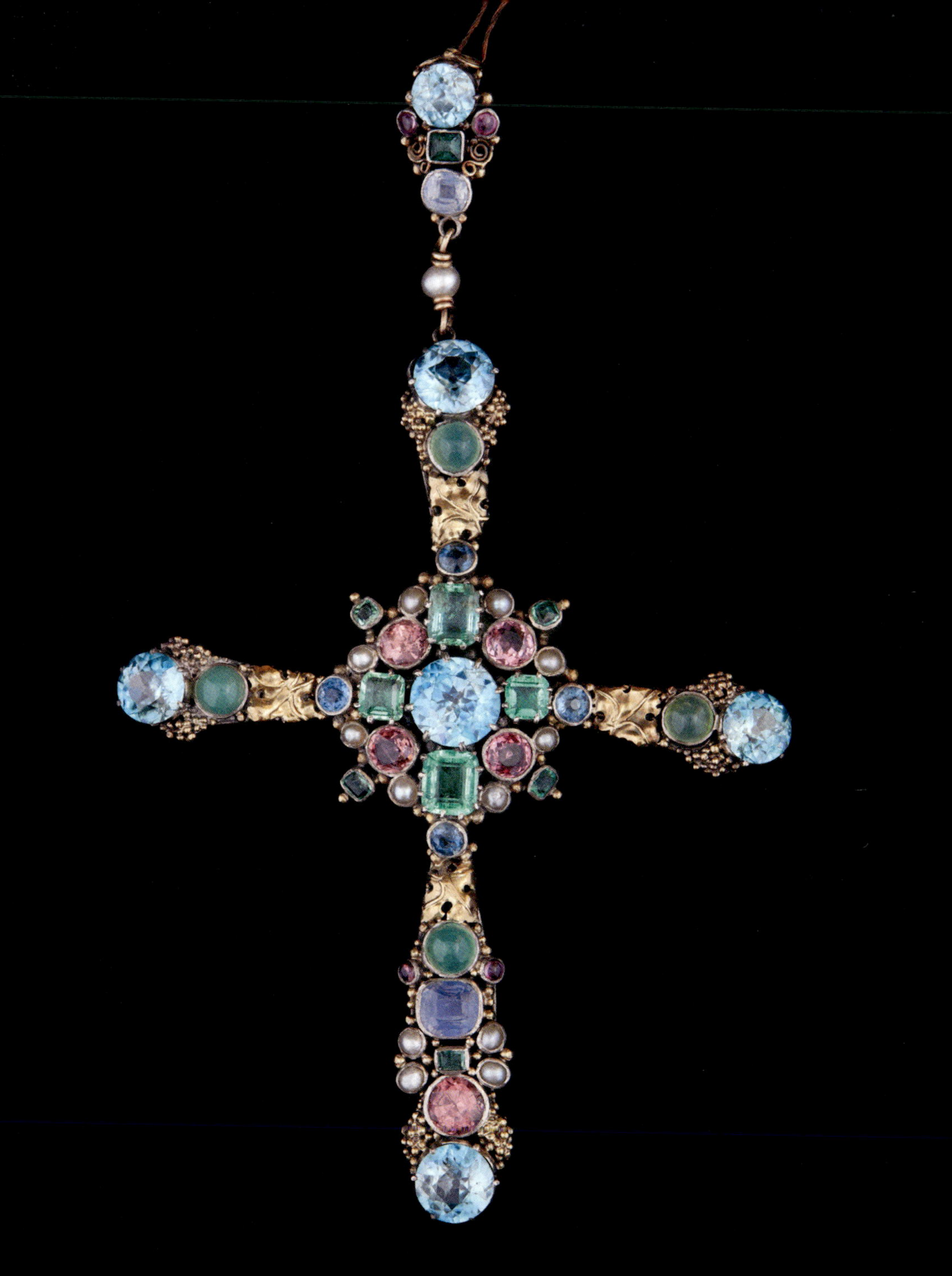

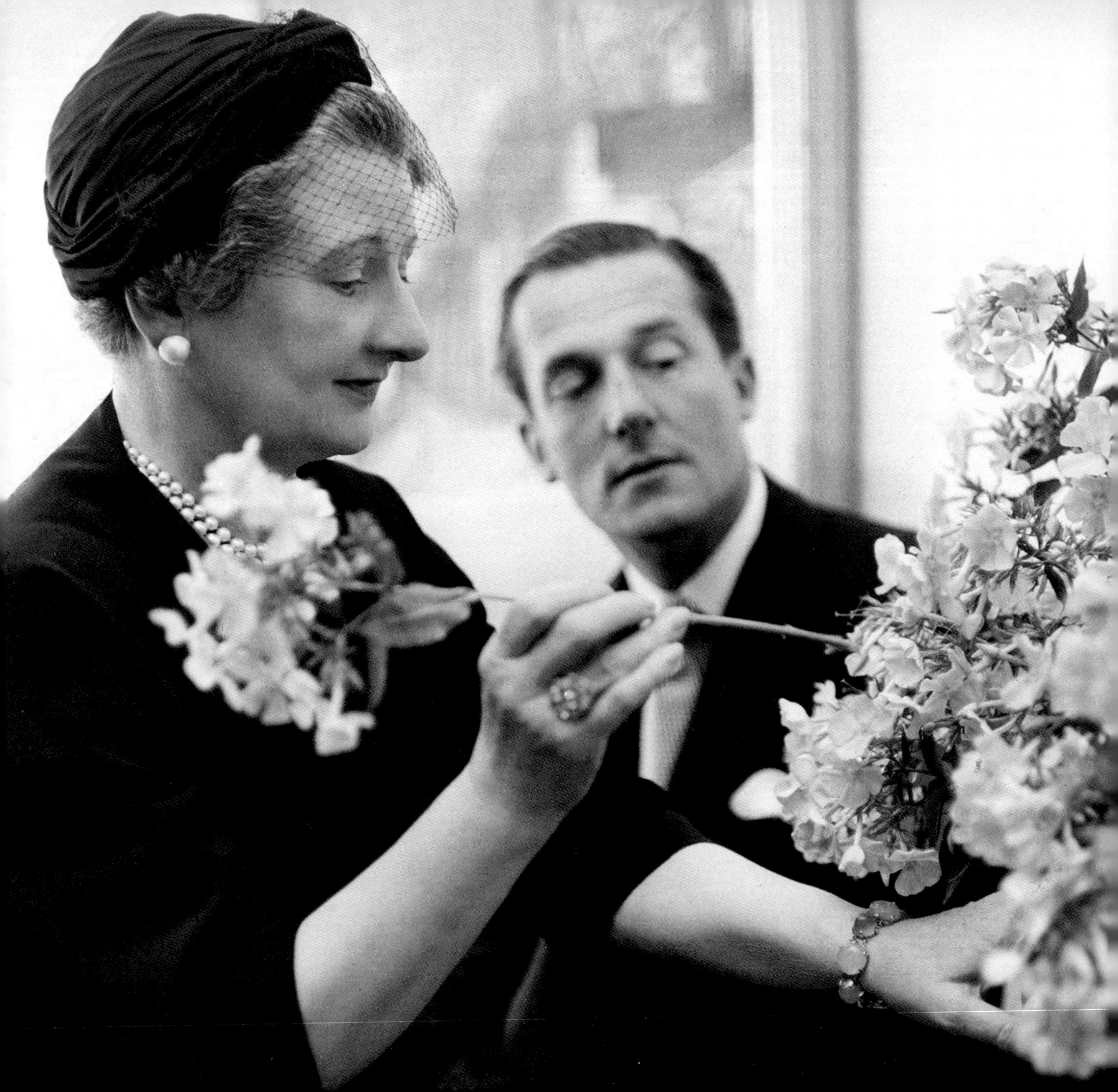

The art of flowers

CONSTANCE SPRY (1886–1960)

In her 1954 book *How to Do the Flowers* Derby-born Constance Spry wrote, '… with living plants as your medium, it is possible to create beauty, even to the degree of making a masterpiece'. Although she is best known for her work as a flower artist, Spry did not enter the profession until she was in her forties, having previously worked in health, social reform and education.

Spry was unconventional in her practice, combining vegetables, foliage and fruit with flowers in dramatic, asymmetrical arrangements led by colour and form. She believed that it was not access to rare and expensive plants that made the best floral artist, but that it was a medium 'for everyone who loves a beautiful thing and will take a little trouble'.

Spry was equally bold in her choice of containers for flowers – advocating the use of, for example, old copper jugs, brass bowls, food tins, antique vases, silver bread baskets and old cooking pots. In the 1930s Spry and her art assistant Florence Standfast collaborated with the Fulham Pottery to design a range of simple but innovative boat-shaped vases, which complemented Spry's open style of arrangement.

Spry later collaborated with Royal Brierley to design ten vases as part of its 'Chunky Crystal' range, which launched in 1959 (page 223). Spry had cautioned her readers against using glass vases for their arrangements, advising that 'confused stems and stained water are an eyesore'. This was certainly borne in mind when she was designing her Brierley range: the marketing material claimed that 'the frozen-water appearance of the Crystal obscures the confused effect liable to arise from stems in a mixed bunch'.

Spry gained international recognition for her art. In 1934, amid this considerable success, she established her shop in London's Mayfair, a suitably chic location for society's most fashionable florist. For a time she created weekly arrangements for the Mansard Gallery in Heal's London department store. Her most important commissions included overseeing the flower displays at Westminster Abbey for the 1947 marriage of Princess Elizabeth, and for her coronation as Queen Elizabeth II five years later.

In the early 1930s Spry was in a relationship outside her marriage with the artist Gluck (born Hannah Gluckstein, 1895–1978), who painted a number of floral paintings inspired by Spry's signature style (overleaf). RC

← Constance Spry with fashion designer Hardy Amies in 1960

↓ *Chromatic* by Gluck (Hannah Gluckstein, 1895–1978), 1932, oil on canvas, 121.9 × 119.4cm, private collection. The painting was inspired by a flower display commissioned from Spry by her friend Prudence Maufe to celebrate the completion of Gluck's new art studio.
→ Vase designed by Constance Spry and made by Stevens and Williams (Royal Brierley), *c.*1959, crystal glass, 15.2cm (height), Berrington Hall, Herefordshire (NT 617438)

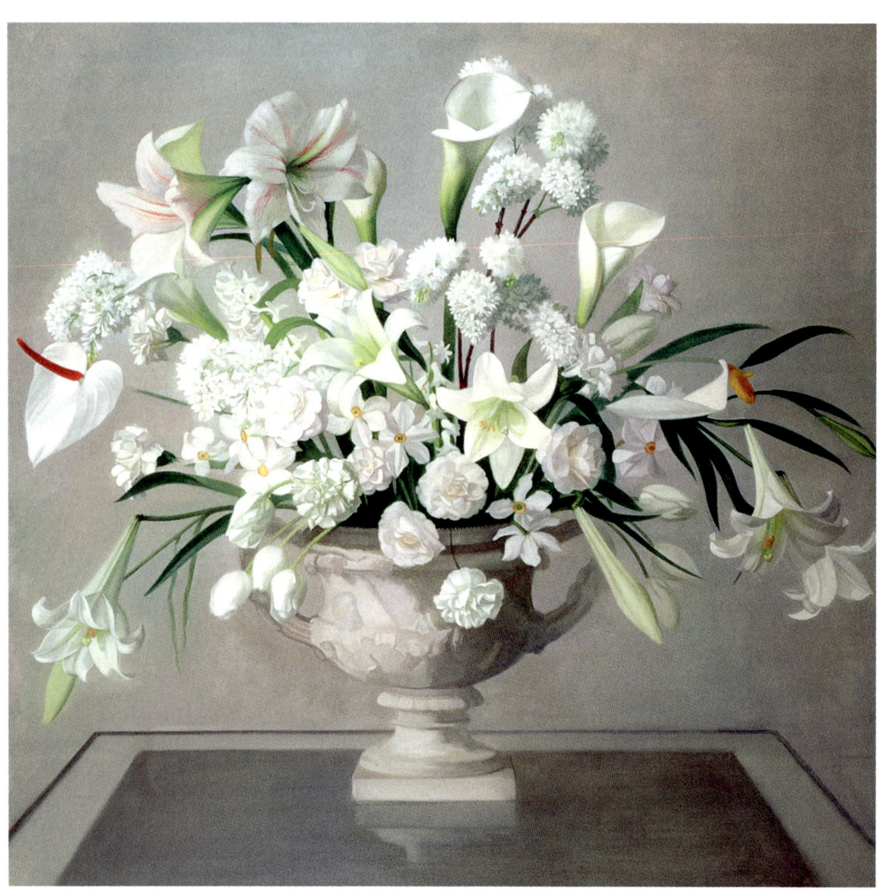

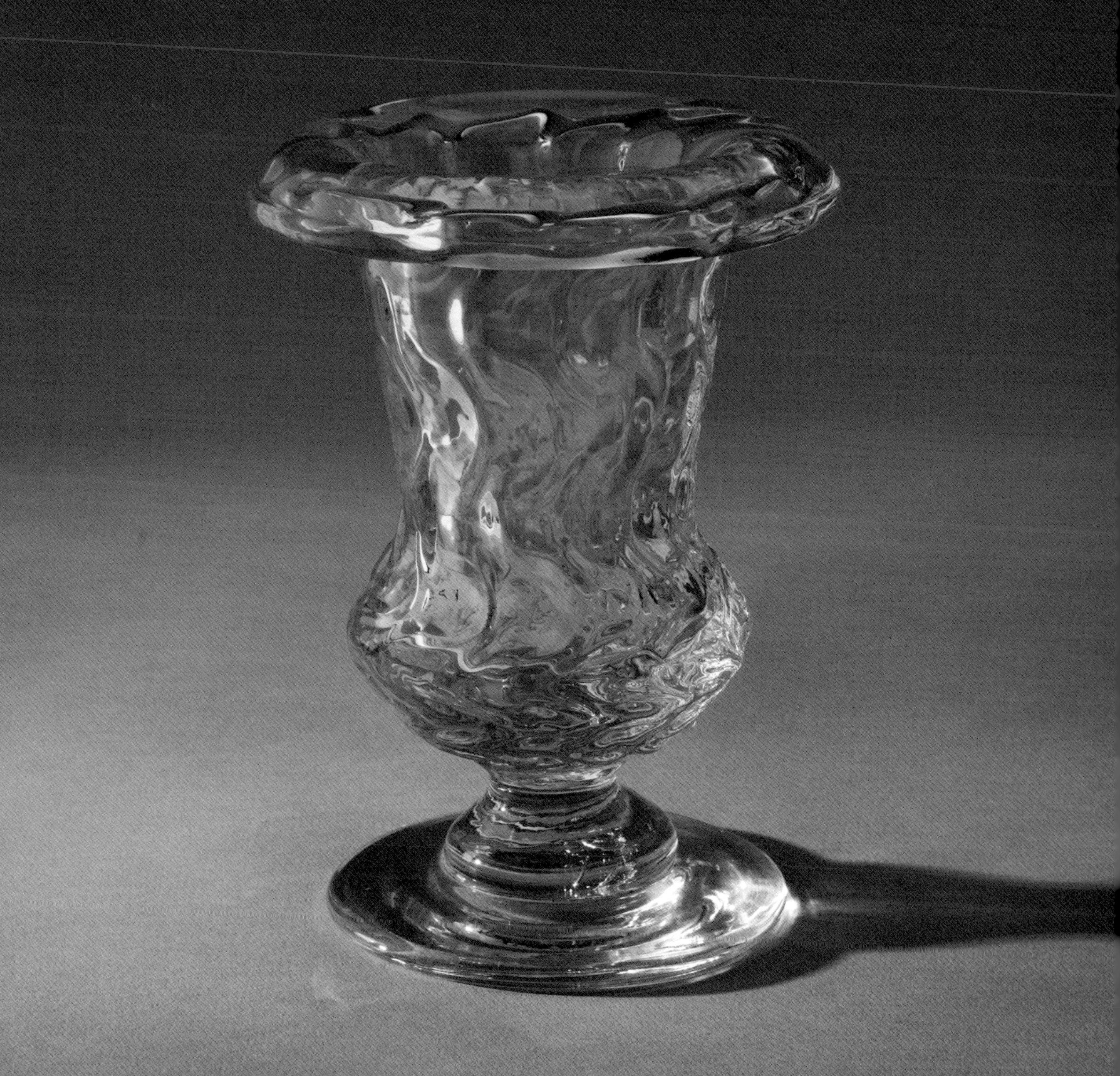

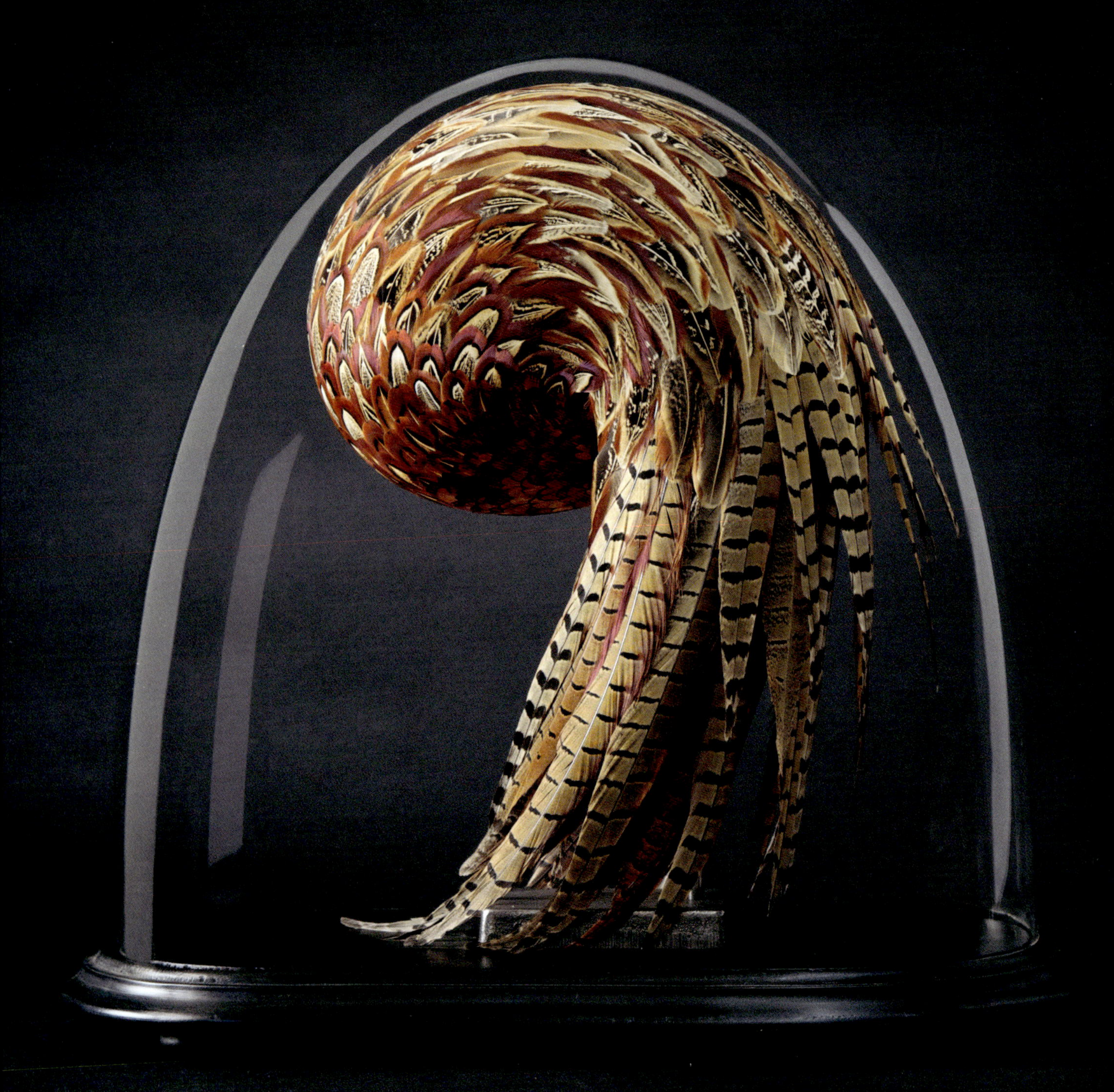

TRUST IN ART

Our collections of 20th-century art are a focus of ongoing research for the National Trust. An important group of works presented by the artist Derek Hill (1916–2000) is at Mottisfont, Hampshire – in addition to earlier works by Gwen John (page 167), it includes paintings and drawings from the mid-to-late 20th century by Adrienne Haig (1929–2010), Barbara Hepworth (page 233), Joan Eardley (1921–63) and Mary Potter (1900–81).

Paintings, embroideries and furniture decorated by Florence Elsie Matley Moore are at Greyfriars, the Worcestershire home she restored with her brother (page 227). Moore was best known for the detailed watercolours she produced to record historic stained-glass windows and other decorative features in Worcestershire, which were at risk of bomb-damage during the Second World War.

The works by Lucie Rie (page 244) and Janet Leach (page 240) at Greenway, Devon – both dating from the later stage of their careers – reflect the continuing importance of women in the British studio pottery movement during the second half of the 20th century. In the 1980s a group of extraordinary young artists from the Royal College of Art, including Elizabeth Fritsch (b.1940), Alison Britton (b.1948) and Jacqueline Poncelet (b.1947), continued to stretch the boundaries of ceramics by creating radically different work, dubbed 'New Ceramics', that was highly conceptual and sculptural. All of these women were

← *Perihelion*, Kate MccGwire (b.1964), 2014, mixed media with pheasant feathers in antique dome, 50 x 45 x 28cm, commissioned by Norfolk Contemporary Arts Society for *The Tourists* exhibition at Felbrigg Hall, Norfolk

pivotal in foregrounding ceramics as an art form – and one that flourishes today. Within the ceramics industry, Susan Williams-Ellis (page 239) was an influential designer and businesswoman, while Susie Cooper (page 214) established her own highly successful ceramics business that went on to become part of the Wedgwood Group. Other prolific ceramic designers during the mid- and later 20th century include Jessie Tait and Eve Midwinter (W.R. Midwinter Ltd), Kathie Winkle (James Broadhurst & Sons Ltd), Truda Carter and Ruth Pavely (Poole Pottery), Peggy Davies and Agnete Hoy (Doulton).

One designer that the National Trust had a close relationship with during this period was Pat Albeck (1930–2017), a talented textile and flat-pattern designer. Albeck was another Royal College of Art alumnus and started working with Horrockses Fashions while still a student in the 1950s. She produced beautiful, illustrative designs for printed cottons that were used for classic, full-skirted dresses. From the 1970s onwards Albeck designed some of the National Trust's most iconic pieces of merchandise, including 300 joyous tea towels, many designed for individual properties, Albeck capturing the essence of each with humour, flair and impeccable attention to detail. The collection at the Victoria and Albert Museum includes an early design for a range of products incorporating the Trust's acorn logo (right). Later in life, Albeck discovered a passion for cut-paperwork, exhibiting intricate flowers on black backgrounds, reminiscent of the work of Mary Delany (page 52) over 200 years earlier.

During recent years, the National Trust has engaged with many women artists, principally through displays and exhibitions. The Foundation for Art programme (1986–2001) commissioned artists to respond to National Trust places and saw the acquisition of works by women. Over 300 emerging and established artists were commissioned to create work in response to our places through the Trust New Art programme (2009–22), supported by Arts Council England. They included Turner prize-winner Lubaina Himid (b.1954), sculptor and installation artist Susie MacMurray (b.1959) and Kate MccGwire (b.1964), who creates remarkable sinuous sculptural works using feathers (page 224). A programme of silversmithing residencies supported by the Worshipful Company of Goldsmiths in 2012–13 saw Miriam Hanid (b.1986), Rauni Higson (b.1970) and Theresa Nguyen (b.1985) displaying

↓ *Acorn*, Pat Albeck, 1970, pencil and felt tip on paper, 36.6 x 26.7cm (Victoria and Albert Museum, London). This sheet includes designs for oven gloves, a chopping board and carrier bags.

→ Embroidered overmantel created by Florence Elsie Matley Moore (1900–85) in 1970, wool crewel work on linen, 137 x 37cm, Greyfriars, Worcestershire (NT 443636)

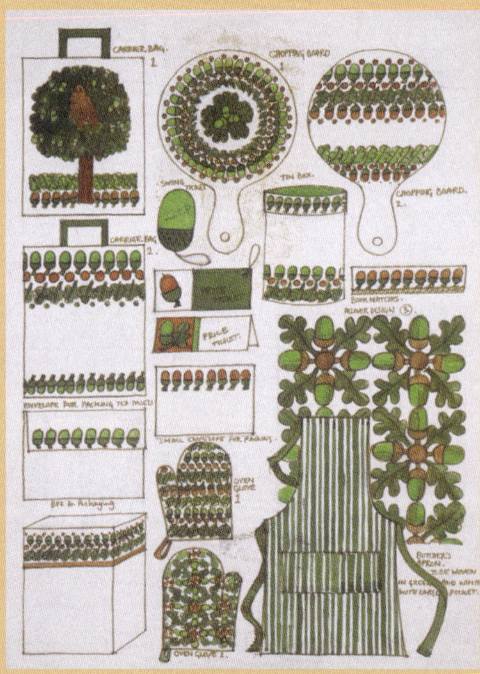

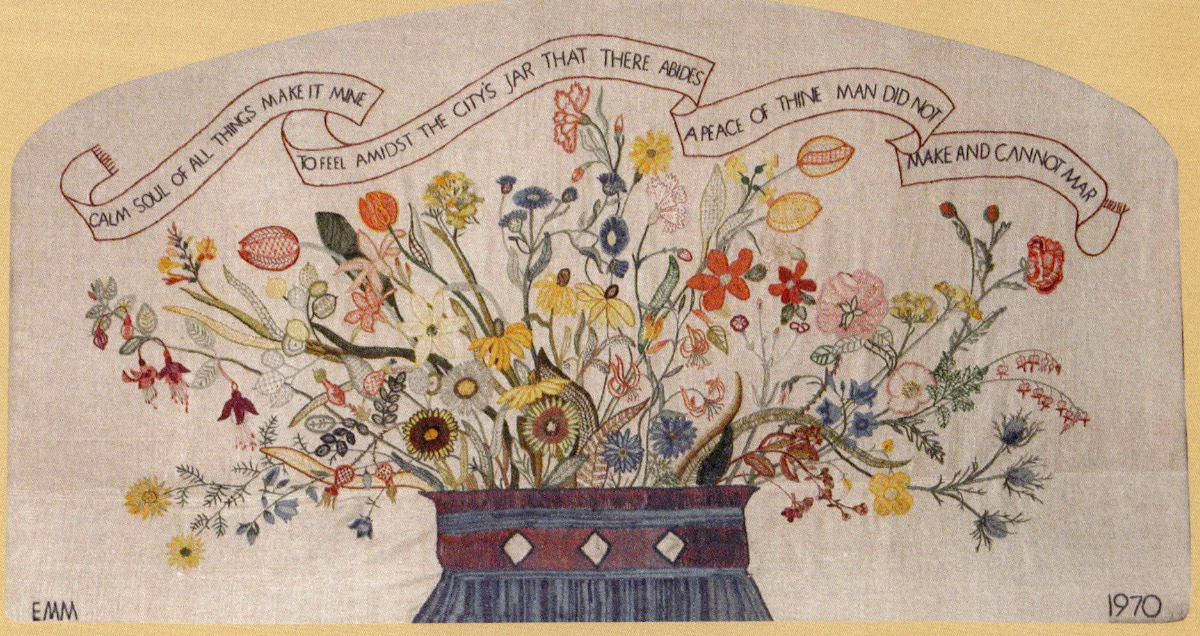

work and demonstrating their extraordinary skills at Ickworth, Erddig and Kedleston. More recently, a partnership between Petworth and the Royal Academy saw work by its first female president, Rebecca Salter (b.1955), exhibited at the property.

Women artists make up only an estimated two per cent of the National Trust's collection of oil paintings. Although this is incredibly disproportionate, as a comparison, the National Gallery estimates half as many for its collection. It feels important for us to continue to develop the National Trust's contemporary holdings in ways that are strategic, ambitious, relevant to place and that foreground public benefit. Recent examples include photographs by Tabitha Jussa (page 248), Dafna Talmor (b.1974) and Ellen Carey (b.1952), which are adding richness and new context to our important collections of historic photography. Meanwhile, at Croome, Worcestershire, Faye Claridge (b.1976) is co-designing four new sculptures with community groups, inspired by originals depicting the four seasons – an exciting opportunity for a socially engaged commission that will reinstate a 'lost' feature of the historic parkland. Perhaps this signals a direction for our future?

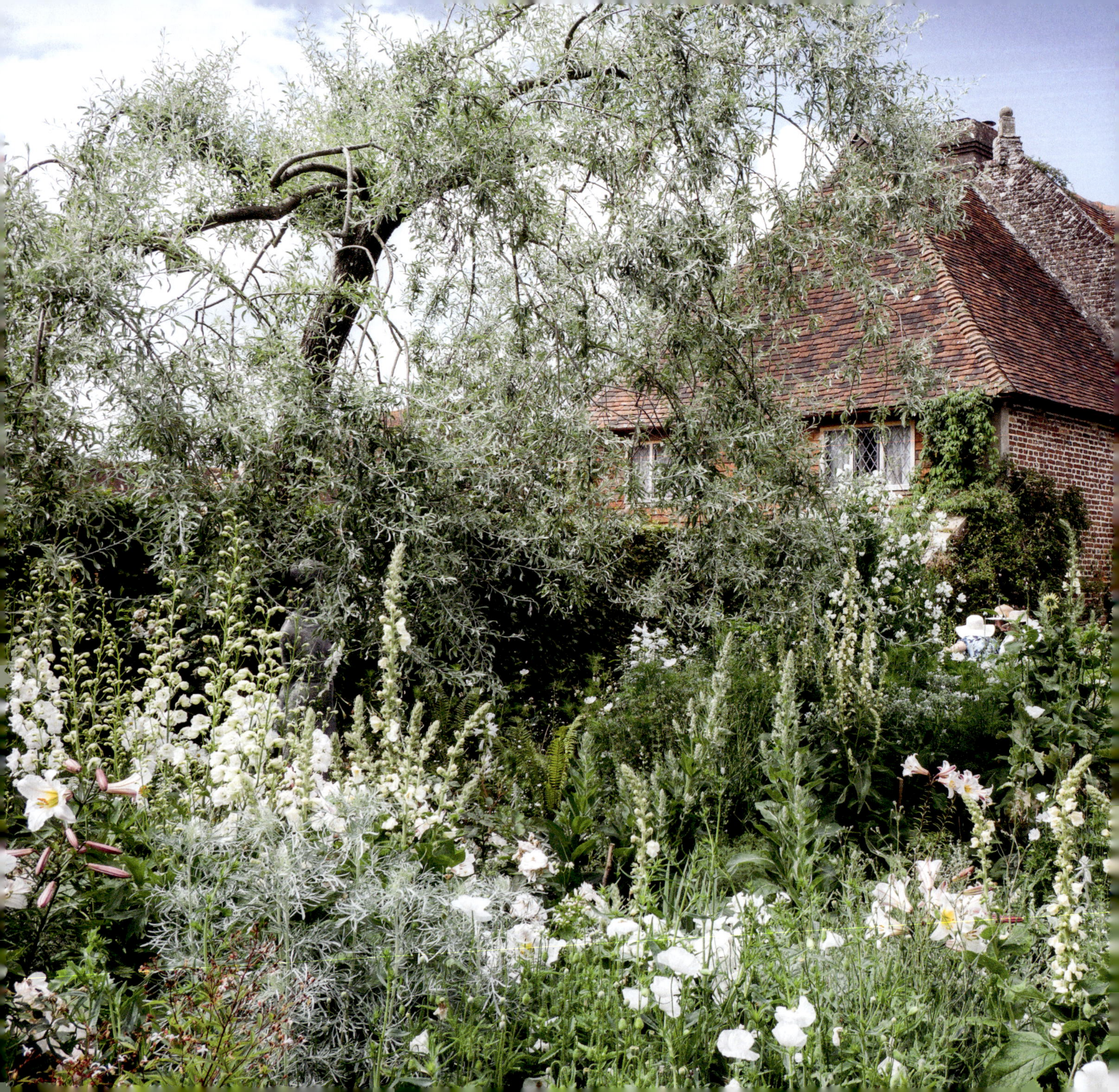

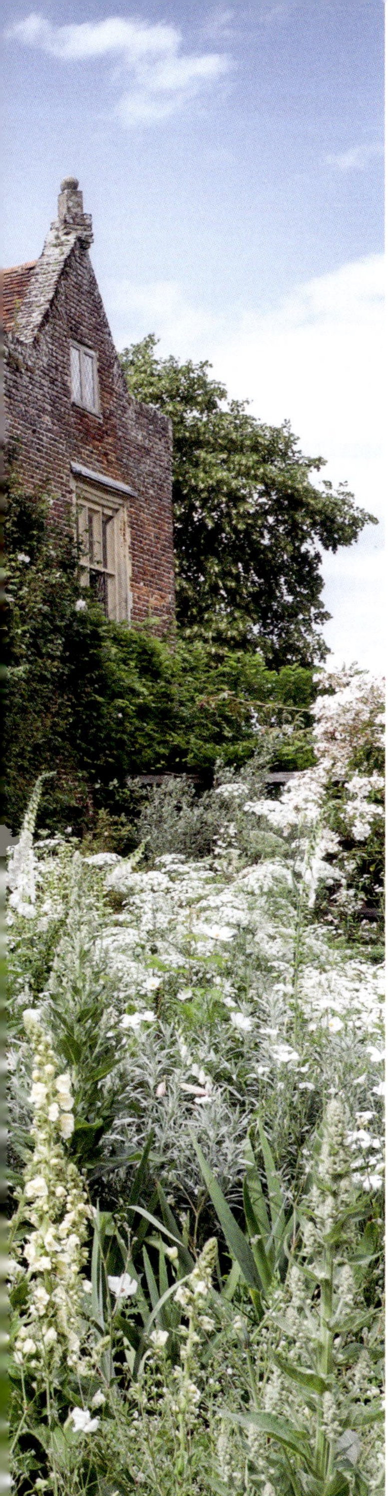

Poetic planting

VITA SACKVILLE-WEST (1892–1962)

Victoria Mary (Vita) Sackville-West spent most of her childhood at Knole, Kent. As a child she read voraciously and wrote novels, plays and poetry. Sackville-West and her husband, Harold Nicolson, purchased their Kent home, Sissinghurst, in 1930. Their partnership was unconventional but ultimately harmonious, with both pursuing same-sex relationships outside the marriage while remaining loving and supportive companions.

The gardens created collaboratively by Sackville-West and Nicolson at Sissinghurst are among the most influential in the world. The buildings and garden were badly run-down – in 1950 she described them as 'Sleeping Beauty's castle with a vengeance' – but they were steadily planned and transformed. Sackville-West was not a professional gardener, but her planting schemes and original style define the gardens. She filled the formal structure of garden rooms and vistas, designed by Nicolson, with romantic, billowing planting, and developed distinct colour schemes, such as the much-imitated White Garden (left). The planting is almost entirely of specimens with white flowers or silvery-grey foliage, including clematis, roses, foxgloves and hostas. Adjoining it is Delos, which has recently been reimagined in the spirit of the couple's original vision. This experimental garden sought to evoke the atmosphere of the Greek island it is named after, which Sackville-West and Nicolson had visited in 1935. It incorporates four Hellenistic marble altars and a Corinthian capital, removed from Delos in the 1830s, arranged to give the impression of the ancient ruins found on the island.

Sackville-West's achievements as a writer and gardener were recognised in her lifetime – she wrote more than 20 books and many articles on gardening, including regular columns for *The Observer*, from her room in Sissinghurst's tower. In 1948 she was appointed a Companion of Honour for her services to literature, was the first woman to win the Hawthornden Prize for poetry, and in 1955 received the gold Veitch medal of the Royal Horticultural Society for her gardens at Sissinghurst. RC

↞ The White Garden at Sissinghurst, Kent
↓ *Victoria (Vita) Mary Sackville-West, Lady Nicolson*, Philip Alexius de László de Lombos (1869–1937), 1910, oil on canvas, 106.7 x 91.4cm, Sissinghurst, Kent (NT 803030)
→ Vita Sackville-West's desk in the Writing Room at Sissinghurst

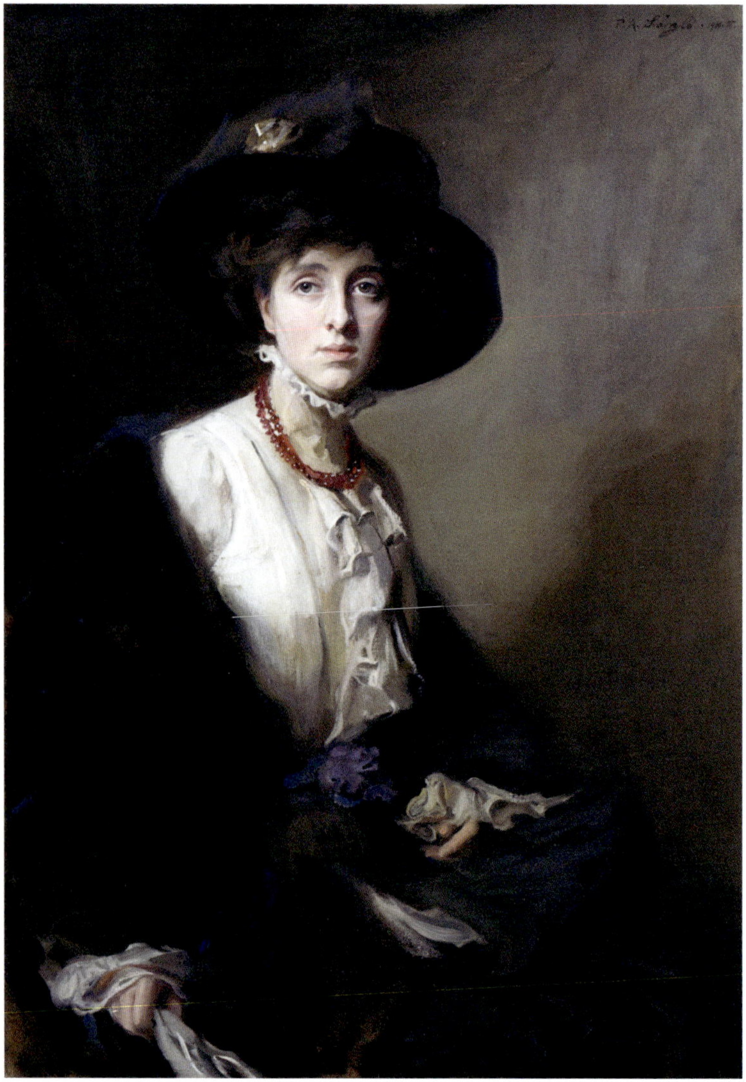

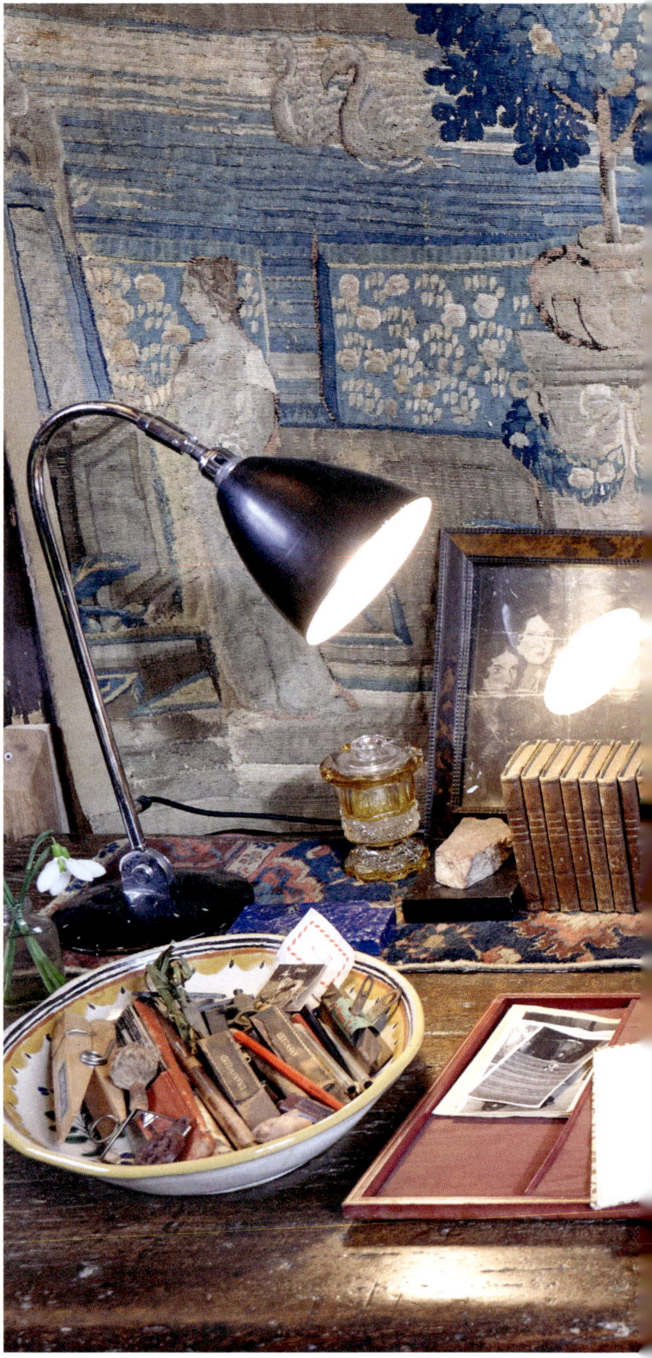

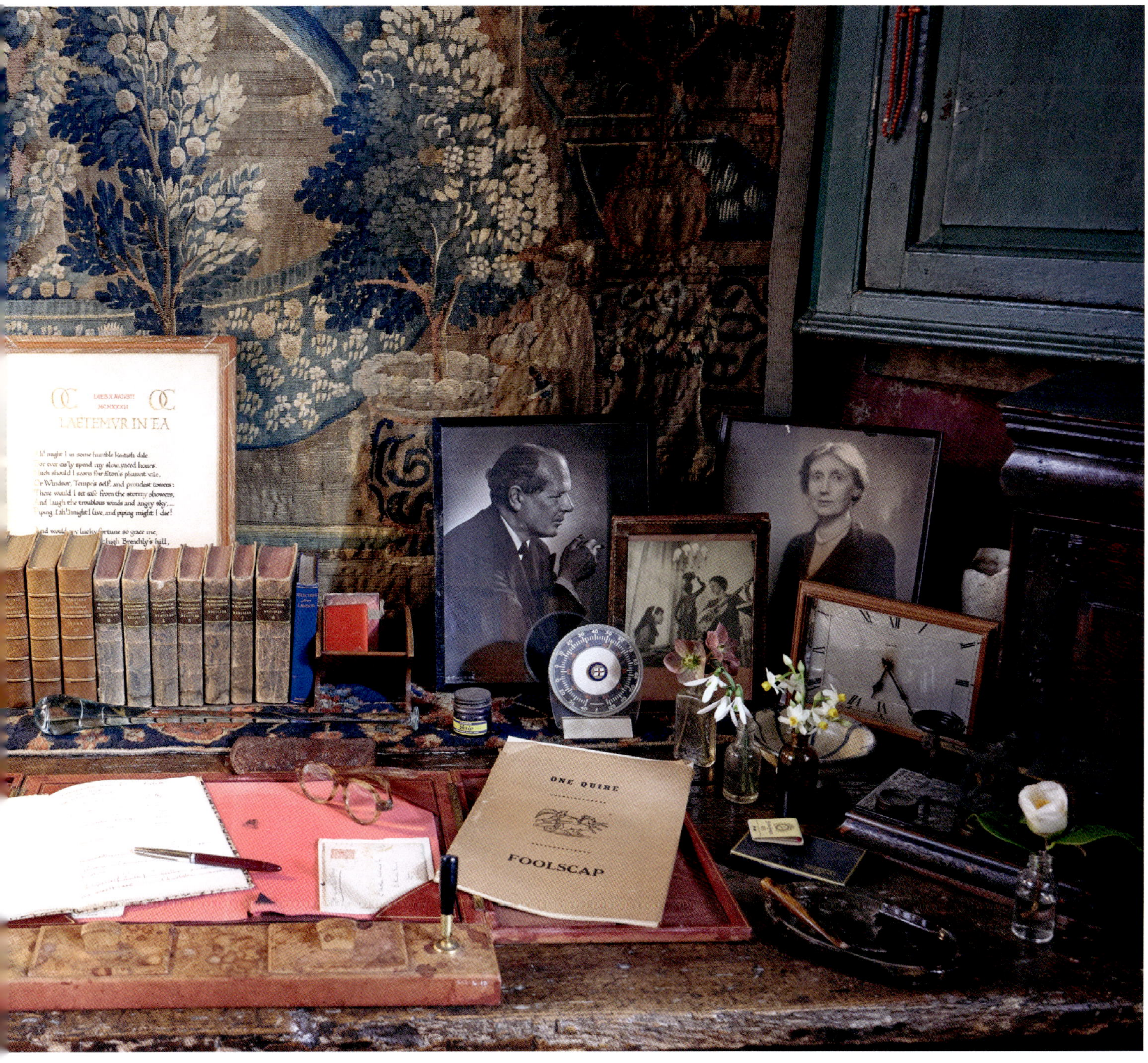
DIES X AVGVSTI
MCMXXXII
LAETEMVR IN EA
h! might I in some humble Kentish dale
or ever easly spend my slow-paced hours.
uch should I scorn fair Eton's pleasant vale,
r Windsor, Tempe's self, and proudest towers:
here would I sit safe from the stormy showers,
nd laugh the troublous winds and angry sky,—
iping, (ah!) might I live, and piping might I die!
ONE QUIRE
FOOLSCAP

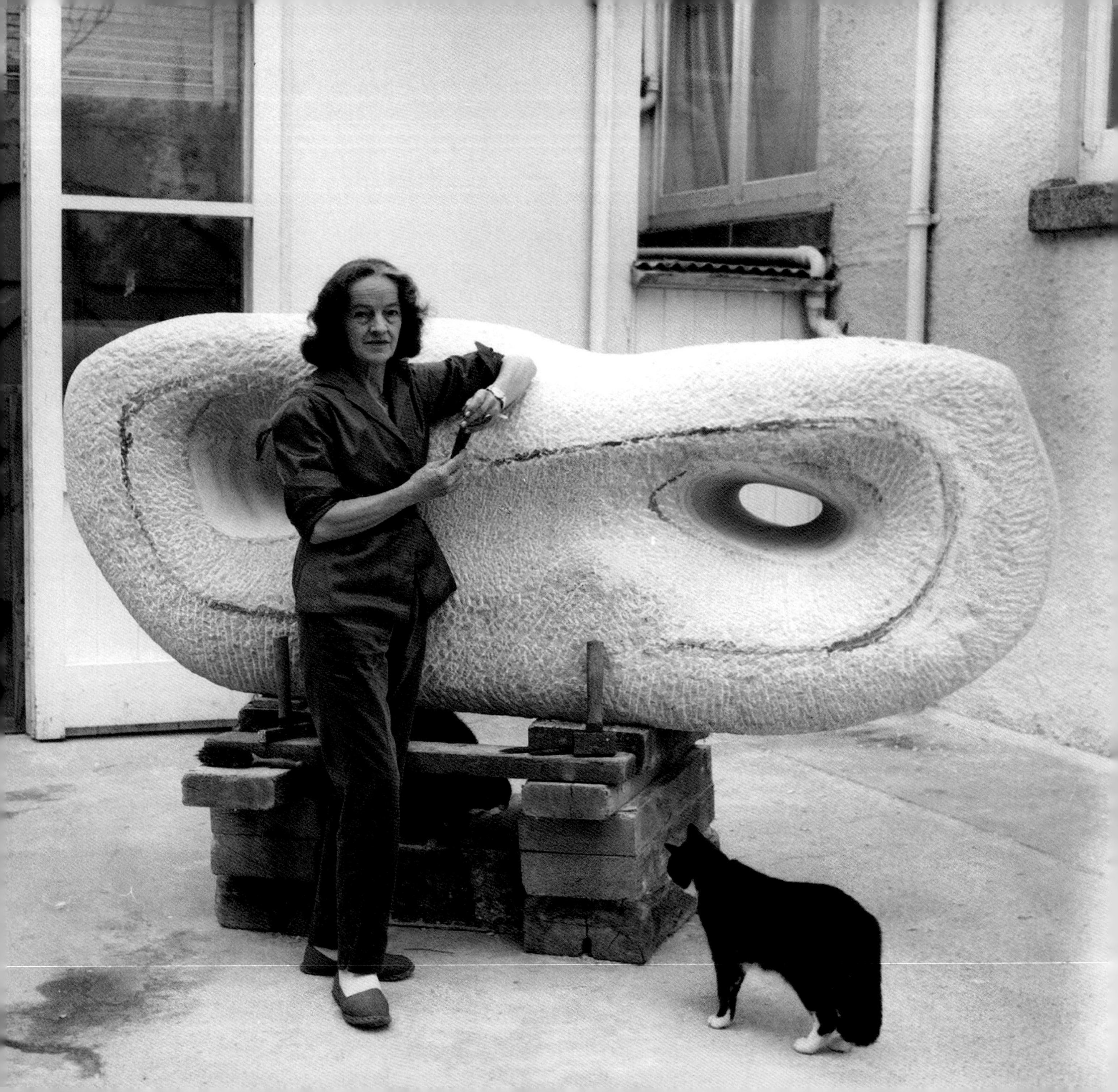

Form and figure

BARBARA HEPWORTH (1903–75)

← Barbara Hepworth with her cat Nicholas and her sculpture *Reclining Form (Rosewall)*, photographed by Ida Kar in 1961 (National Portrait Gallery, London)

Barbara Hepworth is one of the most important and celebrated artists of the 20th century. She produced a remarkable body of work throughout her career, particularly hand-carved sculptures in stone and wood that were later cast in metal. She was a leading figure in a number of avant-garde movements and the first woman to represent Britain at the Venice Biennale.

Hepworth was born in Wakefield and studied at Leeds School of Art before enrolling on the Royal College of Art's sculpture course. A scholarship enabled her to travel to Italy in 1924 – a formative experience that provided her first significant introduction to direct stone carving. Thirty years later, a long-awaited visit to Greece was similarly inspirational and restorative, following as it did the death of her eldest son the previous year. The trip to Greece was arranged by Hepworth's close friend and supporter Margaret Gardiner. Inspired by ancient Greek *kouroi* sculptures depicting male youths, Hepworth's drawing *Figures (Delphi)* (overleaf) is one of a number of her works that respond to the beautiful ancient town on the slopes of Mount Parnassus. She described her experience of being there as feeling 'at ease both physically and spiritually'.

The small, cast-bronze sculpture *Two Forms (Orkney)* (page 235) is another that emerged from her friendship with Gardiner, who lived on the island of Rousay. Like many of Hepworth's sculptures, the relationship between the dual forms, which appear to gently lean into each other, is important – the pierced hole of one mirroring a recess in the other, the polished surfaces creating contrasting light and shade.

Hepworth encountered and challenged overt and implied sexism during her career, particularly in relation to her dual roles as an artist and mother. In her 1970 *Pictorial Autobiography* she wrote, '… the dictates of work are as compelling for a woman as for a man'.

Her legacy is celebrated at the Barbara Hepworth Museum on the site of her former studio in St Ives, Cornwall, and at The Hepworth Wakefield. RC

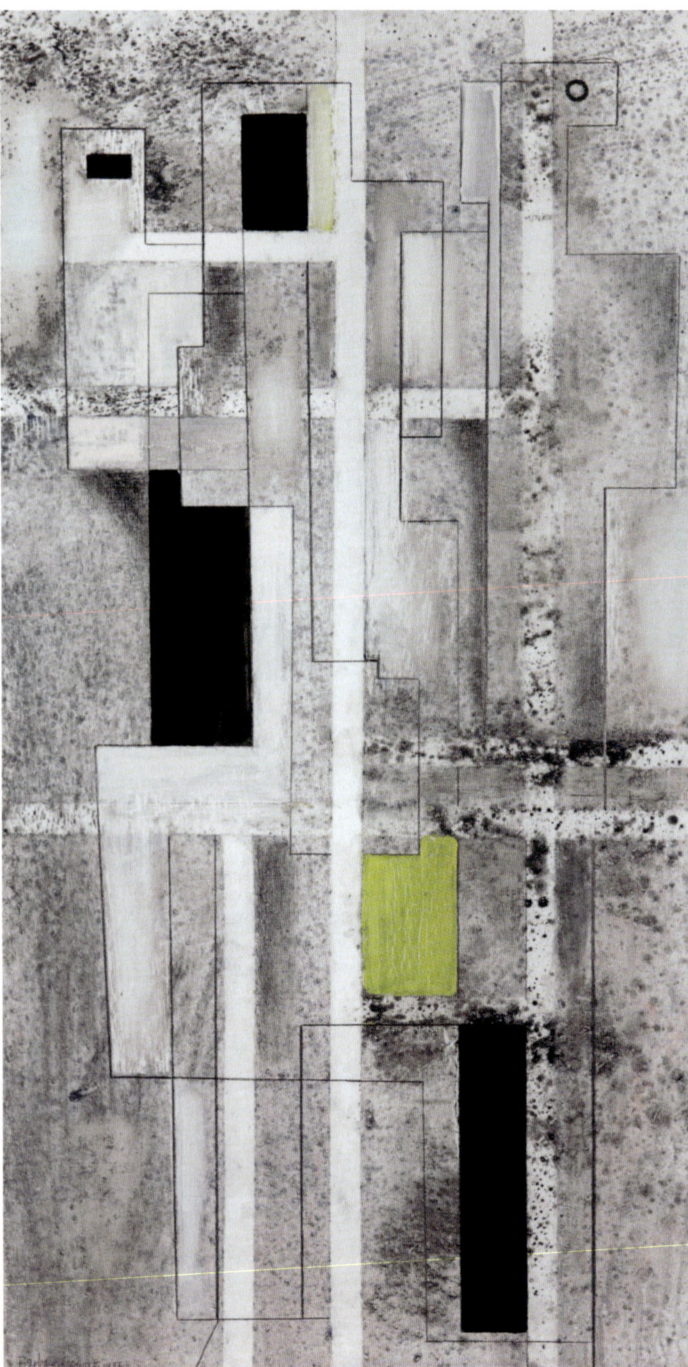

← *Figures (Delphi)*, Barbara Hepworth, 1956, oil, pencil and gouache on fibreboard, 76 x 38cm, Dudmaston, Shropshire (NT 814221)
→ *Two Forms (Orkney)*, Barbara Hepworth, 1967, polished bronze, wood, 19.5 x 29 x 20cm, Dudmaston, Shropshire (NT 814369)

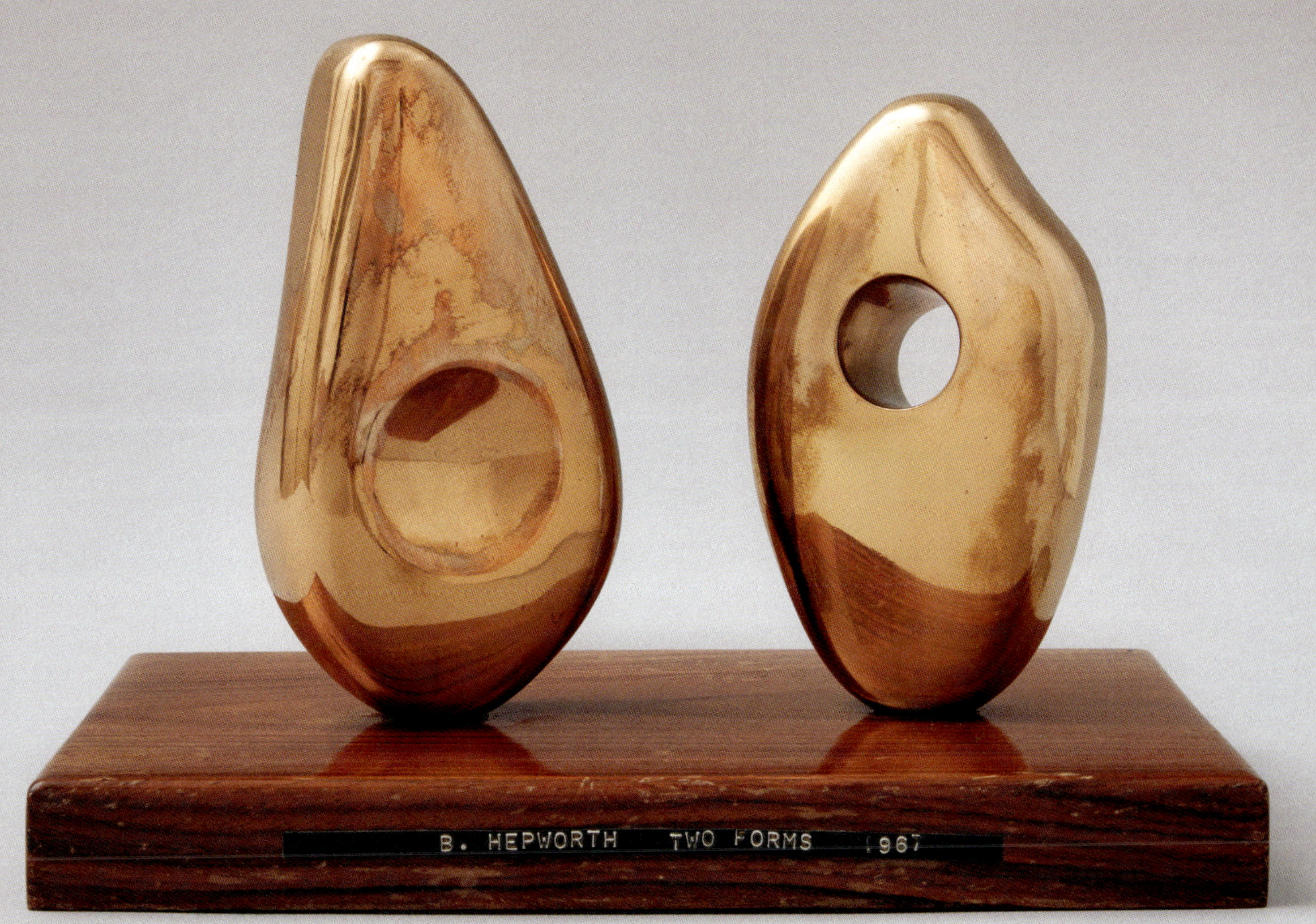
B. HEPWORTH TWO FORMS 1967

Modern comfort

RAY EAMES (1912–88)

Ray Eames is best known for the groundbreaking furniture designs she created in collaboration with her husband, Charles Eames (1907–78). Together, they also worked across interior design, graphics, exhibition design, filmmaking and architecture – most notably the creation of The Eames House, their steel-framed home in Los Angeles.

Eames was born in Sacramento and moved to New York to study with Hans Hofmann (1880–1966), an influential avant-garde painter and teacher. She became a founder member of the American Abstract Artists group, which fought for the recognition of non-representational art, and she went on to study at Cranbrook Academy of Art in Michigan. It was here that she met Charles, whom she married in 1941. Ray and Charles moved to Los Angeles and their remarkable creative partnership began. The understanding of structure and colour that Ray had developed through her training as a painter was a consistently important influence on their work.

The celebrated Eames Office, led by Ray and Charles, focused on the creation of high-quality, practical and affordable mass-produced furniture using modern materials and techniques. After the Second World War they focused, with great commercial and critical success, on the production of chairs in moulded plywood – a material that was strong but pliant – manufactured to their design by the Herman Miller Furniture Company in Michigan. A few years later they developed seating with moulded, coloured shells in plastic – a relatively new material for furniture.

The Lounge Chair (model 670), formed from three linked plywood shells veneered with rich rosewood and upholstered in leather, was in development for two years and marked a departure from affordability into luxury. Launched in 1956 with a matching Ottoman (model 671), it was advertised as 'luxuriously comfortable, completely relaxing, supremely handsome'. Today it is considered an icon of mid-century modern design. RC

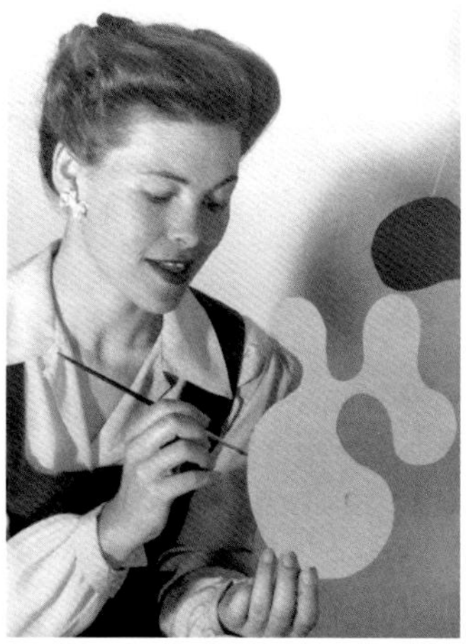

↑ Ray Eames photographed by Charles Eames in the early 1940s
→ Lounge Chair (model 670) and Ottoman (model 671), designed by Charles and Ray Eames, *c.*1953–5, made by Herman Miller Furniture Company, Michigan, *c.*1956–70, plywood with rosewood veneer, leather, steel and aluminium, 92 x 83cm, The Homewood, Surrey (NT 864325.1–2)

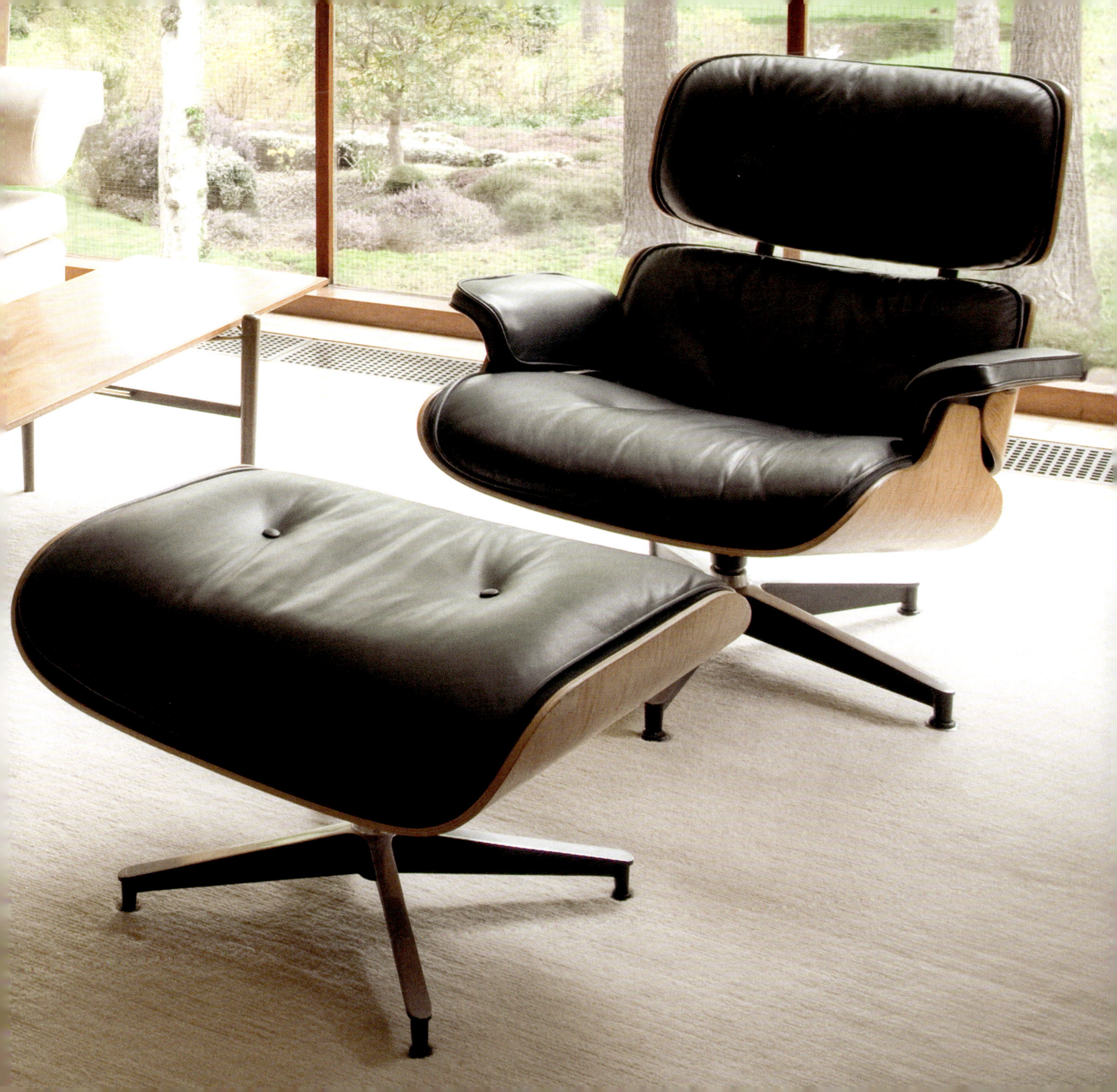

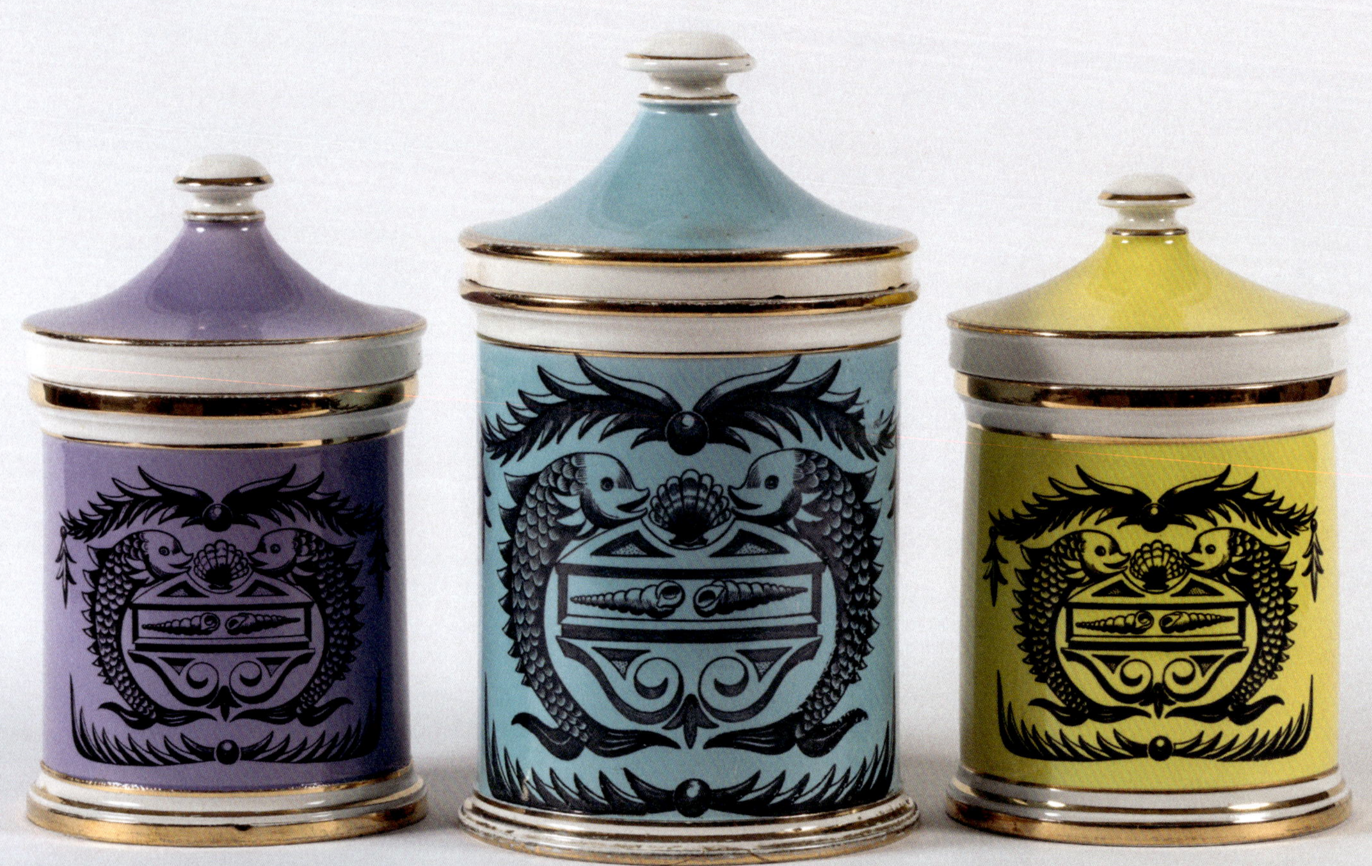

The model of a modern designer

SUSAN WILLIAMS-ELLIS (1918–2007)

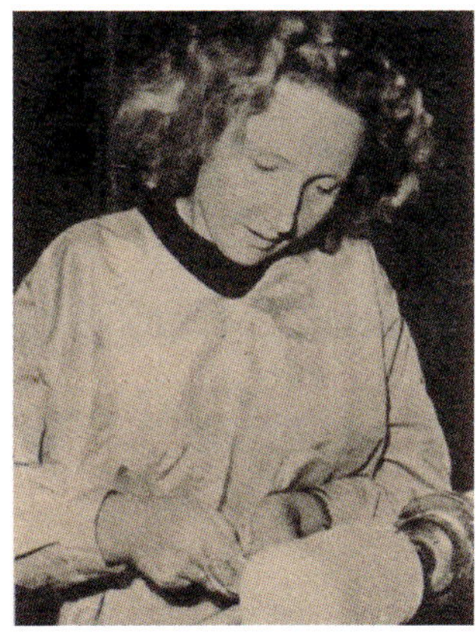

← Group of *Dolphin* pattern 'store' or 'apothecary' jars designed by Susan Williams-Ellis in 1959, made by Portmeirion (Gray's Pottery), Stoke-on-Trent, *c*.1959–68, largest size 14cm (diameter), Chartwell, Kent (NT 1101347–8)
↑ Susan Williams-Ellis at work in her studio, *c*.1965

Susan Williams-Ellis founded the Portmeirion Pottery. She created cutting-edge designs for table, tea and coffee wares that continue to sell across the world.

Williams-Ellis was born into a creative family and was determined to become an artist from an early age. As a child, she attended Dartington Hall School in Devon, where she was taught wood-turning – a skill that she would later put to use making plaster moulds for her commercial ceramics – and wheel-throwing by potters Bernard and David Leach, which developed her understanding of clay. She went on to study at Chelsea Polytechnic's art school, before returning to Dartington to teach art, later working as an illustrator and independent textile and surface-pattern designer. A set of tiles she designed for Poole Pottery was shown in the 1946 *Britain Can Make It* exhibition at the Victoria and Albert Museum, London.

In 1953 Williams-Ellis and her husband, Euan Cooper-Willis (1920–2015), took over the running of the gift shop at Portmeirion, the model village in Gwynedd designed by her father, the architect Clough Williams-Ellis (1883–1978). Sensing an opportunity to improve sales, Susan began to create bespoke ceramic patterns for the shop, which were printed onto blanks (undecorated pots) by the Staffordshire decorating firm A.E. Gray & Co. One of the first designs to be created exclusively for Portmeirion was *Dolphin* (opposite). The colours used were unusual at the time and were intended to harmonise with modern kitchen interiors.

Williams-Ellis took over Gray & Co. in 1960 and, a year later, the pottery manufacturer Kirkham's Limited. The two businesses were amalgamated and became Portmeirion Pottery Ltd. This gave Williams-Ellis complete creative freedom – she was no longer restricted to developing surface patterns, but could design brand-new shapes. Some of her most successful and iconic designs were the 1960s 'cylinder' forms – particularly her tall, elegant coffee pots – that are so closely associated with the Portmeirion style. Her outstanding contribution to the industry was recognised in 2002 with an honorary degree from Keele University. RC

An independent potter

JANET DARNELL LEACH (1918–97)

Janet Darnell Leach is a major figure in British post-war studio ceramics. She was born in Texas and studied sculpture in New York City. In 1941, when the USA entered the Second World War, Leach trained as a welder in a shipyard, becoming highly skilled in this traditionally male occupation. Disillusioned with struggling to make a living as a sculptor, in 1947 Leach visited the Inwood Pottery in New York City, which was run by Leeds-born Aimee Le Prince Voorhees (1874–1951). Here she found her medium.

In 1952 Leach attended a seminar at the avant-garde Black Mountain College in North Carolina. There she befriended potter Bernard Leach (1887–1979), whose groundbreaking philosophical and technical approaches had interested Janet since her time at the Inwood Pottery, and was introduced to Shōji Hamada (1894–1978). Deeply inspired by Hamada's spontaneous approach to working with clay, in 1954 she travelled to Japan to study at his workshop in Mashiko and at the Ichino family pottery in Tamba. For Leach to throw pottery (typically the preserve of men) and travel alone challenged Japanese social

→ Janet Leach in a photograph by Ben Boswell taken in 1982 (National Portrait Gallery, London)

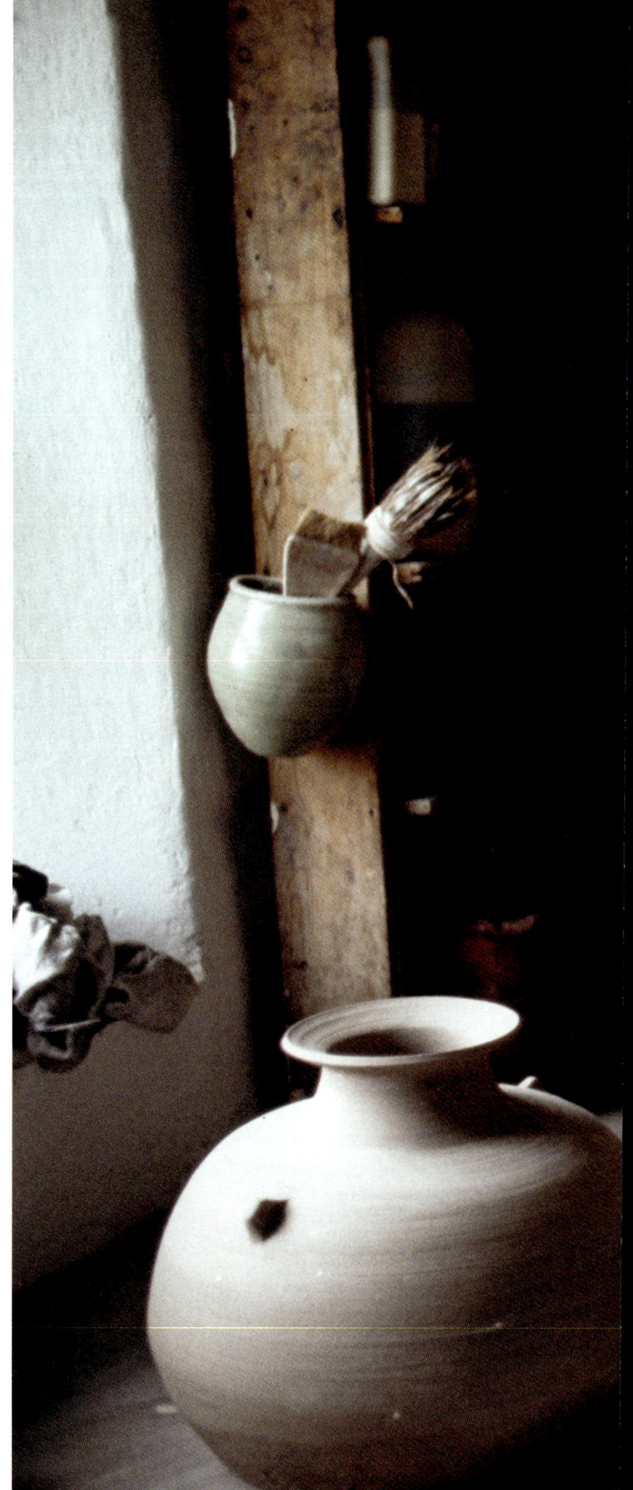

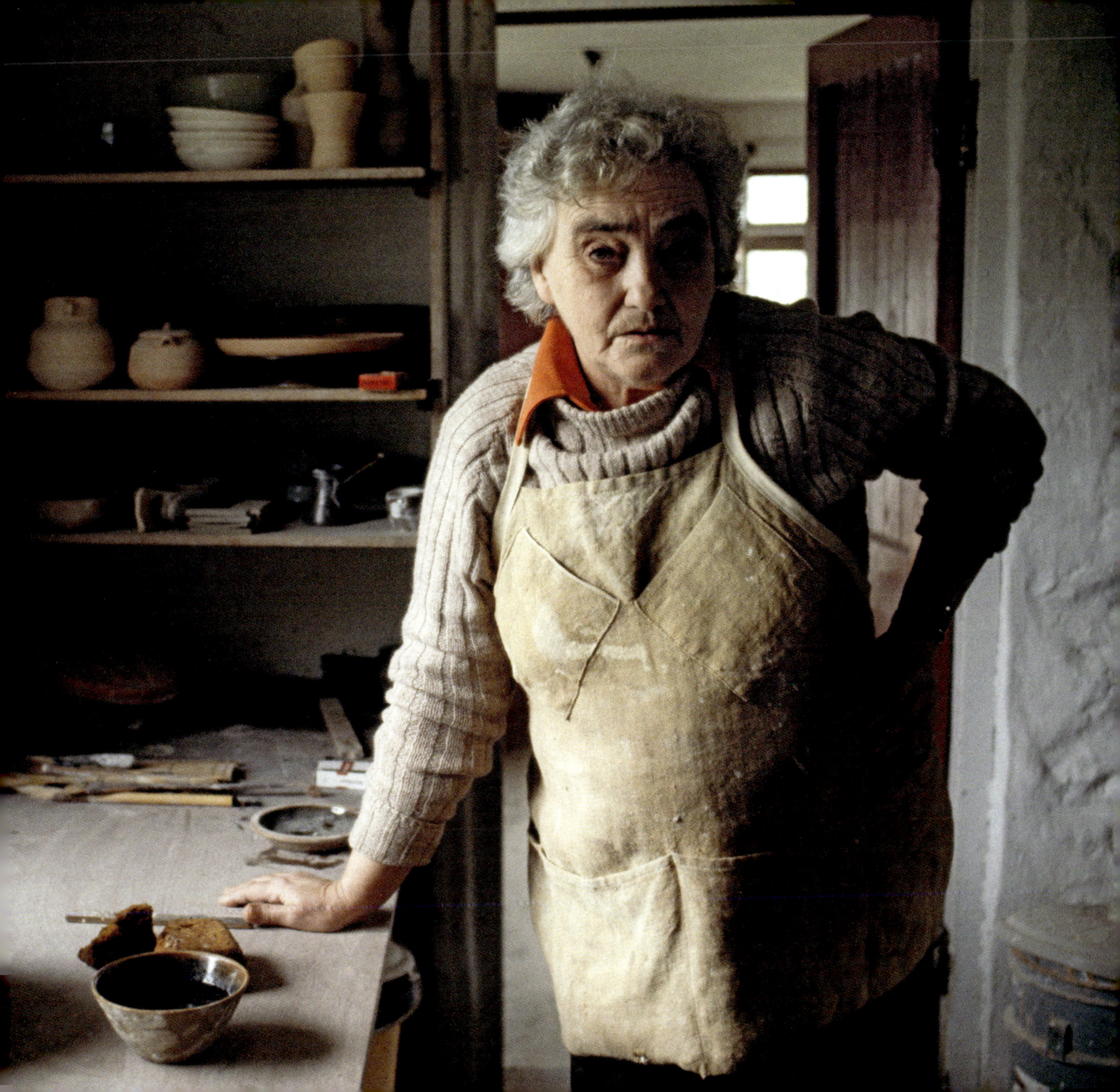

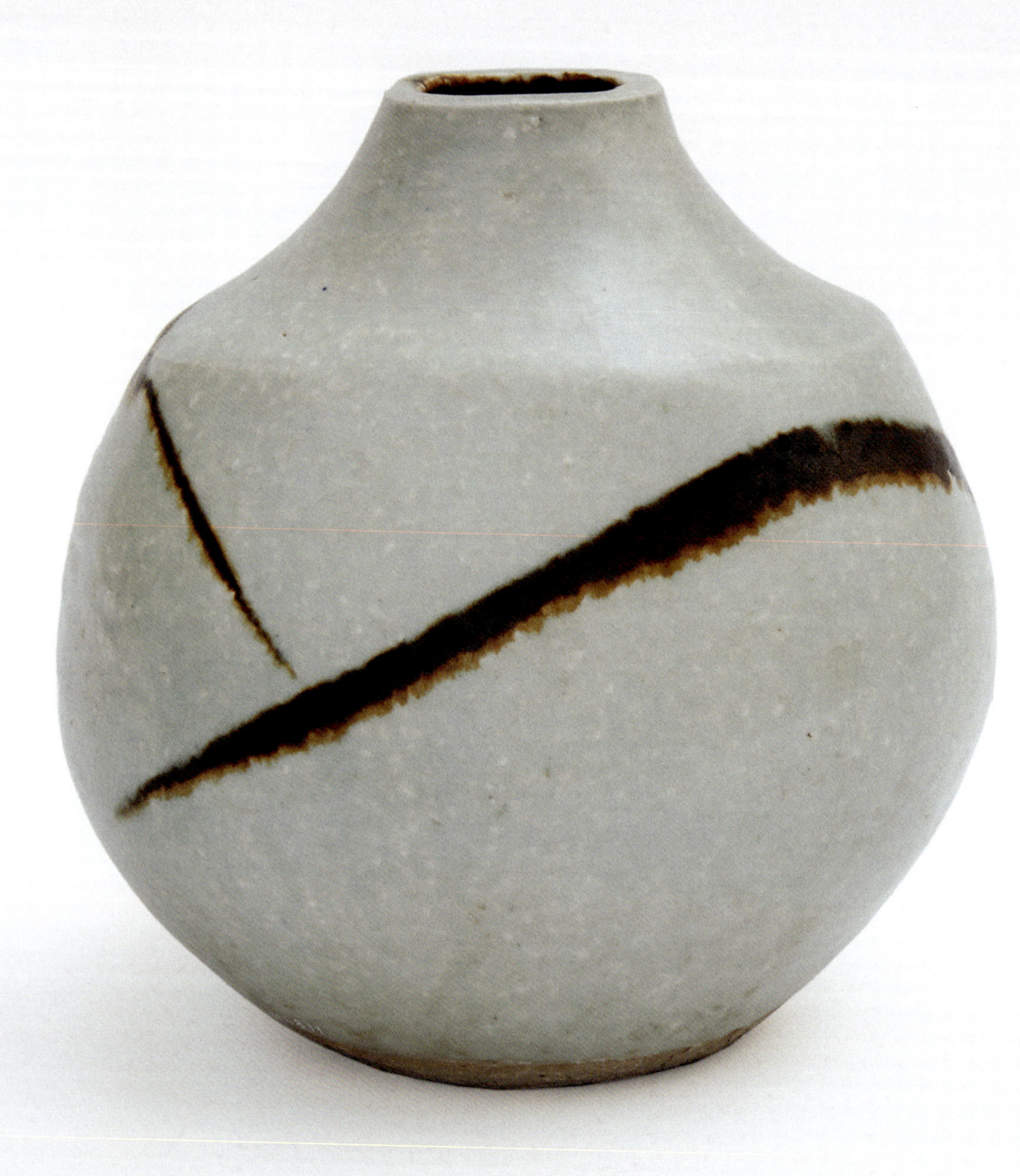

convention, but these were incredibly important, formative experiences for her – she later described them as life-changing. Leach learned a different appreciation of the natural qualities of clay and traditional wood-firing techniques that would have a profound influence on the development of her own, highly individual style.

Janet and Bernard travelled across Japan visiting traditional pottery villages, and married in 1956 – she would eventually agree to adopt his family name. Plans to stay in Japan did not come to pass and they returned to Britain, where Janet took over the management of the commercial Leach Pottery in St Ives, Cornwall. She managed the pottery until 1997 but built her own studio with two Japanese kick (unmechanised) wheels and an experimental wood-firing kiln so that she could continue to develop her own work.

Despite her husband's influence within the discipline and their mutual respect and admiration for Japanese ceramic tradition, Janet was resolutely independent in her practice. Working in stoneware and heavily grogged porcelain, she evolved her own making and decorating techniques to achieve a distinctive, modern potting style that seems influenced as much by abstract art as Japanese ceramic tradition. Her work is often characterised by free mark-making that captures a moment, such as the poured black glaze that flashes across the body of the pot shown here (opposite). RC

← Hand-built pot by Janet Leach, *c.*1970, using grogged porcelain with pale celadon glaze and poured black glaze, 16.5 x 15.5cm, impressed marks of Janet Leach and the Leach Pottery, Greenway, Devon (NT 118915)

‘To make pottery is an adventure to me’

LUCIE RIE (1902–95)

In the early 1950s Lucie Rie wrote: ‘to make pottery is an adventure to me, every new work is a new beginning’. Rie is one of the most important and influential studio potters of the 20th century. She developed a Modernist, minimal aesthetic that caused her work to stand out from that of her contemporaries. Her pots are useful shapes in porcelain and stoneware, thrown on the wheel – particularly bowls, bottles and vases – with a focus on creating distinctive surface effects through subtly layered, textured glazes, or lines of sgraffito incised through dark slips.

Rie was born in Vienna and attended the Kunstgewerbeschule – the art school attached to the progressive Wiener Werkstätte (Vienna Workshop). Students were encouraged to experiment with different materials and Rie chose to specialise in pottery – later describing herself as being ‘lost to the wheel’. Working from a studio in her flat, Rie applied her glazes onto the raw clay (most potters do this after an initial biscuit firing), which allowed her to develop the distinctive textured surfaces that characterise her work. Rie’s reputation grew as she sold and exhibited

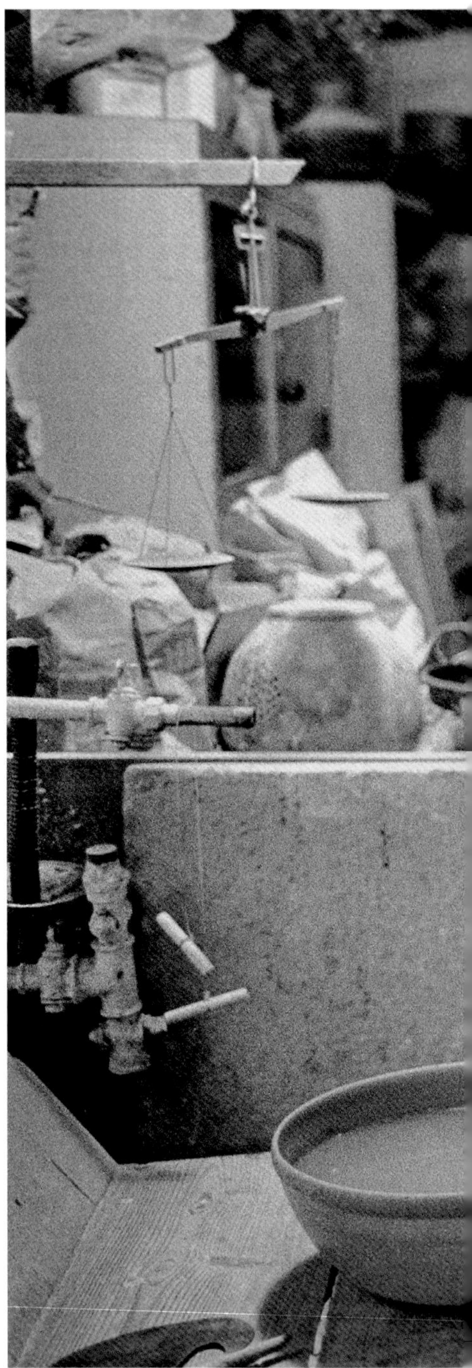

→ Lucie Rie photographed by Ben Boswell in 1983 at her home and studio in Albion Mews, London

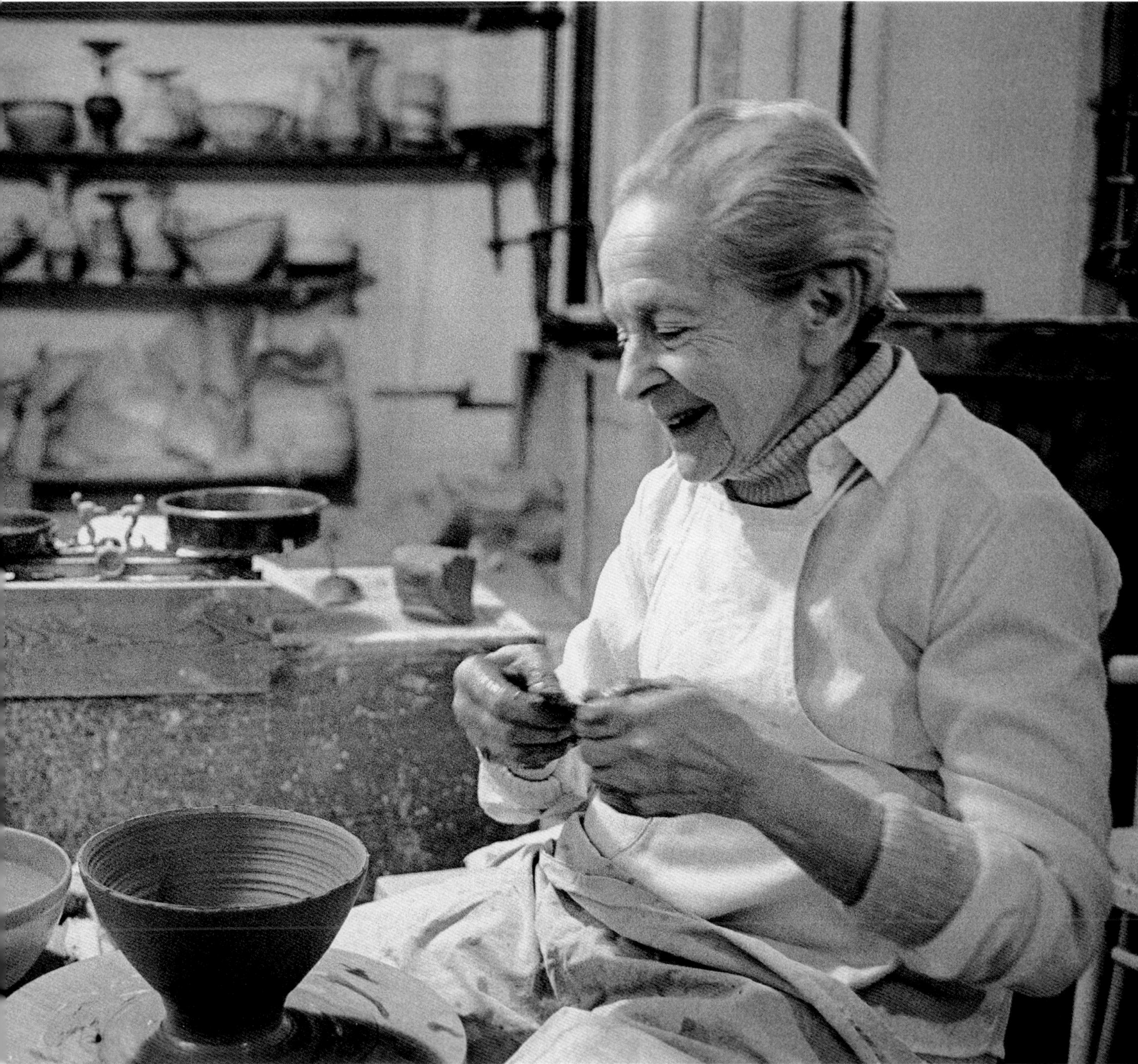

her work internationally, including at the prestigious Milan Triennale in 1936 and the Paris Exposition Internationale the following year, winning medals at both.

Rie, who was Jewish, was forced to leave Austria in 1938 to escape the Nazi regime. She settled in London and remained there for the rest of her life, working from a studio in Albion Mews, Paddington. Her Modernist work was very different from the Leach tradition favoured in Britain, so Rie worked hard to re-establish her profile. Before restrictions on the making of non-essential goods were introduced in 1942, Rie made tableware, as well as small pieces of jewellery and ceramic buttons for fashion houses and high-end department stores. After the war, she resumed her work and established a long, highly successful career. Her work is represented in major collections across the world and has been celebrated in many exhibitions, including retrospectives at the Sainsbury Centre, Norwich, and the Victoria and Albert Museum, London, in 1981. Among her many accolades, in 1991 she was the first potter to be awarded the honour of Dame Commander of the British Empire. RC

→ Wheel-thrown porcelain bowl by Lucie Rie, *c.*1972–80, pale green and brown glazes, 19.4cm (diameter), impressed 'LR' seal mark, Greenway, Devon (NT 118953)

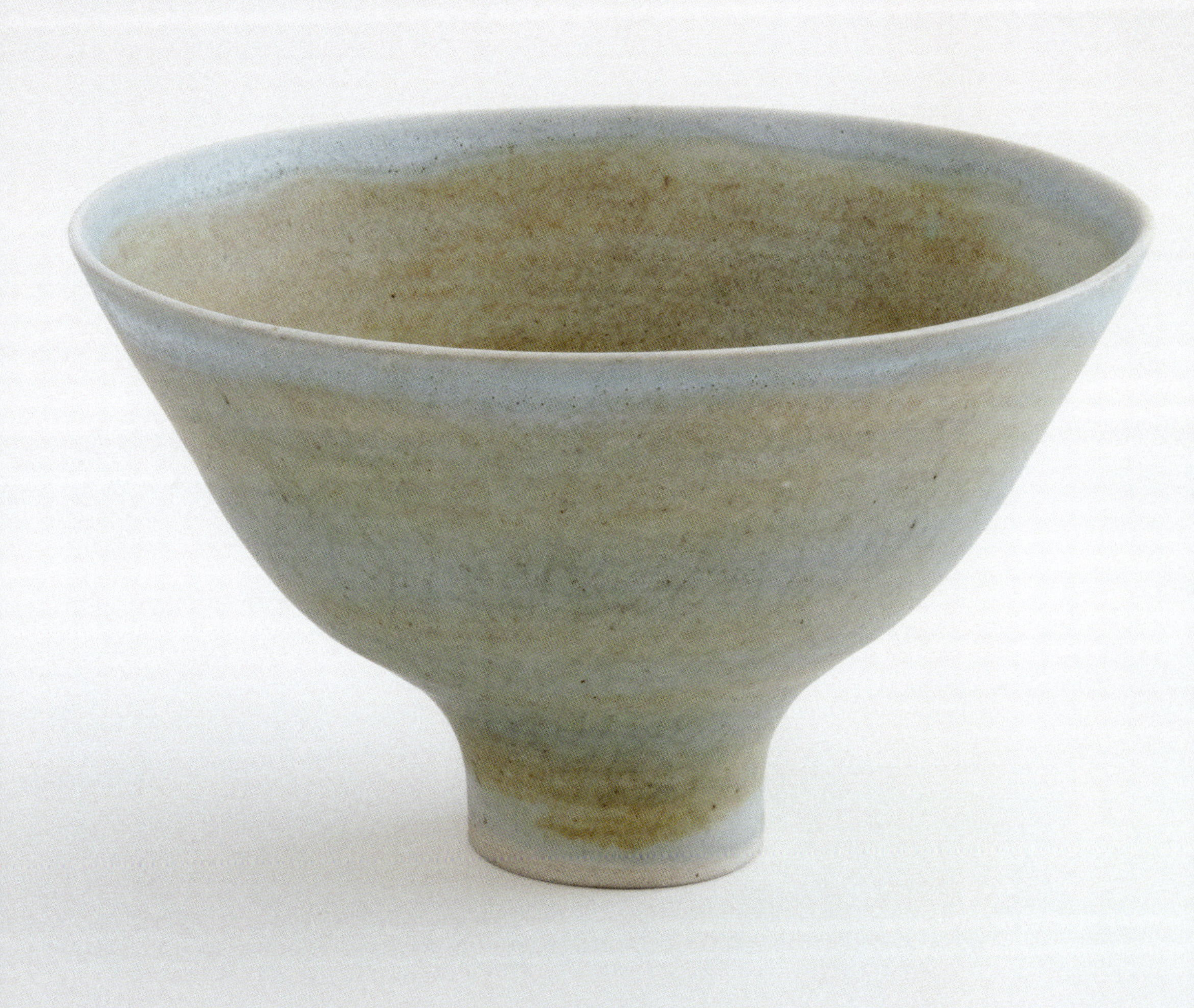

‘Tones of the past’

TABITHA JUSSA (b.1974)

Living and working in Liverpool, Tabitha Jussa is a photographic artist whose work focuses on socio-political issues, which she often expresses by interweaving analogue and digital practice. The passage of time underpins much of Jussa’s photography, whether it be the hours spent crafting a single image or through a visual play between past and present.

Jussa was the first artist in residence at The Hardmans’ House in Liverpool, where Edward Chambré Hardman (1898–1988) and Margaret Hardman (1909–70; page 188) once ran their photographic studio.

The Hardmans’ archive, rich with thousands of monochrome and hand-coloured portraits, inspired Jussa to explore the less visible role women played in their creation. A photographer in her own right, Margaret was fundamental to the business, engaging sitters, overseeing production and managing the studio’s female staff. It was also predominantly women, usually working from home, who painstakingly and precisely hand-coloured many of the customers’ prints.

To amplify these contributions, Jussa invited women at the forefront of Liverpool’s cultural scene to collaborate in forming her series *Agency of Women*. Founders, directors, writers, musicians and artists, including The Singh Twins (opposite), sat for a formal portrait session in the Hardmans’ original mid-20th-century studio – an unfamiliar experience in the context of today’s self-controlled filtering of the way we look.

The Singh Twins remarked on feeling ‘eerily … transported back in time … thinking about all the people who had been in this room in the past’. Jussa’s subsequent meticulous hand-application of tints and tones, echoing the practice of the Hardmans’ skilled hand-colourists, reinforces this sense of bygone times, yet uniquely draws in the contemporary and offers her ‘positive celebration’ of creative women. AS

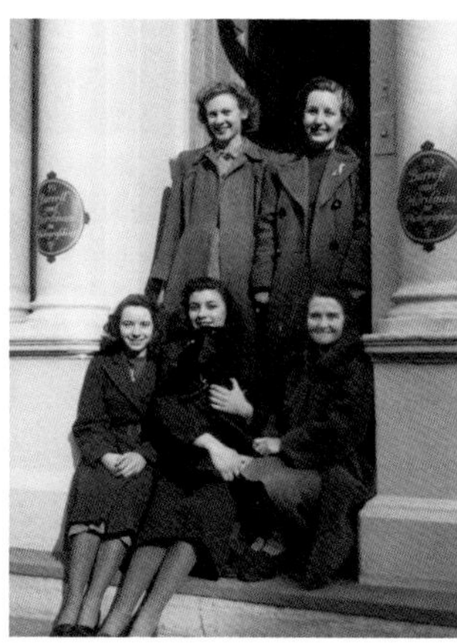

↑ Studio staff, Edward Chambré Hardman, 1950s, gelatin silver print, 12.5 x 10cm (photograph), The Hardmans’ House, Liverpool (NT 973482)

→ *The Singh Twins*, Tabitha Jussa (b.1974), 2019, colour inkjet print, 24 x 16cm, The Hardmans’ House, Liverpool (NT 974227)

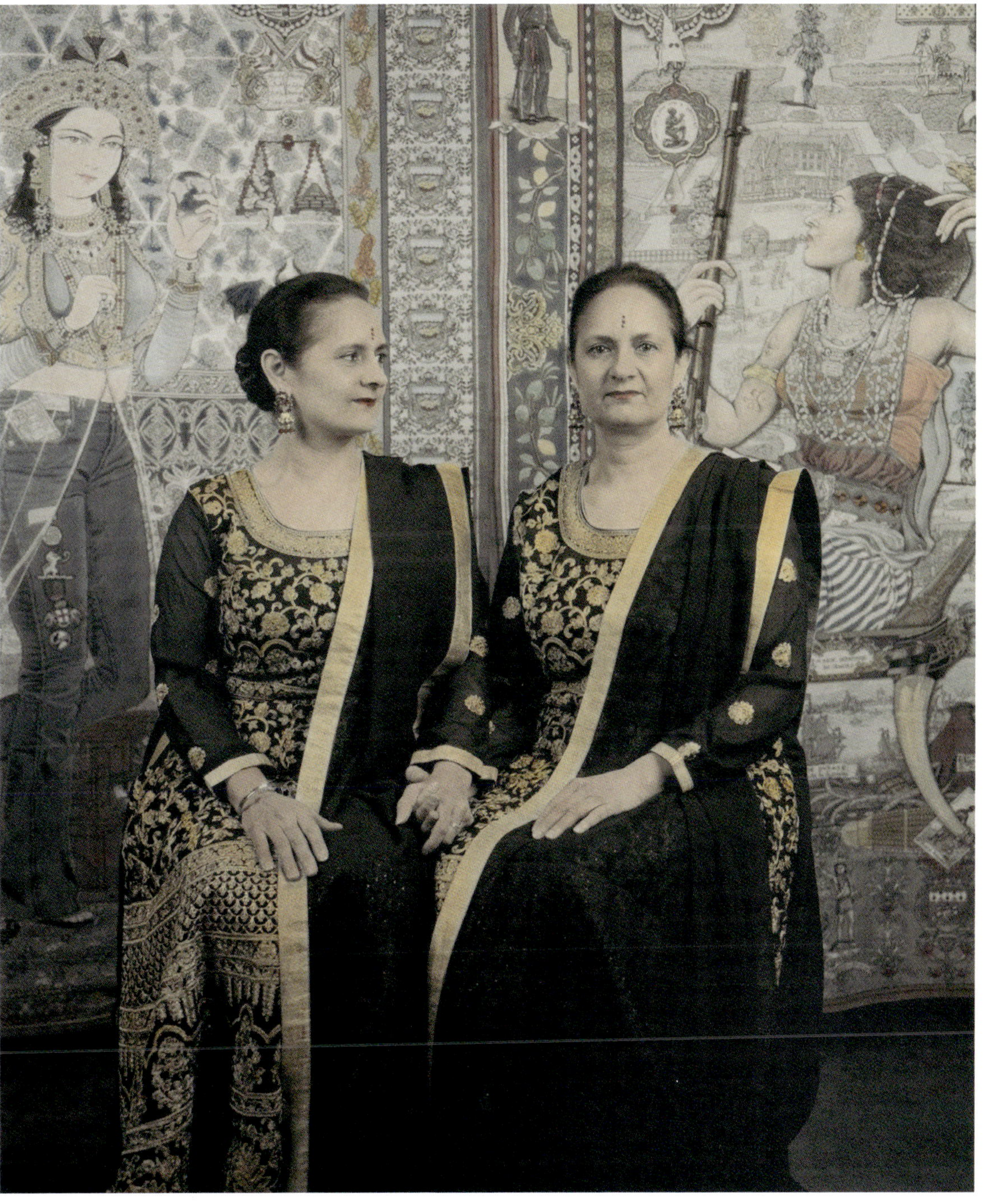

GAZETTEER

For full details of every National Trust property, including further information about collections, opening times, events and facilities, please visit the National Trust website (www.nationaltrust.org.uk) and the National Trust Collections website (www.nationaltrustcollections.org.uk).

A la Ronde, Devon • A 16-sided house built for Jane and Mary Parminter, containing remarkable friezes, shellwork, sand and seaweed pictures, embellished furniture and other artworks by or attributed to the cousins.
Anglesey Abbey, Cambridgeshire • Manor house converted from a 13th-century priory. The collection includes silverwork and jewellery by Dorrie Nossiter and Rebecca Emes, sculpture by Eleanor Coade, Kathleen Scott, Harriet Whitney Frishmuth and Harriet Hosmer, and a woodcut by Gwen Raverat.
Ardress House, County Armagh • 17th-century farmhouse remodelled in the 1780s. The collection includes early Irish furniture, agricultural machinery and a garden urn by Eleanor Coade.
Arlington Court, Devon • Greek Revival house extended in the mid-19th century – the estate was home to the Chichester family for over 500 years. The collection includes photography, paintings, wood carving and painted ceramics by its last private owner, Rosalie Chichester.
Baddesley Clinton, Warwickshire • A moated courtyard house that was home to the Ferrers family for over 500 years. The collection includes works by Rebecca Orpen and Lady Georgiana Chatterton. A rare 1753 silver salver marked by Dorothy Mills may be the only example in a British public collection.
Belton House, Lincolnshire • Late 17th-century mansion, home to generations of the Brownlows and Custs. The collections include work by women in the family, including Lady Sophia Frances Cust, Nina Cust, Elizabeth Cust, Lucy Cust and Marian Alford. Watercolours by Louisa Anne Stuart, Marchioness of Waterford, sculpture by Elisabet Ney, miniatures by Annie Dixon and botanical illustrations by Florence Woolward also feature.
Benthall Hall, Shropshire • 16th-century house, home to generations of the Benthall family for 500 years. The collection includes family portraits by women artists, notably by Ethel Walker,

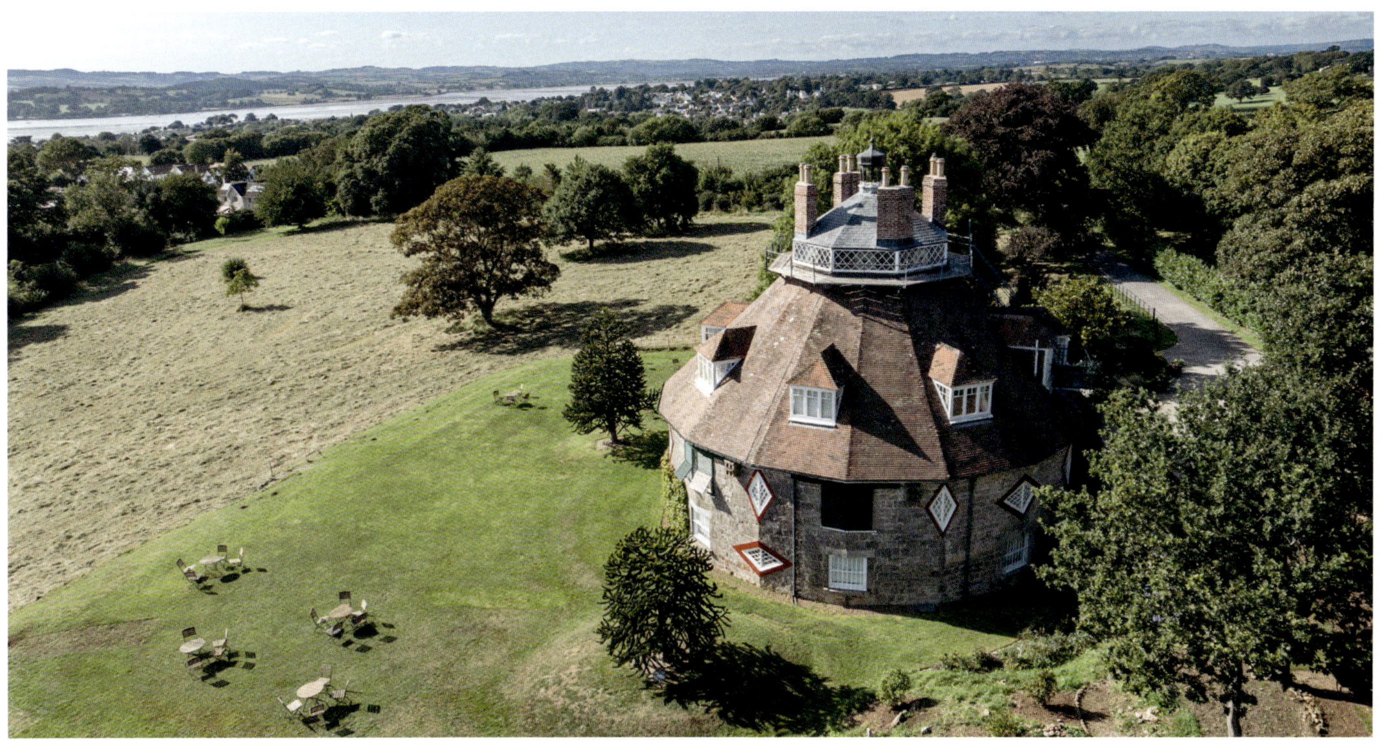

↑ **A la Ronde, Devon**, the 16-sided house decorated and furnished by Jane and Mary Parminter.

Alethea Garstin and the miniaturist Margaret Gillies. Watercolours by women in the family are also in the collection.

Berrington Hall, Herefordshire • Neo-classical mansion built for Thomas Harley and purchased in 1901 by Liberal MP Frederick Cawley. The displays include decorative arts from the Digby Lawson bequest, including a pair of vases designed by Constance Spry.

Blickling Hall, Norfolk • Jacobean house built for Sir Henry Hobart. The library is one of the National Trust's largest and includes two volumes by Maria Sibylla Merian bound together. The gardens were designed by Norah Lindsay in the 1930s.

Calke Abbey, Derbyshire • Baroque mansion presented in a state of 'quiet decay'. The Harpur and Crewe family libraries are at the property and include a volume on apples illustrated by Betsey Ronalds and a 1737 herbal by Elizabeth Blackwell with her engraved illustrations. Other pieces include doll's furniture by The Ladies' Guild, a wine cooler designed by Lady Diana Beauclerk for Wedgwood and a silver salver by Elizabeth Jones.

Canons Ashby, Northamptonshire • Built by the Dryden family using the remains of a medieval priory and largely unaltered since 1710. The collection includes *trompe l'œil* paintings attributed to Elizabeth

Creed, and drawings and watercolours by Clara Dryden.

Castle Ward, County Down • An 18th-century house of contrasts, featuring both Palladian and Gothic Revival architecture. The collection includes paintings by Mary Beale and Mary Hotchkis, silver by Mary Ann Reilly, and drawings, watercolours and illustrated books by Mary Ward.

Chartwell, Kent • The principal residence of Sir Winston and Lady Clementine Churchill from 1924 to 1965. The collection encompasses Churchillian memorabilia that includes paintings, photographs, books, maps, cigar boxes and velvet 'siren suits'. There are also artworks by Dorothy Tennant, Lady Stanley, and Eunice Simeon.

Coleton Fishacre, Devon • Arts and Crafts style country house built for Richard D'Oyly Carte. The collection includes original carpets and rugs designed by Marion Dorn.

Cragside, Northumberland • House built for engineer Lord William and Lady Margaret Armstrong, and the first house in the world to be lit by hydroelectricity. The collection includes objects reflecting the owner's scientific interests, and electrical household gadgets. It also includes a group of family portraits by Mary Lemon Waller and a drawing by Rosa Bonheur.

Dorneywood, Buckinghamshire • 18th-century brick house that is now the official country residence for the Secretary of State and Ministers of the Crown. The collection includes miniatures and oil paintings by Winifred Hope Thomson.

Dudmaston, Shropshire • Country house built *c.*1695 with an outstanding collection of pictures and sculpture with a focus on modern art. It includes work by Barbara Hepworth, Eileen Agar, Sonia Delaunay-Terk, Maria Helena Vieira da Silva and Pauline Norton. Also works by Lady Labouchere, Evelyn Blacklock and Rachel Ruysch

Dunham Massey, Cheshire • Georgian house built in 1720 for the 2nd Earl of Warrington. The collection includes work by Theresia Concordia Mengs, Annie Dixon, Mary Gartside and family members including Jane Grey and Lady Maria Booth Grey. The outstanding silver collection includes pieces marked by Hester and Ann Bateman, Magdalen Feline and Elizabeth Jackson.

East Riddlesden Hall, West Yorkshire • Manor house built in the 17th century, once the heart of a large agricultural estate. The collection holds many needle-work items, including raised work and embroidery samplers.

Erddig, Wrexham • Country house with Neo-classical interiors, including fine Chinese wallpaper and a group of portraits of estate staff. The collection includes a family portrait by Katherine Read, remarkable sculptures and other works by Elizabeth Ratcliffe, and needlework attributed to Anne Jemima Yorke and Victoria Mary Louisa Cust.

→ *Pamela Chichele-Plowden, Countess of Lytton*, Winifred Hope Thomson, *c.*1900, watercolour on ivory, 7.5 x 6cm, **Dorneywood, Buckinghamshire** (NT 1507758). This was one of several works by Thomson shown at the 1900 Women's International Exhibition at Earl's Court, London.

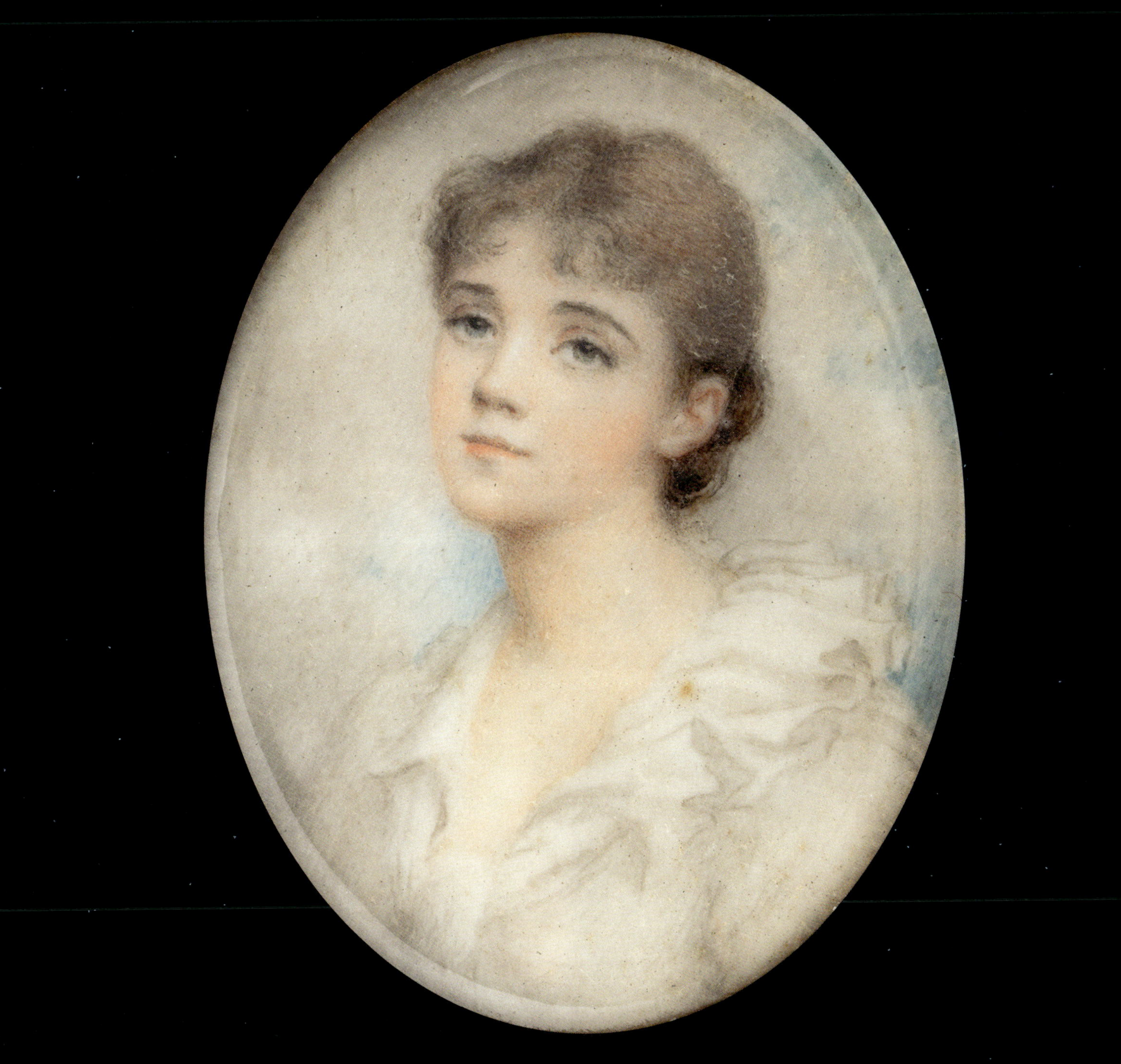

Fenton House, London • Late 17th-century merchant's house in Hampstead with collections assembled by Lady Binning from 1936 and added to by the National Trust through later acquisitions. The collection includes a figure designed by Mary Seton Watts, and pictures by Laura Knight, Clare (Tony) Atwood and Mary Sarah Cohen.

Greenway, Devon • Georgian house that was the holiday home of Agatha Christie and her family. Includes the National Trust's largest group of studio pottery, collected by Christie's daughter, Rosalind, and her husband, Anthony Hicks. Includes works by Lucie Rie, Janet Leach, Norah Braden, Marianne de Trey, Mary Rogers, Denise Wren and Katherine Pleydell-Bouverie. Pictures by Dora Carrington and Winifred Nicholson.

Greyfriars, Worcestershire • Late medieval timber-framed merchant's house, rescued and restored in the mid-20th century by siblings Florence Elsie and Malcolm Matley Moore, who lived there from the 1940s to the 1980s. The collection includes many objects and artworks created by Elsie, including embroidery, paintings, wall hangings, painted furniture, calligraphy and lampshades, as well as historic fixtures and fittings collected and incorporated into the property by the siblings.

Ham House, Surrey • Grand Stuart house on the banks of the Thames with an outstanding and well-documented collection of late 17th-century furniture and paintings, including work by Joan Carlile and Katherine Read.

The Hardmans' House, Liverpool • A Georgian terraced house presented as the photographic studio and home of Margaret Hardman and Edward Chambré Hardman. The collection includes many thousands of prints and negatives, as well as business records and photographic equipment. Most of the photographic collection is cared for in a specialist storage facility by Liverpool Record Office courtesy of Liverpool City Council.

Hardwick Hall, Derbyshire • One of the greatest of all Elizabethan houses with important furniture, tapestries, wall hangings, plasterwork and paintings. Collections include needlework by Bess of Hardwick and Mary, Queen of Scots, and a book by Maria Sibylla Merian.

Hill Top and Beatrix Potter Gallery, Cumbria • Much-loved 17th-century farmhouse purchased by Beatrix Potter in 1905 and featured in many of her illustrations. The collection holds objects owned and acquired by her, including family heirlooms and other items bought at local sales. The National Trust cares for a large collection of photographs, drawings, sketchbooks, watercolours and books created by Potter, as well as archives and memorabilia.

The Homewood, Surrey • Modernist home designed by architect Patrick Gwynne for his family, built in 1938–9. The interiors match the modern exterior, with many luxurious fittings and

↓ *Man of the Sea*, Margaret Hardman, *c.*1930s–40s, gelatin silver print, 50.7 x 40.6cm (mounted), **The Hardmans' House, Liverpool** (NT 974383)

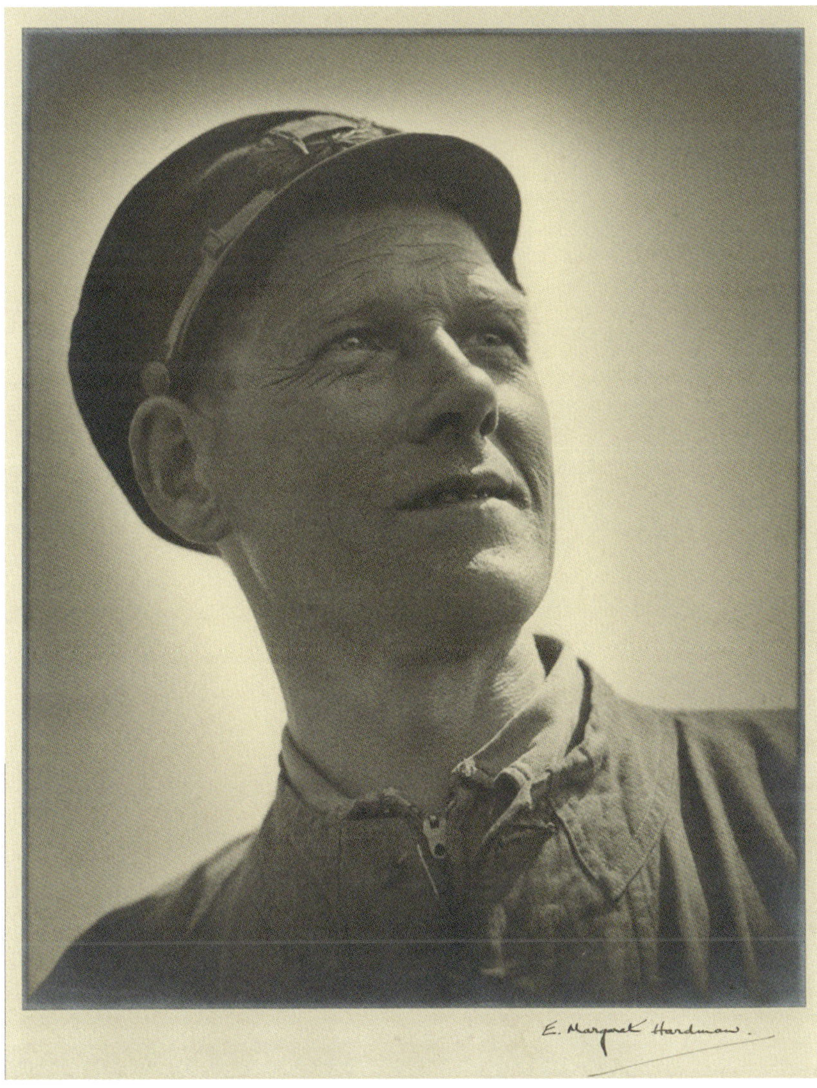

furnishings designed by Gwynne, as well as examples of furniture by Eames, wire chairs designed by Harry Bertoia and made by Knoll (Florence and Hans Knoll), and a sculpture by Bridget McCrum.

Ickworth, Suffolk • Neo-classical house designed to show a remarkable art collection, including work by Angelica Kauffman, Elisabeth Vigée le Brun, Anne Mee and Lady Templetown. The silver includes examples by Elizabeth Aldridge. A rare pair of girl's election dresses embellished by Alice Frances Theodora Wythes, Marchioness of Bristol, also features.

Kedleston Hall, Derbyshire • 18th-century house largely designed by Robert Adam in the Neo-classical style. It houses important collections of paintings, sculpture and books, as well as silver by Louisa Courtauld.

Killerton, Devon • Georgian house set in 6,400 acres of parkland. It is home to a large and varied collection of dress and accessories from the 18th to the 20th centuries. The collection also includes drawings and watercolours by Henrietta Hoare and Frances Ann Acland.

Knole, Kent • Tudor archbishop's palace and home of the Sackville collection for 400 years. The outstanding art collection includes a work by Elisabeth Vigée le Brun (on loan to the National Trust) and a portrait by Anthony van Dyck of Sofonisba Anguissola. The library includes manuscript copies of Virginia Woolf's *Orlando*.

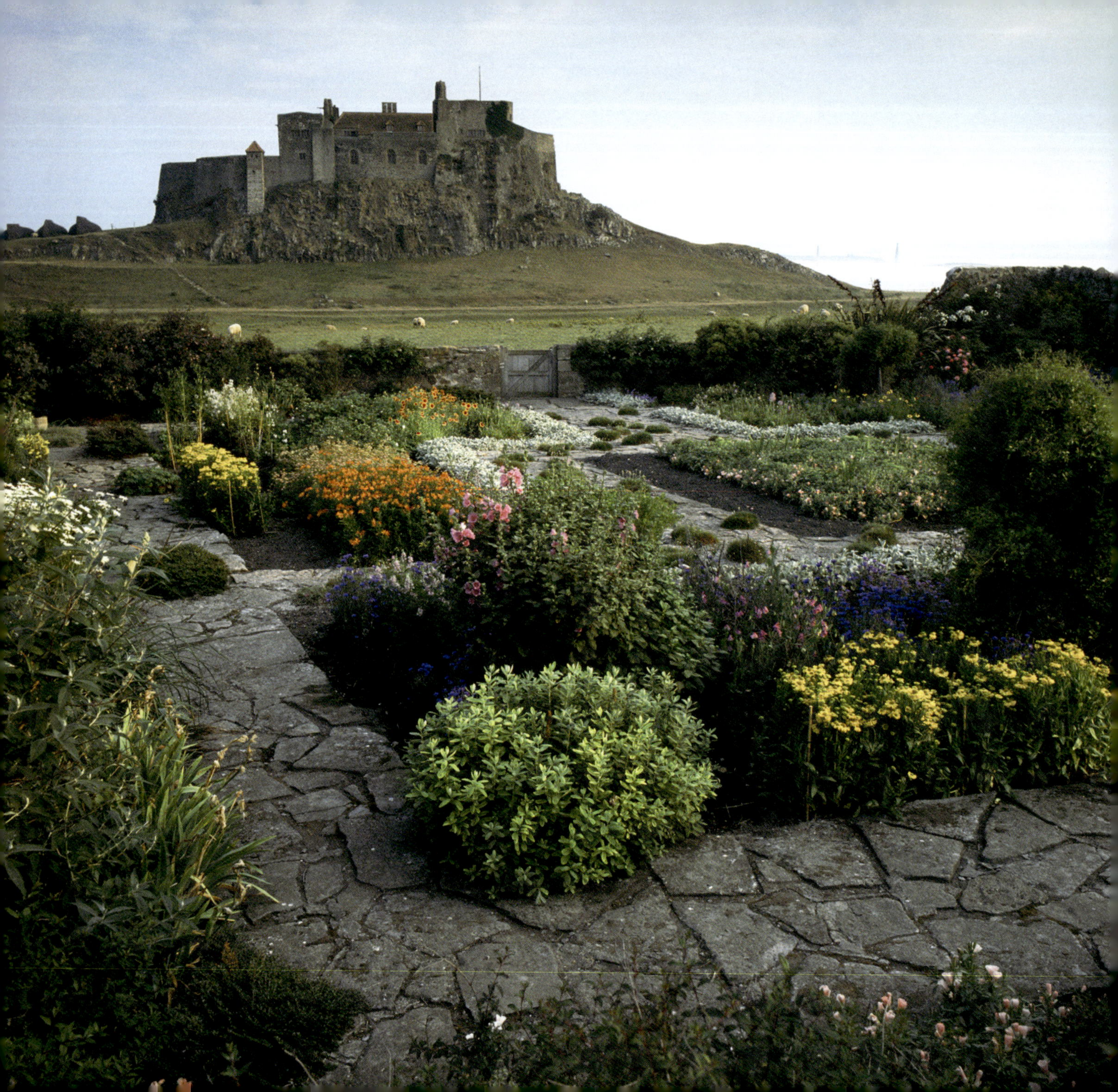

← Designed in 1906 by Gertrude Jekyll in collaboration with Sir Edwin Lutyens, the garden at **Lindisfarne Castle, Northumberland**, was created for Edward Hudson in 1911.

Lacock Abbey and Fox Talbot Museum, Wiltshire • A 16th-century house with later Gothic-style alterations built on the site of a nunnery. One of the most significant sites associated with photography past and present. The collections include the work of Anna Atkins, Olivia Wyndham, Elizabeth Mallett, Yan Wang Preston, Ellen Carey and Dafna Talmor.

Lindisfarne Castle, Northumberland • A 16th-century castle and former garrison on Holy Island, remodelled for Edward Hudson (founder of *Country Life* magazine) by architect Sir Edwin Lutyens in the early 20th century. The walled flower garden was designed by Gertrude Jekyll. As later owners made few changes, it is still largely the work of Lutyens and Jekyll that greets visitors today.

Llanerchaeron, Ceredigion • Georgian villa designed by John Nash in a Welsh country estate. The collection includes the National Trust's only known work by Sarah Biffin, and a group of paintings and drawings by the collector Pamela Ward.

Monk's House, East Sussex • Intimate 16th-century cottage inhabited from 1919 to 1960 by Virginia and Leonard Woolf. The collection includes paintings and objects made or designed by members of the Bloomsbury Group, including Vanessa Bell, Phyllis Keyes, Angelica Bell and Trekkie Parsons.

Mottisfont, Hampshire • Priory converted into a house and transformed in the 1740s. Home of Gilbert and Maud Russell with a major collection of 20th-century art, including works given by Derek Hill. Features works by Gwen John, Barbara Hepworth, Vanessa Bell, Angela Conner, Adrienne Haig, Joan Eardley, Mary Potter and Cathleen Sabine Mann.

Mount Stewart, County Down • Early 19th-century home of the Londonderry family, set within celebrated gardens and with interiors designed by Edith, Lady Londonderry. The collection includes examples of her needlework, as well as silver by Hannah Northcote and Rebecca Emes, sculpture by Margaret Wrightson, miniatures by Beatrice Wainwright and by or attributed to Anne Mee, as well as paintings by Lady Margaret Stewart and her illustrations for *The Magic Ink-Pot*, written by Lady Londonderry for her children.

Munstead Wood, Surrey • Home, garden and plant nursery of Gertrude Jekyll. The Arts and Crafts property was designed for her by Edwin Lutyens and includes interior features made by or attributed to Jekyll, who was skilled in many different creative practices.

Nostell, West Yorkshire • Palladian house built on the site of a medieval monastery housing one of the best surviving collections of Chippendale furniture. The collection includes an important self-portrait by Angelica Kauffman and also works by Sabine Winn, most notably her dressed prints, and drawings by her daughter, Esther.

Nuffield Place, Oxfordshire • The home of William Morris, Lord Nuffield, founder of the Morris Motor Car Company, and his wife Elizabeth. The collection includes a rare plate designed and decorated by Amy Kotzé.

Ormesby Hall, North Yorkshire • Classic Georgian house, home to the Pennyman family. The collection holds work by Ruth Pennyman, including illustrations, drawings and paintings relating to her art training and involvement in the theatre. There are also paintings by Mary Ellen Best and Gwen Brown.

Osterley Park and House, London • Tudor home of Sir Thomas Gresham, remodelled by Robert Adam in 1763–80 for the Child family, with outstanding surviving interiors. The collection includes silver by Rebecca Emes, a wax model by Frances Talbot, needlework, and decorated cache pots attributed to Sarah Child and her daughter Sarah Anne, possibly supplied by John Linnell.

Petworth, West Sussex • Inspired by the Baroque palaces of Europe, Petworth has the richest and best-documented picture collection in the National Trust. It includes work by Lavinia Fontana and Angelica Kauffman.

Powis Castle, Powys • Medieval castle remodelled by generations of the Herbert family, with important paintings, sculpture, furniture and tapestries, as well as a collection of Indian objects owned by Edward Clive. The collection includes works by Anna Tonelli.

Saltram, Devon • A Georgian mansion with saloon and interiors designed by Robert Adam. The collection includes an important group of works by Angelica Kauffman, as well as paintings and drawings by Frances Talbot.

Seaton Delaval Hall, Northumberland • The last great house by Baroque architect John Vanbrugh, built for Admiral George Delaval in *c.*1718–28. The collection includes paintings by Rhoda Delaval.

Shaw's Corner, Hertfordshire • The home and workplace of author and political activist George Bernard Shaw. The collection includes a brass doorknocker depicting Shaw designed by Rosie Banks Danecourt, photography by Julia Margaret Cameron, a Woodburytype print of a portrait by Bertha Newcombe and a watercolour by Laura Knight. There are also ceramics designed and decorated by Louise Powell.

Sissinghurst, Kent • Elizabethan home of Vita Sackville-West and Harold Nicolson, famous for its gardens. The collections include the writers' family photograph albums, their working libraries and personal possessions, as well as artworks by close connections, including Christopher Marie St John, Mary Garman and Gwen St Aubyn.

Smallhythe Place, Kent • A 16th-century timber-framed farmhouse that was home to leading actress Ellen Terry. The collection includes memorabilia relating to Terry and Edith Craig's theatrical careers, including costumes designed by Alice Laura Comyns-Carr and Craig, and pageant costumes by Maud Gibson.

→ Large charger hand-painted by Louise Powell, 1914, earthenware, 41.6cm (diameter), **Shaw's Corner, Hertfordshire** (NT 1274567)

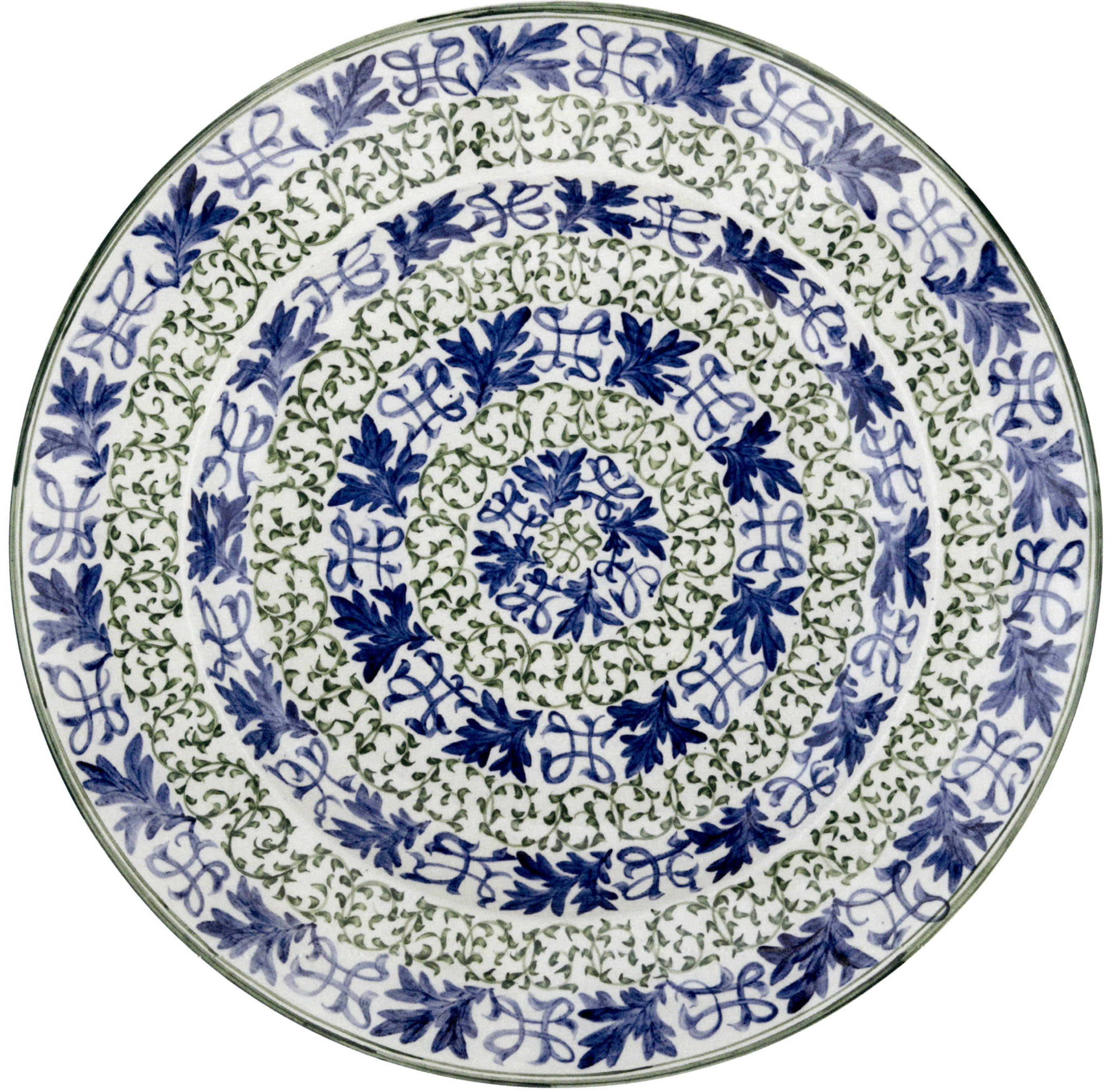

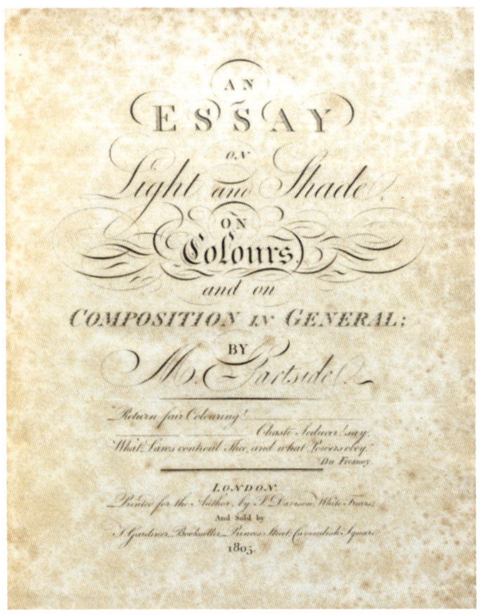

AN
ESSAY
ON
Light and Shade
ON
Colours
and on
COMPOSITION IN GENERAL;
BY
M. Gartside.

"Return fair Colouring! ——
Chaste Seducer! say,
What Laws control Thee, and what Powers obey."
Du Fresnoy

LONDON:
Printed for the Author, by T. Davison, White Friars:
And Sold by
J. Gardiner, Bookseller, Princes Street, Cavendish Square.
1805.

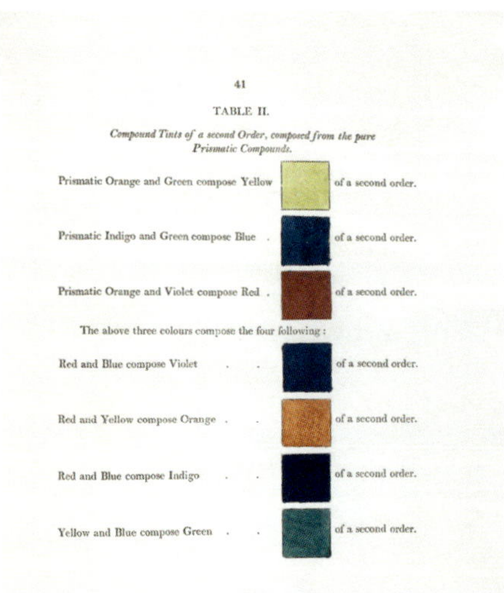

41

TABLE II.

Compound Tints of a second Order, composed from the pure Prismatic Compounds.

Prismatic Orange and Green compose Yellow	of a second order.
Prismatic Indigo and Green compose Blue	of a second order.
Prismatic Orange and Violet compose Red	of a second order.

The above three colours compose the four following:

Red and Blue compose Violet	of a second order.
Red and Yellow compose Orange	of a second order.
Red and Blue compose Indigo	of a second order.
Yellow and Blue compose Green	of a second order.

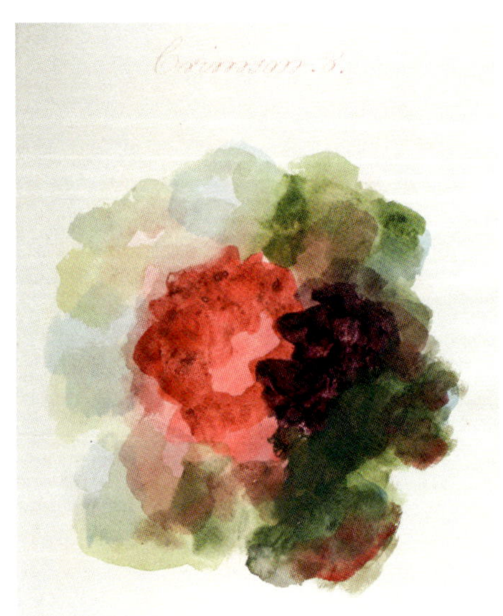

↑ *An Essay on Light and Shade, on Colours, and on Composition in General* by Mary Gartside, 1805, 29 x 22.5cm, **Tatton Park, Cheshire**, ‡ 1966 (NT 3068303)

Artworks by Pamela Colman Smith, photography by Christina Broom and Julia Margaret Cameron, Minton vases decorated by Laura Wilson Barker, sculpture by Doris Lindner and Louise Abbéma, and chair upholstery designed by Nancy Nicholson for Poulk Prints.
Springhill, County Londonderry • Manor house built for the Conynghams in the late 17th century. The collection includes a pair of paintings by Susanna Drury and a print after Elizabeth Southerden Thompson, Lady Butler.
Standen, West Sussex • Arts and Crafts house built in 1891–4 by architect Philip Webb. The collection includes ceramics made, decorated and/or designed by women working at the Della Robbia and Doulton potteries. Rare examples of furniture designed by Agnes and Rhoda Garrett. Painting by Ethel Walker, sketchbooks, watercolours and needlework by Margaret Sarah (Maggie) Beale.
Stourhead, Wiltshire • Palladian home of the Hoare family. The collection includes work by Angelica Kauffman, Margaret Carpenter, Lady Templetown and pastels attributed to Katherine Read, sketchbooks and paintings by Mary Hoare, Frances Annette Hoare and Henrietta Anne Fortescue, and an engraving after Lady Diana Beauclerk.
Sudbury Hall (Children's Country House), Derbyshire • Late 17th-century house with historic collections relating to the Vernon family, housing the Children's Country House Museum. The childhood collections include designs and illustrated books by Mabel Lucie Attwell, Beatrix Potter and Kate Greenaway.
Tatton Park, Cheshire • 18th-century Neo-classical mansion with a landscaped

deer park. The remarkable art collection includes a pastel by Rosalba Carriera and scenic photographs made by Lady Anna Egerton. The library includes an 1843 book on orchids illustrated by Sarah Ann Drake and Augusta Innes Withers, as well as Mary Gartside's groundbreaking book on the theory of colour, *An Essay on Light and Shade* (1805).

The Vyne, Hampshire • A 16th-century manor house built for William Sandys, purchased by the Chute family in 1653. The collection includes work by Rosalba Carriera, and watercolours by Margaret Meen, Eliza Smith and Augusta Smith.

Tyntesfield, North Somerset • Victorian Gothic Revival house, home to four generations of the Gibbs family. The extensive collection includes examples of ceramics designed by Susie Cooper, Jessie Tait (W.R. Midwinter Ltd), Ethel Sleigh and Phyllis Simpson (Old Cheyne Pottery).

Uppark, West Sussex • 17th-century house with Rococo and Regency interiors, devastated by fire in 1989 and later restored. The collection includes a portrait of Sarah Lethieullier, Lady Fetherstonhaugh, by Pompeo Batoni, as well as a small group of her own watercolours. Margaret Glyn, Lady Meade-Fetherstonhaugh, was a pioneer conservator and worked on many of Uppark's historic textiles.

Waddesdon Manor, Buckinghamshire • French Renaissance-style chateau housing the influential collections of the Rothschild family. Includes work by Suzanne de Court, Marie-Louise-Adélaïde Boizot, Adélaïde Labille-Guiard and Elisabeth Vigée Le Brun.

Wallington, Northumberland • *c.*1688 house remodelled in the 18th century with important collections of portraits, the working library of the Trevelyan family, an extensive group of ceramics and Dame Jane Wilson's 'cabinet of curiosities'. Artists include Maria Verelst, Caroline Grosvenor and Dorothy Tennant, Lady Stanley. Needlework by Julia, Lady Calverley, and Mary (Molly), Lady Trevelyan. Sketches and watercolours by Pauline, Lady Trevelyan, and Caroline, Lady Trevelyan. Pauline commissioned the spectacular mural by William Bell Scott in the Central Hall, making a significant contribution to its scheme, including painting many of the floral pilasters.

Wightwick Manor, West Midlands • Late Victorian Aesthetic Movement house with an important collection of Pre-Raphaelite pictures and Arts and Crafts furnishings. The collection includes works by May Morris, Elizabeth Siddal, Marie Spartali Stillman, Lisa Ramona Stillman, Emma Sandys, Evelyn De Morgan and Winifred (Wilfreda) Julia Spencer Stanhope.

Compiled by Rachel Conroy

INDEX

Bold page numbers refer to main illustrated entries for individual artists and designers; *italic* page numbers indicate other illustrations

FURTHER READING

The list below includes a selection of the works referred to by the authors of the current book, as well as some key books on the wider subject of women and the arts that may be of interest to the reader.

Andaleeb Badiee Banta, Alexa Greist and Theresa Kutasz Christensen (eds), *Making Her Mark: A History of Women Artists in Europe, 1400–1800*, Art Gallery of Ontario, Baltimore Museum of Art and Goose Lane Editions, New Brunswick, 2023

Tabitha Barber, *Mary Beale: Portrait of a Seventeenth-century Painter, Her Family and Her Studio*, Geffrye Museum Trust, London, 1999

Michael Bath, *Emblems for a Queen: The Needlework of Mary Queen of Scots*, Archetype, London, 2008

Christine Boydell, *The Architect of Floors: Modernism, Art and Marion Dorn Designs*, Schoeser, Essex, 1996

Aoife Brady, *Lavinia Fontana: Trailblazer, Rule Breaker*, National Gallery of Ireland, Dublin, 2023

Hazel Clark, 'Joyce Clissold and the "Footprints" Textile Printing Workshop' in Jill Seddon and Suzette Worden (eds), *Women Designing: Redefining Design in Britain between the Wars*, University of Brighton, Brighton, 1994

Eleanor Clayton, *Barbara Hepworth: Art and Life*, Thames & Hudson, London, 2021

Emmanuel Cooper, *Lucie Rie: Modernist Potter*, Yale University Press, New Haven and London, 2012

Elizabeth Crawford, *Enterprising Women: The Garretts and Their Circle*, Francis Boutle, London, 2002

Elizabeth Crawford, *Art and Suffrage: A Biographical Dictionary of Suffrage Artists*, Francis Boutle, London, 2018

Caroline Davidson, *The World of Mary Ellen Best*, Chatto & Windus, London, 1985

Serena Dyer, *Material Lives: Women Makers and Consumer Culture in the 18th Century*, Bloomsbury, London, 2021

Martin Eidelberg et al, *The Eames Lounge Chair: An Icon of Modern Design*, Merrell, London and New York, 2006

David B. Elliott, *A Pre-Raphaelite Marriage: The Lives and Works of Marie Spartali Stillman and William James Stillman*, Antique Collectors' Club, Suffolk, 2007

Alicia Foster, *Gwen John: Art and Life in London and Paris*, Thames & Hudson, London, 2023

Philippa Glanville, *Women Silversmiths 1685–1845*, Thames & Hudson, London, 1990

Bendor Grosvenor, *Bright Souls: The Forgotten World of Britain's First Female Artists*, Lyon & Turnbull, London, 2019

Barbara Hepworth, *A Pictorial Autobiography*, Moonraker Press, Bradford-on-Avon, 1970

Katy Hessel, *The Story of Art Without Men*, Hutchinson Heinemann, London, 2022

Louise Lippincott, *Selling Art in Georgian London: The Rise of Arthur Pond*, Yale University Press, New Haven and London, 1983

Anna Mason et al, *May Morris: Arts & Crafts Designer*, Thames & Hudson in association with the Victoria and Albert Museum, London, 2017

Elizabeth Foley O'Connor, *Pamela Colman Smith: Artist, Feminist & Mystic*, Clemson University Press, Clemson, South Carolina, 2021

Emma Slocombe, 'The Embroidery and Needlework of Bess of Hardwick' in David Adshead and David A.H.B. Taylor (eds), *Hardwick Hall: A Great Old Castle of Romance*, Yale University Press, New Haven and London, 2016

Laura Smith and Grace Storey (eds), *Eileen Agar: Angel of Anarchy*, Whitechapel Gallery, London, 2021

Paris A. Spies-Gans, *A Revolution on Canvas: The Rise of Women Artists in London and Paris, 1760–1830*, Yale University Press, New Haven and London, 2022

Zoë Thomas, *Women Art Workers and the Arts and Crafts Movement*, Manchester University Press, Manchester, 2020

Joanna Wason, *Janet Leach: Potter*, Leach Pottery, St Ives, 2021

ACKNOWLEDGEMENTS

The author would like to express her sincere thanks to Sandi Toksvig for her thought-provoking introduction. Special thanks also are due to the following curatorial colleagues who lent their expertise and insight to the entries they have written, as well as offering support, advice and encouragement throughout the process: Benjamin Alsop (Cultural Heritage Curator), John Chu (Senior National Curator), Matthew Constantine (Cultural Heritage Curator), Jane Eade (Cultural Heritage Curator), Miranda Garrett (Cultural Heritage Curator), Mia Jackson (Curator of Decorative Arts), Rachel Jacobs (Curator), Joanne Moody (Cultural Heritage Curator), Alice Rylance-Watson (Assistant National Curator), Anna Sparham (National Curator for Photography), Alice M. Strickland (Curator) and Jonathan Wallis (Cultural Heritage Curator) – the book is infinitely better for their wonderful contributions.

The book has benefited enormously from the input of many dedicated colleagues at National Trust properties and in the consultancy, who have generously shared their knowledge and suggestions throughout the writing of this book. Special thanks are also due to colleagues outside the Trust, including Tabitha Barber, Alicia Foster, Robert Jocelyn, 10th Earl of Roden, Angus Patterson and Zoë Thomas.

Sincere thanks to Christopher Tinker, the National Trust's Publisher for Curatorial Content, who commissioned this book and oversaw the editing, design and production; and to David Boulting, Editor in the Cultural Heritage Publishing team, for his brilliant editorial eye and constant encouragement. Leah Band, Collections Photographer, has coordinated a complex programme of new photography for the book, which has enabled us to show these fantastic artworks at their best. Thanks also to Matthew Young for his design work; Patricia Burgess for her proofreading; Christopher Phipps for indexing; Susannah Stone for clearing image rights; and Richard Deal and Dan Kosta at Dexter Premedia for the origination.

In addition to the texts and sources included in the Further Reading section (opposite), the book has drawn upon digital resources, including *Art & the Country House*, *British and Irish Furniture Makers Online*, *The British Newspaper Archive* and the *Oxford Dictionary of National Biography*, as well as research published by Trevor Adams, Temma Balducci, Emma Bashforth, Julia Buckley, Leslie Campbell Hatfield, Welda LaJean Chaffin, Jessica Collins, Helen Draper, Kathleen Camilla Hawley, Nicole LaBouff, Elise Lawton Smith, Santina M. Levey, Kelly M. McDonald, Martin Postle, Clare Richardson, Beverley Ronalds, Carew Treffgarne and Eileen Wheeler.

The National Trust gratefully acknowledges the generous bequest from the late Mr and Mrs Kenneth Levy that has supported the cost of preparing this book through the Trust's Cultural Heritage Publishing programme.

PICTURE CREDITS

Every effort has been made to contact holders of the copyright in illustrations reproduced in this book, and any omissions will be corrected in future editions if the publisher is notified in writing. The publisher would like to thank the following for permission to reproduce works for which they hold the copyright:

Page 2 © National Trust/Richard Holttum • 4, 20, 38, 41, 48 (left), 48–9, 56, 71, 82, 83, 90, 92–3, 99, 103, 105, 113, 122, 124, 125, 126, 129, 130 (left), 132, 134, 160, 168, 169, 174, 177, 178, 196, 198–9, 204 (both), 210, 212–13, 215, 217, 219, 223, 259 © National Trust Images/Leah Band • 6 © Thomas Aichinger/VWPics/Alamy Stock Photo • 7 © Debbie Toksvig • 8 © Guerrilla Girls, courtesy guerrillagirls.com • 9, 200 © IanDagnall Computing/Alamy Stock Photo • 10 Courtesy National Gallery of Art, Washington DC/Gift of Mr and Mrs Robert Woods Bliss • 11, 34 © National Trust Images/Matthew Hollow • 12, 14, 24 (bottom), 26, 37, 44 (both), 58, 62, 66–7, 85, 100, 118 (right) © National Trust Images • 17, 117, 171 © National Trust/Andrew Fetherston • 19, 108 (left), 137, 146–7, 173, 187, 192 © National Trust • 22, 32 © Waddesdon Image Library/Mike Fear • 24 (top) West Suffolk Heritage Service • 25 © National Trust Images/David Brunetti • 28–9 (all), 31, 55, 61, 63, 87, 88, 94, 102, 136, 141 (right), 143, 157, 164 (left), 170, 172, 202, 203, 230 (left), 238, 253 © National Trust Images/John Hammond • 30 © Photo Scala, Florence • 40, 64, 69, 75, 76–7, 89, 106, 110, 115, 121, 146 (left), 155, 182 (both), 183, 186, 260 (all) © National Trust Images/Robert Thrift • 42–3, 251 © National Trust Images/Paul Harris • 45, 78 © Waddesdon Image Library • 47 Reproduced by kind permission of the Dryden Discretionary Settlement; Image: © National Trust Images/John Hammond • 50–1, 52–3, 194 (left) © National Trust/Bryan Rutledge • 57 © Tatton Park/Cheshire East Council/Peter Spooner • 59 © Santa Barbara Museum of Art, Santa Barbara • 65 © National Trust/Nick Singleton • 68 © National Trust Images/Colin White • 72 © National Trust/Chris Calnan • 73 © National Trust/The Gap Studio • 80 © National Trust/Jaron James • 91 © National Trust/Simon Harris • 92 © National Trust Images/David Garner • 96 (top left) © Eldon House Museum, Ontario • 96 (top right) © National Trust/Andrew McGregor • 96 (bottom right) © National Trust/Rebecca Allen • 108–9 Courtesy of York Museums Trust • 111 Private collection • 114, 123, 142, 152, 165, 166, 175, 205, 232 © National Portrait Gallery, London • 116 © National Trust Images/Paul Highnam • 118 (left) © National Trust/Sophia Farley • 119 National Gallery of Art, Washington DC, Department of Image Collections • 127, 176, 226 © Victoria and Albert Museum, London • 130 (right) Private collection • 131, 133 © National Trust Images/Andreas von Einsiedel • 135 © Look and Learn • 138 originally published in *Gertrude Jekyll: A Memoir* by Francis Jekyll, Jonathan Cape, London, 1934 • 139 © Knight Frank • 140–1 © National Trust Images/Megan Taylor • 144 © De Morgan Foundation • 148–9 © National Trust/Brain Gornall • 150, 216 (both) © National Trust/Sophia Farley and Claire Reeves • 151 © The Trustees of the British Museum. All rights reserved • 154 © National Trust/John Pittwood • 156 © Bodleian Libraries, University of Oxford • 159 © National Trust/Dan Wray • 162, 189, 190, 191, 248, 255 © National Trust Images/Edward Chambré Hardman Collection • 164 (right) British Library • 180–1 © London Museum (digital image) • 181 (right) © National Trust/Sophia Farley and Renée Harvey • 184–5 © National Trust/Liz MacFarlane • 194–5 © National Trust Images/Andrew Butler • 197 Beinecke Rare Book and Manuscript Library, Yale University Library © Van Vechten Trust • 201 © Estate of Vanessa Bell. All rights reserved, DACS 2024; Image: © National Trust Images/Leah Band • 202, 203 © Estate of Vanessa Bell. All rights reserved, DACS 2024; Image: © National Trust Images/John Hammond • 206, 207 © Estate of Dame Laura Knight. All rights reserved 2024/Bridgeman Images; Image: © National Trust Images/Leah

Band • 208 © Estate of Eileen Agar. All rights reserved 2024/ Bridgeman Images; Image: © National Trust/Claire Reeves • 209 © Trevor Leighton/National Portrait Gallery, London • 211 Photographer unknown • 218 Courtesy of David Bryson • 219 Courtesy of David Bryson; Image: © National Trust Images/Leah Band • 220 © Popperfoto/Getty Images • 222 © The Gluck Estate. All rights reserved, DACS 2024; Image: Bridgeman Images • 224 © Kate MccGwire/Photo: JP Bland • 227 © National Trust/Catriona Hughes • 228–9 © National Trust Images/Sam Milling • 230–1 © National Trust Images/ Arnhel de Serra • 234 Barbara Hepworth © Bowness; Image: © National Trust Images • 235 Barbara Hepworth © Bowness; Image: © National Trust Images/Leah Band • 236 © Eames Office, LLC. All rights reserved • 237 © National Trust Images/Stuart Cox • 239 Courtesy of Ymddiriedolaeth Susan Williams-Ellis Foundation • 240–1, 244–5 © Ben Boswell • 242 © The Janet Leach Estate; Image: © National Trust Images/ Leah Band • 247 © Estate of Lucie Rie; Image: © National Trust Images/Leah Band • 249 © Tabitha Jussa • 256 © National Trust Images/Joe Cornish

Front cover, clockwise from top right: © National Trust Images/ Leah Band • © National Trust Images/Robert Thrift • © National Trust Images/Leah Band • Courtesy of David Bryson; Image: © National Trust Images/Leah Band • *Back cover:* © The Janet Leach Estate; Image: © National Trust Images/Leah Band • *Front flap:* © Estate of Vanessa Bell. All rights reserved, DACS 2024; Image: © National Trust Images/John Hammond • *Back flap:* © National Trust Images/ John Hammond

Published in Great Britain by the National Trust,
Heelis, Kemble Drive, Swindon, Wiltshire SN2 2NA

National Trust Cultural Heritage Publishing

Registered charity no. 205846

ISBN 978-0-70-780469-9

A CIP catalogue record for this book is available from the British Library.

10 9 8 7 6 5 4 3 2 1

Unless otherwise indicated, dimensions are given in centimetres, height x width x depth

‡ Indicates objects accepted in lieu of inheritance tax by HM Government and allocated to the National Trust

Publisher: Christopher Tinker
Project editor: David Boulting
Proofreader: Patricia Burgess
Indexer: Christopher Phipps
Page design concept and cover design: Matthew Young
Additional picture research: Susannah Stone

Colour origination by Dexter Premedia Ltd, London
Printed in Wales by Gomer Press Ltd
on FSC®-certified paper

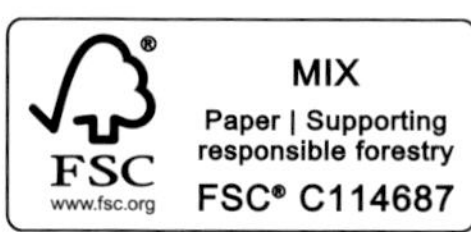

Discover the wealth of our collections – great art and treasures to see and enjoy throughout England, Wales and Northern Ireland. Visit the National Trust website:
www.nationaltrust.org.uk/art-and-collections
and the National Trust Collections website:
www.nationaltrustcollections.org.uk